"Full of psychological good sense and religious wisdom. . . . Dr. Jones puts over against one another 'powerless poise' and 'poisoned power' and points out that these are afflictions of modern man."—*Christian Advocate*

"Sound helps to spiritual and physical well-being . . . rooted in life."—*Presbyterian Outlook*

"Useful . . . conveniently arranged . . . fresh and provocative, and always directed toward reality in daily living problems. . . . Psychological insight and religious instinct combine to make a sensible handbook."—*The Churchman*

"A great book!"—*Christian Living*

The Way to
POWER
AND
POISE

E. Stanley Jones

Abingdon  Nashville

THE WAY TO POWER AND POISE

A Festival Book

Festival edition published October 1978

ISBN 0-687-44190-0

INTRODUCTION

THIS BOOK HAS BEEN WRITTEN TO POINT THE WAY TO MEET TWO modern needs. I say "modern," but they have belonged to all men of all ages. But they have become very acute, painfully acute, in our modern day. They are these: the need of inner poise and the need of inner and outer power. The modern man lacks both.

The modern man will probably acknowledge that he lacks poise. How can he do otherwise? The strained, and hence drained, type of human living which we have developed is issuing in shattered nerves, tangled lives, broken homes, overflowing hospitals and sanatoriums, and overworked psychiatrists. We seem to know everything about life except how to live it.

The modern man will concede his lack of poise, but will probably question his lack of power. Does he not live in "the age of power"? Has not his control over nature gone on by leaps and bounds? True, but what kind of control?

Someone heard me speak on "Poise and Power," and thought I had said "poisoned power." Our power has become poisoned power. We discovered the ultimate physical power in the universe—the power wrapped up in an atom—and the very first thing we did with it was to blow whole cities and their citizens into oblivion. And instead of gaining security by it we are filled with an increasing dread that it may be used on us—on us all. Our power has become power to ruin ourselves. Our very light has turned to darkness.

Man has gained control over nature, but not over human nature. He lacks an inner poise, hence his use of outer power is destructive. He must find an inner poise that will become beneficent outer power.

He must have both poise *and* power. For poise may end in itself and lack a control over outer life. The East has sought poise, but along with it has not sought the power to change outer conditions. The West, on the other hand, has sought power without inner poise and the power is the power to ruin. One is powerless poise and the other is poisoned power. In the "Temple of a Thousand Gods" in Peiping, China, is a figure which is different. All the gods are seated with placid faces, as if eternity were looking through their eyes—looking with disillusioned gaze at passing time. But one figure is standing with his face strained and eager, as if about to possess the earth. That standing god is said to be Marco Polo. The Chinese deified him. There you have the two conceptions dramatically depicted: the East with poise, but with no power to change the passing present; the West with power to change, but with little inner poise to use that power for the individual and collective good. Nothing—absolutely nothing—is so necessary as just this: the combination of power and poise.

But the modern man is not sure of the possibility of finding inner resources, resources out of which poise naturally comes. Skepticism has eaten away his faith not only in God, but in life. This is poignantly put by Eugene O'Neill, the playwright: "But inwardly the war helped me realize that I was putting my faith in the old values, and they've gone. It is very sad but there are no values to live by today. . . . Anything is permissible if you know the angles. . . . There is a feeling around, or I'm mistaken, of fate, of Kismet, the negative fate . . . a sort of unfair *non sequitur*, as though events, as though life were being manipulated just to confuse us. I think I'm aware of a comedy that doesn't stay funny long. . . . The comedy breaks up and tragedy comes on."

How can anyone be inwardly poised and assured with that view of life? With that hypothesis, namely, that there are "no values to live by today," then life is bound to come out just where O'Neill says it will: "Tragedy comes on." Life turns inwardly sick at this prospect.

Romanes, the scientist who lost his faith in God, meditates thus: "When at times I think, as think I must, of the appalling contrast between the hallowed glory of that creed which once was mine and the lonely mystery of existence as I now find it; at such times I shall ever feel it impossible to avoid the sharpest pang of which my nature is susceptible."

It is just this emptiness that Jung, the famous psychiatrist, calls "the central neurosis of our times": "About a third of my cases are suffering from no clinical definable neurosis, but from the senselessness and emptiness of their lives. This can well be defined as the general neurosis of our times." The human personality simply cannot stand living in an empty, meaningless universe. It goes to pieces. A Jewish psychiatrist said this to me: "I have a case where the woman would be well is she could get an inner security, so that no matter what would happen to her on the outside she would still be secure within. As a psychiatrist I can't give it to her, but maybe you as a religious man can." I couldn't, but I could introduce her to Someone who could.

Now the crux of the whole matter is just here: Can we realize God within us in such a way that no matter what happens on the outside we will still be secure? If that can't happen we're sunk. If it can happen we're not only unsunk, but unsinkable.

But there must be no make-believe, no playing with words, no dodging of issues, no skirting of unpleasant realities, no resting in platitudes—it must be real. For inward poise can come only when we are sure that the sum total of reality is backing our way of living. Inner poise is an outgrowth of an inner assurance that Reality approves of us, sustains us, and guarantees our future. Then and then only can we face the past, the present, and the future with serenity.

There are two possible ways we may try to find that inner calm and poise. One is through outer circumstances and the other is through inward conditions. As I write, there are lying on my desk two pictures. One is a description of a tropical isle where people are invited to come and live a community life and find "the way to peace."

> We sing the song of a tropic isle
> That lies in a turquoise sea,
> Of happiness and a peaceful home
> In the shade of a breadfruit tree.
>
> The weather is perfect all the time
> And the air is virgin pure.
> A tropical isle's the place to live
> To be healthy and secure.

There is something very inviting in that picture of peace through circumstances. But the most of our unpeace is within us. And if we went to a tropical isle, it would still be there. In any case the most of us will have to live where we are, and if we find inner poise it will have to be in spite of circumstances.

The other picture on my desk is that of a youth, who with life plans all laid out, including the plan of being a medical missionary, suddenly finds himself a polio victim. A victim? Without inner resources he would have been a victim, but he had what it takes—he literally brought life back to a supposedly dead limb, is walking when it was impossible, and through a radiant spirit is on top of circumstances. He never inwardly cracked. He had God. That fact held him inwardly steady. He had inner poise *in spite of*.

If we cannot get away to tropical isles to find peace, we can live with a center of calm within us *where we are*. This is not mere abstract idea. It works. I have tried it in almost every land of the world and in almost every circumstance. It works. This book is therefore both a treatise and a testimony. I shall keep within the limits of that which has been tried, verified, and found workable.

This Introduction is being written in China. There has been a crisis of some kind in China for twenty-five years, but during this month I have been here there has been occurring, I suppose, the real crisis. The Communist flood, held temporarily at the Yangtze, has broken its banks and has begun to overflow South China. I have been just a step or two in front of that flood for a month—Nanking, Chengtu, Shanghai, Amoy, Canton, not sure just where it might cut me off. I have seen the suppressed tensions of the long-suffering people and of the rough, weather-hardened missionaries. They wait in calm to let that flood go over their heads, and then to straighten up again to face an entirely new way of life. Stomach disorders have increased among the Chinese, I am told. No wonder, for the tensions are great. But through it all has been an astonishing calm within me that had surprised me. The wear and tear of speaking from three to five times a day, and the travel conditions, uncertain as they are, should leave one exhausted, or worse, a wreck. But it has left me neither. I have come through intact. In fact, I have been deepened by the experience. This way works. One can have power and poise *anywhere*.

This book has been written in the same form as *Victorious Living, Abundant Living,* and *The Way*—a page a day for those who want to use it as a daily devotional; a weekly study for those who wish to use it as a basis for class study, for I have endeavored to give a more or less complete study each week; and a book to be read straight through as an ordinary book, for there is one theme running through the whole—the Way to power and poise.

To my readers who are committed Christians, I would suggest that you read the book straight through, but to those who are not inwardly committed to the Christian Way I would suggest that you read through Chapter IV and then skip over to Chapter XXVII, read to the end, and then come back and take up Chapters V to XXVI. The reason for this will unfold as you go along.

I am convinced that the devotional life cannot be developed apart from mental development. That which does not hold the mind will soon not hold the emotion and the will. The devotional life cannot therefore be adequately developed on isolated dabs of spiritual truth read each day. It must be a developing whole. Our theology and our devotional life must grow together. Our conceptions of God and life must get back into the shrine of our devotional life and give it wholeness and direction. And our devotional life must set fire to our conceptions.

That fire must be the fire of the Spirit. This book is really a study and practice of the Spirit. For the Holy Spirit is the secret of both power and poise. The Holy Spirit works in the area of the subconscious, or the unconscious, as it is often called. The subconscious is the area of the battle for the spiritual life. Whatever holds that holds the conscious life. Can the subconscious be cleansed and controlled and be made to work in the purposes of the conscious life? Can the subconscious be converted and Christianized? If not, then poise and power will be weak or absent. We will be undermined from within.

We have tried to answer that question with God's answer. For He has an answer—the Answer. God's way is the Way. This book is a sequel to *The Way*—"the Way" as "the Way to poise and power."

E. STANLEY JONES

CONTENTS

CONTENTS

CONTENTS

CONTENTS

The Way to Power and Poise

THE END OF THE PHYSICAL ORGANISM: INNER STABILITY

The Christian way, often called in early days "the Way," is the way to live. If this means anything, it means that the Way is written not merely in the Bible but also in biology—the demands of religion and the demands of life are the same. The Way, then, is written in our nerves, our blood, our tissues, in the total organization of life. If we live according to that Way, we live; if we don't, we get hurt. You can't live life against itself without disruption. The God of religion and the God of life are the same—one God. The Christian Way is written not merely in texts of Scripture but in the texture of life. It is the way we are made to live.

Is the demand for power and poise a religious necessity, or a life necessity? It is both a religious necessity and a life necessity—it is both a biblical and a biological demand.

First of all, it is written in biological demand. Physical life demands inner stability. If it lacks that, it perishes. The French physiologist, Dr. Charles Richet, says: "The living being is stable. It must be in order not to be destroyed by the colossal forces, often adverse, which surround it. By an apparent contradiction it maintains its stability only if it is excitable, and capable of modifying itself according to external stimuli and adjusting its response to the stimulation. In a sense it is stable because it is modifiable—the slight instability is the necessary condition for the true stability of the organism."

Now note two facts: *(a)* the organism has to be stable to survive; *(b)* it is stable only if it is modifiable. To these two principles we will return again and again.

Bernard, the biologist, says: "It is the fixity of the 'milieu interior' (the interior condition) which is the condition of free and independent life, and all the mechanisms, however varied they may be, have only one object, that of preserving constant the conditions of life in the internal environment." Dr. J. S. Haldane comments: "No more pregnant sentence was ever framed by a biologist."

We see then that all the mechanisms of the physical life work toward one thing: inner stability.

O God, as we begin this quest for inner stability we are grateful to know that Thou hast written this demand first of all in the physical organism. Wilt Thou fulfill it in me? Amen.

AFFIRMATION FOR THE DAY: *When I desire inner stability, I am in line with God's intention in the universe.*

STABILITY BRINGS FREEDOM FROM ENVIRON-MENTAL CHANGE

Yesterday we saw that the whole purpose of the physical organism was to achieve stability. It is organized with that driving purpose.

Dr. Cannon, the Harvard physiologist, to whom I owe much in this section, says: "The nervous system is divisible into two main parts, the one acting outwardly and affecting the world around us and the other acting inwardly and helping to preserve a constant and steady condition of the organism itself." This points to the necessity of both poise and power—a poise that will keep us inwardly steady and a power that can change the outer, or if this is not possible, then not to allow the outer to affect us harmfully.

This is strikingly put by Leon Fredericq: "The living being is an agency of such a sort that each disturbing influence induces by itself the calling forth of compensatory activity to neutralize or repair that activity. The higher in the scale of living beings the more complicated do these regulatory agencies become. They tend to free the organism completely from the unfavorable influences and changes occurring in the environment." Here we note a step further: The end of the inner stability is to produce freedom—freedom from unfavorable changes in the environment. We are inwardly fixed in order to be free. But that fixity can come only if we are capable of change.

Pflinger puts it this way: "The cause of every need of a living being is also the cause of the satisfaction of that need." This means that if we have need for inner stability, that fact calls forth the very agencies that will satisfy that need. Cry and supply are parts of one whole. The universe is physically redemptive.

It preserves. In an experiment a man drank six quarts of water in six hours. The rate of kidney output rose to one and a quarter quarts per hour. And yet in tests of the color of the blood during the period no appreciable dilution of the blood could be observed. Nature saw to it that the normal constitution of the blood was maintained. The end of the organism was fulfilled: stability. Stability and survival are one.

O God, my Father, I live in man-made surroundings which strike at the very center of my life—my inner poise. Help me to keep that center intact. Give me inner stability. Amen.

AFFIRMATION FOR THE DAY: *My need and the satisfaction of my need are inseparable—unless I separate them.*

MORALLY COLD-BLOODED OR WARM-BLOODED?

We continue today the study of how the organism is constructed so that inner stability is achieved amid outer changes.

Men may be exposed to dry heat (239 to 257 degrees Fahrenheit) without an increase of the body temperature above normal. Arctic mammals when exposed to cold as low as 31 degrees below zero Fahrenheit do not manifest any noteworthy fall of bodily temperature, says Dr. Cannon. This is an amazing achievement. I say "achievement," for when I quoted the above facts someone remarked: "But they are made to stay normal," as if an amazing process didn't immediately go into action to preserve the stability. It didn't just happen! The organism worked hard and quickly to maintain stability.

It is reassuring to know that on the hottest day if we take our temperature we are still 98.6 degrees. We are no hotter than usual—we just feel that way. It is also reassuring that in the coldest weather we are as warm as usual! When I said that one day on a chilly morning a lady remarked: "Well, I'm sure if my temperature had been taken between my toes last night the thermometer wouldn't have shown normal!" Perhaps not, and yet the body temperature in general was.

This fact of inner stability makes it possible for us to live in any climate and to move with alacrity in all circumstances. Cold-blooded animals cannot do this. Cold-blooded animals have the temperature of their surroundings: they can act with alacrity only when the weather is warm; the warm-blooded which maintain a fairly fixed high temperature in spite of external cold, can act quickly at all times. By the preservation of constancy they are freed from the influence of vicissitudes in the extrenal environment, says Dr. Cannon.

Many of us are morally and spiritually cold-blooded animals—we are the temperature of our surroundings. We are morally and spiritually warm if others are, but we grow cold if surrounded by cold. The frog sinks into the mud and stays there with a feeble pulse of life until spring warms him up again. Many of us have not achieved an inner stability, so we need to be warmed up by periodic meetings, revivals, conventions. Spiritually we are cold-blooded.

O God, without the glory of Thy life within me I am spiritually cold-blooded. I take on the temperature of the group. I move as they move. Give me Thy life within. Amen.

AFFIRMATION FOR THE DAY: *I must not be environmentally conditioned but God-conditioned.*

HOW NATURE PROVIDES AGAINST EMERGENCIES

We must spend one more day on the fact that stability is the end of the whole physical organism.

Dr. Cannon says that in starvation some tissues waste away, i.e., yield some of their structure, but not the tissues of the heart and brain. These have preferential treatment, and at the end of a long fast are found quite normal. It may be that the heart and brain are well-provided with water, even to the end of a disastrous term of thirsting.

Nature not only holds the interior life stable but discriminates between values in stability. The heart and the brain, being the centers of life, are taken care of when less vital places have to be sacrificed. If we were as wise as nature, we would see that certain moral and spiritual values are vital—if they go the personality disintegrates. We would, therefore, provide that the centers of our moral and spiritual life be kept intact. But often we keep the nonvital centers intact and let the vital centers die.

Nature not only takes care of the vital centers out of the current supplies, but lays up supplies for emergencies. The water supply in the body is of vital importance. The average man has a hundred pounds of water in his composition. The gray matter in the brain is 80 per cent water, while 90 per cent of blood plasma is also water. We can by fasting lose practically all our stored animal starch or glycogen without noteworthy consequences. We can lose all our reserves of fat and about half the protein which is stored or built into the body structure and not be confronted by any great danger. But a loss of 10 per cent of the body water is serious and 20 to 22 per cent is certain death. So water is kept in reservoirs within the body and liberated as needed. Thirsting dogs have the blood state unchanged after several days of water privation.

Salt content is so important that if it is lost in excess there is increased irritability, weakness, paralysis, and then death. The constancy of the concentration of salt in the blood suggests that it, like water, is stored somewhere in the body and released as needed. The end of all the organisms is stability.

Our Father, Thou has been teaching us through Thy handiwork in the physical to discriminate in values. Help me to keep my heart intact for out of it are the issues of life. Amen.

AFFIRMATION FOR THE DAY: *Choose real values and be stable; choose false values and be unstable.*

WE REVIEW THE VARIOUS ATTEMPTS TO GAIN STABILITY

We have seen that the end of the physical organism is to provide for stability in the midst of changes, often violent and disruptive, taking place around that organism. In Alaska there is a peculiar worm that lives in the glacial ice. But the curator of the museum in Juneau assured me that these worms are ordinary earthworms caught on the ice when the glacier was formed, that they did not live on the ice but in tiny pockets of earth gathered in the crevises of the glacier, that they had to reduce their size in order to live so they are the size of a pin. The earthworms pulled in their belts and survived—on ice! They achieved stability in the most adverse surroundings.

If stability is the end of the physical organism, how much more of the spiritual organism! All systems of philosophy and religion have seen that necessity and have provided their answers. When we look at the various systems, we are struck with the fact that they are endeavoring to do spiritually what nature is doing physically, namely, to provide for stability amid changes around one. This one goal is variously named—peace, serenity, inner calm, tranquility, stability, a quiet mind, harmony, unity, integration, realization, poise.

We tried in group discussion to get a better word than "poise," but in the end it held the field as the word that expressed the possibility of a combination of inner serenity and power. The combination was important. In the various systems which we must now examine breifly we find that this combination is almost invariably absent. Except in one.

The Greeks embodied their quest for inner stability in the Stoic philosophy. So impressive was this viewpoint that it persists in our modern vocabulary—the "stoic" attitude. A modern psychiatrist suggests that we "cultivate stoical attitudes" to meet the hard knocks of life. It was the endeavor to match inner, unbent courage against outer circumstances. The Stoics tried to gain poise by hardness of spirit. That proved the fatal defect—it was so hard it could not bend, it could only break. And break it did. We shall see why.

O God, as I begin this quest for poise help me not to take ways that let me down in the crisis. I need something that will stand up under life no matter what the demands of life may be. Take me by the hand. Amen.

AFFIRMATION FOR THE DAY: *This day I shall be Stoic, therefore brittle and breakable; or Christian, therefore bending but unbreakable.*

THE STOIC AND "THE SUPERIOR MAN"

We saw yesterday that the Stoic's quest for poise created a misfit instead of the fit. Why? An authority on Stoics answers: "If the end is tranquility of what use would it be to set the Wise Man's heart free from disturbance by cutting off the fear and desire which made him dependent upon outside things, if one immediately opened a hundred channels by which the world's pain and unrest could flow into his heart through the fibres created by Love and Pity, connecting his heart with the fevered hearts of men all around? A hundred fibres?—one aperture would suffice to let in enough of the bitter surge to fill his heart full. Leave one small hole in a ship's side and you let in the sea. The Stoics, I think, saw with perfect truth that if you are going to allow any least entrance of Love and Pity into the breast, you admitted something whose measure you could not control, and might as well give up the idea of inner tranquility at once. . . . The Christian's ideal figure could never be accepted by the Stoic as an example of his typical wise man."

The Stoic tried to gain tranquility by shutting out love and pity. But to shut out love and pity is to shut out life. So the Stoic inwardly strangled himself to death searching for inner calm. It is no wonder that all Greek dramas ended in tragedy. They put tragedy out of the door and it came back by the window—and mastered the masters of their fate! It failed. It was not the answer. For it produced the man who didn't care what happens to others. That is fatal.

The Chinese "Superior Man" suffered from the same defect as the Greeks' "Wise Man." He, too, tried to achieve tranquility of mind by giving way to no circumstance about him. If soup were spilled on the Chinese "Superior Man," he was not supposed to remove it till he had withdrawn from the presence of others. He would be unmoved and show no emotion. He cultivated an inwardly aloof attitude which degenerated into the phrase that has been responsible for China's downfall more than any other one thing: "It's not on my body"—not my responsibility. Result? What was on nobody's body as responsibility was on everybody's body as calamity.

My Father, as I see the false steps made by man keep Thou my feet. Help me to take Thy way. For Thy ways are paths of peace—and power. I am on a quest so important that I must not fail, for to fail is a life failure. Amen.

AFFIRMATION FOR THE DAY: *I am not superior—except in God.*

THE HINDU QUEST FOR INNER STABILITY

Yesterday we came upon the fatal defect in the Chinese search for poise—it resulted in indifference to what happened to others. I remarked to a Chinese friend: "I cannot understand this. These shops are beautifully clean, electric lighted and the merchants dressed in silks, but these narrow streets are unspeakably dirty." "But don't you see," he replied: "these shops belong to these men and their families, but these streets don't belong to anybody." The streets were not on their bodies as responsibility, hence on everybody's body as calamity. The personal poise was corporate poison.

The Hindu quest for inner *shanti,* or peace, has taken many forms. We will pick out two as typical. One is the pure Vedantist and the other is the modernized Vedantist. The pure Vedantist seeks to be like, or identified with Brahma, God. But Brahma is *nir-guna,* without bonds or relationships, hence without action. He, or rather It, is pure being—actionless and passionless, the Impersonal. The highest man is to be that too. He sits in mediation, attention concentrated between his brows, or at the point of his nose, affirming himself as Brahma. It is better to do nothing good or bad, for all action means fruit of action and fruit of action means rebirth, a coming back into the wheel of existence again. Salvation is extrication from the weary round of rebirth, and becoming Brahma.

What kind of poise does this produce? A very profound poise, the profoundest possible, says the Vedantist. The story is told of a devotee so deep in meditation that an ant hill grew up around him until it covered him over, but his meditation was undisturbed. A more likely story is told of a British soldier in the early days who pricked a meditating devotee with the point of his bayonet, and the devotee opened his eyes and said: "Thou too art He."

This profound philosophy suffers from a fatal defect. It seeks for poise at the expense of power—power to change social conditions around one. It strives to be lifted above action, but life demands action—demands that action be socially beneficial. This has not been.

O God, my Father, I cannot take a path that leads me away from the world's pain and sorrow and toil. I must find my release from inner conflict within the conflict. I would not escape. I cannot. Give me release there. Amen.

AFFIRMATION FOR THE DAY: *Save me from the penury of powerless poise.*

ON TRYING TO BECOME DESIRELESS—THE HINDU WAY

We must continue this week the various methods of search for inner tranquility or poise. We must now look at another, modified or modernized Vedantism. Seeing that pure Vedantism led into an attempt at actionless living, hence was socially sterile, it was modified so that there could be action but without attachment. One is to have no desire attached to action, no desire for the fruit of it.

This attitude has a core of truth in it. Good action that desires fruit or reward ceases to be good action. But no attachment has a fatal defect—it can't be done! When a sunyasi talked with insight and ardor about nonattachment I quietly asked: "Aren't you attached to nonattachment?" He was! You cannot get rid of wrong attachment by having no attachment. "To be is to be in relations." The only way to get rid of one desire is to replace it by a higher desire. You cannot root out all desire, for in doing so the desire to do so is created.

The Christian way believes in desire—it is God-given. But that desire must be fastened upon or attached to the highest—God: "Thou shalt love the Lord Thy God with all thy mind, with all thy soul, with all thy heart." The whole being—mind, soul and heart—is to be attached to God in love. That is our supreme attachment. But then we may be attached to things and persons around us in a secondary attachment, subject to the highest attachment. That cleanses and coordinates them. I can love things and persons provided I love God more than things or persons. I get rid of wrong attachment by a supreme attachment. That is psychologically sound—and possible. The other is psychologically wrong—and impossible. It begins, as all half-truths do, by an initial elation and ends in a collapse.

Swami Rama Tirath seemed the exception. He was a joyous spirit attached to nothing. His way seemed to work—for a while. But the joy subsided, he became moody, and one day walked out into the sacred river and drowned himself. He lived on a half-truth and when the other half finally asserted itself, there was conflict within and the end was tragedy.

O God, I want reality and nothing but reality. I want no peace built up out of half-truths, for I know they will have a whole collapse in the end. Give me a solid rock beneath my feet—a rock on which security can be secure. Amen.

AFFIRMATION FOR THE DAY: *I love Thee supremely, therefore my other loves are safe.*

BUDDHA WOULD CUT THE ROOT OF DESIRE

We must continue our examination of the various answers to the desire for inner stability. We come now to one of the most thorough-going of all—Buddhism.

The gentle Buddha came to "the Great Illumination": existence and suffering are one. The only way to get out of suffering is to get out of existence and the only way to get out of existence is to get out of action, for action makes the wheel of existence turn round, and the only way to get out of action is to get out of desire, for out of desire action comes. So the great remedy is: Cut the root of desire, even for life, and as a consequence you will go out into Nirvana, the state literally of "the snuffed-out candle." If Nirvana isn't the absence of being it is the absence of becoming. I asked a Buddhist monk whether there was any existence in Nirvana and he replied: "There is no suffering there, hence there can be no existence."

Buddha rightly saw that desire was the root of suffering. But he was wrong in trying to get rid of all desire. The only way to get rid of one desire is to replace it by a higher desire. Desire fastened on things which let us down, and cause frustration and suffering must be replaced by desire fastened on things which do not let us down—must be fastened on God. Then under God we can desire things, but with a desire always corrected and cleansed by the highest desire—the desire for the will of God. "Seek ye first the Kingdom of God . . . and all these things will be added unto you." Seek something else first and all these things will be subtracted from you. Since Buddha had no God upon whom desire could be fastened, he had to propose exactly what he proposed, namely, get rid of all desire. He would get rid of the problems of life by getting rid of life itself. He would get rid of our headaches by getting rid of our heads.

It is an escape mentality, a failure of nerve, a denial of the will to live. The people who hold this faith, hold along side it a working faith which is quite different—a faith that salutes the Buddha and his teaching but embraces the world and its affairs. The faith is sterilized by compartmentalization and becomes inoperative. It is inoperative because inoperatible.

O God, my Father, Thou hast given me life. I cannot rid myself of it, nor do I desire to do so. I would not deny life, but dedicate it and thus fulfill it. Amen.

AFFIRMATION FOR THE DAY: *My desires are Thy desires, therefore they are mine.*

ISLAM MEANS SUBMISSION

We continue our search amid the answers given to the quest for inner poise. We come now to the answer of Islam.

The answer of Islam is very simple: Everything that happens to you is the will of God. Bend under it and accept it as such. Islam literally means submission—submission to the sovereign will of God. In submitting to whatever comes, good, bad and indifferent, as the will of God, you gain inner stability. The will of God becomes your peace.

This contains a truth: The will of God is our peace. But it also contains a very dangerous untruth: Everything that happens is the will of God. If everything that happens is the will of God, then what kind of a God is He? His character is gone.

It is true that God in making us free agents is indirectly responsible for what we do with that free agency. He assumes that responsibility and discharges it at a Cross—at a Cross where everything that falls on man as a result of the misuse of that free agency falls on Him. The world's sorrow and sin is "forced through the channel of a single Heart." He bears it and redeems us through it.

But to tell a stricken mother that the taking of her babe, or the loss of a loved one in an automobile accident, is the will of God is to charge God with murder. The time is here when we should be ashamed to have children die, for we know that some law has been broken either by remote parents through heredity, or by the immediate parents through ignorance or carelessness, or by the wrong organization of society producing impossible living conditions, or through the wrong choices of the child. The death is the result of one or more of these wills, but it is not the will of God. God wills health, not sickness; life, not death.

The quest of Islam for inner poise through acceptance of the will of God has produced a patient people, but not a progressive one. Islamic civilization comes up to a certain level—the level of the letter of the Koran and there becomes sterile. To progress they must throw off the letter of the Koran, or submit to it and become stabilized at sterility.

O gracious Father, Thy added cross has been that we have laid on Thee our sins. Thy will, which wills our highest interests always, has been made into the instrument of our torture. Forgive us. Help us to lift that cross from Thee by acceptance of it as our own. Amen.

AFFIRMATION FOR THE DAY: *God's will is my highest interest—always.*

THE HEBREW RESTS FOR SECURITY IN THE LAW

The old Testament answer to inner security rested on the Law. Psalm 119 speaks of the Law in everyone of the 176 verses. The first verse reads: "Happy are they who live uprightly, living by the Eternal's law!" (Moffatt.) Inner poise was to be found by resting in a Law.

There is a truth here. We gain freedom through obedience to law. But the Law is incapable of giving ultimate security because of two things: It is an authority outside of us, imposed on us; and it lacks dynamic to fulfill its demands. No authority is real authority unless it gets within us and becomes identified with us, becomes us. Nothing holds you unless it holds you from within. But there must be something more than a Law within—there must be Life. Divine Life working as dynamic in the depths of us. There must be withinness of authority and withinness of power. The Jewish Law resulted in an outwardism illustrated in the Pharisee. Jesus uncovered the hollowness of the Pharisee. The Law failed because it was a Law. Personal beings cannot rest in an impersonal Law for their inner security. Only Life can answer life.

We now come to some more modern answers. The most obvious modern answer is: Become inwardly secure through outer securities. Plug up all possible cracks in your life through which sorrow and insecurity and old age may reach you, and make yourself secure by material possessions.

In this there is a truth. Worry and anxiety about material needs do cut down life. Those who have annuities live four years longer than those who do not. Securities do secure *up to a certain point.* Beyond that they are a false hope. The most inwardly poised and serene are not the people most financially secure. Wealth doesn't necessarily mean weal-th, it may mean ill-th. Some of the most frustrated and unhappy people on this planet are those who have nothing but material wealth. As one unhappy holder of wealth said: "I've learned how to make money, but I've not yet learned how to live." A poll taken showed that the happiest people were the really religious people, not the financially secure.

O God, I see men seeking for securities that cannot secure. Help me to find secure securities—securities that cannot be undermined by sickness, or sorrow, or old age or death. Help me to find an unshakable inner secu-ity. Amen.

AFFIRMATION FOR THE DAY: *My wealth is ill-th, if not in God.*

MODERN ATTEMPTS AT SECURITY

We saw yesterday that our capitalistic society rested for its inner security on accumulation of material wealth. But the nest is built too low. The floods may reach it. The stock markets may slide and crash, and with it our security. A club room in California is papered with a million dollars worth of worthless securities, lost in the depression.

So the Communist reacts against it and gives his answer: Don't rest in your personal accumulation, rest in the security of the Whole. Contribute to society according to your need. Rest in that.

There is a truth here. The basic principles: To each according to his need and from each according to his ability are New Testament principles. But in Communism these principles are wrapped around with materialistic atheism and political dictatorship. Materialistic atheism says that there are no moral qualities built into the nature of reality and guaranteed by God—morality is that which gets you to your goal, the end justifies the means. That shakes our ultimate confidence in the nature of Reality and brings insecurity. If any means are justified by the end, then what is to keep another group from using any means to oust from power those who used any means to come to that power? There is no morality and no basis for it except expediency. Our greatest security—the moral universe—is gone.

Moreover, materialistic atheism has no security against the decay of the physical and death. I asked a Christian professor in Russia, a convinced communist, whether it wouldn't be possible for some of us to come back to Russia, say in ten years, and put up Christ and His Kingdom. "Yes," he replied, "I think you could. For my students are already asking questions, deeper than communism can answer—ultimate questions about life and destiny and immortality." There the securities of Communism could not reach. It fails us.

O God, I come to Thee to find in Thee my moral universe and my future. I need both. I am orphaned if there is no meaning and no future to life. But in Thee I am secure—eternally secure. I thank Thee. Amen.

AFFIRMATION FOR THE DAY: *My desires, short of God, feed on themselves.*

THE ATTEMPT THROUGH HEDONISM

We come now to another modern answer to inner security and poise—the answer of the modern hedonist, the believer in the pleasure principle as the way to live. Without being articulated it is perhaps the most widely used as a way of life.

It, too, has a truth within it. There is a sense in which the end of life is pleasure. The rhythmical, harmonious working of the human organism does bring pleasure, so that if pleasure is absent something is working wrong. In a sense pleasure is the criterion. But the crux of the matter is: What brings pleasure? The pursuit of pleasure itself? There must be an emphatic, No! Pleasure and happiness are by-products. Pursue them as ends in themselves, and they rot in your hands. The most unhappy people are the people who are seeking most ardently their own happiness. Usually they have to souse themselves with more and more liquor to try to drown their basic unhappiness and frustration. "I don't want you to think I'm happy," said a devotee of this cult, just getting over the results of a bout the night before. I had no illusions about his being happy! The pleasure principle worked out as hangovers and unpleasurable regrets and disillusionments.

The pleasure principle only works when it is linked to something beyond itself. It comes as a by-product of service to God and man. The people who are most inwardly secure from unhappiness are the people who give little or no attention to their own happiness, but seek the welfare and happiness of others. They lose their lives and find them.

A group of people going home from an Ashram were asked by the conductor: "What's happened to you people? You are the happiest people I've seen. What's it all about?" To which the reply was: "We've found God, therefore we've found gaiety." Another group in a large dining room were *gay at breakfast.* The people stared at them as if this were absurd—gay at breakfast! Gaiety had to be worked up through liquor and diversions! But the Christian has a natural gaiety, bubbling from within and needs no diversions. For he has nothing to be diverted from.

O Father, I thank Thee that we can have the pleasure principle within. We can draw water from our own cisterns. I thank Thee that the purest joy known to the human heart is the joy of knowing Thee, of being indwelt by Thee. I thank Thee. Amen.

AFFIRMATION FOR THE DAY: *"In Thy presence is fullness of joy; at Thy right hand are pleasures forevermore."*

SELF-CULTIVATION—ANOTHER ATTEMPT

We come to the last of the ways men take for inner poise and serenity: self-knowledge and self-cultivation. Psychoanalysis is based upon the idea that self-knowledge is self-healing. The ancient Greek saying: "Know thyself" is brought up to date with the addition: "Know thy subconscious self." Self-cultivation is practiced by many modern cults, religious and semi-religious.

Self-knowledge and self-cultivation each have a truth within it. Take self-knowledge. It is necessary to know your self, if you are to grow a self. Psychoanalysis has laid bare the depths. It has contributed much. But it is based upon an illusion: self-knowledge is self-healing. It is not. Some of the most disrupted people of our civilization are the people who have been picked to pieces by psychoanalysis and not put together again in psychosynthesis. Unless you can put people together again on a higher basis by a higher loyalty and love, it is better not to analyze them. Much of this is self-defeating, for it leaves you concentrated on a picked-to-pieces self. To leave you concentrated on your self is unhealthy and bad psychology. I know of a woman who for ten long tragic years has patiently tried to pick herself to pieces hunting for hidden motives which are probably not there. She needs to forget herself in tasks for others. Any system that leaves you occupied with yourself is wrong, however learned it may be.

This is the essential wrong in the cults of self-cultivation. Self-cultivation means self-concentration and self-concentration means self-deterioration—inevitably. It may bring an initial inner boost to begin to cultivate yourself, but it will mean an inevitable letdown. Gordon Allport, professor of psychology at Harvard, says: "Paradoxically 'self-expression' requires the capacity to transcend oneself in the pursuit of objectives not primarily referred to the self." Here psychology and Christian faith coincide: "He that findeth his life shall lose it: and he that loseth his life for my sake shall find it." Self-cultivation is all right and very necessary, provided the self has been surrendered to God. Then it can be cultivated, for it is God-centered and not self-centered.

Gracious Father, Thou art the center of my life. When I find Thee I find myself. For outside of Thee there is nothing but death, inside of Thee there is nothing but life. Amen.

AFFIRMATION FOR THE DAY: *I cultivate and collapse; I surrender and stand.*

SOME CHRISTIAN ANSWERS—HEAVEN

We have examined one by one the various answers, ancient and modern, which men have given to the problem of how to gain inner poise and power. And one by one they have proved inadequate and have left men frustrated or only marginally healed. Doesn't God have an answer?

We take heart when we remember the words of Pflinger: "The cause of every need of a living being is also the cause of the satisfaction of that need." The need calls forth the satisfaction of that need. God created the need in order to satisfy that need. If God's answer to the world's need is Christ, then Christ must have the answer. I believe with the consent of all my being that He has. But before we take His answer we must look at two sub-Christian answers.

A great many Christians rest for inner poise on the prospect of heaven, where all injustices will be righted and all worries and troubles compensated for. This is at the basis of many Negro spirituals—not all, for many saw deeper than this, but it was the hope that gave the Negro slave inner poise and tranquility. He could wait. This hope is being used today. An evangelical preacher comforted the faithful in Russia with the fact that we will soon be in heaven, so we should be inwardly steady in the meantime.

There is a truth here. We are helped to present inner poise by the realization that heaven will wipe out or glorify earth's present troubles. It is good to know goodness will ultimately prevail and heaven will be the scene of it.

But this resting on a future heaven for inner poise is inadequate and precarious. First of all, it is resting on something outside of us. It is resting on an occasional remembrance instead of a continuing realization. You canot gain poise except by a continuing realization now, something that holds you steady from within. And that something must be valid for poise now, even if there were no heaven at all. An inner co-ordination and harmony brings an inner heaven now. Wipe out heaven, and I still have *this*. This puts it where no event in time or eternity can either upset it or let it down.

O God, Thou art my heaven. When I have Thee, I have the future now. All my anticipations become realizations. I live above the possibility of fatal shake or shock. Amen.

AFFIRMATION FOR THE DAY: *No future can guarantee my present; my present must guarantee my future.*

SOME DEPEND ON THE SECOND COMING

We saw yesterday a hope of heaven is an inadequate basis to hold one steady with inner poise. We must look at another marginal answer: the hope of the return of Jesus to set up His Kingdom. Many rest on this as the secret of inner stability.

There is a truth in this: The New Testament uses it as a means for inner poise: "Establish your hearts, for the coming of the Lord is at hand." (Jas. 5:8, A.S.V.) The thought of the immanent coming of the Lord did establish their hearts and did hold them steady. We cannot rule out the possibility of the return of Jesus. He came once—He can come again. History is not exhausted. There may be many surprises in it, among them this one!

But even so, resting on the coming of Jesus is an inadequate basis for inner poise. First of all, it might not happen in our time. For two thousand years it hasn't happened, and millions resting on it have died with hopes unfulfilled. In order to arouse hopes present events and persons are always being fastened on as the precursors of the coming of Jesus. Anti-Christs have come and have gone. In our generation we have had three: the Kaiser, Hitler, and now Stalin. Each time a change has to be made, a rapid shift takes place and a new series of events proclaim the Coming! This is morally and spiritually unhealthy. Fervid hopes have turned to flattened hopes.

But suppose it did happen in our time—would that be a sufficient basis for inner poise? No! For the basis of our poise would be outside of us. No event outside of us is a sufficient basis. It must be within us, holding us within, no matter what happens or does not happen outside of us. Poise and power are dependent on inner conditions, not on outward events, however important they may be. Not that those inner conditions are not resting on and deeply affected by an outward event—the first coming of Jesus. They are. But the historical Jesus has passed over into the Christ of experience. The event has become an experience. The future coming is not an event—it is a hope. It may not happen. But in the meantime we have the experience.

O God, my Father, as we draw near to Thy answer, my heart beats high in expectancy. For we know Thou hast an answer—the Answer—and we would find that. Help me to rest on nothing this side of Thy Answer. Amen.

AFFIRMATION FOR THE DAY: *Today I shall live as if He had come, and then for me He has.*

SOME EXPECT NO INNER PEACE—LIFE IS STRUGGLE

One more sub-Christian answer. There are those who never eypect to find inner poise and power. Life is a struggle. The end is the struggle.

> Awake, my soul, stretch every nerve.
> Fight the good fight with all thy might.

They do not expect to find rest. The seeking, struggling heart will always be within us.

This, too, has a truth within it. "The perfectly adjusted person is the perfectly useless person." We must struggle against the Is in behalf of the Ought-To-Be. We dare not adjust ourselves to circumstances and things as they are, for that adjustment would mean inner decay and death. We must grow, and growth means struggle against environment—inner and outer.

But the Christian conception of struggle is different. "Fight the good fight of faith" (I Tim. 6:12) expresses it. Here there is fight, but it is "the good fight *of faith*"—"of faith" depicts an inner poise and calm amid outer struggle. This is "the *good* fight"—a fight that makes you tense and strained is not a "good fight"; it is a very bad fight. It leaves you exhausted and drained. But the Christian fight, being a "fight of faith," gives you struggle without sapping, fight without fever. The very struggle produces a deeper poise and power. For the strength of the struggle gets into you. "Happy are they who, nerved by thee, set out on pilgrimage! . . . They are stronger as they go." (Ps. 84:5, 7, Moffatt.) Here are people nerved by God, setting out on pilgrimage and instead of exhausting their strength they get stronger as they go! The source of strength is within them—they are "nerved by God."

The idea of the Christian way as a ceaseless, unsatisfied quest with no arriving is a fatal twist that has left a trail of strained, would-be saints, whose piety is a strained piety, and hence unattractive and noncontagious. The Christian way is a ceaseless fountain within, and not a strained, weary pushing on to that next fountain on the roadside.

O Father, I thank Thee that I need not be a strained, struggling soul with no center of undisturbable calm within. "My springs are in Thee." Hence my springs are within. I shall never thirst, for the source of supply is within. Amen.

AFFIRMATION FOR THE DAY: *Today, an open heart, instead of a striving spirit.*

THE CHRISTIAN ANSWER EMBODIED IN CHRIST

We now turn with relief to the Christian answer.

Since Christianity is Christ, the Christian answer to poise and power must be Christ. He is the Word become flesh—the idea become fact. Is He the word of poise and power become flesh—does the idea become fact in Him? To this we can give an unqualified. Yes! In Him we find our quest come to embodiment. In Him poise and power come to perfect illustration—He was poise and He was power. And in Him poise and power are one—His poise was power and His power was poise. This is It!

We have but to turn to the account to find it so. Every line bespeaks poise and every line bespeaks power. And yet the poise and power were manifested in the midst of the problems of men, often with a hostile environment. It was poise and perturbance. His life was one unending struggle and also one unending inner poise.

As a youth He was unperturbed amid the perturbance of His parents and their rebuke. His reply: "Did you not know that I must be in my Father's house?" (Luke 2:49.) Here was assured confidence that He was in the right place, doing the right thing, at the right time—here was poise.

The deeper test of His inner spirit came: Into the wilderness He went for forty days of fasting and temptation. The combination of a prolonged strain upon the body in the fasting and deeper strain upon the spirit in the subtle temptations—temptations which had wrappings of outer good with a core of inner evil—these were enough to leave Him exhausted, a rag. On the contrary, the account says that He "returned in the power of the Spirit." Here was power and poise to the nth degree. A terrific pressure on body and spirit left Him, not exhausted, but exhilarated. Here was physical and spiritual resilience that bounded back into poised power. The very temptations of evil served His purposes. He didn't muddle through; He mastered through. That which intended to weaken Him ended only in strengthening Him. Here is the authentic spirit we have been looking for—a spirit that uses everything, good, bad, and indifferent.

O Father, at last I see what I have been looking for—a spirit that meets everything and masters everything, and does it with poised graciousness. This is the Victory. And this is the Victory which I would have.

AFFIRMATION FOR THE DAY: *Today my mastered spirit shall sit at the feet of the Master Spirit.*

HE ILLUSTRATES POWER AND POISE

We continue our looking at the Answer. When He returned from the wilderness, He went straight into the synagogue and announced His program: "good news to the poor," the economically disinherited, "release to the captives," the socially and politically disinherited; "recovering of sight to the blind," the physically disinherited; the setting "at liberty those who are oppressed," the morally and spiritually disinherited; and the proclaiming of "the acceptable year of the Lord," a fresh world beginning, collective redemption. Here was a new order that would redeem men economically, socially, politically, physically, morally, spiritually, and collectively. It was Good News! The people wondered at the words of grace which fell from His lips!

But He would not go on with a misunderstanding. He would let them know how far He meant to go. God cared especially about widows, lepers, and Gentiles. But every day the pious Jew thanked God he "was not born a woman, a leper or a Gentile!" Here was Jesus cutting across this spiritual snobbery. No wonder the atmosphere changed from admiration to anger. They led Him to the brow of the hill on which their city was built to cast Him down headlong! Did He wilt under this? On the contrary: "He passing through the midst of them went His way"—His way, not theirs! (Luke 4:30, A.S.V.) At the amazing poise the crowd fell back and let Him pass. Here was poise and here was power!

We have seen Him under temptation and strain; now we must look at Him under triumph and success. Will His power and poise be intact there? Many stand bravely with their backs to the wall, but decay when success comes. His came. When He fed the multitudes the crowd hailed Him: " 'This is indeed the prophet who is to come into the world!' Perceiving then that they were about to come and take him by force to make him king, Jesus withdrew again to the hills by himself." (John 6:15.) But why not put His principles and His Kingdom through earthly power? No; He withdrew to pray. He would keep His inner poise intact through prayer. He would not be swept off His feet through herd pressure. Opposition could not break Him, nor success sap Him. Inwardly He was proof against both.

O God, I thank Thee that I see power and poise at work in life—in all ways of life. It works! And now I know it can work in me! I, too, would have a life held steady within by power and poise. Amen.

AFFIRMATION FOR THE DAY: *I lay my failures at Thy feet—and my successes.*

FIVE PLACES WHERE HE SEEMS TO LOSE POISE

We look at one more place, among the many, where power and poise held steady. In the shadow of the cross He turned to His anxious disciples and said: "Peace I leave with you; my peace I give to you. . . . I have said this to you, that in me you may have peace. In the world you have tribulation; but be of good cheer, I have overcome the world." (John 14:27; 16:33.)

A Man who came to set up a world kingdom and to redeem a world is ending in disaster and ending it with power and poise sufficient to hand on to His disciples—enough and to spare! In the white light of this everything else becomes a shadow. He towers over the wrecks of time and over the supreme disturbance of time—the wreck of one's hopes and plans. When all is lost, power and poise remain intact.

But while this is acknowledged, yet there remain at least five places where the power and poise seem absent—perturbance takes possession: *(a)* At the tomb of Lazarus where He "was deeply moved in spirit and troubled . . . , Jesus wept. . . . Jesus, deeply moved again, came to the tomb." (John 11:33, 35, 38.) *(b)* At the coming of the Greeks: "Now is my soul troubled." (12:27.) *(c)* In the synagogue: "And he looked around at them with anger." (Mark 3:5.) *(d)* In the garden of Gethsemane: "He began to be sorrowful and troubled. Then he said to them, 'My soul is very sorrowful, even to death.' . . . He fell on his face and prayed, 'My Father, if it be possible, let this cup pass from me; nevertheless, not as I will, but as thou wilt.' " (Matt. 26:37-39.) *(e)* On the cross: "And about the ninth hour Jesus cried with a loud voice, . . . 'My God, my God, why hast thou forsaken me?' " (27:46.)

In these five places His power and poise seem to have deserted Him. Is there a fly in this ointment of victory—five of them? Or do we come to the very thing that makes the victory more complete—for us? Before we look at that point, let us ask these questions: Suppose He had been unmoved through these crises—would something have been missing? Do these disturbances enhance rather than cancel the victory?

O God, we come now to the very brink of the mystery of Thy Son's pain. Give us insight to see both the mystery and the mastery. For we are certain that mastery is the outcome. Amen.

AFFIRMATION FOR THE DAY: *My darkness may be "the shadow of Thy hand, stretched out still."*

THE ORGANISM IS STABLE ONLY IF IT IS MODIFIABLE

Yesterday we saw that there were five places where Jesus' power and poise seemed dimmed or absent. What is the solution? Must we look on Him as one spotty in His victory?

Let us be reminded of the principle of stability laid down by Charles Richet: "By an apparent contradiction the living being maintains its stability only if it excitable and capable of modifying itself according to external stimuli and adjusting its response to the stimulation. In a sense it is stable because it is modifiable—the slight instability is the necessary condition for the true stability of the organism."

Now applying this to Jesus and to His periods of disturbance we find that it fits in with what we would expect to find. In these five instances we are privileged to look into His processes of adjustment when external stimuli of a catastrophic nature came upon Him. These processes were brief—the adjustment was quickly made, and in each case He emerges with power and poise. To stop at the process and not to see the outcome is to miss the point. The brief disturbance in each case was the process by which His soul adjusted itself to the new and calamitous situation. Had there been no such period of adjustment, then He would not have fulfilled the law which all of us have to obey; namely, we have to be adjustable to survive. That adjustability means disturbance. Without disturbance there is no stability. The brief disturbance is in order to gain stability. That disturbance comes to everybody. The question is, not the coming of the disturbance, but how quickly the adjustment is made and how quickly we emerge having become adjusted and poised. Many take a long, long time to make the adjustment; the period of disturbance is protracted; the suffering is drawn out and devastating.

But in the case of Jesus the adjustment is made very quickly, in some cases almost instantaneously. The place to look is, not at this brief moment of disturbance, but at the quickness of the recovery and the victorious outcome. To linger at the disturbance and not to see the outcome is to miss the point. The point is the quickly adjusted poise.

O gracious Father, I see, I see. I realize that I am now looking at the adjustment periods of the Son of God. Help me to make my adjustment periods brief and victorious. Help me to come out on the right side of calamity. Amen.

AFFIRMATION FOR THE DAY: *Today, by God's grace, shortened adjustment periods.*

THE LENGTH OF THE PERIOD OF ADJUSTMENT

We have noted how the organism can adjust only if it is ex-citable. That is good news to the excitable. They can survive! Jesus was highly organized, sensitized; hence we saw His soul in periods of brief, but intense, adjustments. They had to come. But the real point is, not the periods of disturbance, but their briefness and their outcome.

Take the grave-of-Lazarus disturbance: Jesus was deeply moved and troubled. At what? Apparently at the fact of death. He had come to abolish sin, and death, and here was death striking a loved one. He had to be adjusted to *that*. The distur-bance, however, was brief and soon over. He brushed aside His tears, walked to the tomb, and commanded Lazarus to come forth. And he did. The end is, not the troubled soul and the falling tears, but the command of Himself, the mastery of death, and the risen Lazarus.

Take the coming of the Greeks and His statement: "Now is my soul troubled." Why should the coming of the Greeks to see Him precipitate a crisis in the soul of Jesus? Why, except that they came to invite Him out of the storm which was gathering among the Jews, asking Him to come to Athens to be their honored teacher. It was a crisis over whether it was to be Athens or Jerusalem—Athens with its possible cultured quiet, or Jerusalem with its possible conflict and death. This is not far-fetched, for the account bears it out—the soliloquy of Jesus: "Unless a grain of wheat falls into the earth and dies, it remains alone; but if it dies, it bears much fruit." (John 12:24.) And again: "And I, when I am lifted up from the earth [on a cross], will draw all men to myself." (12:32.) We are privileged to look into this period of adjustment in the soul of Jesus. It was a very shortened period. He gently brushes aside the offer of the Greeks and decides to go on to Jerusalem and die. The end was, not the disquieting adjustment that had to be made, but the ad-justed will. His query "And what shall I say? 'Father, save me from this hour?' " was quickly followed by: "No, for this pur-pose I have come to this hour." He would go through with it. The adjustment was made—He passed through the troubled mind to the tranquil mind.

O God, my Father, I too am tempted to take the easy, un-troubled way—easy but deadly. Help me to make adjust-ments quickly so that my hour of hesitation will be shortened, and I may emerge into tranquility of spirit. Amen.

AFFIRMATION FOR THE DAY: *Today, my adjustment periods so shortened that they become almost automatic.*

HE COMES THROUGH ADJUSTMENT TO ACHIEVEMENT

We must continue our examination of the moments when Jesus had to pass through inner disquietude to inner tranquility. In the passage where Jesus "looked around at them with anger," the added words give the clue to the kind of anger: "grieved at their hardness of heart"—it was, not anger that was personal pique at the attitude of the Pharisees toward Him, but an anger filled with grief that religious leaders could take such an attitude toward a crippled man. The anger was the kind that would redeem both the Pharisees and the crippled man. He passed through it very quickly and healed the man saying: "Stretch out your hand." The period of inner turmoil gave way to healing calm. The end wasn't anger but achievement.

The Gethsemane incident, where Jesus prayed that the cup should pass from Him and where His soul was "very sorrowful, even to death" is not easy to explain on the basis that he shrank from death—that isn't like Him, for He was on His way to death, deliberately so. Then what precipitated the crisis? Was it not that He, who came to save men from sin, was causing men to sin by going on and by making them take sides, knowing they would decide against Him? That is a hard choice: step out, ease the crisis, and thus save men from deciding wrong; or go on, precipitate the crisis, make men decide knowing the decision will be wrong and therefore sinful. Wasn't there another way? "Father, if it be possible, let this cup pass." But it was not possible. He decided to take it. He came to His sleeping disciples and said with poise and calm: "Rise, let us be going"—let us be going to meet the crisis and to face death. He was so poised and so full of quiet power that when the crowd came to take Him, they drew back and fell to the ground. The real point in Gethsemane was not the sorrowful soul, the bloody drops of sweat and the prayer—that was merely the period of adjustment—but the poised, adjusted soul saying, "Rise, let us be going," and actually going out to meet the mob that had come to murder Him. The period of disturbance was brief, but the period of poised tranquility was lasting—lasting through the trial and to the cross. Gethsemane should stand in our minds, therefore, not as the place of sorrow, but as the place of serenity.

God, my Father, when the hour of Gethsemane befalls me, help me to get through it quickly with adjusted will and set purpose. Then I shall be the man of power and poise. Then shall life be adequate for life. Amen.

AFFIRMATION FOR THE DAY: *Today, my Gethsemanes my gateways.*

THE FINAL ADJUSTMENT

We come to the last and most anguished of the periods of adjustment through which Jesus passed—the cry of dereliction on the cross: "My God, my God, why hast thou forsaken me?"

The central cause of that cry must have been this: From the moment He became incarnate there was a deeper and deeper identification with man; here at the cross was the final identification—an identification that meant that He was one with man at the place of his sin. He was dying as a malefactor, a common criminal. That meant that He would feel as the criminal feels—deserted of God and man. So He cried the cry of desertion, for He was identified with man at the place of his sin. So He cried what we cry when we become sinful—but cried it with infinite intensity, for "the whole world's anguish" was "forced through the channel of a single heart." That heart broke.

But only for a moment. He makes the adjustment and passes through to peace: "Father, into Thy hands I commend my spirit. . . . "It is finished." The adjustment was quickly made. His sensitivity suffered infinitely, but not indefinitely. Even amid the anguish He never let go the central fact: "My God"—God was still His Father even amid the anguish of feeling forsaken. There was a center of calm trust even amidst the whirling cyclone of anguish.

And there was power even in the hour of apparent helplessness. For He was master still, even when in the grip of His enemies. He commended His mother to the charge of His disciple; He saved a dying thief and opened the gates of paradise for him; He prayed for enemies: "Father, forgive them," and altogether showed Himself a victor when He most seemed to be a victim.

A man who can make a hard Roman centurion at the foot of the cross beat his breast and cry: "Truly this was the Son of God," is a Man who had both power and poise and had it when in His darkest hour.

Had He not had periods of adjustment to make, had He sailed through every crisis with complete serenity, something would have been lacking. He would not have been Man.

O God, our Father, I thank Thee for these periods of adjustments through which Thy Son passed and passed victoriously. May I, too, do it victoriously and quickly. In His name. Amen.

AFFIRMATION FOR THE DAY: *Today, I shall adjust not to calamity, but to Thy victory over calamity.*

WAS THIS AVAILABLE VICTORY?

We have seen power and poise embodied as fact. The Answer is an answer out of Life to life. It is, not advice, but achievement.

But, someone asks, is not all this unique, incapable of being duplicated? He was He and I am I, and the difference makes Him so different that I admire it but cannot achieve it. On the contrary, He seems to have been able to pass on to those who truly trusted and followed Him the same victory in the same set of circumstances. His power and poise were available to anyone who opened his life to them and received them as a gift. In living fellowship with Him His disciples had the very same power and poise. It was available victory. Had this not been true, then Jesus would have been a monument instead of a movement—a monument to be admired in its cold, isolated achievement, instead of a warm movement to be participated in.

Look at His disciples. They had it. They had what it takes. A nation had murdered their Master; and the very weakest of His disciples—a man who had collapsed under pressure, now reinforced within—is now charging a nation with the murder; and his assurance and power are so overwhelming that thousands with penitent and expectant souls flock to join them to find the same victory.

Take a layman disciple. When they dragged Stephen before the Sanhedrin and lied about him, "his face was like the face of an angel." Lies turned to light. And then when they stoned him, amid the shower of stones he knelt and prayed: "Lord, do not hold this sin against them." This is poise and this is power. The same power that Jesus had has been communicated to the disciples that Jesus had.

And when the tide turned and the disciples became popular, so much so that multitudes began to offer sacrifice to them, they showed the same power and poise that Jesus had when they had tried to make Him a king by force—they refused to be made gods and remained simple, poised men full of divine power. "Thou shalt keep my footing upon the heights" was true of them. Whether buried under stones, or put on thrones, they were not swept from their moorings. They stood inwardly steady, full of power and poise.

My God and Father. I thank Thee that it has happened, not only in Thy Son, but in Thy sons. May it happen in me. Give me that inward Something that insulates me against all that would upset and rob me of peace and power. Amen.

AFFIRMATION FOR THE DAY: *Today, my face shall shine as my heart forgives.*

THE EARLY CHRISTIANS HAD IT

We saw yesterday that the disciples of Jesus were illustrating the Illustration and were incarnating the Incarnation. Take the vitality of this man Paul: "They stoned Paul and dragged him out of the city, supposing that he was dead. But when the disciples gathered about him, he rose up and entered the city; and on the next day he went on with Barnabas to Derbe." (Acts 14:19-20.) Here is a man, supposedly dead from a stoning that must have left him bruised and battered, rising up and going into the city on his own steam. And the very next day walking to another city! We would have had an ambulance take him to a hospital where he would have been laid up for many days, but he had a comeback, a resilience of spirit and body that takes our breath.

But take another illustration. This man Paul could stand before a king and governors and the gentry of a city and say: "I would to God that not only you but also all who hear me this day might become such as I am—except for these chains." (26:29.) Not one word of self-pity, but only pity for the men who did not share his victory. That is mastery. And the graciousness—"except for these chains."

But the last view we get of Paul's mastery is the most overwhelming. A ship is going to pieces under him, and he stands and says: "So take heart, men, for I have faith in God" (27:25, R.S.V.): and then this prisoner takes charge of the ship when the Captain had abdicated, commands the soldiers guarding him what they are to do, and saves himself and the whole company. A prisoner commands a sinking ship and a sinking situation and rescues all. Then as a shipwrecked man he soon had the whole island, including the governor, eating out of his hand, as he healed their sick, and as a result was provided with everything needed when they resumed their voyage. This is power and poise.

We have seen that Jesus had the Answer, and the Answer was communicated to His immediate followers. It would seem that if it worked with them it can work with us. What is the secret, and how can we get hold of it? Will it work in our world now?

Now, Father, I have come to the very center of my quest: Is it possible now, for me? I come with eager expectancy, for I feel that it cannot be for some and not for others. So I open my heart to Thy Answer. Amen.

AFFIRMATION FOR THE DAY: *Life holds no shipwreck now that will leave me a wreck.*

THE SECRET OF THEIR POWER AND POISE?

We now come to ask, What was the turning point in the lives of these very ordinary men who became extraordinary men doing extraordinary things in an extraordinary spirit?

Some would say that it was the fact of the resurrection of Jesus—this turned the tide and gave them inner assurance and power. But while the fact of the resurrection did mentally reassure them, it did not cleanse away the emotions of fear and inferiority. It did not give them power and poise. For after the resurrection it was said: "the doors being shut where the disciples were, for fear of the Jews." (John 20:19.) The news of the resurrection left them still behind closed doors for fear. Emotionally they were uncleansed from fear even after the good news. No amount of good information could produce transformation. Something else was needed. What was it?

The answer is clear: *It was the coming of the Holy Spirit.* A new Power moved into them; took over control; cleansed the depths of them from self-centeredness, fears, inferiorities; reinforced all their natural faculties, co-ordinated them; made them unified persons; and thus filled them with power and poise.

Up to a certain point these men were streaky in their allegiance and in their achievements. Their possession of power and poise was spotty. Sometimes they could rejoice that the evil spirits were subject to them, and sometimes they had to ask with sinking, hearts: "Why could we not cast it out?" They were ready to go to prison and to death with Him and on the way were ready to quarrel over first places. They could whip out a sword and strike off an ear and then could quail before the gaze of a serving maid. They could leave all and follow Him and then "go back and walk no longer with Him." The new life within them was functioning feebly and intermittently. They were not spiritually stablized and the output was meager. They were half-souls trying to produce a whole service. Then something happened. A divine reinforcement took place. They were new men doing a new work.

O God, I see that I, too, am feeble and flickering. My torch is a flickering torch instead of a flaming torch. I would be alight with Thee, reinforced by Thee at the depths. Give me Thyself and I will have all. Amen.

AFFIRMATION FOR THE DAY: *Half-victories are whole defeats—in the light of my Resources.*

THE CRUX OF RELIGION: DYNAMIC

We saw yesterday that the coming of the Holy Spirit into the inner lives of a group of men transformed them from timid believers into irresistible apostles. Draw a line through the pages of the New Testament. On one side you will find spiritual inadequacy and moral fumbling mixed with a good deal of moral and spiritual adequacy and certainty—it is all very sub-Christian. On the other side you will find spiritual adequacy, moral certainty, power of redemptive offense, contagion, healing love, personality a surprise to itself and others, a "plus"—it is all very Christian.

That line runs straight through an upper room where a group of people waited in simple confidence and prayer that the promise that their Master made to them would be fulfilled: namely, that they would receive a divine reinforcement within the total person and the total group. "They were all filled with the Holy Spirit." That line was the dividing line in the moral and spiritual development of humanity. It marked an era. Hitherto men thought that goodness was the exceptional achievement of the exceptional man; but here the ordinary garden variety of humanity found a contagious, powerful type of goodness that transformed the face of humanity. And they found it, not as the whipping up of the will in a strained effort at goodness, but as a relaxed spontaneity from within. Goodness became their native air, the natural output. They were naturalized in contagious goodness. This opened up such an astonishing possibility to morally beaten humanity that multitudes flocked into this new Fellowship where anything that was right was possible. A strange, sober joy went across that sad and decaying world—joy that goodness was here for the asking, that moral victory was possible now, that guilt could be lifted from the conscience stricken, that inner conflict could be resolved and inner unity found, that the total person could be heightened and a "plus" added to one, and that a Fellowship of like-souled persons gave one a sense of *belonging*. It was Good News. And it worked.

It was the coming of the Spirit that wrought this momentous change. For the crux of religion is at the place of—dynamic.

Gracious Father, I am now face to face with my need. I need power—power to live the thing I know. I am weak not at the place of desire but of dynamic. Give me, oh give me, this inner dynamic. Then I shall live. Amen.

AFFIRMATION FOR THE DAY: *My Resources are at hand—can be within me!*

THE HOLY SPIRIT IS GOD WHERE IT COUNTS—WITHIN

The coming of the Holy Spirit within the framework of human nature was the turning of the tide from being a victim to being a victor. What is the Holy Spirit? The *London Times'* literary supplement says: "There are few doctrines more perplexing to the average man than the doctrine of the Holy Spirit." But the Holy Spirit in early Christianity was not a puzzle but a power—the heartbeat of their faith.

The Holy Spirit has been lost in large measure from modern Christianity. We are presenting a Holy-Spiritless Christianity—a demand without a dynamic. A prominent Christian leader said that he did not hear a sermon on the Holy Spirit until he was forty-five, and he had attended Church all his life. A note has dropped out. I read a book entitled *Come, Holy Spirit, Come,* and the only reference in the book to the Holy Spirit was at the end of one sermon: "Come, Holy Spirit, come and dwell with us." That was all. It was a title and not a teaching, a label and not a life. In an exposition of preaching values in the Acts up to the sixty-fifth page the Holy Spirit was not mentioned. Pentecost had been skirted. It was all very brilliant, but it was moonlight instead of sunlight.

Why is it that we celebrate Christmas, Good Friday, and Easter—the birth, the crucifixion, and the rising of Jesus—and yet we pass over the celebration of the coming of the Spirit at Pentecost, the birthday of the Church? Are we more conscious of God with us—the incarnation of Jesus, than of God in us—the Indwelling Spirit? Rufus Jones remarks that by the time the creeds were written all they could say was: "I believe in the Holy Spirit." At great length they outlined the facts of the life of Jesus—the Incarnation—but the Divine Indwelling was mentioned as a belief, a belief instead of an experience. Here is where our faith is faint and anemic. It lacks the red blood of the Spirit's life within our pulses.

For the Holy Spirit is God in action. He is God where it counts—within us. The Holy Spirit is the cutting edge of redemption: He works within, where life is decided.

O God, I thank Thee, that I am on the verge of being introduced to the secret of power. I want to be held from within, for there the issues of life are being decided. Take over my within. In Jesus' name. Amen.

AFFIRMATION FOR THE DAY: *I have believed in the Holy Spirit as doctrine—now as life.*

"FOR THEY WERE AFRAID"

We emphasized yesterday that the Holy Spirit is the missing note in much of present-day Christianity. This was not true in early Christianity. The Holy Spirit was the dynamic by which it was propelled. You couldn't tell where the early apostles ended and the Holy Spirit began. The translators have been puzzled as to whether to use a small *s* or a capital *S* in place after place, for it could be either or both. The human spirit and the divine Spirit had joined forces and seem to be coterminous. And yet the human was not swamped in the divine. It was heightened and released by the divine Indwelling. The Holy Spirit within gave both power and poise.

Suppose there had been no Holy Spirit? Just what kind of Christianity would have faced the world? It would have been the four Gospels without the Upper Room and the coming of the Spirit. Let us glance at the way the Gospels end: Mark ends at chapter 16, verse 8: "For they were afraid." The rest has been added by later writers, so the scholars tell us. Suppose the gospel had ended on that note: "for they were afraid." And that isn't a supposition, for this is what we find in John's Gospel: "The doors being shut where the disciples were, for fear of the Jews" (20:19). Although the resurrection had taken place, yet they were bound by inward fears, and the closed doors were the outer expression of their tied-up condition. Their emotions were stirred by the news of the resurrection of Jesus, but those emotions were not changed from fear to all-conquering faith. No mere event outside of us, however great, can take the place of an indwelling of God, the Holy Spirit within us. Only an Indwelling can rid us of indwelling fears. The Church today is largely there—behind closed doors for fear.

Take the second ending, that of Luke: "And they returned to Jerusalem with great joy, and were continually in the temple blessing God." (24:52.) And dodging the issues! They did not confront the nation with the death of Jesus—did not till the Holy Spirit came upon them. They were "blessing God" but not blasting the soul of the nation for its central crime. Religion made a detour into the temple and stayed there—innocuous.

O God, how often we have retreated behind closed doors or retreated into the temple instead of facing life. Forgive us, and help us to leave closed doors for the open road. Amen.

AFFIRMATION FOR THE DAY: *Today I leave cloisters and closed doors—for me, the open road.*

REFINED INEFFECTUALITY

We have looked at two endings of the Gospels—Mark and Luke. We look at the other two. John ends by saying: "But there are also many other things which Jesus did: were everyone of them to be written, I suppose that the world itself could not contain the books that would be written." (21:25.) Suppose the gospel had ended with a speculation and a consequent controversy as to whether the world could contain the books? How inadequate that ending would be. That doesn't fire the soul for conquests—it leaves us with an irrelevant speculation.

The only Gospel that ends with a well-rounded note is Matthew: "Teaching them to observe all that I have commanded you; and lo, I am with you always, to the close of the age." (28:20.) While this is beautiful, it is inadequate, for it is "with" instead of "in." He is with us but not in us, and anything short of "in" is inadequate and too far away.

If the gospel had ended with the Gospels it would not have been a gospel—not a gospel that would have conquered the world. The whole of these outer events depicted in the Gospels had to move on the inside of them as dynamic power—then the gospel became, not a fear, a worshiping, a world library, a "with you," but a redemption and power within. That changed the world.

We see a Holy-Spiritless Christianity in Ephesus. When Paul arrived here, he sensed a central lack, so his first question was: "'Did you receive the Holy Spirit when you believed?' And they said, 'No, we have never even heard that there is a Holy Spirit.'" (Acts 19:2.) There were twelve men in that group, and without the Holy Spirit what were they doing? Apparently holding their own—noncontagious and without moral offensive. Their spiritual leader, Apollos, was the picture of a present-day highly trained city pastor: "He was an eloquent man, well versed in the scriptures . . . , though he knew only the baptism of John." (18:24-25.) He knew the outer baptism, not the inner. The result was refined ineffectuality. The other Twelve, filled with the Spirit, were turning the world upside down; those twelve filled with a cultured emptiness were barely holding their own.

O God, save me from this refined emptiness that makes of the Christian gospel a culture, but not a conversion. Give me the real thing—the power of the Holy Spirit within. Amen.

AFFIRMATION FOR THE DAY: *I'm through with a cultured emptiness; I'm out for a consecrated fullness.*

FROM IMPOSITION, TO IMITATION, TO INDWELLING

Since the coming of the Holy Spirit was the climaxing of redemption, making redemption effective where it counts, Jesus took great pains to prepare them for His—the Holy Spirit's—coming.

I say "His," for the Holy Spirit is not just an impersonal influence, nor is He just a sense of fellowship when we are together, nor an enthusiasm over ideas or causes—the Holy Spirit is a Person with whom we can commune, from whom we can draw resources, who can be the Life of our life. The coming of the Holy Spirit inaugurates a new era in humanity—the era of the Spirit.

It is impossible to designate well-defined eras in humanity, but in general the stages may be marked as: *(a)* The Old Testament Stage—the childhood stage. *(b)* The age of the Incarnation—the youth stage. *(c)* The age of the Spirit—the mature stage. In the age of the Spirit the authority moves into the center of our beings, and we do from within what was demanded from without. We are, not compelled, but impelled. In the Old Testament stage religion was an imposition, a Law; in the incarnation stage religion was an imitation, trying to do what Jesus was doing; in the age of the Spirit religion is an indwelling, a spontaneous imperative from within. So religion passes from imposition to imitation to indwelling.

To put the three stages another way: God the Father is God *for* us; God the son is God *with* us; God the Spirit is God *in* us. I cannot be satisfied with "for," nor with "with," nor only with "in." God the Father is the Creator; God the Son is the Redeemer; God the Spirit is the Creator-Redeemer within.

The Father's love, the divine intention; the Son's approach, the divine invasion; the Spirit's coming, the divine indwelling. God dwelt in a holy temple, then in a holy Person; now He dwells in us who want to be holy. God in the Old Testament is Light; God in Jesus is Life; God in us is Power. Each time He comes closer, until finally He comes to the ultimate place—within. Authority is never authority until it is within. But when the authority is within, and when that authority is the Holy Spirit, then it must be spelled Authority.

O Father, that is where I want Thee to be—within. I am grateful that Thou art above me, that Thou art with me, but I can never rest until Thou art within me. Then I shall have all. In Jesus' name. Amen.

AFFIRMATION FOR THE DAY: *I'm leaving my spiritual immaturities for God's maturities—I've decided to grow up.*

A RELIGION OF THE SPIRIT

We noted yesterday the various eras. The Law of the Old Testament became the Life in the Incarnation, which became the Liberty in the era of the Spirit.

The Christian faith is a religion of the Spriit. Jesus was conceived of the Spirit; the Spirit descended on Him at the Baptism. He was led of the Spirit into the wilderness, came out in the power of the Spirit, began by saying, "The Spirit of the Lord is upon me." He cast out evil spriits by the Spirit of God, was offered up as a sacrifice through the Eternal Spirit (Heb. 9:14). He was raised by the Spirit of holiness (Rom. 1:4); He issued commandments by the Holy Spirit after His resurrection; He said John baptized with water, but He would baptize with the Spirit, the Church was born of the Spirit at Pentecost; the whole of the Christian faith is a "dispensation of the Spirit" (II Cor. 3:8, A.S.V.). Only those led by the Spirit of God are the children of God (Rom. 8:16); we are made into His image from glory to glory by the Spirit (II Cor. 3:18); the group forms a habitation of God in the Spirit (Eph. 2:22). He guides us into all truth; we are given power by His Spirit in the inner man (Eph. 3:16). The fruits of our Christian lives are fruits of the Spirit (Gal. 5:22); our mortal bodies are quickened by the Spirit dwelling in us (Rom. 8:11). The law of the Spirit of life delivers us from the law of sin and death (Rom. 8:2); we receive power to witness to Jesus when the Spirit comes upon us. From first to last the Christian faith is a religion of the Spirit.

But it is a religion of the Spirit conditioned by the content that Jesus puts within it by His life and teaching. If Jesus reveals the nature of the Father, He also reveals the nature of the Spirit. If God is a Christlike God, then the Spirit is a Christlike Spirit. For men have queer ideas of the nature of the Spirit and His possession. I saw in South India a man, fantastically dressed, seated on the shoulders of another and drinking the blood of goats just sacrificed, and then shaking with the possession of the spirit. The god within was wanting blood and shook the man in approving gratitude. The nature of divine power needed correction and clarification.

O Jesus, Thou hast purified our conceptions of the nature of the Spirit. For we see now that the Spirit is the Holy Spirit and after the nature of the holiness we see in Thee. Amen.

AFFIRMATION FOR THE DAY: *The religion of the Spirit is now my religion.*

THE CONTENT OF DIVINE POWER—IMPORTANT

We saw yesterday that the nature of the Spirit is determined by what we see in Jesus. The fact is that the Holy Spirit and the Spirit of Jesus are used interchangeably: "Having been forbidden by the Holy Spirit . . .; the Spirit of Jesus did not allow them" (Acts 16:6, 7). The Holy Spirit seemed to the disciples to be the Spirit of Jesus within them—they were one.

This is very important, for men have made the divine Spirit into the queer. A holy man in India was drinking charas, an intoxicating drink. When I asked him why, he replied: "It makes me see God." When I suggested it made him drunk, he replied: "An ordinary man like you it makes drunk, but it makes me see God." I saw people falling at the feet of a spastic in India, thinking that his lack of co-ordination was a sign of God within him. Even in the Old Testament there are not the New Testament standards of the meaning of divine power. Witness: "The Spirit of the Eternal inspired him mightily; he went down to Ashkelon, where he killed thirty of the citizens, plundered them." (Judges 14:19, Moffatt.)

This is why God could give the Spirit only sparingly to men until Jesus had fixed the content of the Spirit. Then He could give the Spirit without reservation or limitation. For in Him we see the ultimate character revealed. But the Spirit apart from the Spirit of Jesus is often the spirit of queerness, of unbalance, of the weird. Even today men are afraid of surrendering to the Spirit, for they are afraid that to do so will be to surrender to emotionalism, to get off-balance. But not only was Jesus sanctity—He was sanity. There was nothing psychopathic about Him. He never went off into visions or dreams; He got His guidance through prayer, as you and I get our guidance, and this always when in control of Himself. There were no *samadhis*, or trances, such as the Hindus look for. He was always balanced, and sane, and poised. In fact, He was the most balanced character that ever moved down through human history. And if we are possessed of the Holy Spirit, we will be made like Him, or it won't be the Holy Spirit but some other spirit.

O Jesus, I am not afraid of being made like Thee—I am afraid I'll not be like Thee. For if I am not like Thee, I shall not live. If I am like Thee, I do. Amen.

AFFIRMATION FOR THE DAY: *"We shall be like Him"*—*"Every one who thus hopes in Him purifies himself as He is pure."*

JESUS WAS NO MIRACLE-MONGER

When the early Christian spoke of the Holy Spirit, the content of Jesus was in it. Paul puts them together in these phrases: "the help of the Spirit of Jesus Christ" (Phil. 1:19) and "the law of the Spirit of life in Christ Jesus" (Rom. 8:2). "The Spirit of Jesus Christ" and "the Spirit of life in Christ Jesus" were used for the Holy Spirit. This is why the Incarnation had to take place before the Indwelling, for the Incarnation fixed the character and nature of the Indwelling. It was power exercised after the nature of Jesus' power. So Jesus is the revelation of God's nature and also revelation of God's power. Do not expect God to exercise any power that is not power that Jesus would exercise.

Jesus refused to exercise any magical power to impress people or to validate His claims; so the Holy Spirit will operate within you, not as magical power, but as moral power. Jesus used outer miracle sparingly. If He had power, He had power to restrain that power. He used outer miracle just enough to let us know God was ruler over the total life, and that the universe was not fixed but open; but He threw His emphasis upon God working in the moral and spiritual to produce changed lives. In the Old Testament, Elijah cried on Mount Carmel before the prophets of Baal: "The God that answereth by fire, let Him be God." We now say, in New Testament light: "The God that answers by healed men, let Him be God."

The emphasis in the power of the Holy Spirit is, not on outer signs and wonders, but on the inner signs and wonders of morally crooked men made straight, spiritually impotent and barren people being made victorious and fruitful.

As one modern saint put it: "If God used too much outer miracle, we would become lazy; if he used none, we would be sunk." So the purpose of God seems to be this: just enough outer miracle to let us know that there are open possibilities, but not enough to make us spiritually and morally lazy, depending on God to do everything by miracle instead of doing things by "muscle." But muscle heightened by the power of the Spirit. The Holy Spirit is, not a miracle-monger, but a moral manager.

O God, I need a moral and spiritual cleansing and reinforcement that will make me all-glorious within and adequate for anything without. Amen.

AFFIRMATION FOR THE DAY: *I am determined to be God's moral miracle.*

STEPS IN THE PREPARATION

Since the Holy Spirit is God in action, then we must expect Jesus to put His disciples through a deliberate course of moral and mental training for the reception of the Spirit. We find this course of training unfolded best in John's Gospel. In this Gospel, written later, the whole course was seen in perspective and recorded. There are twelve steps.

1. *The revelation of One upon whom the Spirit descends and remains and One who imparts the Spirit.* "He on whom you see the Spirit descend and remain, this is he who baptizes with the Holy Spirit." (John 1:33.) This is our first necessity: to have One who, though divine, possessed the Spirit in human surroundings, demonstrated its meaning there, and who gives the Spirit to others in the same human surroundings and in the same moral and spiritual manifestations—One who possesses and provides. This would not be, mere teaching, but demonstration in Himself and impartation to others.

John struck two vital notes about this Coming One: "Behold, the Lamb of God, who takes away the sin of the world!" (1:29), and "he . . . baptizes with the Holy Spirit" (1:33). Here are the two characteristic things in the Christian gospel: clearing the way between man and God, by the atonement; clearing the way between man and himself, by the Indwelling. One is atonement, the other is attunement. We need to get right with God and to get right with ourselves, to be at one with God and at one with ourselves. The Christian gospel makes it possible to live with God and to live with ourselves, therefore with others. If you won't live with God, you can't live with yourself, and hence you can't live with others. The gospel makes you live—in every direction and in ever portion of your being.

John says that the special baptism which Jesus gave was the baptism of the Spirit. John specialized in the baptism of water: "I came baptizing with water" (1:31). But Jesus specialized in the baptism of the Spirit: He "baptizes with the Holy Spirit." He never baptized with water; He saved himself to give the "one baptism" with the Spirit. He was to usher in the era of the Spirit, where God works in, and from within, us.

Gracious Father, I thank Thee that Thou art moving straight within me in the Spirit. I cannot be satisfied with Thee anywhere except within. For there I would draw on my Resources. Amen.

AFFIRMATION FOR THE DAY: *The baptism of the Spirit—His baptism— and mine.*

OUTWARDLY, NOT INWARDLY IN?

We continue our examination of the twelve steps in Jesus' preparation of His disciples to receive the Spirit.

2. *The birth of the Spirit.* "Unless one is born of water and the Spirit, he cannot enter the kingdom of God." (John 3:5.) We saw that the first step was to have a Saviour, who himself was full of the Spirit and could impart that fullness to others. Now the first step in imparting that fullness is to impart the new birth of the Spirit. You cannot know the meaning of the Kingdom of God, nor receive its powers to live by, until you are born into it. And how are you born into it? By two things: "born of water and the Spirit." Being born of water means an outer birth into a Christian fellowship—you join a community by an outer rite. Being born of the Spirit means an inner joining of the Kingdom.

It is possible to be outwardly born of water, but not born of the Spirit. You may join a community, but not the Kingdom. Simon Magus was baptized with water (Acts 8:13), but did not have the birth of the Spirit, for Peter had to say to him: "You have neither part nor lot in this matter, for your heart is not right before God" (8:21). He was outwardly in, but not inwardly in. Jesus therefore put His finger on this first step in the In-dwelling—the birth of the Spirit. Without that the rest of the program is impossible. For you cannot make a golden age out of leaden instincts. A big, hulking couple, poorly dressed, came to buy a player piano of a piano dealer. They had sold their crop, were intending to separate; but before they did, they decided to buy a player piano, to listen to its music, to go on a drunken binge, and then to part. As they talked about it, they began to berate each other then and there with the vilest language. My friend said: "Look here, you don't need a player piano, you need God." They admitted it, knelt with him there in the store, and found God, or rather God found them. They were radiant, took the piano home, joined the Chruch, became leading members and respectable citizens. Now the outer music expressed the inner. But to impose music on the inharmonies of their lives was absurd and futile. They needed to be born of the Spirit.

O God, my Father, I see that without the birth of the Spirit I cannot have the blessings of the Spirit. On the very threshold of this quest give me that birth. In Jesus' name. Amen.

AFFIRMATION FOR THE DAY: *I pass from the once-born to the twice-born.*

A MEASURELESS COMING

We saw yesterday that as far as we are concerned, the first step is the birth of the Spirit. In another passage John unfolds how we are not born of the Spirit, and how we are: "Who were born, not of blood [not by inheritance through heredity—by blood] nor of the will of the flesh [not by the strivings of human endeavor—by lifting oneself by his bootstraps] nor of the will of man [no man can confer this on another—no priest, or pope, or parson—not of the will of man], but of God." (1:13.) You find it direct from God or not at all; for neither ancestors by blood, nor you by striving, nor any man by conferring, can give it to you—it is the gift of God by grace.

We would define this birth of the Spirit as that change, gradual or sudden, by which we who are the children of the first birth, through a physical birth into a physical world, become children of the second birth, through a spiritual birth into a spiritual world, by the power of the Holy Spirit, who applies the grace of Christ to us within. Humanity is thus divided into the once-born and the twice-born.

Just as you have to have brains to enter the kingdom of knowledge, an aesthetic nature to enter the kingdom of beauty, an emotional nature to enter the kingdom of love, so you have to have a spiritual birth to enter into a spiritual world—the Kingdom of God. And Jesus said this, not to the gutter type, but to the good type. He said it to a religious Pharisee: "You must be born anew." If he needed it, then we all need it. We come now to the next step:

3. *The coming of the Spirit without measure.* "For he whom God has sent utters the words of God, for it is not by measure that he gives the Spirit." (John 3:34.) Scholars tell us that this last "he" can refer either to God or to Him "whom God has sent." In the latter case it means that Jesus promises to give the Spirit without measure. That fits into exactly what happened—Jesus did give the Spirit without measure to those who sought.

In the new birth the Spirit's coming is by measure. But it is a fact of experience that while new life is present in the birth of the Spirit, it is limited—usually lacks an overflow, an abundance.

O God, my Father, I am grateful for the new life within, and now I want more. My flesh and my spirit both cry out for more. This that I know sets my heart afire for a fullness. Amen.

AFFIRMATION FOR THE DAY: *In myself I am measured; in God I am measureless.*

"LIFE, LTD."

We meditated yesterday on the coming of the Holy Spirit without measure. Jesus said, "I am come that they might have life," the first stage of His coming within us, the stage where He imparts life; "and that they might have it more abundantly," the next stage where, having imparted life, He now inundates us with life. (John 10:10, K.J.V.) In the new birth we had joy, now we have joy with a bubble in it; we had peace, but it was measured, now it is like a river; we possessed love, now it possesses us.

This living on an overflow is what is so lacking in the Church of today. A sign could be put up over our individual and collective lives: "Life, Ltd." And yet Jesus said that the purpose of His coming was to give life "more abundantly." It is that margin that counts—it measures the difference between muddling through this business of living, and living with abounding energy, abounding peace, abounding power. Some of us are living too close to our margins—we are just getting by. When someone asked the little girl how she came to fall out of bed, she replied: "I slept too close to the place I got in." Many of us have tumbles because we have very little margin or moral and spiritual power left. A bit of pressure and we are pushed over into defeat. Most of us can go the first mile, but it is the second mile that counts; we can give the coat, but it is the cloak also that measures the victory; we can bear being smitten on one cheek, but it is the turning the other cheek that makes the difference. Someone has said that "the victory belongs to the one who rots last." The man who has the Spirit doesn't rot at all.

This is what a radiant missionary said: "I had lost my mother in 1929, and I didn't have what it takes to meet the loss, for mother was all the world to me. I struggled and grieved until I felt it was impossible to stay in India without the goods. I didn't have enough of the real essence of Christianity to keep me on top. You spoke on the Holy Spirit; there was a period of silent prayer. Something inside of me snapped into place. Connection was made with the Powerhouse, and the Holy Spirit was mine. I walked down the hill on air. Mother was nearer than she had ever been."

O God, I am so grateful that Thou hast promised to enlarge my margins. I have been living on skimpy resources, have been scraping the bottom of my barrel. Now give me life abundantly. Amen.

AFFIRMATION FOR THE DAY: *From life limited to life unlimited—that is my open door.*

THE OUTFLOW WITHOUT MEASURE

We come now to the next step in the training of the disciples concerning the coming of the Holy Spirit.

4. *The outflowing of the products of the Holy Spirit without measure.* "He who believes in me, . . . 'Out of his heart shall flow rivers of living water.' Now this he said about the Spirit, which those who believed in him were to receive; for as yet the Spirit had not been given, because Jesus was not yet glorified." (John 7:38-39.) The last step told of the inflowing of the Spirit without measure. This step tells of the overflowing of the products of the Spirit without measure. One was intake—the other outgo. Both of them equal—without measure.

This is the rhythm of the life of the Spirit—intake and outflow. If there is more intake than outflow, then the intake stops; if there is more outflow than intake, then the outflow stops—exhausted. The doors open inward to receive only to open outward to give.

Life is no longer a reservoir with only so much resources that if we draw on them we have only so much left, so that therefore we must husband our resources—life is now a channel, a channel attached to Infinite Resources. The more we draw upon those Resources the more we have. So there is no danger of exhausting one's resources. We do not have to harbor them, for the more we give the more we have. We are living the inexhaustible life.

Now, the account says, "Out of his heart shall flow rivers of living water." The Greek word is not a spiritual entity only, the "heart," but a physical entity as well, the "belly" (K.J.V.). In other words, the writer did not hesitate to say that the effects of the Holy Spirit were both spiritual and physical—results will flow. There will be a cleansing and a unifying of the inner life of the spirit and a cleansing and revivifying of the life of the body. The whole being is rejuvenated. And the output of the physical life is heightened and multiplied. A man filled with the Spirit is a man physically filled with the Spirit too. The physical takes on a brightened appearance. A face lifting and a total body lifting takes place.

O Spirit divine, come within this being of mine and work in every part. Quicken my brain cells, give me a better functioning body. Then I shall live—live to my fingertips. Amen.

AFFIRMATION FOR THE DAY: *My body—an organ of the Spirit.*

THE FIRST MAN IN HISTORY REALLY FREE

We meditated yesterday on the stage of the life of the Spirit in which we become outgoing and creative. This is psychologically healthy. For we are made, in the very structure of our being, for creative activity, for contribution; and unless we are contributive, we are in conflict with ourselves. A wife or husband who is always demanding and not donating is a tied-up person.

The world's word is "into"; the Christian words are "out of." Therefore, the Christian personality is a healthier type. The one fits into life, and the other fights it.

The account says that " 'out of his heart shall flow rivers of living water.' Now this he said about the Spirit." The rivers of living water are nine: "The fruit of the Spirit is love, joy, peace, patience, kindness, goodness, faithfulness, gentleness, self-control." (Gal. 5:22.) Note that they begin with "love" and end with "self-control." The Christian method of self-control is, not to sit on yourself in a vain endeavor to keep yourself under control, but to express yourself under the law of love—you love God supremely, and then every other lesser love falls into its place naturally and normally. You are only self-controlled when you are Spirit-controlled. Then every faculty, every passion, every desire, is directed toward the ends for which it is created; and therefore the person is a harmonized person, a fulfilled person, as well as a full person. Paul adds: "Against such there is no law" (5:22); there is no law, there is only a liberty—a liberty to express yourself. Ernest F. Scott, the great New Testament scholar, says, "It is not too much to say that Paul was the first man in history who was really free." He was really free, for "where the Spirit of the Lord is, there is freedom" (II Cor. 3:17)—freedom to be at your best.

And yet while we are free, we are under the deepest exactions ever laid upon the human spirit; for you cannot think a thought, resolve a thing, or even long for anything without the Spirit's intimate approval or disapproval. What bondage! And yet what freedom!

O Spirit Divine, I thank Thee that the moment of Thy coming within me is the birthday of my freedom. Then I begin to live in every cell. I am reinforced and reinvigorated and rejuvenated. I live fully and I live freely. Amen.

AFFIRMATION FOR THE DAY: *In myself—bound; in Thee—free.*

THE PATTERN OF TRIUMPH

We must again look at this passage in John 7:38-39: "Now this he said about the Spirit, which those who believed in him were to receive, for as yet, the Spirit had not been given, because Jesus was not yet glorified."

Why couldn't the Spirit be given until Jesus was glorified? Apparently for two reasons:

a) If the power of the Spirit was to be Christlike power, then it was necessary to see that power manifested through the whole gamut of life, from a carpenter's bench to the throne of the universe, from the denial, betrayal, and crucifixion on the one hand to the triumph of the resurrection on the other. For we had to see this power manifested on a cross as forgiveness of enemies; and we had to see it manifested as supreme modesty and humility, which when he triumphed over His enemies in the resurrection, made him refuse to appear in His triumph before them to cow and overwhelm them—he was humble in every circumstance, and yet almighty in that humility. We had to see this power in its total range, for it was universal power.

b) But there was another reason that the Spirit could not be given until Jesus was glorified: The disciples had to see that this power manifested in Jesus was the ultimate power—it took its place at the center of the universe when Jesus went to the right hand of the Father and was "glorified." This was not obvious to the disciples, for they had been nurtured in the idea that messianic power would be manifested in overwhelming display that would compel acceptance. But the reality was so different! In Jesus love was overcoming evil with good, hate by love, and he would overcome the world by a cross. This was incredible. Was this power final? Would it have the last word? The disciples had to see this power face everything, overcome everything, and go to the place of ultimate power. Then they knew that when this Spirit which was in Jesus came into them, it was ultimate Spirit with ultimate power. The Spirit could not be given in the days of Jesus' humiliation, for that would have set a wrong pattern. He could be given only in the day of His triumph. That set the right pattern.

O God, my Father, I thank Thee that the Spirit within me is the Spirit of triumph. When I live the life of the Spirit, I live the life of triumph. My life becomes "a pageant of constant triumph." Amen.

AFFIRMATION FOR THE DAY: *The power at work in me is Final Power.*

"THE SPIRIT OF GRACE"

Last week we studied the first four steps in the preparation which Jesus gave to His disciples for the coming of the Holy Spirit.

5. *The Spirit's coming would not be a temporary coming—coming for temporary purposes—He would abide in them forever.* "And I will pray the Father, and he will give you another Counselor, to be with you forever, even the Spirit of truth, whom the world cannot receive, because it neither sees him nor knows him; you know him, for he dwells with you, and will be in you." (John 14:16-17.)

The pattern the disciples had of the coming of the Holy Spirit, taken over from Old Testament patterns, was that of temporary afflations of power for temporary tasks. Here Jesus reversed this and gave them the breath-taking news that the Holy Spirit's coming would be a permanent coming—this foreverness of the coming of the Spirit was new. We see it intimated in the Spirit's coming upon Jesus: "He on whom you see the Spirit descend and remain, this is he who baptizes with the Holy Spirit." (1:33.) Note: "remain" and "to be with you forever"—same note.

The idea of an occasional coming is replaced by a permanent coming. The Holy Spirit would not come and go—a kind of furtive, hide-and-seek, sporadic coming. He would move within the recesses of the inner being and stay there forever. The only way He would leave would be by being sinned out by conscious, purposeful, continuous sin. An occasional fall that brought contrition and repentance would not break the relationship. It might cloud it, but He would still be there, ready to restore and heal and re-establish the interrupted intimacy. He is "the Spirit of grace."

There is almost nothing so necessary to get hold of as this, for so many think of the possession of the Holy Spirit as tentative and momentary. But that would defeat the very purpose of redemption, for the Holy Spirit is applied redemption, and His coming must be permanent or the redemption itself is impermanent and hence unsatisfactory and futile. It is "forever" or it is futile. The Holy Ghost is the Holy Guest, and a permanent Guest.

Gracious Spirit, I now see something that I have always wanted to see—Thyself as taking up Thy permanent abode. With Thee there forever I need for nothing, shrink from no task. Amen.

AFFIRMATION FOR THE DAY: *Thou art as permanent within me as my choices—and beyond!*

"HE SHALL ABIDE WITH YOU FOREVER"

Yesterday we meditated on the Holy Spirit as the Spirit of permanence. In a plane I once went over what is known as the "Singing Sands" in Colorado, dunes that were constantly shifting under changing winds, and as they changed they sang. The pilot pointed out a river that disappeared under the sands but emerged at the other side of the dunes, flowing out of sight under the dunes. in spite of the outer dryness, underneath there was the flowing river. It is so with those who have the Holy Spirit—underneath apparent dryness, and amid the winds of outer strife that blow life hither and yon, there is always the gentle flowing of the Spirit's life within. He shall "be with you forever."

Now note that the first work of the Holy Spirit in the life is not a "work" at all—it is "to be with." The important thing is not what He does for you or through you—it is just to be with you and in you. This leads to this conclusion: Don't seek the Holy Spirit for the gifts, but for the Giver. If your attention is concentrated on the gifts of the Holy Spirit—power, effectiveness, joy—then when you have these "gifts," you feel you have the Spirit; but it you haven't any manifestation of the gifts, then you feel the Spirit is absent. This is a mistake, for He shall "be with you forever." Jesus was "led by the Spirit in the desert, while the devil tempted him." (Luke 4:2, Moffatt.) He was led of the Spirit during temptation and hunger, and yet many of those moments must have been soul depressing and dark. And yet the Spirit was *there*, leading and reinforcing *amidst* the temptations. But if the emphasis is upon the gifts of the Spirit instead of upon the Giver, then we go up and down according to the manifestations of the gifts.

In marriage if the attention of the wife is concentrated on the gifts the husband brings, instead of on himself, then the marriage is precarious—it goes up and down with the gifts or the absence of them. The gifts are by-products of a relationship— seek first that relationship, and all these gifts will be added. Seek first the Giver, and the gifts will take care of themselves. For He is *the* Gift!

O Spirit of truth, I thank Thee that Thou hast come to abide with me forever. I am grateful for Thy gifts, but I am more grateful for Thee. For in Thee are all gifts. Amen.

AFFIRMATION FOR THE DAY: *I shall pay attention to the Giver—He pays attention to the gifts.*

"THE STRENGTHENER"

We turn again to the Holy Spirit in John 14:16 and note that He is called the counselor. I say "He," for the Holy Spirit is more than an influence—an impersonal entity. He is a person who counsels, guides, cleanses, empowers, and, most of all, just abides with us and in us. An impersonal influence, an It, doesn't do that!

Here He is called the "Counselor." The translators were all scholars and would therefore lean toward a word having a content of advice, of verbal direction. But the Greek is *para* (beside), *kaleo* (call)—one who is called beside us. For counsel? Yes! For strength? Yes! For everything? Yes! There isn't a single thing needed for life that He isn't there to provide—not merely advice, but asserts. The word used in older translations, the "Comforter," is nearer to it if you take the literal meaning of the word—*con* (with) and *fortis* (strength)—one who strengthens you by being with you.

But there is a further emphasis to be found in the "Strengthener," the emphasis that He strengthens all our natural powers, brings them up to their highest, gives them a "plus." The natural is only at its best when it is reinforced by the Supernatural. When the powers of the inner life are co-ordinated under the Spirit's control, then those powers are no longer canceling themselves out by conflict between them. The man becomes *a man,* not *many* men, each fighting for the mastery within and leaving the whole a consequent cipher. He is the Strengthener!

But note further that the Strengthener is called "the Spirit of truth." He not only brings truths to you, but He himself is the essence of truth, the Spirit of truth. So the Spirit of truth doesn't free us by magic—He frees us by making us be identified with truth, and then "the truth" makes us "free." He cleanses us from all lies, all evasions, all make-believe, all false fronts, from all except complete sincerity. He brings a crystal clarity that makes for power. It is no magic—the laws of well being are fulfilled, and therefore well being flourishes.

O Spirit of truth, make me to be so truthful that I become truth, so pure that I become purity, so loving that I become love. I cannot do this. Thou canst. Amen.

"WITH" OR "IN"

We must pause another day on the passage in John 14:16. Concerning the Spirit of truth it says that "you know him, for he dwells with you, and will be in you."

Note the difference in the prepositions "with" and "in." Before the outpouring on the Day of Pentecost the Holy Spirit was "with" the disciples; afterwards He was "in." You can see the difference: on the other side was effectiveness mingled with ineffectiveness; they cast out devils at times, and at times the devil possessed had a better case of devil possession than they had of Spirit possession. They forsook all and followed Him—all except themselves, for they were constantly being entangled with their unsurrendered selves. They were loud in their assertions of loyalty and louder in their collapses. The Spirit was with them, inspiring, guiding, cleansing, but only *with,* for they had not yet surrendered the depths—He was not *in.* Their Christian lives had not found an inner poise, and hence they lacked outer power. Then the Spirit came upon them, in them, and fitful living became faithful living; erratic loyalty became everlasting loyalty. The Spirit was functioning *in* them.

Today the Holy Spirit seems to be more "with" the average Christian than "in." He comes now and again to illuminate in a crisis, to censure in a fall, to urge against our sloth, to point out duties undone, and to keep us going, although it is at "a half-dying rate." The average Christian lives under the lash of demand rather than under the liberty of the Spirit. He lives under the "ought" instead of the "can."

The life of the Spirit is a life that lives on Resources within. It is natural just because it is within. It is the expression of human nature illuminated, controlled, and directed by divine Nature. It is supernaturally natural. The most natural man that ever lived was the supernatural Man. For, as Chesterton says, "if the natural will not submit to the Supernatural it becomes the unnatural." Jesus was perfectly surrendered and hence perfectly natural. We must move from the "with" to the "in"—the difference in a preposition will make a difference in our personality.

O God, the Spirit, Thou hast been with me and I am grateful; now be in me and I shall be more than grateful—I shall be forever Thine. I have tasted of Thee, and now I cannot rest till Thou art within forever. Then I shall live. Amen.

AFFIRMATION FOR THE DAY: *The Spirit within makes adequacy without.*

THE MAGICAL AND THE MORAL

Another phrase beckons us: "another Counselor," or another Strengthener.

That word "another" fixes the character of the Strengthener. For the Strengthener was to be like Jesus—"another." Without that word "another," the Strengthener is unanchored. Strengthen you to do what? See how men stumbled in pre-Christian days when they described the work of the Spirit: "The Spirit of the Lord came upon Jephtah. . . . And Jephtah vowed a vow. . . . If thou shalt without fail deliver the children of Ammon into my hands, then it shall be, that whatsoever cometh forth of the doors of my house to meet me, . . . I will offer it up for a burnt offering." His daughter came out, and after a great deal of hesitation he "did with her according to his vow." (Judg. 11:29-31, 39.) Obviously that was pre-Christian and sub-Christian. The content of Jesus had not yet gone into the Holy Spirit.

The fact is that the Holy Spirit is a distinctly Christian conception. The Spirit of God is the Old Testament word. The Holy Spirit is the New Testament word. The content of Jesus has gone into it.

Today I picked up the paper, and it told of people who allowed a child to be bitten by a snake in order that the power of God might be manifested in her healing. The healing didn't take place, and it shouldn't have taken place, for this is contrary to what we see in Jesus. He refused to perform a miracle to show power or to convince His enemies. When Herod asked Him to show a miracle, all He showed was the miracle of His silence. His was, not a magical revelation, but a moral revelation. He used no power except in behalf of human need. It was always under moral control. It is true that Paul shook off a serpent into the fire and was unharmed, but he was bitten in the course of duty. Had he bought a snake to let it bite him to prove his Master's power and to convince the people, he would have died. For that would give religion a fatal twist—the magical would take the place of the moral.

So Jesus had to say "another" in speaking of the Spirit. The Spirit's power is the same as Jesus' power.

O Spirit Divine, Thou art the Spirit of Christlikeness. Thou wilt work only according to His character. I thank Thee, for I can trust Him wholly, hence trust Thee wholly. Amen.

AFFIRMATION FOR THE DAY: *I shall not look for miracles —I shall be one; then the miracles will come naturally.*

THE SILENT BUT ULTIMATE FORCES OF GOD

We are now at the crux of the whole question concerning the power of the Holy Spirit. A great many people are afraid to surrender themselves and their powers to the Holy Sprit; for they are afraid they will become queer, off-center, unbalanced.

But if the Holy Spirit is "another" Strengthener, then this means that the power He exerts produces the same character as we see in Jesus. The Holy Spirit will make you Christlike, or it is some other spirit—the spirit of unbalance or the spririt of intolerance. Are you afraid of being Christlike, afraid of being like the most balanced Character that ever moved down through life—the only Sane Man in an insane world? He is so balanced that He makes the rest of us seem off-balance. If we are not like Jesus, then we are neither good, nor wise, nor balanced. If we are not like Him, we are bad, unwise, and unbalanced. For here is life just as it ought to be—or, better still, just as it is. For anything that is un-Christlike is un-life.

Here we can let go with abandon, complete abandon, knowing that when we have the Spirit of Jesus, then the moral laws of the universe have come to embodiment in us, and with the moral laws the moral stability of the universe. The sum total of reality is behind us. When we act Reality acts. All our actions are guaranteed by the moral universe. The stars in their courses fight for us. We do not have to fight—all we have to do is fit—to fit into God's purposes as revealed in Jesus, and then the moral universe guarantees the rest. This brings inner poise—knowing that the silent but ultimate forces of God are guaranteeing us and our way of life. We need not fussily try to hold things together, for they hold themselves together—in Him.

The Holy Spirit is the Spirit of Jesus become intimate and operative within. That is good news. The ultimate Character and the ultimate Power are at work in the recesses of our beings, making us into the image of Jesus. We can ask for nothing higher, we can be content with nothing less. This is *it*: Ultimate Power producing ultimate Character.

O God, my Father, I am not afraid of being like Thy Son—I am afraid I won't be like Him. For to be like Him is the highest possible. So I surrender to the processes of the Spirit—surrender to be like Him. Amen.

AFFIRMATION FOR THE DAY: *To be under the control of a Christlike Spirit—this is the highest destiny possible.*

FINAL BUT UNFOLDING

We come to the next step in the preparation of the disciples to receive the Holy Spirit.

6. *The Holy Spirit would become Teacher and Remembrancer.* "But the Counselor, the Holy Spirit, whom the Father will send in my name, he will teach you all things, and bring to your remembrance all that I have said to you." (John 14:26.)

This is an important step. A prominent agnostic said that there is an irreconcilable conflict between science and religion, for science is never fixed—it is open and progressive; religion, on the other hand, becomes fixed in absolutes, and non-open dogmas. This observation is true of some interpretations of Christianity. But it is not true of the Christianity of Christ. For in it He provides for a continuing revelation—"He will teach you all things."

It is true that the Christian faith is that in Jesus we have God's final because of God's complete self-disclosure. We do not see in Jesus God's total omnipotence—that would do us no good, for it would frighten us to death to see what the omnipotent God could do. Nor do we need to see in Jesus God's total omniscience—it would overwhelm us to see all that God knows. The revelation of God's omnipotence and omniscience would not be redemptive—it would be paralyzing. What we do want to know is: What is God, like in character? For what He is like in character we must be like. God's character we have seen in Jesus. If we haven't, then we are not interested, for if God is not like Jesus, He is less than good. A thoughtful Hindu said: "When you said that you would not even accept God if He were in any way unlike Jesus, I wondered at your all-devouring passion for Christ. This is *Bhakti* [devotion] par excellence." In Jesus God's final unfolding of Himself.

But if this revealtion is final, it is unfolding. The Holy Spirit continues the revelation—"He will teach you all things." But His teaching is according to a pattern: "He will bring to your remembrance all that I have said to you." The revelation is unfolding, but unfolding according to what we see in Jesus.

O God, I have just what I want: something fixed and yet something unfolding. For I want to rest in something and yet be spurred to more by that very assured rest. Amen.

AFFIRMATION FOR THE DAY: *The one point of my compass is fixed in Thee, the other sweeps the horizon of reality.*

"MORE," BUT NOT "OTHER"

We ended last week on the necessity for a final but unfolding revelation. Here is the tragedy of the movements not anchored to the historic Jesus. They emphasize the universal Christ with little emphasis upon the historic Jesus. They read into this unincarnate universal Christ their own vague contents instead of the very definite content which Jesus Himself put within it by His own life and teaching. John puts it: "By this you know the Spirit of God: every spirit which confesses that Jesus Christ has come in the flesh is of God, and every spirit which does not confess Jesus is not of God." (I John 4:2-3.) Unless the Jesus-content is in God, in Christ, and in the Holy Spirit it is not of God.

This anchoring to the historic Jesus saves Christianity from a vague theosophy which wanders from the novel to the novel without fixity, and at the same time it saves it from the fixity that becomes rigid dogmatism by providing the continuing revelation of the Spirit.

The Holy Spirit will teach us all things, but in the teaching will call to our remembrance all that Jesus has said. He will teach us *more* than Jesus taught, but not *other* than Jesus taught. Here is conservatism, conserving all that Jesus taught; here is radicalism, applying to new areas of life the universalism of Jesus. The word "radical" comes from the Latin word meaning "the root." Here in Christianity is the real meaning of radical: its root in the past, its fruit in the past, present, and future.

Note again: "He will bring to your remembrance *all* that I have said." Note the "all." When we are not under the Spirit's guidance, we tend to become fastened on some thing or things Jesus taught and neglect the "all." The consequence is a lopsided Christianity with an overemphasis on some things and an underemphasis on others. Whole denominations are built around one truth. They live on a truth instead of on the Truth. They have to be controversial to justify their lopsidedness. Christians under the Spirit are not controversial, but creative.

O Spirit of God, take from my heart all living on a truth, or on a cluster of truths—I want to live on the Truth. For I know I will become what I feed upon. Amen.

AFFIRMATION FOR THE DAY: *In others there are truths; in Christ there is the Truth.*

ON BECOMING CREATIVE AND CONTAGIOUS

We continue our study of the steps in the disciples' preparation to receive the Holy Spirit.

7. *The Holy Spirit witnesses to Jesus and produces witnesses who do the same.* "But when the Counselor comes, whom I will send to you from the Father, even the Spirit of truth, who proceeds from the Father, he will bear witness to me; and you also are witnesses." (John 15:26, 27.) Here is a step further: the Spirit is the Witness to Jesus and the creator of witnesses to Jesus. He not only unfolds truth—He unfolds persons. He makes them creative and contagious. Wherever the Spirit is, there creation continues.

This verse was fulfilled after the Holy Spirit came upon the disciples: "And we are witnesses to these things, and so is the Holy Spirit whom God has given to those who obey him." (Acts 5:32.) Here were human spirits and the divine Spirit working together for the same purposes, witnesses to the same Person and with the same power. The creative Spirit makes creative persons who in turn make creative persons.

This is the line of apostolic succession. Those who have the apostolic success are in line with the apostolic succession. They transmit not merely truth but the very Spirit of truth—the creative activity of God. If a minister or bishop has the Spirit of God, and he lays his hands on you, then you will receive the Spirit of God if you are surrendered and receptive. But if he has, not the Spirit of God, but only the spirit of ecclesiasticism, then when he lays his hands on you, you will receive that spirit and nothing more. As a humorous friend of mine put it: "If a bishop hasn't the Spirit of God but has the measles, and he lays his hands on you, then you will not get the Spirit of God, but you will get the measles!" You can give only what you have.

The Spirit is "the Spirit of truth"—there is no make-believe, no hocus-pocus, nothing but reality. Others bring truths; He brings not only truths but the Spirit of truth. Under His sway we become so truthful we are truth; we become so loving we are love.

O Creator Spirit, live within me and make me creative. For I am made for creative activity, and I cannot rest until I am outgoing and creative. I surrender all my dead powers to Thy Life. Make them live. In Jesus' name. Amen.

AFFIRMATION FOR THE DAY: *I have witnessed the Truth; now I shall be a witness to the Truth.*

51

CONVINCING WITNESSES

8. *The Holy Spirit not only makes us witnesses but convincing witnesses to Jesus.* "It is to your advantage that I go away, for if I do not go away, the Counselor will not come to you; but if I go, I will send him to you. And when he comes, he will convince the world of sin and of righteousness and of judgement." (John 16:7-8.) Here the Spirit creates convincing Christians. Two people speak the same thing: the words of the one fall upon the heart and mind but leave little or no impression; the words of the other are not only convincing but creative—newborn souls and new impulses and movements arise.

But before there is a coming to newness, there must be a break with the old. The Holy Spirit precipitates a crisis. Sin must be faced and effaced. The Spirit convinces of three things: sin, righteousness, and judgment. Sin is what you have done wrong; righteousness is what you might have done right if you had not done wrong; judgment is in regard to both. We will be judged not only for what we have done wrong but also for what we might have done right had we not done wrong.

Now note: "Of sin, because they do not believe in me" (16:9)—the very center and essence of sin is not believing in Christ, not making Him the center of your life. For if you don't make Him the center, then you make yourself the center—you are God—and making yourself God is the essence of sin.

Further: "Of righteousness, because I go to the Father" (16:10)—I go to the Father to give you the Holy Spirit, making possible righteousness, a righteousness that comes from the Spirit within. So you will be judged for the righteousness you might have had through the Spirit.

Finally: "Of judgment, because the ruler of this world is judged" (16:11)—the ruler of this world, the very center of evil, has been judged. Evil has met its match, has been defeated, and now we face no evil that hasn't the footprint of the Son of God on its neck.

O Jesus, I thank Thee that I face nothing which Thou hast not faced and hast not conquered. That gives me the glorious sense of victory as I go into life. I am afraid of nothing, for I've bowed to Thee. Amen.

AFFIRMATION FOR THE DAY: *Today I shall be a convincing demonstration of Christ's saving power.*

GOOD NEWS, OR MUSTY VIEWS?

We saw yesterday that when the Holy Spirit comes within us, He makes us convincing Christians. When we speak, there is a sense of moral power in what we say; when we act, we act with the sum total of reality behind us. We have power and are convincing. That is lacking in the modern Chruch. It is all explicable, can be accounted for by the human resources available. There is no unexplainable Plus. It is the human spirit instead of the Holy Spirit. It is not convincing. I glance up from my writing, and across the street on a third-rate hotel is a sign with letters washed out and made dim with age: "Newly Furnished Rooms." It isn't convincing! There is no sign of newness. The average church makes you think, not of good news, but of musty views. Nietzsche said: "The Christians must look more redeemed before we can believe in redemption." The coming of the Holy Spirit gives a face lifting so we look redeemed, gives an inner assurance so we feel redeemed, empowers us at the place of the will so we act redeemed, and reinforces every portion of us so we are redeemed. Now another step:

9. *The Holy Spirit guides us into all the truth*: "When the Spirit of truth comes, he will guide you into all the truth." (John 16:13.) This is a step beyond the stage 14:26, where "He will teach you all things"—here He not only teaches you the truth; He guides you into the truth, guides you into the possession of it. In the first stage you see; in this you seek—and find! The one is illumination, and the other is illustration; one is the word, the other the word made flesh.

Here is the weak place in contemporary religious life—it is informed but not inspired; it knows all about life but doesn't possess it. The preacher is a guidepost instead of a guide—he tells you what to do but does not show how to get the power to do it. The Holy Spirit is not in control. For He guies you—takes you by the hand and guides you—in the possession of all the truth. He turns the ideal into the real, aspiration into acceptance, and makes the whole operative now. As in Jesus through the Holy Spirit the Word became flesh, so in us the Word again becomes flesh.

O Holy Spirit, this is what I want. I want to have all my longings become actuality. So I surrender to Thy guidance now. Guide me into the possession now. Amen.

AFFIRMATION FOR THE DAY: *Today: illumination becomes illustration.*

DESTINY IN DIRECTIONS

10. The Holy Spirit will give you the prophetic spirit. "He will declare to you the things that are to come." (John 16:13.) There are two ideas of prophecy—one where a person tells by almost magical foresight what is going to happen. He imposes his declaration on events. The second declares, more by insight than foresight, that certain ways fit in with God's way, and the future is with them—reality backs them.

The Old Testament prophecy illustrates the first, the New Testament the second. The difficulty with present-day "prophetic" preaching is that it is more often the Old Testament type than the New. It is trying magically to prophesy events, instead of morally discernment that certain events are bound to follow certain causes. New Testament prophecy, instead of trying to direct destiny, sees destiny in directions.

And it sees that Jesus determines destiny—whatever fits in with Him lives, and whatever goes in opposition to Him perishes. "For the testimony of Jesus is the spirit of prophecy." (Rev. 19:10.) If you testify to Jesus and point men to Jesus as having the final word, then you have the spirit of prophecy. You are forecasting the future, for you see the present. You see that the way of Jesus is the Way—the Way unqualified. It is the way to think, to act, to be, in every conceivable circumstance. There are only two things—the Way and not-the-way. The Way of Jesus is always the Way, and every other way is not-the-way. Therefore you can write the destiny of everything, and you can write it now: Everything that fits in with Jesus is destined to rule, and everything that does not fit in is doomed to ruin. This is the "sure word of prophecy."

So those who possess the Spirit of God are not behind the times, nor with the times, they are ahead of the times. For they see the future in the past—see it in the revelation of Jesus. They know that He is the "Alpha," the Christ of the Beginning; and the "Omega," the Christ of the Final Word. Therefore they project His word into that future, knowing that heaven and earth may pass away; His word never. They have the Spirit of prophecy.

O Jesus, I know that in Thee the past, present, and future are unfolded. Thou art final. Help me then to boldly proclaim Thy victory, even when it is not here. Amen.

AFFIRMATION FOR THE DAY: *Today I shall act as though the Kingdom were already here.*

A SEVEN-DAYS' WONDER?

11. The Holy Spirit will glorify Jesus. "He will glorify me." (John 16:14.)

This statement in the process of education of the disciples for the receiving of the Holy Spirit points up the whole purpose—the end of the coming of the Holy Spirit is, not to glorify the person who receives, nor the Person who is received, but to glorify Jesus. That puts the emphasis in the proper place. For if it glorified the person receiving, making him a seven-day wonder in spiritual things, that would make religion egocentric—the wrong center. And, again, if it glorified the Holy Spirit, that would glorify something without character content, for it would be cut loose from the Incarnation. It is the Incarnation that gives character content to God, to the Holy Spirit, and defines what we must be like. Hence the final emphasis is on Jesus, the Incarnate.

In India in a marriage procession the people often walk alongside the bridegroom, seated on a horse, and hold up torches to light up the face of the bridegroom. The work of the Holy Spirit is to light up the face of Jesus. "No man can say Jesus is Lord, but by the Holy Spirit."

This saves religion from going off onto tangents of subjectivity. For it is possible for the subconscious mind to give suggestions to the conscious mind which we may interpret as the Voice of the Spirit. This is particularly true in matters of sex. Our own subconscious desires may be projected as the Inner Voice. For instance, a very sincere person hears a "Voice" saying: "Your marriage relation is dissolved, and a new one will be formed." If subjectivity is not checked by something outside as a divine Standard, then this is authentic. But the moment that "Voice" is tested with Jesus, then it becomes worse than doubtful, for He said that only adultery or death dissolved the marriage bond. And there is neither in this case. A very sincere girl hears a "Voice" saying that a certain person is to be her life mate. But nothing had been communicated to the other person! Subconscious desires projected as guidance have to be tested as to whether they fit into Jesus—our objective standard.

O God, my Father, here I walk on delicate ground and shall need Thy clarity. Give me the clear vision of Jesus so that I shall always decide according to Him. Amen.

AFFIRMATION FOR THE DAY: *Today, none of my light shall turn to darkness.*

"TAKE THE HOLY SPIRIT"

We come now to the last step in the teaching of Jesus in John's Gospel concerning the finding of the Holy Spirit:

12. *"Receive the Holy Spirit."* (20:22.)

The end of the eleven steps was the twelfth: the reception of the Holy Spirit as a personal gift. The quest ended in finding. This was not a case of "ever learning and never coming into the knowledge of the truth"—the end of the learning was the creation of a yearning, which became receptivity, which became finding.

But the finding did not take place when He breathed on them and said, "Receive the Holy Spirit." It did not take place for nearly fifty days afterwards. Then, where is the reality of the saying "Receive the Holy Spirit" when they did not receive? It is in the fact of Jesus' character. When he says "Receive," then you have received, even though the manifestation does not take place till later. The space in between is the space where you rest on Him, not on your subjective realization. It is the period of intensive schooling, teaching us that faith and not feeling is the basis of the life of the Spirit. For Him to say "Receive" is to receive. His word is our sufficient assurance. "Heaven and earth will pass away, but my words will not pass away."

This period of waiting for the manifestation is the weaning period—it wears us from all dependence on our own emotions and throws us fully on Him. We learn that emotions are unstable—He abides forever. We learn that if we depend on emotions, we will be temperamental Christians, going up and down with our emotions; but when we depend on Him, then we are trustful Christians, holding steady amidst changing of emotions—"believing where we cannot see."

But note that the word "Receive" is not passive but active. It could be translated, "Take the Holy Spirit." Here was active receptivity, a reaching out by faith in the character of the One who invites us to take. There were forty-seven days of resting on His word and an eternal lifetime resting on His word, plus corroborating experience! The experience was richer and sweeter because it had faith in it.

O Jesus, I know when Thou dost speak, it is done then and there. Help me to accept it and to walk in it, even though I walk by dry faith. For I know that faith will turn to fact and fact to feeling. Amen.

THE SEVEN PILLARS OF THE CHRISTIAN FAITH

We have traced the preparation which Jesus gave to His disciples concerning the coming of the Holy Spirit, as recorded in John's Gospel. Before we look at the actual fact of the coming of the Spirit, we must look at one more step in the preparation.

Before Luke describes the coming of the Spirit, he sums up the facts upon which the Christian gospel rests. For he could not describe this power until he had fixed in the mind of the reader the *type* of power which came in the Holy Spirit. That type could be fixed only by his reminding us that it was a Jesus type of power. The same power that was working in Jesus would be working in us—the same *quality*. That sets everything in the right direction.

So Luke fastens upon seven facts as the pillars on which the Christian faith rests. He sums these up in the first three verses of the Acts.

1. *The Word becomes flesh:* "All that Jesus began to do" (Acts 1:1). The gospel begins with Jesus—the Incarnate. It is first of all a *fact*—the fact of Jesus. It begins, not with a Word, but with the Word made flesh. Had it begun with a Word, it would have been a philosophy. It began with the Word made flesh, so it was a fact, not a philosophy. Had it been a philosophy, it would have been good views. It was a fact; hence it was good news. To present the Christian faith as primarily a philosophy of life is to place it alongside of other philosophies of life—above them, but one of them. This makes the issue of question of the best ideas. But Jesus never presented good views—He announced good news. And He was the good news. The gospel lies in His person. He did not come to announce good news. But He came to present Himself as good news. He did not come to announce the forgiveness of God—He was the forgiveness of God. The word of forgiveness became flesh in Him. He did not come to announce God's love to man—He was that Love.

If the gospel were primarily a set of good ideas, then the end would be intellectual assent and acceptance. But if the gospel is primarily a Person, then the end is a surrender to, and a following of, that Person.

O Jesus, I see that Thou art the good news. I also see what I must do about it—surrender to, and follow, Thee. I do—with all my being. I would give, and give all, and would do it now. In Thy name. Amen.

AFFIRMATION FOR THE DAY: *Today, all of my good views shall grow out of the Good News.*

THE WORD BECOME FLESH

We saw yesterday that the primary thing in the Christian faith is: the Word made flesh—an incarnate Fact.

The gospel is primarily founded, not on the universal Christ, but upon the incarnate Jesus. You cannot say "Christ" until you have first said "Jesus." For Jesus puts contents into Christ—the content of His own life lived out among us. A Hindu swami in India said: "We can all accept the universal Christ." Why? Because you can read into the universal Christ any content you want, but you cannot read into Jesus any content you desire. For it is fixed—fixed by the historical facts. He put His own content into it by His life, deeds, and teaching. It is anchored in history. That saves the gospel from meaningless theosophies that wander here and there amidst ancient ideas and new intellectual fads without any fixed conent. "We are the congregation of the queer," said a leading theosophist to me one day. Why? Because they were at the mercy of the latest novelty, and that produces the unstable queer.

Note that the cults that emphasize self-cultivation, discovering the Divine within you, are all based on the universal Christ—not on the incranate Jesus. Why? Because the universal Christ does not demand self-surrender, but the incarnate Jesus does. The universal Christ is an idea to be accepted; the incarnate Jesus is a fact to be surrendered to and followed. The one appeals to the intellectual conceptions, the other to you—to the whole you.

Do not misunderstand me. I believe in that universal Christ; but, I repeat, you cannot say "Christ" before you have said "Jesus," for the universal Christ is defined by the historic Jesus. You cannot say "God" or the "Holy Spirit" or "Christ" until you have first said "Jesus." The gospel begins at Jesus. In Him you are confronted with God's offer and demand—an offer of redemption and a demand to take sides.

"There are many religions, there is but one Gospel." So the gospel does not stand alongside other religions and philosophies—it confronts all religions, all philosophies, all life, with the good news.

O God, how grateful I am that in Jesus Thou dost offer me Thy all. In Him I find the fullness of the Godhead bodily. And here I find what I need most—redemption. I thank Thee—thank Thee. Amen.

AFFIRMATION FOR THE DAY: *The first law of my being is self-surrender; the second law, self-cultivation.*

THE WORD BECOME GUIDANCE

We come to the second fact upon which the Christian gospel rests:

2. *The Word become guidance:* "All that Jesus began to do *and teach*" (Acts 1:1, italics mine).

We said yesterday that the gospel was, not primarily a philosophy, but a fact—the fact of Jesus. But it has a philosophy, and the philosophy grows out of the fact—the teaching is based on the doing: "All that Jesus began to do *and* teach." It was, not primarily a teaching, but a doing. The teaching is the unfolding of a doing, something that was operative within Himself. He taught nothing that He had not been practicing. That makes His word come with power, "He taught them as one who had authority, and not as the scribes." They quoted authorities, and He spoke with the authority of His own life behind everything He said. The newness of the teaching of Jesus is not merely in what He said but in the illustration He gives to everything He said. People didn't merely hear the Word—they saw it.

"The Word became flesh," and then the flesh became Word. The message was verbal from His lips, but also vibrant in every portion of His being. His words were deeds, and His deeds were words, and coming together with what He was became the Word made flesh. His words and His deeds blended like the words and music of a song. He was so truthful that He was truth, so loving that He was love, so good that He was goodness, so morally beautiful that He was beauty, so living that He was life, so godlike that He was God.

So His teaching was not idealism imposed on life—it was realism exposed from Life. The Christian Way has been realized—in Jesus. And when it was perfectly realized, it produced the perfect Character. The teaching was testimony— an unfolding of something operative in Himself. So Jesus is not a signpost pointing to the Way—He is the Way, and to follow Him is to find oneself on the Way.

"Jesus is nowhere out of place," for everywhere He is light to that situation. "As long as I am in the world, I am the light of the world"—nowhere is Jesus not light. He has the answer, for He is the Answer.

O Jesus, I thank Thee that I follow, not a ghostly idea, but an incarnate Fact. Make Thy ideas to become fact in me. Give me everything Thou hast—to my capacity. Thou art doing it now. Amen.

AFFIRMATION FOR THE DAY: *Today I shall demonstrate the realism of the Kingdom of God.*

THE WORD BECOME VICARIOUS

We continue our study of the seven facts upon which the Christian gospel rests:

3. The Word become vicarious: "After his passion" (Acts 1:3).

When this Word becomes flesh and then becomes guidance, then we come to the next obvious development—that Word meets sin in the loved one, and of necessity suffers, turns vicarious. For it is the nature of love to make the sins of the loved ones its own. If it is love, it is bound to suffer in the sufferings and sins of the loved ones. All love has the doom of bleeding upon it when sin develops in the loved one.

The moment God created, that moment the unseen cross was upon His heart, for the sins and sufferings of His loved ones were His own. If, as Augustine says: "Christianity is as old as creation," then the Cross is as old as creation. The outer cross was lifted in history to let us see the inner Cross which is always upon the heart of God. Jesus is "the Lamb slain from the foundation of the world." "The Son of Man will be in travail as long as creation lasts," says Pascal.

"Creation, redemption and sanctification are all one and the same indivisible fact. The death of Him who is Himself eternal God is the final creative act," says C. E. Holt. The Cross, then, is not something imposed on life—it is Life exposing Itself at its deepest depths. "For Him to create was to enter into His creation, wearing its sorrows, as a garment, its joys as a crown of glory—nay more, thrilling with its joys and dying upon its bitter cross," says Mrs. E. Herrmann. The Cross, then, is the ground plan of the great Architect of the universe. "Turn to the heights, turn to the depths, turn within, turn without—everywhere thou shalt find the cross," says Thomas à Kempis.

So the Cross is not an afterthought of God—it is the scarlet thread running through the whole garment of creation. "A cross that operates in the little patch we have fenced off from the whole coherent field of life is a depleted cross. . . . The essential glory of the cross is that it is the most characteristic expression of the Being of God and not merely an expediency to meet an emergency," says Herrmann. The Word is bound to become vicarious when it meets sin.

O God, I know that on Thy heart is this unseen Cross. I see that through this outer cross. I know that the Cross is the price that Thou dost pay to get to me in spite of my sins. I'm grateful. Amen.

AFFIRMATION FOR THE DAY: *The Cross is the center of my faith; today it shall be the center of my actions.*

THE WORD BECOME VICTORIOUS

We come to the next fact upon which the gospel rests:

4. *The Word become victorious:* "To them he presented himself alive" (Acts 1:3).

It is not enough for the Word to become flesh, to become guidance, to become vicarious—it must also become victorious. If it is crucified, dead, and buried—it must rise again. If that Word which became flesh lies in ashes in a tomb, it is not the Word for this sad and defeated world. It must meet everything and triumph over everything. In the Resurrection it has. The last word of God is not the Cross—His last word is the Resurrection—victory! I could not worship a dead Christ except with a dead heart. In that case the chords of my worship would be a sigh instead of a song. But with the bursting of the tomb there is a bursting of my heart—with joy.

A Hindu student said to me: "Every day my life gets sadder and sadder. For every day that I live I know I am getting that much nearer to death." And there is no escape from that if you think that death has the last word. But we know now that it hasn't. Jesus arose! That is the answer, for in Him I too shall rise. When George Santayana the philosopher, said, "There is no cure for birth and death save to enjoy the interval," he was speaking as a philosopher and not as Christian. For philosophy there is no other word than that, but for the Christian there is another: Look forward to death, enjoy death, for death can be nothing other than an entrance to large life. The Resurrection lights that darkest area of life—death—and lights it, not with a verbal word of encouragement, but with a vital word of incarnate victory: He arose! That is the most luminous fact of history. It lights up all history—and it lights up me. The music of the spheres is not a funeral dirge—it is the song of victory of the creative God bringing His recreated Creation back to life. When a tomb has an angel in it announcing good news, then every other place in earth and heaven has an angel in it announcing the same good news. Creation is vibrant with the new song—the song of the worst being met and vanquished.

O Christ, I thank Thee that my heart is tuned to victory; for in Thee I see what I want to see—nothing can stop Thee, not even death. The end of life is, not death, but more Life. I praise Thee. Amen.

AFFIRMATION FOR THE DAY: *The Resurrection shall be re-enacted in me today.*

THE WORD BECOME FINAL AND TOTAL PROGRAM

We now look at the next fact upon which the Christian faith rests:

5. *The Word become final:* "Until the day when he was taken up" (Acts 1:2); and Peter adds: "Exalted at the right hand of God" (2:33).

Here the Word goes to the right hand of the Father—to the center of the universe and there has the final word. It is not enough that the Word be victorious in a single event like the Resurrection—we want to know whether the Word will be victorious in all events, will have the last word in every situation for all time. This verse says that it will, that this Word is at the very center of the universe, and no matter who has the first word, or the intermediate word, the Word will have the last word. "I am the Alpha," the Christ of the Beginnings, "and the Omega," the Christ of the final Word. When we are dealing with Jesus, we are dealing with one who is not imposed on life, but one who is at the very heart of life—is Life itself.

6. *The Word become total program for the individual and society:* "Speaking of the Kingdom of God" (1:3). It is not enough for the Word to become flesh, to become guidance, to become vicarious, to become victorious, and to become final—that Word must be projected back into life as a total way of life for the individual and for society.

Men need something to command them, something to command them totally, for the primary law of life is obedience—obedience to something higher than themselves. The primary law of life is not freedom—it is obedience, and then through that obedience you gain freedom. "Seek ye first the kingdom of God, ... and all these things shall be added unto you," including your freedom (Matt. 6:33, K.J.V.). Seek first freedom, and bondage will be added to you. Seek first the Kingdom, and freedom will be added unto you. Here is a complete totalitarianism which when you obey, you find perfect freedom. When you obey any lesser totalitarianism, you find perfect bondage. God's totalitarianism means our perfect freedom, for we are made for it, and when we obey it, we obey ourselves.

O God, I thank Thee that Thy Kingdom is my homeland, the order for which I am fashioned and made. Here I am at home, and here I live and live abundantly. I am grateful that I am at home always and everywhere. Amen.

AFFIRMATION FOR THE DAY: *Perfect freedom through perfect obedience.*

THE WORD BECOME DYNAMIC

We come now to the last fact on which the Christian Gospel rests:

7. *The Word become power within us:* "After he had given commandment through the Holy Spirit" (Acts 1:2).

The first six facts of the Christian faith are all outside us: The Word become flesh, guidance, vicarious, victorious, final, and total program—all outside us. If it remains outside of us, then it is good but not good enough. For no authority is authority till it gets within us, and until we obey it from within as identified with us.

In the Holy Spirit all the first six things move within us and become realized there. For "the doctrine of the Holy Spirit is nothing else than the intensification and extension of the doctrine of Christ within." The Holy Spirit is again the Word made flesh within us—subject to our limitations, of course.

Without this moving within us of the power of the Spirit the Christian faith is a counsel of perfection demanding of men to do what cannot be done. It lays an intolerable burden on the human will. The "ought" becomes more than the "can," so that our faith is an irritation. But when the Holy Spirit comes within us, then anything becomes possible. For the same Power which worked in Jesus works in us. The Holy Spirit takes over our natural powers, cleanses and heightens them and makes them go beyond themselves. There is a "plus" added to life. Ordinary men do extraordinary things—all out of proportion to their powers. They are a surprise to themselves and to others.

If we drop out of our teaching the Holy Spirit, then our faith becomes a belief in historic facts as seen in the historic Jesus. It becomes a creed about life—life outside of us. But in the Holy Spirit the creed passes into a deed. Now you don't quarrel over correct statements about objective fact, you let the same Life that was in the objective fact of Jesus course within you, producing the same fruits. The Roots are within you, so the fruits are brought forth through you. The Christian faith becomes naturalized within you—the Supernatural producing the natural.

O God, my Father, I thank Thee that Thou hast provided power where I need it most—within. Give me the reinforcement of the Spirit within, and then I am capable of anything—the "ought" becomes the "can." Amen.

AFFIRMATION FOR THE DAY: *The power that raised Jesus from the dead will work within me today—to the degree I let it.*

THE PROMISE OF THE FATHER

Before we go into the examination of what happened at the coming of the Holy Spirit on the birthday of the Church—Pentecost—we must gather up several pre-Pentecost passages not found in John's Gospel.

"And behold, I send the promise of my Father upon you; but stay in the city, until you are clothed with power from on high." (Luke 24:49.) There are four outstanding things in this verse: (*a*) The necessity of the coming of the Holy Spirit upon them—the last thing Jesus said on each and therefore the most emphatic. (*b*) What He was talking about was "*the* promise of my Father"—God had nothing better to give. (*c*) The place where it was given—"in the city"—was important. (*d*) This power was from "on high"—its source was not within them.

Take the first thing: (*a*) The last impression will be the lasting impression. What would be the last thing He would say to them? He had said many deathless things to them—love your enemies, be the servant of all if you would be the greatest of all, lose your life to find it again, and many others, all of which are of great importance. But what did He pick out as of the greatest importance—the last thing of which He would speak? Both Luke's Gospel and the Acts of the apostles are agreed on this: He urged them to stay in the city until they were "clothed with power" (Luke 24:49), and "you shall receive power when the Holy Spirit has come upon you" (Acts 1:8). In both cases it was described as the last thing He said: "Then . . . he parted from them" (Luke 24:50-51); "and when he had said *this*, . . . he was lifted up" (Acts 1:9, italics mine).

Jesus knew if they missed this, they had missed the whole point of redemption. For the Holy Spirit is redemption—continuing redemption within us. Apart from the Holy Spirit the redemption is outside of us—in history in the historical Jesus, but the historical becomes the experimental in the Holy Spirit. The redemption would not be complete unless it becomes experience. So the last words of Jesus were: "You believe it, now experience it! Lo, I am with you always—in you always in the Holy Spirit. Tarry till He comes within."

O Jesus, Thou hast come a long way—now come the full way, into the depths of me. There I would realize Thee. And Thou art pressing in the Spirit upon my spirit. I yield, I accept. Come. Amen.

AFFIRMATION FOR THE DAY: *The Holy Spirit is God's redemptive intention working where it counts—within me.*

THE GIFTS AND THE GIFT

We saw yesterday the four important last things Jesus said in Luke 24:49. We have looked at one: The very last thing Jesus spoke of on earth was the necessity of the coming of the Holy Spirit upon them. The last words of our passing loved ones are the most treasured—and the most heeded. This last word of Jesus is the point of redemption, and to miss this is to miss the point.

We come now to the next thing in His last statement: (*b*) "I send the promise of my Father upon you." God gave many promises to humanity. We have picked them out of the Old and New Testaments and have put them into mottoes on our walls. We sing them in our anthems and treasure them in our hearts. But the Man who never missed the point, never got off on the irrelevant or the unworthwhile, picked out this promise and called it "*the* promise of the Father." Of all the promises the Father gave, this is *the* promise. Why?

Because all the promises He gave were usually about gifts— the gift of peace, of comfort, of guidance, of sustenance—but here was the promise of the gift of the Giver. The Giver was giving Himself. The Father could not give anything higher than Himself. In the giving of the Spirit He was giving just that— Himself. No wonder it was "*the* promise"! This focused all the scattered promises into one—a burning glass that gathered all the scattered rays into one burning focus. The gifts become one—the Giver! Having Him we have all the gifts too. Had this not been emphasized by a final emphasis, we might have had the disciples each concentrating on individual gifts they needed and wanted—one would want forgiveness; another, peace; another, guidance; another, power. Each might have gone off into the marginal. Here Jesus concentrates them at the Center—the gift of the Giver Himself. It is like the lover who has given many gifts to his intended bride now coming to the sacred marriage day when he gives himself. It is *the* gift. Without that the gifts would be bare—this gift of himself consummates all the gifts. So the Father, having given many gifts, comes now to the consummating moment—the moment of giving Himself, imparting His very self to the receptive loved one.

O God, my Father, I thank Thee for his hour—the hour of the consummation of all the process of redemption. My heart is open. Come, Spirit, Come. And take possession of my inmost being. I have a tryst with Thee there. Amen.

AFFIRMATION FOR THE DAY: *Thy last promise shall be my first concern.*

VICTORY AT THE PLACE OF "THE CITY"?

We come to the third of the four things in the last words of Jesus: (*c*) "Stay in the city." Why did He tell them to stay in the city? Would it not have been better for them to have retired, say to a mountain in Galilee, and there in the quiet to wait upon God?

But suppose they had found the Spirit there in the solitude; would they not have had the lurking doubt as to whether this would work in the storm and stress of the city? That doubt would have eaten like a worm into their new-found joy. In Retreats and Ashrams many people during the last days say with almost monotonous regularity: "Now that we are going down from the mountain top, what will happen in the valley?"

Jesus wiped that whole thought out of their minds by commanding that they stay in the city. The "city" is the place not only of concentrated populations but of concentrated problems. It is said: "There met him a man *from the city* who had demons" (Luke 8:27, italics mine)—the devils in him were city devils. The evils of the city moved into him and became personalized there. The city morally exhausts itself by its evils and, if not revitalized from the moral character of the country born, soon festers. If, then, this new power which was going to operate within them could operate while they were living in the city, it could operate anywhere.

But there was something else about this city which had peculiar significance to them. In this city of Jerusalem the disciples had failed. They all had forsaken Jesus and fled in the crisis. The burning shame of that must have made them blush every time they thought of it. It must have produced an inferiority complex about the city. Jesus would wipe out that feeling of inferiority by making them a success right where they had been failures. If they could meet Jerusalem, they could meet anything. Someone has said: "Whenever you raise a question, raise it in its most acute form—solve it there, and then you have solved it all down the line." Jesus raised the question of the workability of this new life in its most acute form—Jerusalem—solved it there, and hence solved it all down the line.

O God, I thank Thee that Thou canst help me to walk up to the most difficult thing I know and canst give me power to solve that, so I'll be afraid of nothing else. How thorough is Thy grace. Amen.

AFFIRMATION FOR THE DAY: *Today I shall not escape my problems—I shall encompass them with God.*

NOT AN ANESTHETIC BUT AN ANSWER

We continue our meditation on Jesus' insistence that the disciples "stay in the city, until you are clothed with power from on high." Why in the city?

Well, religion is often an escape mechanism, a dodging of issues, a drugging with devotion and emotion. Jesus saw to it that this was scotched in the very beginning. He would get the disciples to face up to the hardest situation; and if they could meet that, then all feelings of inferiority, all tendencies to dodge out of issues, would be wiped out. They would become positive, outgoing, creative persons, afraid of nothing. When they found that they could call Jerusalem to repentance—the Jerusalem whose hands were red with the blood of their Master—then they knew that the Answer led through life and not around life. They became the doing, not the dodging, type. The Christian faith was, not an anesthetic, but an Answer.

I received a letter with this paragraph in it: "The neurotic personality seems to be as afraid of success as of failure and afraid of freedom in its greatest connotation." And this the writer spoke of herself. This is profoundly true. Then the disciples were cleansed of all neuroticism, for they were not afraid of success. Five thousand responded to their appeal in one day. And freedom? They were out from behind closed doors. They were free from fear of success or failure. They were "out"—out from cramping inhibition and all personal hesitation.

There was another thing to be considered in staying in Jerusalem. This city, the center of their national hopes and pride, stood for all that was corporately dear to them. When the Holy Spirit came on them, it would be not only a deliverance from fears and inhibitions and failures but also a deliverance from what they held highest. The victory would be not only over the worst but over the best as well. They would offer not only their failures and fears but their highest loves. Their highest now could not keep them back from His highest. Jerusalem, their national idol, was dethroned that the new Jerusalem might descend upon them. There was victory at both ends of life—the lowest and highest—and all between.

O God, I thank Thee that now I need be afraid of nothing. For the Spirit is going to deliver me from the Jerusalem of my failures and fears and the Jerusalem of my hopes and loves. I'm free, I'm free. Amen.

AFFIRMATION FOR THE DAY: *Today I shall enter the Jerusalem of my fear, or of my pride, with the confidence of a conqueror.*

FROM WITHIN OR "FROM ON HIGH"?

We must pause a little longer on: "And behold, I send the promise of my Father upon you; but stay in the city [of Jerusalem], until you are clothed with power from on high."

(*d*) Note that the power was from "on high." There are two outlooks and approaches to this matter of finding spiritual power within. One is the approach of discovering the power within you. The other is to receive it from on high.

The first is the approach that many are turning to today: "Awaken your hidden resources." "Discover the God within." "You are a part of God." "Cultivate the Christ-consciousness within." "You are determined from within—your thoughts determine the within. "You are, if you think you are." This emphasis has given birth to innumerable cults for self-realization and self-improvement. They contain a truth and are a reaction against the worm-of-the dust, self-abasement emphasis in many orthodox bodies. This self-affirmation with its positive attitudes of affirming health instead of disease, of life instead of death, of victory instead of defeat, has a very salutary effect on many people. It is a Yes instead of a No, and as such it is more healing.

But the benefit is limited. Self-realization, self-affirmation, and self-suggestion, even though you spell the self with a capital S, soon come to the end of the resources of the self. For though you may affirm the self as Self, a part of the Divine, it is still the self. No amount of affirmation will turn the self into the Self. We are we, and God is God; and while we can co-operate and interpenetrate and become so unified that we can scarcely tell where we end and God begins, nevertheless we are we, and God is God.

An American girl came to India as a disciple of a swami who claimed he was divine. Disillusionment set in when she discovered he was very human, like the rest of us. She developed spasms in her stomach; her hair fell out; she began to get fever. It all came out of disillusionment and a loss of spiritual security. We are not God; and the end of life is not to realize yourself, but to renounce yourself as central and to make God, God.

O God, I want to live in a paradise, but not in a fool's paradise. I want Reality. Save me from any false hopes that let me down. For I know that Thou canst give me Reality. For this I pray. Amen.

AFFIRMATION FOR THE DAY: *Today I shall first consecrate, then cultivate.*

SELF-CULTIVATION OR SELF-SURRENDER?

We must continue our meditation on the phrase "clothed with power from on high." We saw yesterday that all systems based upon your identity with the Divine will let you down eventually. After the effect of the wine of your wordy assertion of identity with the Divine wears off, then the aftereffects of disillusionment set in. So people wander from cult to cult hoping to get a bigger shot in the arm to keep up their sinking spirits. It is all under "the law of decreasing returns"—you have to put in greater affirmation each time to get out the same returns in self-created exaltation.

We return with relief to this promise of being "clothed with power from on high." Note the "on high." This power is, not from within us, but from "on high." At the very moment God is going to be most intimate, coming within us in the Spirit to become Thought of our thought, Love of our love, Life of our life, Being of our being—at that very moment He reminds us that this is from "on high" and not from within us. What does this emphasize? It emphasizes the fact that to find this power you are, not to cultivate yourself or assert yourself as divine, but to surrender yourself to the Divine.

That is important. For no matter how much you cultivate yourself or assert yourself as divine, you are still the center. And any system that makes you the center is off-center—is "eccentric." For you are not the center—God is! No matter how you may dress that self up in fancy religious garments, it is still the self. And self-centeredness is the central sin in life. To make yourself God is the supreme idolatry. Self-worship is sin. Hence, the first demand of the Christian faith is self-surrender. The first law of life is to lose your life that you may find it again. "He who loves his life loses it"—it will disintegrate, no matter how much rouge of assertion of divinity is put upon the pallid cheeks of the self to make it appear blooming.

The attitude must be that of receptivity to God instead of assertivity of the self. The self must get into the right place: surrender—then anything can happen.

O God, my Father, I thank Thee that Thou art uncovering my ego, not to humiliate and shame me, but to lift and save me. For Thou art cornering me to loose me. Amen.

AFFIRMATION FOR THE DAY: *I shall give my ego a dressing-down instead of a dressing-up.*

SELF-CONTROLLED SELF CANNOT BE SAFELY EXPRESSED

We spend this last day of our week in a further meditation on "from on high."

At the very moment God is to exalt us, He has to put us in the dust. He has to get us to die to live. When He offers His highest gift—Himself—which is an amazing divine Self-surrender to us, then of necessity He must demand a self-surrender from us. For without that self-surrender we would use this new power in the purposes of the old self.

A very brilliant and forceful woman has said: "All my life I've been a go-getter—I've gotten what I wanted. Then suddenly it all turned to ashes. I saw it was all done for myself. My religious work all had a self-reference—it was to dress me up as pious and devoted. I've never said: 'O God, you've got me.' It was always: 'O God, I've got you.' I have never surrendered this ugly self. And now today I'm inwardly limp, my self-confidence gone; I'm in the dust." But the next day: "I'm new, I'm resurrected. I'm alive again. Yesterday I was in the depths; today I'm in the heights. God is filling every fiber of my being with power." Why? She changed from self-assertion to self-surrender. But the self-surrender brought self-realization.

You cannot find yourself in yourself—you find yourself in God. The process by which the change is made is self-surrender.

Now an important step takes place: After the self is surrendered to God, you can cultivate the self around this new center. For the self is in its place. In this new place you can safely cultivate the self; for it is not all just a sitting on the lid of self—God has that self—He cleanses and controls and guides it; therefore you can cultivate a God-controlled self. It is in the right hands. You are off your own hands and into the hands of God. Then true self-expression sets in. A Spirit-controlled self can be safely expressed, but a self-controlled self cannot safely be expressed.

So Jesus said that this power was from on high, and its central law is self-surrender. With that clear, everything was clear. Without that clarification, everything was muddled. God could give the Spirit without measure.

O God, I thank Thee that Thou dost cast a dart at my central problem—myself. Thou dost wound me mortally, to heal me vitally. So I accept. I surrender. Amen.

AFFIRMATION FOR THE DAY: *Today I shall look up, not in; my eyes are on Thee, not on myself.*

THE END OF OUR CALLING?

We thought that we could leave this emphasis upon self-surrender as a condition of finding a Spirit possession, but we must tarry a little longer on it. For to get this clear will mean full steam ahead. What is the end for which we live? The end is important; for if the end is clear, the means to that end will be clear. The center of our call is simple: "Called to belong to Jesus Christ." (Rom. 1:6)

There are those who by emphasis would say that our calling is to get to heaven. I heard a congregation in Malaya singing: "When we all get to heaven, what a day of rejoicing that will be," and at that very time reports were coming in of flying Communist bullets only ten miles distant. Both the singing of the hymn and the singing bullets were inadequate answers. If you make getting to heaven the goal of life, it turns into a reward morality—you are bribed into goodness. Heaven is not the end—it is a by-product of something deeper. You get it "thrown in" as it were.

Nor are you "called" to be holy as the end of life. For that leaves you the center—*you* are holy. A self-conscious holiness is not holy—it is unholy.

Nor are you called to be happy. For that centers on you and your happiness. And the people who center on themselves and their happiness are not happy. A poll was taken to find out who were the happy. It found that the religious were happier than the nonreligious, and the truly religious were the happiest of all.

Nor are you called to be useful. For in that case you are still the center—*you* are useful. Those who center on being useful often end in being self-conscious uplifters of others—not a very attractive type.

Nor are you called to serve God. In that case you are serving Him—you are still the center. Jesus said: "If any man serve me, let him follow me." (John 12:26, K.J.V.) It is possible to serve Him and not follow Him—you serve Him, but *you* are the center, unsurrendered to Him.

Gracious Christ, Thou art clarifying my vision so that Thou canst clarify me. I want my eye to be single; then my whole body shall be full of light—with no part dark. Give me that. Amen.

AFFIRMATION FOR THE DAY: *Today, I must keep my eye single that my whole body may be full of light.*

CALLED, NOT TO BE, BUT TO BELONG

Let us continue our meditation on the end of our calling. We are not called to be like Jesus Christ. For in that case we are still the center—*we* are to be like Jesus Christ. That produces self-striving efforts at copying something. It is off-center.

We are not called to be—we are called to belong: "Called to belong to Jesus Christ."

The primary thing in the Christian faith is, not to be, but to belong. If it is "to be," then that centers on the self; if it is "to belong," then that centers on Christ. The basis of one's life is shifted from a self-centered person to a Christ-centered person.

As long as the universe was looked on as geocentric—centering in the earth with the rest of the worlds revolving around it, as in the Ptolemaic system—none of the sums would add up right; everything was awry. When men discovered, with Copernicus, that the earth was not the center, but the sun was—that our universe was heliocentric, and we revolved around it—then everything began to add up, to come out right.

If any system of religion keeps you centered on yourself and your own status of mind and body, it is off-center, and your sums won't add up. You are perpetually thwarted and frustrated. You will be driven to the disconcerting conclusion: Religion won't work. That is true—from that center!

For the first law of life is this: You must lose your life to find it. If you find it by centering on yourself, in no matter how religious a way, you will lose it; it will disintegrate through conflict. You are an off-centered person—"ec-centric." The universe doesn't back that way of life. Hence you always are "up against it." But when you decide "to belong"—to surrender to Christ and to make Him the center—then you are not "up against it"; you're "with it"; the sum total of reality works with you and not against you. You are aligned. When you "belong to Jesus Christ," then everything belongs to you—everything works with you and for you. Only evil, which is the word "live" spelled backwards, works against you.

O Christ, I thank Thee that at long last I've found my way to my center—to Thee. For Thou art the center of everything for me. My all. I want no life apart from Thy life. I rest here and here only. Amen.

THE THERAPEUTIC VALUE OF SELF-SURRENDER

Yesterday we came to the goal and end of our calling: "called to belong to Jesus Christ." But the process by which we pass from belonging to ourselves to belonging to Jesus Christ is self-surrender. A great many shy at this term: A young man wrote: "I don't like your word self-surrender. Seems to me to be weak—an escapist mentality. You turn over your life to Another because you haven't enough nerve to face life yourself."

When we turn to the New Testament, we do not find the term "self-surrender." But the idea is profoundly there. It is central. And it is becoming central in life as a working way to live. A psychiatrist comes out with an article on "The Therapeutic Value of Self-Surrender." He saw that the human personality works badly when centered on itself, works well when surrendered to Another. And gets well in the process!

But let us clear the debris of wrong thought from around self-surrender. (a) It is not weak to surrender to Another. The adolescent attitude is an insistence on independence; the mature attitude is to take one's independence and delegate it, or surrender it, to a higher entity. The individual surrenders his sovereignty to the union in marriage—loses his life and finds it again in a fellowship in the union. The citizen surrenders his sovereignty to the nation and finds a larger fellowship in the brotherhood. The individual surrenders his sovereignty to God—seeks first the Kingdom of God; and, lo, all these things are added to him again, including Himself.

When you most belong to Him, you most belong to yourself. Lowest at His feet you stand straightest before everything else. Bound to Him you walk the earth free. Fearing Him you are afraid of nothing else. You bow to Him, but you do not bow to anything else. You are God's freeman, for you are God's slave. The strongest persons are those most surrendered to themselves. This works with a mathematical precision, and there are no exceptions. If you are centered in yourself, you are a problem—if you are centered in God, you are a person.

O Christ, Thou art teaching me how to live by teaching me how to surrender. For in Thee I am in myself—I am myself. Now I know the way; help me to take it absolutely. Amen.

AFFIRMATION FOR THE DAY: *Today I am strong in Him, to whom I have surrendered.*

NOT SELFLESS, BUT UNSELFISH

Let us continue to look at self-surrender. To surrender oneself is not to cancel out the self—it is to heighten it. In India the word "selfless" is often used for "unselfish." The use of the word "selfless" is perhaps from the dominant philosophy of India, Vedanta, which looks on the highest as the loss of the personal self into the Impersonal. The final goal of life is to be merged into the Impersonal Brahma. Vedantists are afraid of personality. It is a compliment to say a man is selfless.

But in the Christian Way a man never becomes selfless—his self is heightened and affirmed. Jesus was the most self-surrendered person that ever lived: "I seek not my own will but the will of him who sent me." And yet Jesus was the most self-assertive self that ever existed: "I am the way, and the truth, and the life." He was the most self-assertive because the most self-surrendered. Now it was safe to assert the self; for it was asserted, not for self-purposes, but for God-purposes. His self hits you with all the weight of God behind it. So to surrender to God does not mean you will be mush.

> Oh, to be nothing,
> Just to lie at His feet,
> A broken and empty vessel,
> For the Master's use made meet.

This song is a caricature of the surrendered soul. For the surrendered soul is not "nothing"—it is very much something, a somebody now. Jesus took the nobodies and turned them into the somebodies. But only after they made a full surrender.

In my Quiet Time today I read: "And his garments became glistening, intensely white, as no fuller on earth could bleach them." When whiteness came in contact with Him, it became whiter, "intensely white;" when love came in contact with Him, it became lovelier; when strength came in contact with Him, it became stronger; when beauty came in contact with Him, it became more beautiful. Everything is heightened. When joy comes into contact with Him, it becomes Joy; love becomes Love; life becomes Life. Life on our own hands dulls and decays; life in His hands delights and dances. We surrender to survive.

O Christ, I'm seeing that I must belong to Thee before anything belongs to me—including myself. So here I take the one thing that is mine, and I surrender it to Thee. Amen.

AFFIRMATION FOR THE DAY: *Today all my bad shall become good, all my good shall become better, all my better shall become best.*

SELF-SURRENDER IS NOT GIVING UP THIS OR THAT

We saw yesterday that surrender was not mush—it produced a heightened personality. Jesus does not reduce people to their zero. He raises them to their zenith. He is not a strong man making men around Him weak. He is the Strong creating the strong. He doesn't use a "broken and empty vessel"—He uses surrendered vessels, and those surrendered vessels are neither broken nor empty; they are whole and full. Life has come to its maximum in Him—it is not "nothing"; it is something, and something significant!

We pursue what surrender is not: (*b*) It is not giving up this, that, and the other thing around the self and leaving the self intact. Don't bother with self, and let that go. That carries with it the margin. (*c*) Surrender is not tentative—it is decisive, once and for all. There are no "ifs" in surrender—"if God will do this, I will do that"—there is a once-and-for-all attitude in it. To sink or to swim, to survive or to perish, for better or for worse, for life or for death—that is the attitude. Of course, there is a daily surrender of things—before unknown—which keep coming up; but that is different from the central surrender, which is permanent. In a real marriage you don't say, "Now, dear, let's be married over again today"; that is once and for all; but around that central surrender to each other there is a daily adjustment—little things are daily surrendered. So real surrender is once and for all, and yet it is continuous.

There is a disease known as erythroblastosis fetalis, in which the child inherits incompatible blood types from its parents. It will die from the incompatibility unless the old blood is completely drained away and simultaneously an entirely new and compatible type of blood is infused. In surrender to Christ you surrender completely the old incompatibilities—a self that wants mutually incompatible things—and you accept the inflow of a new compatible life which now takes over from the old and carries on. Surrender eliminates all inner incompatibilities and gives inner unity. Hence it must be complete and once and for all.

O Christ, my blood is full of contradictions; I consent to surrender it all to Thee. Let Thy new blood, so rich and pure, take complete possession of me and be life of my life. Take over everything. Amen.

AFFIRMATION FOR THE DAY: *Today, my life for Thy Life.*

"LORD, WILL YOU . . . BUT YOU . . ."

We must now look at one or two more things before we see the actual coming of the Spirit at Pentecost. When Jesus "charged them not to depart . . ., but to wait for the promise of the Father," the disciples started off on a tangent with this question: "Lord, will you at this time restore the kingdom to Israel?" His reply: "It is not for you to know times or seasons. . . . But you shall receive power when the Holy Spirit has come upon you." (Acts 1:4-8.)

This was a necessary correction for them and for us. They had the pattern of Daniel in mind, of whom the king said: "All the wise men of my kingdom are not able to make known unto me the interpretation: but thou art able; for the spirit of the holy gods is in thee." (Dan. 4:18.) So Daniel foretold the future. The "spirit" was the spirit that could discern future events.

Jesus scotched that conception: "It is not for you to know times or seasons"—that is prognostication. But you are to be witnesses of me—that is power. Here He turned the eyes of the disciples from prying into the future toward redeeming men in the present. He turned religion from the magical to the moral—from reading future events to redeeming present events.

Had we taken that correction seriously, we would have been saved from useless controversies over "times and seasons" which have laid waste the powers of sincere Christians. Jesus gave us no map for the future—He did give us power for the present. Our business is witnessing to Christ now, not witnessing to times and seasons. That is a fatal twist that sends you to controversy instead of to conversions.

Note another emphasis in these last words: "Lord, will you . . .? But you . . ." (Acts 1:6, 8). They had been looking to Him; now He was looking to them. They had been looking to Him as a person to do this, that, and the other; now He would not do anything except from inside of them and through them. They would be His hands, His feet, His brain, and His heart—He would work through them. In other words: "Don't expect me to interfere with miracles imposed from without—I'm going to do my miracles through you."

O Christ, Thou art washing out my eyes with Thy clarity and Thy simplicity of purpose. Thou art saving me from the extraneous and confining me to the eternally worth while. I thank Thee. I thank Thee. Amen.

AFFIRMATION FOR THE DAY: *Today, my eyes Thy eyes, my hands Thy hands, my feet Thy feet.*

THE SPIRIT FOR EXTRANEOUS PURPOSES

There was another correction which Jesus was compelled to give before the Spirit could come with abandon.

The disciples asked: "Lord, will you at this time restore the kingdom to Israel?" (Acts 1:6.) He had been talking for forty days discussing the affairs of the Kingdom of God (Acts 1:3). The disciples watered this down to a restoration of the kingdom to Israel—a universal Kingdom was being confined to a Jewish mold. And the power that was to be loosed with the coming of the Spirit was a power to glorify national ambition—so they thought. Had that not been corrected, the Spirit would never have come.

That spirit and attitude is still among us. We still want to use the Spirit for extraneous purpose. Back of a good deal of urging us to pray for the Spirit is the hope that He may bring revival, that numbers might be gained, that prestige might come to our denomination. "Lord, will you at this time restore the kingdom to the Methodists? To the Baptists? To our Group? To me?" And the heavens are silent and unresponsive. And we wonder why no Pentecosts are ours.

Andrew Murray says: "We want to get possession of the power and use it. God wants to get possession of us and use us." You can see the difference in the disciples: before Pentecost they possessed the Spirit, but after Pentecost the Spirit possessed them. This refinement of purpose is decisive, for if we still hope to use God in purposes of the self, individual or collective, then we wonder why religion doesn't work. We try to work it for wrong purposes.

Until this national egotism was cleansed out of the disciples, God could not let the Spirit come. It took them ten days to get to the end of themselves and their nationalistic egoism. For ten days they tarried, not to make God willing, but to get themselves in a place where God could give His best—the Holy Spirit. The time limit was theirs, not God's. If in ten minutes they had offered their all, then His all would have come. In ten minutes, or ten seconds, if we say "Yes" with our all behind it, then Pentecost is present—now.

O God, Thou seest my heart—Thou seest whether I say "All" and mean it. I do mean it, and I do say "All." So from this hour I belong to Thee and belong to Thee without reservation. I thank Thee for this inner willingness. Amen.

AFFIRMATION FOR THE DAY: *Today, I shall not use Thee; I shall let Thee use me.*

THE PULSE BEAT OF ALL WE DO

We come now to the holy place of the Christian faith—the Upper Room. It was the holy place, for there this group of believers became wholly His, wholly filled and therefore holy. The Upper Room was the birthplace of the Chruch. It was there that power was loosed that changed the world.

But the Upper Room has often become in our present-day Christianity the Supper Room. The different is profound: In the one they "waited," in the other they are waited on; in the one they waited for "the promise of the Father," in the other they wait for the promise of the menu; in the one they looked up, in the other they look down into their plates; in the one God was first, in the other food and fellowship are first and God is second; one ends in making humanity different for all time, the other ends in a good time.

The Supper Room is all right, provided it is second and the Upper Room is first. For Jesus was "eating" with them (Acts 1:4, margin) when He charged them to "wait for the promise of the Father." The Holy Spirit was to be associated with the commonplace happenings of life—like eating. He was going to make every meal sacramental and every place "where they were staying" (1:13) into a shrine.

It was very important that the Holy Spirit came upon them, not in the Temple, but in a home. If the Spirit had been given in the Temple, then His coming would be associated with a sacred place, sacred services, and sacred occasions. The Holy Spirit came in the most common place—the home. Therefore He is to be given not for special "spiritual" occasions, but for all occasions, for all life. The Holy Spirit, then, is not a spiritual luxury to be imported into the unusual, but a spiritual necessity for the usual. He is to be the pulse beat of all we do—the Life of our living. In the coming of the Holy Spirit the insignificant relationships of life were touched into divine significance—the family becomes the Family of God. When the Holy Spirit moves within, then every bush is aflame with God, every moment is packed with eternity, and every contact is redemptive.

O God, I thank Thee that I do not have to wander from sacred place to sacred place in search of Thee. Thou dost come into me, and, lo, my heart is aglow with shekinah glory. Everything sings. Amen.

AFFIRMATION FOR THE DAY: *Today the Holy Spirit turns all my seculars into sacreds.*

THE SIGNIFICANCE OF THE UPPER ROOM

We say yesterday that the fact that the Holy Spirit came upon the ordinary place, the home, and made it into the extraordinary naturalized the Holy Spirit in all life.

There is another significance to the coming of the Holy Spirit in the Upper Room. This room was associated in their minds with the Last Supper, for in this same room Jesus sat with them and unfolded the redemption He would make in the self-giving on the cross. The Upper Room stood in their minds as a reminder of His supreme self-giving. Now this same place would find them confronted with the same necessity of their self-giving. The divine Self-giving—the coming of the Holy Spirit—would mean their initial self-giving as a preparation for the Spirit's coming. In the Upper Room He offered His all, and in the same Upper Room they offered their all. God and man were offering the supreme sacrifice—their all. Out of that all offering came all power. For God only can give All to all. We offer "some" and expect God to overlook the reservation and to give us all. But the heavens are silent. They open with only one key—all.

So in the Christian faith the Upper Room has a double content—the Cross and the Spirit. They are closely associated. If you do not bear within you the spirit of the Cross, you will not bear within you the Spirit of God. You must die to live. We are crucified followers of a crucified Lord and yet by that very fact are risen followers of a risen Lord and "endued with power from on high" (Luke 24:49, K.J.V.). When the spirit of the Cross becomes faint in us, then our power grows faint. When we are "all on the altar," then we are all on fire with the fire of that altar. When we become self-pampered, self-referenced, self-centered, then we have only the power of a decaying self. But all His—we have all of His.

In the Upper Room two movements meet—the movement of man's offer upward of himself and the movement of God's offer downward of Himself. Heaven and earth kiss and are wedded forevermore. Life becomes eternally fruitful. The creative life begins. For the creative Spirit is within.

O God, in this Upper Room where I am today I offer my little all, and I take the great All. Here I exchange—exchange my poverty for Thy Riches, my emptiness for Thy fullness. How rich and full I am in Thee. Amen.

AFFIRMATION FOR THE DAY: *Today, my all on the altar, and my all on fire with the fire of that altar.*

THE FIRST FRUITS OF THE CHRISTIAN MOVEMENT

We have looked at the place, the Upper Room, now we must look at the occasion, Pentecost. The occasion was very befitting for the coming of the Holy Spirit. For Pentecost was the Feast of the First Fruits, the festival when the first fruits were offered to God in thanksgiving and prayer for the rest of the harvest.

As the nation was offering the first fruits of the harvest, so they were offering the first fruits of the harvest of the Christian movement—themselves. The first fruits of the harvest which Christ would reap from the whole world was there in that little company of a hundred and twenty men and women. Five hundred brethren saw Him after His resurrection (I Cor. 15:6), and yet only a hundred and twenty obeyed His charge for them to tarry for the Spirit. Three hundred and eighty were "brethren," but they were brethren unfilled and therefore unfulfilled. They dropped out, victims of arrested development. They probably excused themselves from the waiting for the ten days to be endued with power by saying that they were too busy. They were the practical minded.

But no amount of fussy busyness can atone for the first business of the Christian: namely, to be the kind of person God can use. Time spent in seeking the Holy Spirit is the most fruitful time of one's life. It saves one from needless repentances, inward preoccupation with inner unsolved problems.

The proportion of one hundred and twenty out of five hundred is about the same proportion of one soil out of the four bringing forth fruit in the parable of the sower. These one hundred and twenty out of five hundred, roughly one out of four, were the ones who changed the history of humanity. For their all was taken up into the All of the Spirit and cleansed, reinforced, and heightened, and used. As the nation offered at Pentecost things to God, so they offered themselves to God. The one ended in a religious festival; the other ended in a religious fervor that set the world on fire. The one ended in a momentary meeting of individuals at a festival; the other ended in an eternal fellowship, the deepest on earth—the Chruch.

O God, on this day of giving I give the one thing I have—I give myself. Let this day be my Pentecost, for I want to take from Thee Thy All in exchange for my little all. Amen.

AFFIRMATION FOR THE DAY: *My first and my last and all between— Thine.*

SOME OF THE SCAFFOLDING OF PENTECOST

We saw that the setting of the Day of Pentecost created faith in the waiting group that something would surely happen on that day of *giving*. The day helped. But having looked at the day, we must dismiss it, less it becloud the central fact.

The use of the word Pentecost to describe the coming of the Spirit throws the emphasis on an event. It sends our minds off on the tangent of trying to reproduce that event with all its accompaniments—sends us to outer phenomena.

Pentecostalism has failed to be the pulse beat of the churches precisely because it was Pentecostalism instead of a movement of the Spirit. It tried to duplicate what happened at Pentecost, was drawn off to phenomena, looked for signs and wonders, became an outwardism. Instead of seeking the Spirit they sought the gifts of the Spirit—the gifts instead of the Giver— therefore they became a movement of the margin instead of a movement of the center, produced cults outside the church instead of conversions inside the church, often produced the queer instead of a peculiar people.

A great deal of the phenomena surrounding Pentecost was temporary scaffolding which was taken down when the building emerged. That scaffolding has its use for that time—it served a needed purpose. God was teaching certain principles with kindergarten methods, but the kindergarten method was laid aside when the principle was established.

For instance, what was the use of the phenomena of the "sound . . . like the rush of a mighty wind, [filling] all the house where they were sitting," except to arouse in them a general expectancy that the group as a whole was going to receive the Spirit? And what was the meaning of the cloven tongues like as of fire sitting upon the heads of each of them, except to arouse in each individual the expectancy that he as a person was to receive the Spirit? When the principle had been established that the group and the individual would both receive the Spirit, then the outer scaffolding of events could be removed; the principle remained—the scaffolding temporary, the principle permanent.

O God, I am grateful that Thou hast put together in the coming of the Spirit collectivism and individualism and harmonized them in one Spirit. Let me be the meeting place of that harmony. Amen.

AFFIRMATION FOR THE DAY: *In me and in my group the Spirit will work today.*

"STREWN WITH THE WRECKAGE OF HOPES"

We saw yesterday that the sound of the rushing mighty wind and the tongues of fire brought home to the waiting group that the group and the individuals were to receive the Holy Spirit. Thus collectivism and individualism came together in one experience of the Holy Spirit.

There is another temporary phenomenon which we must face—the speaking directly in the languages of the peoples who heard—the speaking in other tongues. We can see the necessity of this, for without this there would have been the tendency to insist that those who received the gospel through the Jews would have to adopt the Jewish language and culture—Christianity would be identified with the medium through which it came. That had to be scotched at once. It was scotched—"each one heard them speaking in his own language . . . the mighty works of God." (Acts 2:5, 11.) That meant that God was going to use every language and every culture to be the medium through which the universal gospel would come. There would be no imposing of a foreign culture and language on people with the coming of the gospel. The universal gospel would be expressed in local forms and local cultures, and thus a rich variety would be brought into the Kingdom of God. It would be a unity of diversity instead of a unity of uniformity.

This question became acute in the early Church, and a Church council had to be held over it (Acts 15), and it lingers today. Some missionaries, returned from Africa, were asked in what language they preached the gospel; and when told that French and Laconian were used, the hearers replied: "Oh, no, the gospel of grace can be preached only through English."

This tendency to put the universal gospel into national molds and to confine it there was struck a blow by this miracle. A unity with all races was put into an experience of God. To be one with Him was to be one with them, but it was a unity of diversity. This miracle was unique. An unknown type of tongues appeared at Corinth, but that needed an interpreter—this needed no interpreter; they spoke directly in the language of those who heard. The Corinthians type appears today—the Pentecostal type does not appear. India is strewn with the wreckage of hopes that the Pentecostal type would be duplicated.

O God, I thank Thee that Thou hast made us of one blood but of many cultures and languages. We are one amidst difference. Help us to be tolerant of differences and yet one among them. Amen.

AFFIRMATION FOR THE DAY: *My tongue shall be Thy tongue today.*

THE SEEKING FOR SIGNS

Yesterday we saw that the special miracle of the power to speak directly in the languages of the people who were gathered there from all that ancient world was for a special purpose. To teach that one hasn't the gift of the Spirit unless one can duplicate this special miracle encumbers the gift of the Spirit with an impossible burden.

We must not confound the gift of the Spirit with the gifts of the Spirit. The gift of the Spirit is for all, but the gifts of the Spirit He divides "severally as He will" (I Cor. 12:11, K.J.V.)—they are not for all. Paul makes this plain in 12:29-30: "Are all apostles? Are all prophets? Are all teachers? Do all work miracles? Do all possess gifts of healing? Do all speak with tongues? Do all interpret?" The answer is, No!

Paul urges: "But earnestly desire the higher gifts" (12:31). And then he goes on in the thirteenth chapter, and expounds the higher gift of love, and adds to it this: "Make love your aim, and earnestly desire the spiritual gifts, especially that you may prophesy" (14:1). Prophecy here is, not fore-telling of events, but forth-telling of the good news. So the power to love and to share the divine Love in speech—these are the gifts to desire earnestly.

One more passage needs to be looked at: "And these signs will accompany those who believe: in my name they will cast our demons; they will speak in new tongues; they will pick up serpents, and if they drink any deadly thing, it will not hurt them." (Mark 16:17-18.) But this passage is not a part of the original Gospel which was broken off and lost at verse 8. Moffatt gives three "second century attempts to complete the Gospel," among them the one from which this passage is quoted. The Revised Standard Version adds it marginally, omitting it from the text.

This second-century attempt to complete the gospel has sent men on a tangent of looking for signs. It results in an outwardism that is foreign to the gospel. "The fruit of the Spirit is love, joy, peace, patience, kindness, goodness, fruitfulness, gentleness, self-control" (Gal. 5:22, 23); and all these are moral qualities—not one is an outer sign.

O God, I thank Thee that the manifestations of Thy Spirit are, not magical, but moral. Thou hast held us to the impressiveness of holy living, instead of impressing by magical happenings. Amen.

AFFIRMATION FOR THE DAY: *The sign of the Cross upon me—let that be my "sign."*

THE FRUIT OF THE SPIRIT—MORAL QUALITIES

We saw that three principles were established in a dramatic, primary way at Pentecost: (*a*) All races and languages and cultures would be used of God in the new Order, the Kingdom. (*b*) The group as a group would be filled with the Spirit and be under His guidance. (*c*) The individual as an individual would receive the Spirit and be under the Spirit's guidance. Thus, the equal worth in the sight of God of all races and His intention to use all, the group as a group to be the organism of the Spirit and to be guided and used as an organism, the individual as an individual not to be swamped in the race or the group but to be filled and used of God—all these, which were the solidarity of humanity, collectivism, and individualism, were put together in a living blend in an experience of God.

Thus the doctrines of the solidarity of the human race, collectivism, and individualism are not imposed on the Christian faith but are inherent in it—bone of its bone—inescapable.

The fruits of the Spirit are not just an emotional overflow, though deep emotions are engendered; they are moral qualities; love, joy, peace, patience, kindness, goodness, faithfulness, gentleness, self-control. None of these are magical signs—they are moral qualities, beginning with love and ending in self-control. Love God, and the self is controlled by that love. But this is the opposite of a great deal of teaching that the Spirit's control is a loss of self-control, that going off into trances, seeing visions, hearing voices, speaking in an unknown tongue, are fruits of the Spirit. The fruits of the Spirit are to be found in the nine qualities of life.

But these personal fruits of the Spirit are added to by the social fruits of the Spirit—a life lifted above race, a life that becomes a part of a collectivism, used of God, and yet with a deep sense that I as a person am worth while and not lost amid collective emphases. We often get off on an exclusive emphasis on one or more of these emphases, become lopsided, but the Spirit-controlled life is a life of complete balance. All virtues and all right emphases inhere in the Spirit.

O Spirit of God, Thou in whom all is found, may I be found in Thee, not mechanically trying to hold things together, but joyously and spontaneously living out life from within—with Thee, the Source. Amen.

AFFIRMATION FOR THE DAY: *All my wrongs righted, all my virtues balanced.*

ALL PLACES SACRED

Let us pursue this week the study of how the barriers went down at Pentecost and a universal faith and movement emerged.

1. The Holy Spirit made all places sacred. The Spirit came upon them, not in the Temple, but in an Upper Room. We capitalize that Upper Room now, but it was just an upper room, a home "where they were staying" (Acts 1:13). God's most precious promise—"the promise"—the promise of Himself was given in the most commonplace place, a home.

This lifted religion out of the tyranny of sacred places where God is said to be found especially. I say tyranny, for it is just that. Millions in money, years in time, are spent in various lands to get to sacred places—Jerusalem, Mecca, Bernares, Gaya, Rome—all to get a special touch with God through a touch with a sacred place. Weary, wasted pilgrims trudge from sacred place to sacred place to rub off something of the sacred place and to keep it for their own. Lifetime earnings and lifetime energy is spent upon these fruitless searches for God in sacred places. The people return exhausted in body, mind, and spirit. For God cannot approve of giving Himself in some specially sacred place; for if He did, how would the poor, those who are tied up in families, the busy, find Him? That would send religion off on a wrong tangent—run it into local grooves.

When the Holy Spirit came upon that group in a home, it lifted God's availability out of the hands of priests, places and the paraphernalia of organized religion. These things and persons may be useful in helping us to find God, but not one of them is necessary. God has not tied His hands by anyone's cords of validity and sanctions. Wherever the human heart meets the inner conditions, there God is available. This is the most freeing thing that ever happened in religion. God will use any person, any building, any rite or ceremony, that looks beyond itself and is the instrument of the Divine; but He has not confined Himself to anything except two—He comes through Christ and He comes to a person, whoever and wherever that person may be, provided that person lifts up a surrendered, trusting heart to God through Christ.

O God, I thank Thee that I need not move from where I am, except in attitude, to find Thee coming in Thy fullness and power. Here, where I am, I offer to Thee my all, and I take Thy all. I thank Thee. Amen.

AFFIRMATION FOR THE DAY: *My attitudes alone determine my altitudes.*

ALL PERSONS SACRED

Ve saw yesterday that the Spirit came upon the disciples
ile they were in a home, not in the temple. That naturalized
Christian faith within the natural. The Holy Spirit was given
live life out in the ordinary relations. He is power for life,
l not power for special occasions connected with special
ces.

The mother, father, children, in the home find power to live
: the highest spirituality in the lowliest of relationships and
ies. The prophet saw this when he said: "On that day the
y bells on the horses shall be inscribed with 'Sacred to the
rnal'; the very pots in the house of the Eternal shall be as
red as the bowls in front of the altar; indeed, every pot in
usalem and in Judah shall be sacred to the Lord of hosts."
:ch. 14:20-21, Moffatt.) The Holy Spirit makes sacred all we
ch. That means that all work if lifted out of the secular into
sacred; all duties are temple duties, all areas of life under
; control.

'. *The Holy Spirit makes all persons sacred.* We saw that the
ly Spirit came on people in a home and not in a temple. The
t thing to notice is that the Holy Spirit came, not on the
elve, but upon the one hundred and twenty. Suppose the
rit had come on the Twelve and not upon the hundred and
nty—what would that have done to religion? It would have
l up the Spirit's presence and power to people specially
ed to specially sacred tasks. The addition of zero to twelve,
king the hundred and twenty, was one of the most important
litions in human history. It lifted the gifts of God from
:sts and prophets and put them on people. The prophets and
:sts could have them too, but not as prophets and priests—
y as people. All distinctions based on sacred classes were
ie. Sacredness attaches to a person and not to his duties. He
:acred if he is sacred—inherently. A priest can be holy, a
phet can be holy, and a person can be holy—all on the same
iditions and with no special favors. Sacredness is found in
racter, not collars; in value, not vestments.

) Divine Spirit, I thank Thee that I as a person, apart
m everything else, can receive Thee and live out Thy
: in my vocation. That will be the area of the Spirit's ac-
ity in me. Everywhere, everywhere, I shall take Thee.
ien.

IRMATION FOR THE DAY: *My person made sacred by Thy Person will
ok on all persons as sacred.*

THE FOUNDATION OF DEMOCRACY

Let us pursue that thought that the Holy Spirit came on the hundred and twenty instead of on the twelve.

We need to regain the sense of mission in all life. Some occupations are considered sacred and some secular. This sends a moral sag into every so-called secular occupation—the layman is in a second-rate occupation and hence is expected to live a second-rate Christian life. This has impoverished daily life—it has no sense of divine calling within it.

For instance, the political life of this nation has been lowered because we haven't had enough—there have been some—men who feel a divine urge to go into politics. We need to put God down through the corporate decisions of our nation—to become a God-guided nation through God-guided political servants. We should have courses in our Christian colleges and seminaries on Christian statesmanship—how to relate the Christian faith to corporate life. We should have services of dedication as Christians go into public life, just as we have such services when they go into the ministry. They should go forth with the blessings of the Chruch upon them as they go to function as Christians in the life of the country.

A supreme-court judge heard me say that in a meeting with the city officials of a large city. I urged the Christian laymen go into the public life to change it. He inwardly accepted the challenge, gave up his supreme-court job, ran for governor, was elected, and is now trying seriously to put God into public decisions, and is doing a magnificient job of it. He is lifting the tone of the whole state.

If the highest gift of God—Himself—is available for a person as a person, then that makes everybody important, lays the foundation of democracy in a spiritual experience of God. This makes democracy, not an expedient, but an experience. Democracy is founded on a faith in God which produces a faith in man, which produces a faith that man is capable of governing himself, which produces democracy. But it is more: it makes the man stand up and say: "If I stand equal before God, I stand equal before man, anywhere, everywhere."

O God, I thank Thee that when Thy Spirit comes upon me, it puts back my shoulders, for if I am equal to obtaining the highest gifts of life, then I must be equal to obtaining all the lesser. They are all mine. Amen.

AFFIRMATION FOR THE DAY: *The sense of mission in all I do today.*

THE HIGHEST OPEN TO WOMAN

We now continue the leveling process through the coming of
e Holy Spirit.

3. *The Holy Spirit makes both sexes equal.* There had been a
ecially sacred sex—the male sex. "Every male that opens the
omb shall be called holy to the Lord." That was as far as
daism went, but the Christian faith went beyond this: a
oman as a woman received the highest gift of God—the Holy
irit—and if this is true, then all the lesser gifts must be open
her. "All these with one accord devoted themselves to
ayer, together with the women. . . . And they were all filled
th the Holy Spirit." (Acts 1:14; 2:4.)

This is breath-taking in its significance, for it was a completely
w departure. Mrs. V. Pundit, the present Ambassador of
dia to the United States, was with her two daughters when a
an got out of a bus, put up his umbrella, walked ahead with his
fe behind with a baby astride her hips and a bundle on her
ad. "Look Mother, what's that?" asked one of the girls.
hat's India," quietly replied the mother. The younger said:
Vell, if I were in her place I'd give him the baby and the
indle, and I'd take the umbrella and walk ahead of him"—that
is the young radical. The older daughter said: "I wouldn't. I
ould give him the bundle, and I'd walk alongside of him under
e umbrella with my baby"—that was the young liberal. But
at isn't India alone—that was the whole ancient world. Then
mething happened—the Holy Spirit came upon a woman
iually with a man, and that planted the equality of woman in
experience of God. If the highest gift of God is open to a
oman, then all the lesser gifts of God must be open to her too.
iis outflanked all the arguments of antiquity about man's
periority and placed man and woman on the basis of equality
fore God and hence in all the rest of life. Now wonder Paul
ms up the Christian attitude in these words: "There is neither
w nor Greek, there is neither slave nor free, there is neither
ale nor female; for you are all one in Christ Jesus." (Gal.
28.) To take any other attitude was to blaspheme the Holy
irit.

O Gracious Father, Thou art wiping out our barriers and
aking us see life through Thy eyes—and what a vision we
:t when we do. Help us to be true to the heavenly vision
id act upon it in all relationships. Amen.

THE CONSERVATIVE AND THE RADICAL

As the barriers go down before the coming of the Spirit, we stand amazed. But the end is not yet.

4. *The Holy Spirit made both ages—youth and old age—equal.* When Peter spoke after the coming of the Spirit, he said:

"God declares,
that I will pour out my Spirit upon all flesh,
and your sons and daughters shall prophesy,
and your young men shall see visions,
and your old men shall dream dreams." (Acts 2:17.)

There has always been a sacred age, and it has always been old age. In every religion power and sanctity have gravitated toward old age. It has therefore tended to become conservative.

But the Christian faith is so dynamic that it cannot be expressed by conservatism alone. To conserve values is good, but not only does Christian faith conserve values; it pushes those values into more and more realms of life and makes them operative there. Hence it demands a radicalism as well as a conservatism to full express itself—both old age and youth must combine to show its true nature. The Christian faith as conservatism is weak; the Christian faith as radicalism is also weak—but as both conservatism and radicalism is a living blend, then it is truly strong. We need both. But the Christian faith leans toward the radical: "Therefore every scribe who has been trained for the kingdom of heaven is like a householder who brings out of his treasure what is new and what is old." (Matt. 13:52.) Here is says that both the new and the old are to be brought forth—both radicalism and conservatism are to be the working forces of the Kingdom. But note the "new" is first. The Christian faith leans toward the radical. And further note that this is said of a "scribe." But the scribe was a copyist—one who recorded—he didn't create. But here even the scribe—the copyist—would become so creative that he would bring forth the new. The Holy Spirit is the redemptive Spirit, pushing upon more and more areas of life to redeem them. Hence the young men shall see visions and the old men dream dreams—both radical because both redemptive.

O God, Thou art within me, the ceaseless urge toward the new. Keep me forever responding to that urge. May I never settle down to what is. Keep me on my toes with anticipation of the good things to come. Amen.

AFFIRMATION FOR THE DAY: *All I touch this day becomes new, for Thy creative touch is upon me.*

ALL CLASSES EQUAL

We saw yesterday that both youth and old age would be used in the Kingdom, but that the radicalism of youth should carry over into old age and keep it young. There is no place for hardened arteries in the Kingdom of God. Someone has said, "America has dough, but it has no leaven." If the leaven is taken out of us, we are but soggy dough.

But note that it is, not just young men, but young women too who are to prophesy. As we saw, prophecy is not fore-telling, but forthtelling—an aggressive downright pressing home of the word of God upon the consciences of people. Here is where young men and young women can be alike and be alike creative. If the "daughters" would cease spending their time and attention on being like the "sons" in dress and habits of smoking and in guzzling liquor, and if both would become like each other in the forth-telling of the Good News, then a new era would begin. There is another barrier that went down with the coming of the Holy Spirit:

5. *The Holy Spirit made all classes equal.*

"On my menservants and my maidservants in those days I will pour out my Spirit, and they shall prophesy." (Acts 2:18.) The menservants and the maidservants were those who belonged to the so-called lower classes of society—the serving class. They were to become prophetic, creative, the makers of a new world.

R. H. Tawney says: "The foundation of democracy is the sense of spiritual independence which nerves the individual to stand alone against the powers of this world, and in England, where squire and parson, lifting arrogant eyebrows at the insolence of the lower orders, combined to crush popular agitation, as a menace at once to society and to the Church, it is probable that democracy owes more to Nonconformity than to any other single movement." But conformity was only an attempt to get back to the original Spring—to the coming of the Spirit upon believers at Pentecost. There a sudden sense of individual worth was introduced into life—a man was a man, a man for whom Christ died. Class went down under that. A classless society arose out of the impact of the Holy Spirit.

O Spirit Divine, I thank Thee, when Thou dost dwell within me, that I am no longer able to despise myself, nor others. Thou art the great Leveler. This makes me grateful to my fingertips. Amen.

AFFIRMATION FOR THE DAY: *I look on a man today, not as a man, but as a man for whom Christ died.*

NO DISTINCTIONS BASED ON BLOOD

We must pause at one more barrier that went down with the coming of the Spirit:

6. *The Holy Spirit canceled all distinctions based on blood.* The account says that among those who "devoted themselves to prayer" were "Mary the mother of Jesus, and . . . his brothers."

It would have been easy to build up a special, privileged line through blood and to make this line specially sacred and authoritative. Had Mary the mother of Jesus and His brothers been set aside in any special way to special consideration, this would have happened. They were not. Mary and the brothers of Jesus waited along with the rest, paid the same price for the coming of the Spirit, and received the Spirit on the same conditions as the rest. At the moment of the receiving of God's highest gift, the Spirit, there were no favorites, no exceptions—all were equal. This canceled out superiorities based on blood. One branch of the Christian Chruch, the Roman Catholic, has gone against this and has put Mary as the mother of Jesus in a privileged position as an intercessor. This is foreign to the Christian faith. The last mention of Mary in the gospel account shows her bowed in prayer along with the rest. That fits in with the spirit of this new movement.

"At the foot of the cross the ground is level." That remark was made by Dr. Abernathy when Chief Justice Hughes and a Chinese laundryman stood to be received into the church at the same time.

In Islam descendants of the prophet Mohammed are numerous and honored as such. In the Christian faith no such hierarchy was ever attempted. We find none claiming blood relation with Jesus. Why? Because that was all canceled at the coming of the Spirit. What was the use of claiming special blood when no privilege was attached to blood? A new heredity came into being—all could directly partake of the divine Nature through self-surrender and appropriating faith. The Blood of the Son of God made us all sons of God the moment we accepted it. Human blood was irrelevant.

O God, my Father, I thank Thee that Thou hast opened the highest to the lowest, the greatest to the least. My heart dances with anticipation of what I shall be—in Thee. For an endless Life pulsates within my veins. I belong to the twice-born nobility. Amen.

AFFIRMATION FOR THE DAY: *I am inferior if I think myself superior.*

THE BARRIER DOWN BETWEEN FLESH AND SPIRIT

Let us note the coming down of another barrier:

7. *The Holy Spirit broke down the barrier between flesh and spirit.*
"I will pour out my Spirit upon all flesh." (Acts 2:17.) Here
"Spirit" was to come upon "flesh." It is true that "flesh" is often
used as "people," but the very fact that "flesh" was used instead
of "people" was significant and fits in with the genius of the
gospel. For that gospel is founded on "the Word made
flesh"—the Incarnation.

If the Word had become printer's ink, it would have become
a code. If the Word had become idea, it would have been a
philosophy. But the Word became flesh and therefore became a
gospel—the good news.

This Incarnation becomes reincarnation in us—in the Holy
Spirit. Here the Divine again moves into flesh—this time partial
and limited, for we are partial and limited. But in a real way the
Incarnation is re-enacted. We do not become Christs, nor do we
become Divine, but there is a real Divine indwelling in flesh.

I talked to a French lady, a disciple of Aurobindo Ghose, who
shows himself to his disciples only four times a year, and she
said: "He is trying something that has never been tried before:
he is not only realizing his soul as divine, but he is making his
body divine." Here by various disciplines he was trying to take
the flesh up into the Spirit. That is commonplace in the Christian
gospel—it is its very heart and soul. The body is not "a reeking
mass of festering matter" to be sloughed off so the spirit can be
free; it is a part of redemption and is to be the agent of redemption. "Do you not know that your body is a temple of the Holy
Spirit within you . . . ? So glorify God in your body." (I Cor.
6:19-20.)

If the Word is to become flesh in us, then the flesh is to
become Word. Through our very flesh the Word is to be
revealed and respoken. Our bodies take on the likeness of the
Spirit and speak the message of the Spirit. The dualism between
soul and body is broken down, and both are under a single control. All life is unified under the control of the Holy Spirit.

O God, I thank Thee that Thou hast made the material,
wilt redeem the material and through the material redeem
others. This body of mine is Thine—and Thine to redeem
and use. I give it to Thee anew. In Jesus' name. Amen.

AFFIRMATION FOR THE DAY: *Today my flesh shall become Word.*

AN ABOUNDING SENSE OF VITALITY

We saw yesterday that the Holy Spirit is to have as one of the areas of redemption—the flesh. He is to indwell it, to quicken it, to make it function well continuously, and to make it a redemptive agent. These four things are important.

(*a*) The Spirit is to indwell it—the flesh. The body and the Spirit are not alien—they are made for each other. The laws that underlie the body are the laws of God written in flesh, in nerve and tissue. "The body is . . . for the Lord, and the Lord for the body." (I Cor. 6:13.) The body works well and harmoniously when it does the will of God—it obeys its own laws. The body works badly and with discord when it does not work with the will of God—it is a frustrated body. "The body is . . . for the Lord"—finds its fulfillment and is at its highest best in Him. "The Lord for the body"—He is asking you, not to despise it, to suppress it, but to offer it as the agent of God's will and purpose. He is *for* it. The body and the Spirit are affinities. Only when the body is used in anti-Spirit ways is it an enemy to the Spirit and to itself.

(*b*) The Spirit quickens the body: "will give life to your mortal bodies also through His Spirit which dwells in you" (Rom. 8:11). The body can be quickened or quenched according to the control behind it. Let it be controlled by fears, worries, anxieties, resentments, self-centeredness, guilts, and it will be quenched. Its sparkle will leave, and the body will be a burden and a subject of disease and functional disturbance. But let it be controlled by the Spirit, and all the lines of the face will turn up; the organs will function better; the blood will circulate more freely; the nerves will be steadier; the glands will secrete more normally; disease will drop off as a dead leaf; the whole being will have a sense of well-being. The body is being quickened by the Holy Spirit within. Tiredness, which is often chronic in those who are not quickened by the Spirit, now drops away, and an abounding sense of vitality takes possession. We live—in Him. And that life goes to our fingertips. We are alive in every cell.

O Spirit Divine, I yield all my members to Thee. They are Thine—quicken them, bring them to Thy best, and may they become the happy agent of Thy purpose. For Thou art the life of their life, the Being of their being. Amen.

AFFIRMATION FOR THE DAY: *My flesh, quickened by the Spirit, shall be alive in every cell today.*

ON WAKING UP WITH A GRIN

We saw that the Spirit quickens the body. We go a step further: (c) The Spirit makes it function well continuously. The quickening is not merely putting pep in us—there is a pep with no kickbacks or hang-overs.

I often say to young people's groups: "I don't have any hangovers from being a Christian. I won't wake up tomorrow morning and say to myself, 'Stanley Jones, why were you a Christian last night—what made you do it?' " They invariably laugh. They know instinctively that the Christian faith and health are one—at that point—that you should get up with a sense of well-being, a sense of adventure with God. As one man put it after giving himself to Christ: "For the first time in my life I woke up with a grin." It's a grin or a grouch, according to the inner control.

Jesus was indwelt by the Spirit, and His vitality was amazing. A rough woodsman looked at one of the paintings of Jesus by Sallman, and he said: "Gosh, that Man could cut twenty cords of wood a minute." He illustrated that statement regarding Pentecost: "Each one heard them speaking in his own language . . . the mighty works of God." This man was expressing in a woodsman's language the wonderful works of God as seen in the face of Jesus—vitality, health, power.

A radiant friend, full of the Spirit and seventy-five years of age, said: "The Holy Ghost puts back my shoulders." He does. He takes the droop out of the spirit and hence out of the body. For the mind of the spirit becomes the mood of the body. The body is the outer manifestation of the spirit—it gradually becomes like the spirit behind it. If the spirit behind it is healthy, radiant, outgoing, then the body tends to become healthy, radiant, outgoing. The body becomes more and more the show window of the soul. Every emotion, every act, every desire, is registered in the tissues, however faintly, and the sum total begins to emerge as the body, befitting the soul behind it. Even disease cannot fully obliterate or check this process. For some are beautiful in spite of bodily disfigurements. The soul, blow by blow, chisels the body to its own likeness.

O God, I thank Thee that there is nothing hid that shall not be revealed—revealed in flesh. Help me then to keep my soul inwardly clean and simple and unaffected. For I want the total man to be clean. Amen.

AFFIRMATION FOR THE DAY: *My body, shaped by my spirit, shall be a better body today.*

THE FLESH BECOME WORD

We now spend another day on this thought: When the word becomes flesh in us, then the flesh becomes word. The flesh becomes the vehicle of revelation.

Whatever word becomes flesh in us, then the flesh becomes that word and reveals that word. Suppose it is the word of self-centeredness that becomes flesh in us. Then the tissues will contract, become tense, and will turn in. Every self-centered person is tied in knots—physically. When the word of self-centeredness becomes flesh, then the flesh becomes the word of self-centeredness, expresses it in a tied-up, tense body. Suppose the word of resentment becomes flesh in us; then the flesh becomes word—the word of resentment. The conflict of the soul will pass over into the body. Every resentful soul is full of conflict with others, but mostly with himself, not merely as spirit, but as body—the face takes on the conflict within, sign of the conflicting organs. Jesus said of the servant who mistreated other servants that the master would "cut him in pieces" (Luke 12:46, margin). That is true now. They are cut in pieces now—by inner conflict.

Take the word of fear when it becomes flesh; then the flesh becomes word—the word of fear. The flesh becomes pale; the blood has retreated; the muscles contract ready to run away; the brain cells that preside over foresight actually become so corrupted by fear and retreatism that in extreme cases operations have to be performed so that the rest of the brain can function without them.

Take the word of guilt when it becomes flesh; then the flesh becomes word—the word of guilt. The body takes on a guilty appearance—the eyes become shifty; the flesh shrinks; the whole being is furtive, lacks straightforwardness.

On the other hand, when the word of purity becomes flesh, then the flesh becomes word—the word of purity. The facial expression becomes the expression of purity—it is self-verifying. You can tell at a glance a person of purity. When the word of love becomes flesh, then the flesh becomes word—the word of love. The very flesh expresses love—the person has a lovely countenance, no matter how plain.

O God, I thank Thee that life, inner and outer, soon becomes one. For our outer expresses, sooner or later, our inner. We grow a body that expresses us. Help me to be at Thy best. In Jesus' name. Amen.

AFFIRMATION FOR THE DAY: *Today my flesh and my spirit shall speak the same message.*

THE WORLDS OF MATTER AND SPIRIT BECOMING ONE

8. *The coming of the Spirit attunes the two worlds—material and spiritual.*

We saw a great deal of physical phenomena surrounding the coming of the Holy Spirit, each having meaning and purpose. But we observed further that the material phenomena had its counterpart in the spiritual—these two worlds were saying the same thing. Note:

(*a*) The Day of Pentecost was the day of offering the first fruits of the harvest. The group was offering the first fruits of Jesus' sowing—themselves.

(*b*) There was the sound of a rushing mighty wind. *Ruach* or *pneuma* both mean "wind" and "spirit." So the Wind or Spirit was sweeping through them like a cleansing breath from heaven.

(*c*) Tongues of fire were resting on their heads. The Flame of the Spirit came into their hearts and set them afire with God.

(*d*) They spoke with other tongues. They were speaking with new motives, new clarity, new certainty, new fire, new converting power. Their tongues were not the same, for they were not the same.

(*e*) They appeared "drunk." They were intoxicated with God. All inhibitions, all fears, and all inferiority feelings were taken away, and they were "filled with the Holy Spirit."

(*f*) They were all together in one place. They were spiritually together in one place—God. The barriers were all taken down and they were a unified group—in one Spirit.

(*g*) The cloven tongues as of fire rested upon the heads of each: "distributed and resting." The Holy Spirit came upon them and *rested* on them—a permanent coming, abiding with them forever.

The two words of matter and spirit were thus shown to be one and reacted upon each other. When things happen in the spirit, the material universe responds. The material takes on the image of the spiritual—your body becomes like your spirit. When miracles take place in the spirit, then miracles begin to happen in the material. The universe is a universe and not a multiverse.

O God, my Father, I thank Thee that Thou art creator and redeemer of both worlds of matter and spirit, and Thou canst make my flesh not only to dwell in hope but to be the agent of redemption. I thank Thee. Amen.

AFFIRMATION FOR THE DAY: *My worlds are one—in Thee.*

NATURE AND HUMAN NATURE REFLECTING EACH OTHER

Yesterday we saw that there was a physical counterpart of the spiritual experience: If there had been no physical counterpart of the spiritual experience, then we could come to the conclusion that it was a severely spiritual experience and did not affect the material.

But this shows that "creation waits with eager longing for the revealing of the sons of God; . . . because the creation itself will be set free from its bondage to decay and obtain the glorious liberty of the children of God." (Rom. 8:19, 21.) A converted farmer will convert his farm. A converted workman will convert his workmanship. "Every change in the character of the molder is reflected in these precision castings," said the head of a molding factory. "If the person is inwardly upset, the molding will reflect that upset. We have to have good men to make good moldings."

So nature and human nature reflect each other. But having noted the physical phenomena that surrounded the coming of the Holy Spirit, let us not ourselves try to repeat that physical phenomena as a sign of the coming of the Spirit. That will lead to the queer and to the off-center. The connection between the physical having been shown, this particular scaffolding of physical phenomena was taken down—after the principle of the connection was established.

Pentecostalism has failed in large measure in so far as it has tried to repeat Pentecost. When its emphasis is on the day and its surroundings, the attention is called away from the fact to the phenomena. The fact is the coming of the Holy Spirit, and not how He came. Pentecostalism has emphasized Pentecost—the day and its phenomena—and has become a movement of a day and its phenomena instead of a movement of the Spirit, the Spirit expressing Himself through forms suitable to this day as the forms were suitable to that day. If, instead of trying to duplicate Pentecost, the Pentecostals had let the Holy Spirit express Himself through them in creating manifestations of redemption in terms of today, they would have swept redemptively through the Church. "To each is given the manifestation of the Spirit for the common good." (I Cor. 12:7.)

O Christ, I want the Spirit within me to duplicate nothing—nothing except Thee. For I want no manifestation that doesn't manifest Thee—manifest Thee in Thy sanctity and Thy sanity. For Thou art life. Amen.

AFFIRMATION FOR THE DAY: *Not Pentecost, but the Spirit of Pentecost, shall be manifested in me today.*

NOTHING NECESSARY EXCEPT THE SURRENDERED WILL

We saw yesterday that the coming of the Holy Spirit is not bound up with any outer manifestation. There is no "sign" except the nine fruits of the Spirit (Gal. 5:22), and they are all moral.

Another fact must be noted before we pass from this: The disciples were going through no rite or ceremony when the Holy Spirit came. Suppose they had been undergoing baptism or the Lord's Supper, or any other rite or ceremony; we would have made that rite or ceremony a necessary condition or accompaniment of the coming of the Holy Spirit. That would have made the Holy Spirit rite bound or ceremony bound. We use the rites and ceremonies as aids, but not as necessary aids. There is nothing that is necessary except the surrendered heart and the appropriating faith. That universalizes the Gift.

It is true that the disciples went down to Samaria and "prayed for them that they might receive the Holy Spirit. . . . Then they laid their hands on them and they received the Holy Spirit." (Acts 8:15, 17.) But the laying on of hands did not produce the coming of the Spirit—it was the prayer that did it. If we say the laying on of hands did it, then we are guilty of the fallacy in logic "with, and therefore on account of." The Holy Spirit might come at the time of the laying on of hands, but not necessarily. For the prayer of faith on the part of the minister and the receptivity of the one who seeks may be absent.

The Holy Spirit sometimes came with the laying on of hands, as in the case of Paul laying his hands on the Ephesians (Acts 19:6). But He sometimes came without any laying of hands, as at Pentecost and as in the house of Cornelius: "While Peter was still saying this, the Holy Spirit fell on all who heard the word" (Acts 10:44).

That brings "a freedom of the Spirit"—you can be free to use human help or to go to God without it. Nothing is necessary except the surrendered will and the appropriating faith. No posture, such as kneeling, was necessary for the Holy Spirit came upon them "where they were sitting" (Acts 2:2). Never was the Highest so open to everybody, everywhere.

O God, I thank Thee that Thou hast put no strings to Thy Gift. Freely Thou dost give. This puts the latchstring so low that even a child can reach it and open the door into Life. I thank Thee, thank Thee. Amen.

AFFIRMATION FOR THE DAY: *Today, nothing between, Lord, nothing between.*

THE COMING OF THE SPIRIT MEANT INNER CLEANSING

We come now to the kernel of the experience of the Holy Spirit at Pentecost. As we take off the temporary wrappings, we come to the permanent. Some things passed away with the hour, but some things remain. We pick out two permanent results.

The first is that the coming of the Holy Spirit brought inner cleansing of heart. Peter, in interpreting what happened at the coming of the Holy Spirit upon the Gentiles said: "God who knows the heart bore witness to them, giving them the Holy Spirit just as He did to us; and he made no distinction between us and them, but cleansed their hearts by faith." (Acts 15:8-9.) Here was something common to both Jews and Gentiles: "He made no distinction between us and them, but cleansed their hearts by faith"—cleansing of the heart came as a result of the coming of the Spirit.

When we speak of cleansing of the heart, we usually mean cleaning from the impurity of sex. It does mean that; but it means much more—it means cleansing from all inner conflict and division. The pure heart is the undivided heart.

We now know that the center of our inner conflict is between the conscious and the subconscious minds. Psychology tells us that about one tenth of the mind is conscious and about nine tenths is subconscious. Like the iceberg, which is nine tenths submerged, life is largely in the submerged portion of our being—the subconscious. This is important, for if that nine tenths is not working with the conscious purposes in the one tenth, then here is a serious division—a division so serious that it becomes decisive. Whatever controls the subconscious controls us.

The subconscious has been so interpreted by some modern psychologists that it leaves a sense of determinism—we are determined by the subconscious. We are powerless, since the dark subconscious desires color and control all we think and do. To the determinisms of heredity and environment is added a new determinism—the determinism of the subconscious. Man is enslaved—unless the subconscious can be redeemed, cleansed, and controlled.

O God, Thou hast fashioned me in my inmost being—hast Thou fashioned me for slavery or for freedom? I know it is for freedom, for Thou couldst not be God and fashion me for anything else. Show me that freedom. Amen.

AFFIRMATION FOR THE DAY: *If I am determined by the subconscious, I am determined by a subconscious controlled by the Spirit.*

AT WORK IN THE SUBCONSCIOUS

We saw yesterday that life was in large measure determined by the subconscious. This is startlingly illustrated in the following: A very devoted missionary got into the train in India and found the lower berth occupied by an Indian, so that he had to take the upper. He went to sleep resentful. He woke up during the night finding himself putting the Indian out of the door, had him halfway through the open door. Another push and he would have been thrown out upon the tracks. The missionary was shocked, apologized profusely saying that he did it in his sleep. But the Indian could not trust himself to such a man and got out at the next station. What had happened? This missionary had dropped into his subconscious mind a resentment just as he was about to go to sleep. At the moment of passing into unconsciousness the subconscious mind is very susceptible of influences. This resentment worked while he slept and precipitated an act which would have horrified him when he was conscious.

A little girl said: "I want to be good, but I don't want to be obedient"—her conscious mind would like to be known as good; but her subconscious mind, where self was one of the driving urges, did not want to obey anything except itself.

The minister who preaches a gospel of self-surrender to God, but would like to be complimented and praised for preaching that gospel, is suffering from a division between the conscious and subconscious minds.

The question of questions for religion is: Can the subconscious mind be redeemed? If it cannot, then religion will deal with the conscious motives and leave unredeemed the depths. If that be true, then it is only a half-answer. But if its power and redemption can reach to the subconscious and there cleanse and control it, then it is not an answer—it is *the* answer.

The Christian gives the answer in the Holy Spirit. The area of the work of the Holy Spirit is largely, if not entirely, in the subconscious. In the Holy Spirit we are provided with a divine presence and power adequate for redeeming and controlling the subconscious.

O God, my gracious Father, I thank Thee, for Thou hast provided for my deepest need—the need of cleansing and controlling the depths of me. Without this I would sink into the depths of despair; with this I rise to any height. Amen.

AFFIRMATION FOR THE DAY: *The subconscious is no longer an enemy—it is in friendly Hands.*

"ARCHED AND BUTTRESSED FROM WITHIN"

Without the emphasis on the Holy Spirit, religion works partly with the historical, in the presentation of the historic Jesus, and partly in the experimental, in the conversion and control of the conscious mind. But the emphasis on the redemption of the subconscious is dim or absent. Even where the Holy Spirit is emphasized, the connection between the Holy Spirit and the subconscious is unrecognized. Two recent books on the Holy Spirit do not even mention the subconscious.

Marcus Aurelius says: "Man must be arched and buttressed from within, else the temple crumbles into dust." Jesus puts it stronger: A "house divided against itself shall not stand." (Matt. 12:25, K.J.V.)

An occasional touch and reinforcement is not sufficient. The power and the redemption must be there as continuously as the subconscious itself. I visited Aurobindo Ghose, a Hindu devotee who shows himself to his followers four times a year. The go-between is a French lady, who told me she had been in a trance, during which time she had left the body and had entered into the inner life of some of the devotees "to set us at rights," but it is pitifully inadequate. For no human being can redeem the human from within; even so, the visits are limited and occasional.

Nor would the fulfillment of the words of Jesus be wholly adequate: "Lo, I am with you always even unto the end of the world." (Matt. 28:20, K.J.V.) That must go deeper, for it is "with"—only an "in" can be adequate. In the Holy Spirit this passage became: "Lo, I am in you always, even to the depths of the subconscious."

Paul puts his finger on this work of unifying the personality in these words: "To unite all things in him, things in heaven and things on earth" (Eph. 1:10). Does this "all things" include the uniting of the conscious and the subconscious minds? If not, then the circumference unitings without a center uniting is beside my need. But if "all things" include the conscious and the subconscious, then this verse is fulfilled: "If then your whole body is full of light, having no part dark, it will be wholly bright" (Luke 11:36).

O God, I want an inner being with "no part dark," no part unredeemed. My heart tingles at the thought that I can have an inner life which will be wholly full of light. I take it. Amen.

AFFIRMATION FOR THE DAY: *My conscious and my subconscious dance to Thy music—together.*

"BARREN AND ABSOLUTELY DRY"

Nothing less than the Divine can unite the inner life—conscious and subconscious—and make it function as one.

Ezekiel puts it this way: "A new spirit will I put within you"—that is man's own spirit made new by grace. But when this is done, there is the further work: "I will put my Spirit within you" to dwell in that new spirit and to make the subconscious a part of that newness (Ezek. 36:26, 27, K.J.V.). It is this indwelling of the Spirit in the total being that is the steadying force within. A little girl, three-and-a-half years old, put it this way: "I wish God would stay inside me where He belongs, because whenever He goes away, I do something I oughtn't." "Where He belongs"—that is the revealing insight, for God and I are not alien—I belong in God, and God belongs in me.

Now note this passage: "Walking in the fear of the Lord and in the comfort of the Holy Spirit it was multiplied" (Acts 9:31). There are two sides to his passage—"Walking in the fear of the Lord"—that is the historical, a faith based on the historic Jesus. Then: "In the comfort of the Holy Spirit"—that is the exprimental, an experience based on the Holy Spirit within. Unless these two things are kept in balance, danger sets in. If it is all based on the historic Jesus, then it becomes a set of beliefs. But if it is based only on the Holy Spirit within, without the correction of the historic Jesus, it becomes subjective emotionalism, going off into visions, impressionism.

Dr. M. L. Dolbeer, a Lutheran missionary, writes, "We landed in Colombo and crossed to India, and as we passed along the barren sand flats I thought to myself: 'My soul is like that, barren and absolutely dry.' I wondered why I was coming back, and what I had to give to India. Then I read your book, *The Christ of Every Road*. It was just the answer I needed. And when you came to the later chapter concerning the receiving of the Holy Spirit and gave illustration of the lady who found it just as simple as taking a book, I said to myself: 'Well, I can do that too,' and I did. It was a wonderful experience. The outstanding things in it were joy, fellowship, and co-ordination." The historical had become the experiential.

O Spirit Divine, I know thou art making real this wonderful Historical—making it real within me. Now redemption is within. Now I am redeemed and co-ordinated—at one with myself and with Thee. Amen.

AFFIRMATION FOR THE DAY: *Thy offering I take—and give, today.*

DRIVING URGES, NOT SUPPRESSED, BUT REDEEMED

We noted that the gospel offers an inner life with "no part dark." When you study the psychology of the subconscious as found in modern writers, you feel that, like the "throne of the beast, . . . its kingdom was in darkness." The depths are unlighted save by the pale light of information shining on it—the powerful light of transformation is not there. You feel that you walk through life with a Trojan horse within, ready to betray you at any weak moment.

But the gospel offers freedom. "Where the Spirit of the Lord is, there is freedom." (II Cor. 3:17.) So if the Spirit of the Lord is within us, there is freedom—freedom from the conflict between conscious and subconscious. Does conversion bring this freedom? Partly.

At conversion there is introduced into the conscious mind a new love, a new loyalty, a new life. But down in the depths of the subconscious is the residing place of the driving urges: self, sex, and the herd. These urges have come down through a long racial history, and they have been contaminated by long association with racial evil through heredity. They drive for their completion, their fulfillment, often apart from, or against, the moralities and loyalties built up in the conscious mind through conversion. So a conflict ensues between the conscious and the subconscious. Paul describes this conflict in these terms: "For I delight in the law of God, in my inmost self, but I see in my members another law at war with the law of my mind and making me captive to the law of sin which dwells in my members." (Rom. 7:22-23.)

Redemption seems to proceed through stages—the first stage is conversion, which introduces the new life into the conscious mind and transforms it. The disciples had this before the coming of the Holy Spirit at Pentecost: "They are not of the world." And yet "the world" had hostages within them. Self was still there, ready to assert itself as to who should be first. The fear of the herd was there, for "the doors [were] shut . . . for fear." The driving urges were repressed but not redeemed.

O God, Thou hast made my driving urges; now redeem them—redeem them from all perversions, and direct them to Kingdom ends. For I know that these urges can urge me—to Thy Kingdom. Amen.

AFFIRMATION FOR THE DAY: *My urges, surrendered to Thy purges, shall urge me toward Thee and Thy purposes.*

THE THREE LEVELS OF LIFE

We saw yesterday that the disciples had a new life before the coming of the Spirit at Pentecost—they had a new life; but the new life didn't have them, not completely.

There are three levels of life: the instinct level, the duty level, and the grace level. Before they came to Christ, they were living on the instinct level. Paul put it this way: "We all once lived in the passions of our flesh, following the desires of body and mind." (Eph. 2:3.) Most people live on that level—the impulses of the instincts determine their conduct.

Then comes religion with its "Thou shalt not do this; thou shalt do that"—here is the introduction of duty. Many live on this level—religion introduces a struggle with the instincts. That level of life is filled with people who have clenched fists, knit brows, set jaws, and pain. It is artificial instead of artesian. They sigh and look for heaven as release from the tense struggle. But heaven is at hand—and the release can be now.

The third level is the level of grace. Here the disciples found that if they would surrender their all—all they knew, the conscious, and all they did not know, the subconscious—then the Spirit of God would move in and cleanse and control them at the depths. The Spirit is called "the Spirit of grace" (Heb. 10:29). What a name! And what a function! The Spirit is to apply grace at the place it counts—at the depths, at the unconscious. There grace is redemptive, taking over the instincts, and cleansing away all wrong bents and intents, directing the driving urges toward new ends with new power within.

After Pentecost the disciples weren't suppressing their instincts—they were expressing them. They were letting nature caper, because it was controlled by the Holy Spirit. The Holy Spirit pulled out the stops and played them all over. They could let nature caper because it wasn't capricious—it was controlled and directed. The thing they needed had come: the Spirit of grace—grace working in the subconscious.

O Spirit of Grace, I thank Thee that Thou hast come to me, for I know that in Thee I find all I need and more—redemption and redirection. My heart is glad with a strange, wild gladness—the gladness of victory. Amen.

AFFIRMATION FOR THE DAY: *The Spirit of grace will make me gracious today.*

PERFECT FUNCTION IS PERFECT HEALTH

The three levels of life have been described as the instinct level, duty level, grace level. These levels also could be described as the sewer level, the street level, and the sky level.

The sewer level is the level where we simply obey our driving instincts without question or inhibition. Life descends to the level of the animal or below. The instincts are perverted from the natural good to the unnatural evil.

Then there is the street level, where we do as life around us does. We are herd controlled. "Everybody does it," decides life for us. I was once caught in a fear-controlled mob on the streets of Shanghai when bombs began to fall. I had to run with them, for to go against them would have meant to be trampled and crushed. But as soon as possible I extricated myself from the mob and became a person again. But some people surrender themselves to the herd and never become persons again—they are herd centered. Once when it was announced that our plane would be indefinitely delayed, someone suggested going to the bar—all followed. Met by a frustration, they took to an escape method, and all followed the herd.

Then there is the sky level—your feet are on the earth, but your head is in the sky, and you listen to God and are directed by Him.

Here the instincts are, not sewer controlled, nor street controlled, but God controlled. And when they are God controlled, they come to their own.

In the Spirit-controlled life self is still there but now, not self-centered, but God centered and therefore rhythmical and harmonious. "Perfect function is perfect health," says Dr. Hay. The self functions perfectly and is therefore perfectly healthy—a self you can live with. Sex is still there, but now being God centered it functions as God intended it to function, so functions into health and harmony. The herd instinct is still there, but now it is fastened on the Kingdom of God as the supreme loyalty, and as a result you can enjoy the herd because you don't belong to it.

Someone has defined music as "wild sounds tamed to time and tune." You are musical now.

O God, I thank Thee that these wild urges can be cleansed and redirected and harnessed to Thy purposes and thus find their freedom. For Thy will is our freedom. I surrender them now. Amen.

AFFIRMATION FOR THE DAY: *My wild urges, tamed to time and tune by Thee, will make music today.*

THE DRIVING INSTINCTS CANNOT BE ELIMINATED

We said last week that the driving urges were cleansed, redirected, and dedicated. Note that we did not say that they were eliminated or even suppressed. By no known process can the driving instincts be eliminated, and any philosophy or religion founded on the attempt to eliminate them or to suppress them is bound to fail. Put the instincts out at the door, and they will come back by the window, often dressed up in garments of disguise. The philosophy of Buddhism and many of the philosophies of Hinduism are built on the possibility of not only wiping out all the instincts but also wiping out all desire. I asked a Hindu ascetic: "What is your desire?" "Nothing," he replied. "Where are you going?" "Nowhere." "Where have you come from?" "Nowhere." He was afraid of desire and wanted to be a blank—and was! But not quite a blank, for he ardently desired to be a blank; so desire was still there, turned toward the absence of desire.

When the attempt is made to get rid of desire through philosophy, then compartmentalism sets in, and you fence off your philosophy of no desire and pay tribute to it there, while life and its desire function in other compartments. The Buddhists of Burma are an illustration—they pay tribute to desirelessness as a religion in one compartment and then manifest the deepest interest in life in the others. They salute the philosophy in special ways and then proceed to follow their desires. We Christians do the same—we praise the Sermon on the Mount and then practice the sermon of the mart. A Hindu nationalist expatiated at length upon the self-sacrifice and honesty of the congress leaders of India and glowed with enthusiasm. When about to leave the train, he reached up, unscrewed the electric bulb, and remarked: "I need it," and walked out. He compartmentalized his patriotism and his personal desires. The bane of religion is, not infidelity, but inconsistency. Why? Because it is usually presented as suppression. Only when it is presented as expression at its highest, and so it is to the interests of the urges to obey, will real consistency be achieved.

O Spirit Divine, I know I am fashioned in my inmost being for Thee and Thy ways, and that my ways are Thy Ways. So help me to give myself to Thy will with complete abandon and complete joy. Amen.

AFFIRMATION FOR THE DAY: *Today—nothing compartmentalized, but all conformed to the purposes of God.*

PLAYING TRUANT FROM OURSELVES

We discussed yesterday the fact that our urges are fulfilled only when they are surrendered to the will of God. When we obey them we obey ourselves—our interests and God's will are one. Our wills and God's will are, not alien, but affinities.

An old gentleman asked a little boy: "Whatever are you crying for, sonny?" Sonny: "I've been playing truant all day, and I've just found out that it is Saturday." When we play truant against God, we play truant against ourselves.

One passage vividly describes this identity of interest in the will of God and our own wills: "Without him was not anything made. . . . That which has been made was life in him" (John 1:2; 1:4 margin). Note two things: (*a*) That God made our instincts—His stamp is upon them. They are made to work in His way. Their way and His Way are one. (*b*) When those instincts are in Him, they are life: "That which has been made was life in him." When we by choice surrender our driving urges to the Holy Spirit, who in Christ in us, then they become "life in Him"—they live; they live abundantly; they live at their maximum best. But they not only live—they *are* life. They are life; hence they live and cause others to live.

But suppose by choice we surrender the instincts to themselves and their own impulses; then they are death. They die themselves, and they produce death. Outside of God there is nothing but death; inside of God there is nothing but life. And life becomes so living that you have to spell it with a capital *L*.

A school boy on his examination quoted the statement of Jesus this way: "I have come that ye might have life and have it moribundantly." That is the outcome of self-centered driving urges—they promise to give us life, but they give it moribundantly. They promise life and produce death. They "keep the word of promise to our ears and break it to our hope." These are the two ways of life: in Christ you live more abundantly; outside of Him you live moribundantly. There are no exceptions. Life knows its Master and lives when it hears and obeys its Master's Voice.

O Spirit Divine, when Thou art within me I live and live to my fingertips. Life glows with life. And the joy of it is that Thou art there—there—taking over charge and infusing life into every cell and every nerve tissue. Amen.

AFFIRMATION FOR THE DAY: *Today, that which has been made—my body, my mind, my spirit—shall be life in him.*

"THEN WE BECOME GOD"

We must continue to study how the driving urges are completed when they are completely God's.

Paul says: "Your old nature . . . is corrupt through deceitful lusts." (Eph. 4:22.) The nature which God has made is not "old," and it is not "corrupt"—it becomes old and decaying and becomes corrupt through deceitful lusts. The desires of the instincts become lusts when they are drawn away from their natural functions and become ends in themselves. The self becomes egotistical; sex becomes sensuality; the herd instinct becomes the worldly mind, obeying the herd around one. In this process they become corrupt. They are not corrupt in themselves—they are God made and God ordained and God blessed. But when we take them into our own hands, then we become God, and that is the center of sin. When that happens, life is corrupted at the center. An abscess forms at the center of our being and just as an abscessed tooth is liable to give you rheumatism and other ailments, so an abscessed or corrupted self will bring pains and aches into the entire self. We give ourselves a pain.

There is a banana blight caused by an insect that blights the leaves so they don't unfold, and hence no fruit ripens. The leaves are not spread out to the sun and air, so get no nourishment, and hence the plant cannot fulfill its function. So the "bug" that bites us is the idea that to have our way is freedom, that God's way is bondage. When we are bitten by that idea, we are immediately tied-up souls, filled with inhibitions and fears and complexes. Life turns in on itself, doesn't unfold, and hence we become stunted and runted.

Psychology agrees with this. Dr. Gordon Allport, professor of psychology at Harvard, says, "Paradoxically 'self-expression' requires the capacity to lose oneself in the pursuit of objectives not primarily referred to the self." In other words, you must lose your driving urges, lose them in a higher Will; and then you will find them again, find them in self-expression. For its self-expression is Spirit-expression. The subconscious and the conscious have one control, the control of the Spirit, and have one output, harmony.

O Spirit Divine, I make Thee Lord at the Center— everything under Thy control. Now Lord of the subconscious and Lord of the conscious, express Thyself through them. Then they live. Amen.

AFFIRMATION FOR THE DAY: *Today, no fears, no inhibitions, no suppressions, for nothing unsurrendered to God.*

LIFE AFFIRMING AND WORLD AFFIRMING

We continue our meditation upon the work of the Spirit in the subconscious1 This passage tells of the attempt at suppression as a way of life instead of expression: "The Spirit expressly says that in later times some will depart from the faith by giving heed to deceitful spirits . . . , who forbid marriage and enjoin abstinence from foods which God created." (I Tim. 4:1, 3.) Here the Spirit foresaw the whole movement of asceticism which swept the Church in the early centuries and blighted it. For it was centered in self—self-mutilation, self-cultivation, but nevertheless the self.

When the Church lost the way of self-dedication, it took to the way of self-suppression. There are two ways to try to get rid of yourself—one is by self-suppression and the other is by self-surrender leading to self-dedication. In apostolic days there was the healthy self-expression through dedications of the powers to be used of God. When that became dimmed or died, men tried to get rid of the self by sitting on it, by mortifying it. Marriage was taboo; certain foods were taboo. The story goes of a bunch of grapes that went the rounds of the monasteries, each monk passing it on to the other, for each wanted to prove he was too good a Christian to eat them.

A young evangelist of India approached marriage three times and found some reason why it shouldn't take place. Each time it was in the girl. But the real reason was that his subconscious mind held the idea that marriage and being an evangelist were incompatible—he couldn't assimilate it into his spiritual life. At that time he began to be unable to digest anything made of wheat. I pointed out the connection between the inability to assimilate marriage into his life and the inability to assimilate wheat. He had transferred his moral and spiritual fear to a physical object. He surrendered to God his fear of marriage and found that he could now assimilate wheat—it no longer made him ill. He passed from a sub-Christian attitude toward life to a Christian attitude. For the Christian attitude is life affirming, world affirming and relationship affirming—provided they are under the control and guidance of the Spirit.

O God, I thank Thee that tensions and fears about myself are letting down. I am no longer afraid of myself, for I am made for Thyself; and when I have Thee, I have myself. Amen.

AFFIRMATION FOR THE DAY: *God is saying Yes to what is good for me, No only to what is bad for me.*

THE DRIVES DRIVING IN THE RIGHT DIRECTION

We saw yesterday that the life of the Spirit is, not a life of asceticism, but a life of assertion. You get rid of one desire in the only possible way: replace it by a higher desire. I get rid of self-centeredness by God centeredness, through surrender. I get rid of sex domination by surrender of sex to God, seeking His way and guidance, and, lo, sex serves me—makes me creative, full of creative well-being. I get rid of herd dominance by surrender of it to God, and, lo, now the herd comes back—I love people the more just because I'm no longer dominated by them. My heart is free—to love. The expulsive power of a new affection casts out the lower loves by fastening them on higher objects.

Hence we find expressions like these in the Scriptures: "Consecration by the Spirit" (II Thess. 2:13); "who through the eternal Spirit offered himself" (Heb. 9:14); "sanctified by the Spirit" (I Pet. 1:2). These verses give the divine strategy of redemption: the powers of the inner life are, not condemned, but consecrated by the Spirit. But a word is used which is deeper than consecrated: the word "sanctified"—"sanctified by the Spirit." The word "sanctified" has the double meaning of cleansed, or made holy, and consecrated—the negative and the positive. The Holy Spirit cleanses away the wrong attachments and motives which have gathered around the driving urges and then consecrates those urges to supreme loyalty to God and service to man. They are unfastened, from all wrong, and refastened, to all good. Now they can drive ahead, because they are driving in the right direction and not toward the ditch. Now a man can live with the stops out, for the result is, not discord, but harmony.

The passage which is the acme of the work of the Spirit is this one: "Who through the eternal Spirit offered himself." Here the eternal Spirit gives the impulse not only to offer one's powers to God but also to give oneself redemptively for man. Just as the Spirit gave the inner urge and power to Jesus to go to the cross for man, so He gives that same urge to us to do the same thing. Life becomes sacrificial, outpouring.

O Holy Spirit, I come to Thee for this cutting loose and setting free. Free from all that ties me up, and loose me to live freely and fully—for others. For life must be living—full to the brim. Amen.

AFFIRMATION FOR THE DAY: *Now I am free through giving—free to give.*

THE STEPS FROM CONVINCING TO CONTROLLING

The work of the Holy Spirit in the subconscious mind can be summed up in those words—convincing, constraining, cleansing, co-ordinating, consecrating, contributing, comforting, controlling.

The first work of the Spirit is *convincing*—He brings us to the point that we see that the depths of us are out of our control, and that only divine power can reach and make sense of those depths. We are at the end of our resources.

He then presses no further, *constraining* us to hand over to Him the depths which are too much for us. So we inwardly surrender.

When that is done, then there is a *cleansing*. The Holy Spirit came on Jesus "like a dove," but upon the disciples "as of fire." Why the difference? They needed cleansing, so He came like cleansing fire. But Jesus needed no cleansing, so the Spirit came "like a dove"—the symbol of peace, expressing the divine approval.

After the cleansing comes the *co-ordinating*—life is unified at the center. The soul forces are fused into one. All the conflicts, the pulling in different directions, are taken out, and life is directed toward one great end. We become inwardly unanimous for God.

Then comes the *consecrating*. The cleansed and co-ordinated soul forces are now consecrated to the purposes of the Kingdom. They take on purpose and mission. Life is no longer hanging at loose ends.

Then life is *contributing*. The Holy Spirit turns the forces of life outward to contribution. The self is off its own hands and is now at leisure from itself, so it can give itself to others. This is emancipation for participation—participation in helping others.

A schoolteacher who had found the full life put it this way: "Inside of Him everything is safe and sanctified; outside of Him all is bewildering and treacherous." Now your powers are "safe and sanctified" and usable. You are in the hands of the eternally Creative. He is *comforting*.

All of this is the result of the last: *controlling*. He does all these only when He is in control.

O Spirit of Grace, I give Thee control. My control is chaos—Thy control is cosmos. So I turn over to Thee everything, for when Thou hast the kingdom within, then peace and power reign there. And all in order. Amen.

AFFIRMATION FOR THE DAY: *The Spirit's sevenfold work at work in me perfectly today.*

ONCE AND FOR ALL AND CONTINUOUS

Before we leave this first permanent fact of Pentecost—cleansing—we must ask these pertinent questions: Is cleansing something beyond conversion? Is it once and for all, or continuous?

In answer to the first, the usual experience is that cleansing of the subconscious takes place after conversion. The fact is that it is usually only after conversion that we feel the conflict with the subconscious. For before conversion life is often unified on a very low level. Then comes conversion—a new life and a new loyalty is introduced into the conscious mind. But the subconscious mind does not accept the sway of this new loyalty and love. There is inner revolt—conflict ensues. It is then that we are driven to seek redemption of the subconscious. It is then that we know that a house divided against itself cannot stand. It is the converted who see and feel the conflict and seek a remedy.

It is true that the disciples had a measure of cleansing before the coming of the Holy Spirit: "You are . . . clean by the word which I have spoken to you." But it was the word of anticipation rather than of realization. Only when the Holy Spirit came upon them were they cleansed in any deep sense.

Was this all at once, or a continuous act? Both. There is an all-at-onceness about it, and a continuity. Just as there is an all-at-onceness in marriage—you don't get married again every day if you are really married; it is once and for all—yet there are daily adjustments to be made around the great central adjustment of marriage. You can be married all at once, and yet it takes a long time to be married well. For larger areas and deeper depths have to be brought under the marriage relationship.

"Surrender" is the initial word, but "gladly yielding" and "response" are the words we use after the initial surrender. As a friend put it: "I surrender to surrender, and I yield to yielding, and I respond to response." The initial surrender brings an attitude of wanting to respond to God's daily advances of love. The points at issue are met in surrender, and then the whole weight is thrown on response.

O Spirit of the Living God, give me that once-and-for-all cleansing. And then give me the daily cleansing from accumulations that gather in my being from my daily mistakes. Amen.

AFFIRMATION FOR THE DAY: *Since I have made my surrender, today there will be nothing but response.*

DELIVERANCE FROM SELF-HATE

We have been studying the fact that the Holy Spirit cleanse primarily from inner division, especially the division between the conscious and the subconscious minds. These minds, under His cleansing and control, become one mind—the mind of Christ. The mind of Christ supplants two self-centered mind and gives a single pointedness to life. Our energies are not wasted on an inner civil war. We have a heart at leisure from self—and its conflicts.

Jesus said: "But if it is by the Spirit of God that I cast of demons" (Matt. 12:28). This was connected with disruptions—house divided against itself (12:25). The greatest demon is division. Many are canceling themselves out by inner division. The man possessed of evil spirits said in reply to the question of Jesus as to his name: "My name is Legion; for we are many (Mark 5:9)—"my name . . . we are many." Here was a man who was many men. The Holy Spirit saves us from many-mindedness and gives us the "single-eye," because we have a single mind.

In order to give us this single mind He delivers us from a sense of fear, inferiority, and all wanting to run away from life. Someone has suggested that there ought to be another Beatitude: "Blessed are they who save us from our self-despising." When the Holy Spirit is within, then there can be no sense of self-despising, for you have within you nothing less than the Divine. You cannot tell where He ends and you begin, and where you end and He begins. For your thoughts are His and His are yours—life is one, and yet separate. So it is impossible but to be humbly proud and proudly humble. For the Holy Ghost is the Holy Guest.

This deliverance from self-hate is just as important a deliverance from other-hate. "Bitterness, taunting and criticising, saying cruel things that wound the heart of friends, one may be sure he is dealing with someone who hates himself, who loathes and despises himself, says John S. Bonnell. Your bitterness to others is hatred to yourself that you have projected on to others and to God. The Holy Spirit saves from all self-despising. You reverence the within, for Another is there.

O Spirit Divine, within me—I fear nothing, not even my self, for Thou art controlling me too. So under Thy control I am out from under the control of everything. I thank Thee. Amen.

AFFIRMATION FOR THE DAY: *I shall love myself in Thee this day.*

THE TWO WITNESSES

Let us look at another important passage before we move on: "It is the Spirit himself bearing witness with our spirit" (Rom. 8:16). Linked with that another passage: "I am speaking the truth in Christ . . . ; my conscience bears me witness in the Holy Spirit" (9:1).

Here is a double witness: the witness of the Spirit and the witness of our own spirit. We would have expected the word "to" instead of "with." But the "with" makes it a double witness—the Spirit witnessing downward, and our spirits witnessing upward, and both saying the same thing. These two witnesses combine the religious approach, the Spirit bearing witness, and the scientific approach, our spirit bearing witness. The witness of our spirits is the witness of the facts—the inductive method.

We find our spirits now different—free from conflict, and fears, and inhibitions. When the Spirit whispers, "You are pure," our spirit answers in antiphonal response, "I am pure—I feel it; I know it." When the Spirit says, "You are mine," our spirits answer, "I am thine." When the Spirit says, "You are victorious," our spirits reply, "I am victorious."

Suppose there was only the witness of the Spirit without the witness of our spirits. Then it would lack inward confirmation from the facts—it would be a faith but not a fact. Then suppose there was only the witness of our spirit. Then we might be drawing prejudiced conclusions in favor of ourselves. But when the Spirit of God and the spirit of man say the same things, then this is the strongest possible confirmation. There is no possibility of fooling ourselves when these two witnesses agree. John Dewey says: "There is only one method of revelation, and that is the revelation from scientific facts." This is weak. Suppose the Divine does not approve of your facts, then? But suppose the facts do not approve of the divine witness, then? Both are weak. We are strong only when the Fact from above and the facts from below kiss each other and are wedded henceforth and forevermore. This is assurance—plus!

O Holy Spirit, I thank Thee that Thou dost witness with my spirit. My spirit is filled with a sense of divine-human assurance. So I exult—exult with the deepest assurance a mortal can know. I thank Thee. Amen.

AFFIRMATION FOR THE DAY: *Today, the unfolding witness of my spirit and the enfolding witness of Thy Spirit—the one up and the other down—shall more and more coincide.*

THE CONSCIENCE CORRECTED

Yesterday we quoted: "I am speaking the truth in Christ . . .; my conscience bears witness in the Holy Spirit." (Rom. 9:1.)

This passage brings together the objective standard, "The truth in Christ," and the subjective standard, "My conscience bears witness in the Holy Spirit." We often find people saying, "Well, I'm living according to my conscience—isn't that enough?" But conscience is not necessarily a safe guide. Conscience is the capacity to distinguish between right and wrong according to the standards you teach. It can be taught to approve directly opposite things. Two professors meet, one a Hindu and the other a Mohammedan; they shake hands each day as they have done for years, and after shaking hands each goes and washes his hands, for the other is unclean. The conscience of each was trained to approve directly opposite things. Conscience therefore is unsafe unless it has in it the highest content—the Holy Spirit. Into the Holy Spirit has gone the content of Christ—the Holy Spirit is a Christlike Spirit. When, therefore, your conscience bears witness in the Holy Spirit, then it bears witness according to the highest standard ever seen upon our planet—namely, that of Christ. It is a safe conscience—the highest conscience—when it bears witness in the Holy Spirit.

We need to be cleansed, and our consciences need to be cleansed. "How much more shall the blood of Christ, who through the eternal Spirit offered himself without blemish to God, purify your conscience from dead works to serve the living God." (Heb. 9:14.) Here is a conscience purified. Here the very thing that judges and purifies us is itself judged and purified. He purifies our very standards.

So with the heart cleansed, and the standards of the heart cleansed, and the inner spirit and the divine Spirit witnessing to the same things, then we are all set—set for power and poise. When the motive and the monitor are both cleansed, then we come to a morality which is morality—plus. Spirituality and morality have become one. Unmoralized spirituality is a danger. Unspiritual morality is dead. Together they live—abundantly.

O Spirit of God, I surrender myself and my standards to Thee for cleansing. Thou art the Strengthener, for Thou art the Cleanser, for I am strong only as I am pure. In Thee I am. Amen.

AFFIRMATION FOR THE DAY: *Today, my morality and my spirituality shall become the alternative beats of my heart.*

POWER TO THE TOTAL PERSONALITY

We have dwelt at length, since page 99, on the first of the two things permanent in the coming of the Holy Spirit—purity of heart. We come now to the second permanent things in Pentecost: power. "You shall receive power when the Holy Spirit has come upon you; and you shall be my witnesses in Jerusalem and in all Judea and Samaria and to the end of the earth." (Acts 1:8.) Here is something that will be permanent—something that will persist from Jerusalem to the end of the earth—namely, power.

We usually say this is the power to witness to Jesus. It is. But it doesn't say so. It says, "You shall receive power"—power in general. Under that general power is the specific power to witness. But it is power to the total personality, the strengthening of total forces of life. The best translation of the Paraclete, or the Comforter, is probably the Strengthener—*con* (with) and *fortis* (strength)—One who strengthens us by being with us. When He is within us, then we are no longer canceling ourselves out by our inner divisions. We are unified, hence fortified. We go places; we do things; for we are integrated persons.

The difference between a person before and after the coming of the Holy Spirit within is the difference between a sailboat and a steamboat. The sailboat depends on environment, on circumstances; the steamboat depends on "inner-stances"—it has power within and goes ahead with or without the help of environment. Some are sailboat Christians, and some are steamboat Christians. Some are circumstance-directed and some are Spirit-directed. In the sailing-vessel days the doldrums in the southern mid-Atlantic were a terror to the sailors, for they were liable to be becalmed there with no breezes blowing. Now the doldrums have lost their terror, for steam power within carries the vessels through. Many Christians are in the doldrums, for they are without the Spirit's inner power. But with the Spirit's inner power, we go through the becalming dead spots that stop so many: Power to meet any emergency, and with a margin to spare.

O Spirit Divine, give me the inner resources so that I do not go dead when life goes dead around me. Give me love when hate surrounds, peace when disturbance prevails, life amidst deadness. Amen.

AFFIRMATION FOR THE DAY: *I shall have power today because I shall not depend on my powers, but on Thy power working through my powers.*

THE HOLY SPIRIT IS POWER—WHERE IT COUNTS

The modern emphasis on psychology in the remaking of personality is good, but not good enough. Psychology lays bare our problems and our motives. But it lacks power to solve those problems and to unify those motives. It lacks central dynamic. The method of psychology is only successful where it is combined with religious faith that provides dynamic—one provides information; the other transformation.

But religion without the Holy Spirit is also inadequate. It imposes a set of rules and regulations but doesn't give power to perform. The Holy Spirit, however, when consented and surrendered to, moves in to be the spring of action and motive. This divine reinforcement within makes the ideal real, the impossible possible. The Holy Spirit is power—where it counts. "He may grant you to be strengthened with might through his Spirit in the inner man. . . . Now to him who by the power at work within us is able to do far more abundantly than all we ask or think." (Eph. 3:16, 20.) It is the inner man that makes the outer man. If the inner life is weak, then weakness spreads to the outer—a weak personality confronts the world. If the inner life is confused, then confusion is written on the face. We gradually chisel our exterior after the image of the interior. When someone remonstrated with Lincoln for judging a man's character by his face he replied: "A man is responsible for his face after forty." He was right, for by that time the interior has been exteriorated—the inner facts have become the outer facial. And not only the outer facial but the outer life.

So the Holy Spirit strengthens us with might where it counts—"in the inner man." Other remedies strengthen us with ultimate weakness—a shot in the arm that lifts us temporarily and lets us slump permanently. But this is strengthening us "with might"—inherently we become strong. All the life forces are quickened under the impact of Life. You feel alive in every fiber of your being.

Psychology can explain; religion as precepts can exhort; the Holy Spirit makes us exult. For the Spirit gives above "all we ask [religion] or think [psychology]."

O Spirit of God, when Thou art at work in my depths, I am safe and serene and secure. Nothing can make me inadequate or afraid. I am possessed where it counts—at the center. I thank Thee, thank Thee. Amen.

AFFIRMATION FOR THE DAY: *Serenity, not in myself but in Thee, shall be my inner climate this day.*

"INTELLECTUAL, SPIRITUAL, AND MORAL"

We continue our study of the Holy Spirit as power. The sole psychological emphasis leaves you with yourself on your own hands to cultivate. That does not release you from yourself. The Holy Spirit gets you to surrender yourself—"who through the Eternal Spirit offered himself" (Heb. 9:14)—and that takes the self off your hands into the hands of God. The center is shifted. Now that you have the right center, power can be entrusted to you. For if power should be entrusted when you are on the basis of self you would use it in the interests of self. So the whole psychological approach when it depends on that alone is shut off from the resources of God and must depend on its own resources. It is earth bound. And hence its results are meager. When it is linked to religion its results are amazing. It has dynamic at its disposal.

Religion in order to be effective must have: "Intellectual penetration, spiritual insight, and moral power." The first two without the last are moonshine. The last without the first two is wild-fire. The combination is light and power.

Some Christians emphasize the Word. Others emphasize the Spirit. There must be a combination. The Word without the Spirit is light but no power. The Spirit without the Word is power, but no light. The two together are light and power—knowing and doing.

Jesus said: "Is not this why you are wrong, that you know neither the scriptures nor the power of God?" (Mark 12:24.) You go wrong if you don't keep close to the Scriptures—the historical revelation of God in Christ. But you also go wrong if you don't know the power of God within. One is historical, and the other is exprimental. Barthanism emphasizes the historical, the Scriptures, but shies away from the experimental, the mystical. Mysticism unanchored in the historical revelation of God in Christ is liable to go off on tangents. Both are weak. Together they are strong. The Scriptures for light, the power of God for dynamic—that is the Christian faith. I need to see, and I need power to follow what I see. The Holy Spirit gives both.

EXPERIENTIAL

O Spirit of Truth and Spirit of Power, live in me as both. For I need to see the Truth and to know the Power. Give me Thyself for Thou art both. In Thee I have everything necessary to live and to live abundantly. Amen.

AFFIRMATION FOR THE DAY: *Today, the Truth shall make me serene, and the Power shall make me serve.*

IT MUST WORK OR BE WORTHLESS

We continue the meditation on the Spirit as power. It is at the place of power that religion becomes vitiated or vital. "Men do not want a formula for water—H_2O—they want a drink." So men want to know whether faith works as power. A sign over an establishment in Russia read: "Committee on the Electrification of all Russia"; but beneath it another sign said, "Bell out of order. Rap." All our big signs making vast claims are canceled out if the thing doesn't work as power day by day—if the electricity doesn't make our doorbells ring. If our faith doesn't make us sing amidst sorrow and laugh at daily obstacles, then it lets us down. The Holy Spirit is religion as power—power available within.

Paul could say: "Our gospel came to you . . . in power and in the Holy Spirit and with full conviction." (I Thess. 1:5.) At the center of that "power" and "full conviction" was the Holy Spirit. That is lacking in much of modern Christianity—it lacks power and it lacks full conviction because it lacks the Holy Spirit. A man of insight studied a picture and remarked: "Its perspective is good; its coloring is correct; its conception is excellent; but it lacks that," snapping his fingers. The same can be said of a lot of our preaching: It is correct in style; its subject matter is good; its intentions are right, but it lacks one thing—the Holy Spirit. Without that we are preaching, unquickened truth—truth that doesn't fall upon the soul with quickening and converting power. It falls dead upon the soul. Two men say the same thing: one falls upon the hearers with awakening, kindling power; the other falls upon them flat. Our Christianity is not bad—it is just dull. And that is bad, for the gospel is good news—the greatest good news that ever fell upon human ears. We make it into something that is as mechanical as a Buddhist prayer wheel. Hence our people do not have enough conviction to share it. Our faith is noncontagious. The Holy Spirit, when accepted and obyed, turns all that insipidity into inspiration, that dullness into dancing. He makes one *alive*—alive to his fingertips. The Holy Spirit is the Strengthener—when He comes we speak strong words, have strong convictions, for we are inwardly strong.

O Strengthener, strengthen me. Take out of my vocabulary all weak, negative words, out of my thought all excuses and alibis, out of my inmost spirit all that saps my strength. In Jesus' Name. Amen.

AFFIRMATION FOR THE DAY: *What counts is not my ability, but my usability.*

UNITY WITH GOD

We have seen that the coming of the Holy Spirit meant purity and power. To these two must be added another: unity. We seldom think of Pentecost as bringing unity into being—it brought sharp division. But unity? Yes, amazing and far-reaching unity. At least eight great unities came into being with the coming of the Spirit.

1. *Unity with God.* "They were all filled with the Holy Spirit" (Acts 2:4). God, the Holy Spirit, and they were all one in purpose and life. They were longer working at cross-purposes with God—life was merged at the center.

Merged, but not submerged. Here is the essential difference between the Hindu conceptions and the Christian conception. In Adwaita Vedantism immanence is so thoroughgoing that God is looked on as the only Reality. All personality is to be looked on as an illusion. Separateness is the central evil. Not only are you one with God—you are God. You are a part of the universal Essence.

The only sin is that which separates one from this universal Essence. I asked a Hindu, "What is sin?" And he reached up, broke a twig from a tree, and said: "That is sin." He had sinned against the universal Essence which was equally immanent in the twig and the heart of man. The impersonal It is there, consent or no consent, moral conditions being what they may. "God is the Naught; God is silence, rather than Speech. God is Being itself, . . . without a Second, . . . Unchangeable, without Quality, without Form, neither this nor that," say the Upanishads. When it is said: "God is . . . without a Second," the meaning is, not a second God, but without a second anything—It is the All. Salvation is the recognition of the unity with the All. Your separate personality fades out, and with it all your problems and sufferings. You are merged in the ocean of Being.

In the Christian conception of unity there is a unity of purpose and life between the human spirit and the Divine, but no submerging in the ocean of impersonal Being.

O Divine Spirit, I know my unity with Thee will never be at the expense of my real being. I am made by Thee, not to be canceled by Thee, but to be fulfilled and perfected. I thank Thee for Life and Life Abundant. Amen.

AFFIRMATION FOR THE DAY: *My spirit and Thy Spirit separate, but interpenetrating this day.*

UNION AND YET SEPARATENESS

We saw yesterday that the Hindu Vedantism would extinguish personality; the Christian faith would heighten personality. The incarnation of Jesus is not a greater degree of immanence of God. It is a descent into matter. "Immanence, at its highest, can never yield Incarnation. Immanence admits of degrees; Incarnation of none. The Incarnation was not the maximum revelation of God through humanity; it was an absolute revelation. Between unique inspiration and Incarnation lies an unfathomable barrier," says E. C. Dewick. Jesus is, not man at his highest, but God at His lowliest; He is, not man reaching up, but God reaching down.

The union, then, with the Holy Spirit is not a heightening of divine immance—it is a created being, created in God's image, accepting by an act of the will and an attitude of faith the offer of God's indwelling in the Spirit. When that unity with God comes, it is a unity resulting in a community of life. Your thoughts and His thoughts are so intertwined that you cannot tell which are yours and which are His. A couple married late in life and very much in love with each other were so one that when the husband related a dream he had, the wife spoke up and said: "Frank, did you dream that dream or did I?" Their waking hours were so one that their dream became one. They were one. A little girl in an ecstasy of love for her grandfather took his face in her hands, looked up at him, and said, "I am you." And the grandfather could have answered: "Yes, and you are I."

But there is a deeper unity between the fully surrendered and the Holy Spirit. Jesus said: "In that day you will know that I am in my Father, and you in me, and I in you." (John 14:20.) Here in a union and a separateness: "You in me"—that is your union with Me. But "I in you"—that is My union with you. Your personality is, not lost, but heightened. Paul puts it thus: "It is no longer I who live, but Christ who lives in me; and the life I now live . . ." (Gal. 2:20.) He didn't live, and yet he did live. Christ was there living, and he was there, living.

O God, my Inmost, I bow in my heart to Thee—so intimate and yet so beyond. Thou art my life, and yet my life is never so much mine as when most Thine. For this mystery of the Intertwining, I thank Thee. Amen.

AFFIRMATION FOR THE DAY: *Today, one in purpose and therefore one in Person.*

"WHEN I GROW UP, I WANT TO BE ALIVE"

The first unity to get straight is your unity with God. For if disunity is there, then disharmony spreads itself all down the line of human relationships, with oneself, with others, with nature. A young missionary said very sadly in one of our Indian Round Table Conferences; "God and I are not getting along very well, and hence my life is tasteless and sad."

The central difficulty in the world today is that we are trying to adjust to one another without any adjustment to God. But the jigsaw puzzle of life will not make sense until you get that piece straight.

Emerson said a profound thing when he said: "The baptism of the Holy Spirit is a free possession of you." It is. God fully possesses you, and you fully possess God. And when you fully possess God, you fully possess Life and yourself. Some young people were talking about what they wanted to do when they grew up. Some wanted to be doctors, lawyers, ministers, and so forth. One little fellow spoke up and said: "When I grow up, I want to be alive." He was right. Some have grown up and are not alive—they are infected with decay and deadness. For they are not alive in God—their first unity is not assured.

A radiant person, alive to God and man as few men are, has a saying, a kind of life conclusion with him: "I have one, and only one, business in life—to live in union with God. All else follows." He is profoundly right, for if I live in union with God, I share His thoughts; I align myself with His purposes; I am one with Him in resources; we share a common life. The wonder is, not that I dwell in Him, but that He dwells in me. Andrew Murray says: "That a pure holy body should be found for the Son of God ... is indeed a great miracle. But that the same Spirit should now come and dwell in the bodies of sinful men is a greater miracle"—of grace. But He does and does it so graciously. To be able to live in union with Him in spite of what we have been and are—that is pure grace. Life is one continuous attitude of gratitude for grace. We are exalted to the highest heaven and at once put in the lowest dust of gratitude—humbly exalted.

O Spirit of my spirit, Life of my life, Joy of my joy and Being of my being, I adore Thee, and I love Thee: adore Thee for Thou art beyond me, love Thee for Thou art intimate, and near, and dear. I thank Thee. Amen.

AFFIRMATION FOR THE DAY: *My one business today—to live in union with Him.*

EVERYTHING YOU SAY AND DO IS HEIGHTENED

When one lives in union with God, then he takes on the significance of the One with whom he is united. To be conscious that when you work, God works; when you think, God thinks; when you go ahead, you are not alone—that is the cure for inferiorities, for hesitations, for weak personality. "In Him who strengthens me, I am able for anything." (Phil. 4:13, Moffatt.) "In Him" anything right can happen; out of Him everything wrong is bound to happen.

Now, in God your life takes on weight, moral authority. You move ahead with sure tread, knowing you walk His ways. It says in the ancient Scriptures: "He made his glorious arm to go at Moses' right hand." (Isa. 63:12, *American Translation.*) When Moses lifted his arm, God lifted His, God's strength his strength, God's life his life. Men like that have significance far beyond themselves. They are a constant surprise to themselves and others.

I write this as India still mourns the tragic death of the father of this land. Perhaps never in human history has there been such an outpouring of universal grief born of a deep affection for their leader—and ours. Why? The reason is that Mahatma Gandhi was and is identified with the cause of India's freedom—the person and the cause coincide. So the Mahatma had a significance beyond himself—when he spoke, the cause of India's freedom spoke. The cause of India's freedom came to embodiment in him. Therefore, people by the millions hung upon his words as upon an oracle. Gandhi as a person has little significance, but Gandhi as embodying the cause of India's freedom has the significance of that cause.

Identified and allied with yourself, you have the significance of your self—a decreasing significance. Identified and allied with prevailing society, you have the significance of that society—you become its echo. Identified and allied with your work, you have the significance of that work. But identified and allied with God, then you take on divine significance to the degree you are identified with the Divine. Everything you think, say, and do is heightened—a Plus is added. Life is alive—with God.

O Spirit of God, I take my littleness and ally it with Thy greatness, my insignificance and ally it with Thy significance, my love and ally it with Thy love. Now I am set to go—anywhere. Amen.

AFFIRMATION FOR THE DAY: *My weakness, allied to Thy Strength, can go anywhere and do anything today.*

UNITY WITH ONE'S OWN SELF

We are noting the unities that come into being when the Holy Spirit takes possession of us. In that unity Vedantism would say: "God is wholly you." Barthanism would say: "God is wholly other." We would say: God is wholly you and wholly other. The identity is real, and the separateness is real. I rejoice in my unity with Him, and yet I kneel in the shrine of my heart and worship Him. He is God, not I. The word for enthusiasm can mean either "in God" or "on fire." It is both. We are in God and therefore on fire with God. But at the center of that fire is a shrine where we kneel. This God-possession is a humbling experience and a hallelujah experience.

We look now at the second unity resulting from the Spirit's coming.

2. *The unity with one's own self.* "They all began . . . to express themselves." (Acts 2:4, Moffatt.) Now the group had a self which they could express. Here was true self-expression, for that self was, no longer a self divided against itself, but a self unified under the Spirit's cleansing and control. The self had found itself when it lost itself under the Spirit's control. It had obeyed the deepest law of the universe: "He who finds his life will lose it, and he who loses [it] will find it."

A lady telling of her needs at the morning of the Open Heart at the Ashram said: "My self-centered life has resulted in fears and anxieties. I want to have a Christ-centered life." Why did her self-centered life result in fears and anxieties? A very simple reason: The universe doesn't back our being its center, therefore, we are uneasy with fears and anxieties, for we are instinctively afraid that we are off-center.

A soul centered on itself is a lost soul, estrangled from God and man and itself. It is lost to itself. It doesn't know how to live with itself. Now the Spirit has moved into the inmost shrine and has taken control; and just as cosmos came out of chaos when the Spirit moved across the face of the deep and a new universe arose, so the Spirit now makes a harmonized self arise under a new creative dynamic. We are on-center, settled down in God—rhythm, harmony, inner poise, begin. We have a self we can live with. The soul is at home.

O gracious Spirit, I thank Thee that with Thy coming within I am at home in the house of my soul; I am at home with myself. I love myself, for I love something beyond myself. I am free. Amen.

AFFIRMATION FOR THE DAY: *I am centered in Thee, therefore at home everywhere, especially with myself.*

LIFE IS REDUCED TO SIMPLICITY

We saw yesterday that when the Spirit dwells within us, then we can express ourselves. We can do so because we then become natural. Sin is the unnatural; therefore, anyone living in sin is off-center, is unnatural. When we are most possessed by the Supernatural, we are most natural, most ourselves.

As Coventry Patmore says: "Religion is not religion until it has become not only natural, but so natural that nothing else seems natural in its presence." And again: "Religion has no real power until it becomes natural." Under the Spirit's cleansing, all unnatural evil is taken out of us, and we are supernaturally natural. Life is reduced to simplicity. Evil is very complex; the good is simple. The universe is against one and backs the other. Therefore, when we are possessed by the Spirit, we feel at home, universalized, and can go forward with a sense of confidence.

The idea that religion is imposed and unnatural is perhaps the chief hindrance to its wholehearted acceptance. A little boy sampling a new and delicious Thanksgiving pudding said: "I know this must be bad for me, for it is so good." But the good is good for us, and the bad is bad for us. We are made by the Spirit for the Spirit; and therefore when we receive Him, we find ourselves. All self-expression which is centered on the self as in starting point bound to create clash with others and with the self. It is off-center and therefore off-circumference. But the Spirit-centered life spreads harmony within and without. When the soul is Spirit-adjusted, then it is self-adjusted and life-adjusted.

The person who is adjusted to the Spirit fits the Chinese saying: "To big for worry, too noble for anger, too strong for fear, too happy to permit the presence of trouble." And we may add: Too respectful of one's self to despise one's self, and too at home with God not to be at home with one's self. For when you can live with God, you can live with yourself, love yourself, and rather like yourself. Self-surrender to God brings self-respect to yourself.

O God, my Father, I thank Thee for the privilege of surrendering to Thee and of obeying Thee, for in those two things I am but fulfilling the law of my being. Thou art my Home, my Companion, my Self. I thank Thee. Amen.

AFFIRMATION FOR THE DAY: *I am naturalized in the Supernatural, therefore natural.*

"LOOK ON US"

We linger another day upon the unity with oneself when the Spirit takes control. In saying if you are Spirit-possessed you are self-possessed, are you reading into the account something not there? No!

Look at the fact that the first reaction of the crowds was that these people were "filled with new wine." We all know that to come under the influence of liquor is to have the controls taken off. That is what happened to these people—the inhibitions, the fears, the self-consciousness, were taken away, and the people were so natural they appeared intoxicated. The natural seemed the unnatural to unnatural men. People off-center thought people on-center were off-center. A man who heard Rufus Moseley, a Spirit-intoxicated man, yet one as sane and natural as a child, said: "The first time I heard him I thought he was crazy; the second time I heard him I knew I was crazy." The ages have judged these men at Pentecost the only sane men in an insane world.

Look again at the fact that it describes these people: "They partook of food with glad and generous hearts" (Acts 2:46). They were "glad" because they were "generous." To be generous means to be openhearted, openhanded, outgoing—going out of themselves, they went into gladness. Going into oneself is to go into sadness. But the word "generous" comes from the same root as "generate" (create). The generous are the creative; the self-centered are the noncreative. We get bored with ourselves unless we are outgoing and creative. The useless person is the unhappy person. These men had aligned themselves with the process of creation and were alive in it—and happy.

Again, we see how natural and at home with themselves they were when they said to the impotent man at the Beautiful Gate: "Look at us." To look on them was to create faith—and they knew it and said so! Before the coming of the Spirit, if they had said that to the multitude, it would have created doubt, not faith. For they didn't look redeemed; now they knew that redemption looked out of their eyes and glowed in their countenances. People like that can respect and love themselves safely.

O Spirit of God, Thou dost make it possible for me to love myself and to be at home with myself, for I love Thee more and am at home with Thee. So I inwardly dance with joy. Amen.

AFFIRMATION FOR THE DAY: *Today I shall look redeemed, for I shall be redeemed—by Thee.*

UNITY AMONG THE IMMEDIATE BODY OF BELIEVERS

We come to the third unity brought into being with the coming of the Holy Spirit:

3. *Unity among the immediate body of believers.* "Peter stood up along with the eleven." (Acts 2:14, Moffatt.)

Peter had stood against the eleven. The disciples had just been celebrating the Passover—a deliverance from bondage. But immediately they showed they had an inner bondage unresolved: "A dispute also arose among them, which of them was to be regarded as the greatest" (Luke 22:24). This happened after they were communing with Christ and one another in commemorating a deliverance from slavery. But they soon showed they were in slavery to themselves and to their own position, and power, and prestige. The dispute was really over prestige; for it was over, not who *was* greatest, but who should "be *regarded* as the greatest." Peter, in the forefront with his claims, stood against the eleven.

Then, when they waited for the coming of the Holy Spirit, "Peter stood up among the brethren" (Acts 1:15). This was closer—he wasn't "against," nor was he "with," the brethren; he was "among the brethren." He was melted from his antagonism but had not been melted into amalgamation. Then the Spirit fell upon them; and, the barriers going down within themselves, they went down between the group—one with themselves, they were one with one another.

The barriers within us are the very barriers that divide us from others. The Chinese have a saying, "He who is not at peace with heaven cannot be at peace with himself; therefore he is never at peace with his neighbor." In union with God you are in union with yourself, therefore in union with others.

The most difficult group to be in union with is the group who are in the same set or occupation, where interests clash. Doctors can get along more easily with teachers than they can with doctors, where interests clash. A Christian has been defined as "one who gets along well with others, according to Jesus Christ." A good Christian is one who is able to get along with immediate associates according to Jesus Christ.

O Spirit of God, who art the Spirit of Concord and Harmony, help me live in concord and harmony with my immediate associates. Help me in the give-and-take to be big, generous, and Christlike. Amen.

AFFIRMATION FOR THE DAY: *Today I shall not ask for generosity from my associates—I shall give it.*

"GREAT . . . FIRST . . . THE SON OF MAN"

Let us meditate on the unity that came among the immediate associates—the Twelve—when the Holy Spirit came upon them. Peter stood up "along with the eleven." (Acts 2:14, Moffatt.) When he spoke, the eleven spoke in him and through him—it was corporate preaching and a reaping of corporate results. When the disciples thus merged themselves in Peter, they did not lose authority with the crowd; for when he finished, the account says: "Now when they heard this they were cut to the heart, and said to Peter and the rest of the apostles" (2:37). The repentance was toward "the rest of the apostles" as well as Peter. You do not lose yourself and your authority when you merge yourself in others and produce a corporate result. You lose yourself if you refuse to corporate. Your personality disintegrates.

It was said "Diotrephes, who likes to put himself first" (III John 9)—he liked to put himself first; hence no one else put him first. No one today bears the name of Diotrephes. He remembered himself, and hence everybody forgot him.

But is there no way to be great in the Christian scheme of things? Yes. Jesus told us: "You know that those who are supposed to rule over the Gentiles lord it over them, and their great men exercise authority over them. But it shall not be so among you; but whoever would be great among you must be your servant, and whoever would be first among you must be slave of all. For the Son of man also came not to be served but to serve, and to give his life a ransom for many." (Mark 10:42-45.) Here are the degrees of greatness: "great . . . , first . . . , the Son of man"; and these three degrees were achieved by the degree of self-giving: the "servant" becomes "great"; the "slave of all" becomes "first"; and the One who gives "his life a ransom for many" becomes "the Son of man." Degrees of greatness come through degrees of self-giving. That is the open door to greatness—a beneficent greatness, for the greatness is harnessed to the uplift of others.

Some high-school young men were talking about who was boss in their homes, their fathers or their mothers, when one boy spoke up: "God is boss in our home"—a beautiful home as a result.

O Spirit Divine, melt from my heart all that keeps me from being at my best with others. Make me resilient and adaptive, and yet let me be strong when worth-while issues are at stake. There let me stand. Amen.

AFFIRMATION FOR THE DAY: *Today I shall be great as I greatly give.*

"STREET ANGEL AND HOUSE DEVIL"

The task of getting along well with immediate associates is the most delicate task of the Christian life. A very honest Christian said: "I'm a street angel and a house devil." The very honesty was a step to its solution.

A person who has difficulty in getting along with others is projecting his own conflicts into the situation. The inwardly snarled-up soon snarl up relationships. The inwardly at-peace soon make peace around them. Peter and the rest were not fully surrendered before the coming of the Spirit, so there was much inner tension in the group. But the coming of the Spirit let down those tensions, wiped out the area of conflict, turned them away from themselves—from self-loyalty to the Kingdom loyalty. All adjusted to the Kingdom they were adjusted to each other. They sought first the Kingdom; and all these things, including themselves and the fellowship, were added to them. They were straightened out, and then their relationships were straightened out too. I sat in an Indian train one day, and looked out of the window, and remarked to myself that the whole sky was laden and murky. But I soon found I was the cause: my glasses were laden with dust, and I saw everything through dust-filled glasses, and everything was murky. Many of our difficulties are within us. We can't get along with others because we can't get along with ourselves. We project our inner snarls into our outer relationships with others. A lady in our Ashram said that her "child had asthma with sneezing and coughing, was thought to be allergic to this and that. We gave up the cat. Then I surrendered to God; my tensions gone, the child has never had a return of the asthma. The child was then eight; now she is twenty." Our inner tensions spread to our group; and when tensions set in, then relationships snarl up. Being self-centered puts sand in the machinery of our relationships; being Spirit-centered puts oil in the machinery. "It is these who set up divisions, worldly people, devoid of the Spirit." (Jude 19.) Where groups or individuals are devoid of the Spirit, there divisions, strife, jealousy, set in and break the fellowship. When the Spirit came upon the group, then they had to create a new word, *koinonia,* fellowship.

O Spirit of God, descend upon my heart and take out all that separates between Thee and me, and between me and my associates. For I cannot live with Thee unless I can live with them. In Jesus' name. Amen.

AFFIRMATION FOR THE DAY: *Today, no street angel and house devil—all angel.*

ORGANS OF ONE ANOTHER

If the whole group becomes an organism of the Spirit, then the individuals are organs of one another. Peter was the organ of speech for the early group. They all preached in him—a corporate result. So the group life functioned with various manifestations of the Spirit for the common good.

On the wall of a choir room of a great church was the banner: "Love one another." That is needed in most choirs! They could love one another in real sincerity only as they felt they were producing a corporate result, each contributing to a central harmony. So our group living must be based on the recognition of differences, with all working for a corporate harmony of differences.

Paul says, "Welcome one another . . . as Christ has welcomed you." (Rom. 15:7.) Treat one another as Christ treats you—this is a higher standard than "Love your neighbor as yourself," for your standard of self-love may be low. This is the highest conceivable—take the same attitude toward each other as Christ takes toward you. This is the high-water mark of social morality. Then is brought into being the highest conceivable society: "In whom the whole structure is joined together and grows into a holy temple in the Lord; in whom you also are built into it for a dwelling place of God in the Spirit." (Eph. 2:21-22.) A dwelling place of God in the Spirit—this is the new Society.

In this new Society we yield to each other because we yield to the Spirit. My friend, a gracious soul, wanted to pull out my chair at the table and to push it under me as I sat down. I refused and stood behind his chair! We stood there canceling each other out. He yielded, and I pushed the chair under him; and as I sat down, he got up, and he pushed the chair under me! We were even, but he came out morally ahead, for he yielded first!

To do this "we must carry each other in inward upholding prayer"; then we will have "a peace that not only passes understanding, but that passes misunderstanding as well."

O Spirit of the Lord Jesus, bathe our relationships with Thy presence and Thy Spirit, and then it will be easy and natural to live with each other. In Thy name. Amen.

AFFIRMATION FOR THE DAY: *I can afford to yield to others, for I have supremely yielded to the Spirit.*

DESTROYING THE TEMPLE

We take the next step in the unities that came into being with the coming of the Spirit.

4. *Unity of all believers:* "The believers all kept together." (Acts 2:44, Moffatt.) All the believers kept together; now they keep separate—"you in your small corner, and I in mine." They were Christian minded—we are denominational minded. Paul cried out in these words against the beginning of demoninationalism: "Each one of you says, 'I belong to Paul,' or 'I belong to Apollos,' or 'I belong to Cephas,' or 'I belong to Christ.' Is Christ divided?" (I Cor. 1:12-13.) The idea of dividing into denominations around teachers with their special emphasis was outrageous to Paul. His position was this: You don't belong to Paul, or to Apollos, or to Cephas—they belong to you, a part of your heritage. You belong to Christ. So all great teachers belong to you—why divide over them? "All belongs to you: Paul, Apollos, Cephas [all great teachers], the world, life, death [all great facts], the present and the future [all time]—all belongs to you; and you belong to Christ, and Christ to God." (I Cor. 3:22-23, Moffatt.) His position was that in Christ there was a central unity, but around that unity and within that unity there was room for difference of emphasis as found in Paul, Apollos, and Cephas.

Paul cried out again against this division in these words: "Do you not know that you are God's temple and that God's Spirit dwells in you? If any one destroys God's temple, God will destroy him." (I Cor. 3:16-17.) This is usually taken to mean that the body is the temple, for a parallel passage does refer to the body (6:19). But here the context shows that the destroying of the temple was a destroying of the temple of believers by divisions. He said that if you destroy the temple by divisions, God will destroy you. And He does—He cancels out our power and influence when we are divided. The Chruch today is a fulfillment of that—its influence is destroyed by its divisions. When the Spirit becomes dim in the Church, denominational differences become dominant—the spirit of division replaces the Spirit of God.

O Spirit of God, cleanse away all that divides us from each other and hence from Thee. For the Spirit of God can dwell only where there is a spirit of unity. Save us from a divisive spirit, for we want Thy Spirit. In Jesus' name. Amen.

AFFIRMATION FOR THE DAY: *I can betray with unity with other Christians, but I cannot deny it.*

UNITY NOT A UNITY OF ECCLESIASTICAL MECHANICS

We continue our meditation on the Spirit uniting all believers. That unity is a unity of the Spirit, and not a unity maintained by a mechanical, tactual succession.

A theosophist Hindu said to me one day: "We in theosophy have a straight line of succession back to the apostles in the ordination by the bishop of the Old Catholic Church of Bishop Leadbeater and Arundale, as bishops in the Theosophical Liberal Catholic Church. We have found by occult means that a line of magic runs from Christ through the Apostles, and that if someone from the outside, or a woman, enters that line, the line is broken. This magic inheres in the line and is apart from the character of the persons concerned." He was sound, if the Spirit is given through an unbroken line, for the Old Catholic Church bishops came over from Rome without break. So the line was intact. But at the end of that line were two men who to all intents and purposes were Hindus—believing in karma, and transmigration, and the central Hindu concepts. Two Hindus were authentically in the line of apostolic succession! This is the *reductio ad absurdum* of the theory. Such mechanics are foreign to the Christian faith, where the Holy Spirit came upon the group of a hundred and twenty without rite, ceremony, or meditation of any kind, and where He came upon the Gentiles in the house of Cornelius while Peter was speaking. It is true that the Holy Spirit came on the Samaritans and on the Ephesians through the laying on of hands by Peter and John in the one case and by Paul in the other. But there is no evidence that Paul was in any line of tactual succession with the original Twelve; for it was a layman. Ananias, who laid his hands on him, and he received his sight and the Holy Spirit (Acts 9:17). The Holy Spirit was given with or without the laying on of hands, and the people who laid the hands could be in a line of tactual succession with the Twelve or outside of that line.

The unity of believers is a unity of believers and not of ecclesiastical mechanics. We are united because we share a common Life and not a common "line."

O God, the Spirit, draw our hearts together at the place of central loyalties and not at the place of marginal loyalties. For in Thee we do not seek for unity, we have it—have it intrinsically and inherently. I thank Thee. Amen.

AFFIRMATION FOR THE DAY: *I belong to all believers, for I belong to the Lord of all believers.*

A UNION OF DIVERSITY—FEDERAL UNION

We are meditating on the unity of the Spirit. That unity is not uniformity. It provides for difference.

The rich variety of the gifts of the Spirit: "Now there are varieties of gifts, but the same Spirit. . . . To each is given the manifestation of the Spirit for the common good. . . . All these are inspired by one and the same Spirit, who apportions to each one individually as he wills.

"For just as the body is one and has many members, and all the members of the body, though many, are one body, so it is with Christ." (I Cor. 12:4, 7, 11-12.)

Here the unity is a unity of diversity—in other words, a federal unity. In a federal unity there is corporate unity, for the federal entity can act as one corporate entity; it can act as one organism; therefore there is organic unity.

All life in its higher phases is a federal unity. The amoeba is a single cell. When we come to man we find a unity of diversity, a federal unity; for man is made up of body, mind, and spirit, and yet he is one personality. God, the highest life of all, is a federal unity: Father, Son, and Holy Spirit.

All higher relationships are federal relationships. Marriage is a federal union, a union with diversity under it—a common name and separate names, a common life and yet separate lives. Federal union puts together two apparently contradictory instincts or urges—a desire for union with the whole and a desire for local self-expression or self-government. It therefore satisfies human nature. Any attempt to get us into one undifferentiated whole is an attempt to return to the amoeba. It is to reverse life, for life moves from the simple to the complex and yet to a great unity amidst that complexity. The future belongs to federal union in every branch of life, including the Church. We can have unified diversity now, provided we sail past "the Scylla of segmentation and the Charybdis of regimentation."

"The tree of life with its twelve kinds of fruit" (Rev. 22:2)—one Tree; but the branches inhering in the Tree are diverse with diverse fruit. The Tree of Life is a federal union.

O Spirit Divine, make us one not only in spite of our differences but on account of them. For Thou art the author and lover of diversity. Make our diversities blend. Amen.

AFFIRMATION FOR THE DAY: *"Unreservedly given to God, unbreakably given to each other."*

UNITY OF ALL RACES

We continue our study of the unities that came into being with the coming of the Holy Spirit.

5. *Unity of all races:* "All who believed were together." (Acts 2:44.) If we look at the races present in that "together," we will see that the whole of that ancient world was represented—men from Mesopotamia, Africa, Europe (2:9-11). All races and all colors were represented in that togetherness. Under the Spirit's touch mankind felt its essential kinship and its essential oneness. They looked on people of another race, not as a problem, but as a possibility. A new sense of the worthwhileness of a man as a man had come into life.

We are now discovering that the differences between races is, not inherent, but cultural. Given the same stimulus, the races will come out at about the same place. The differences are in the cultural inheritance and the response to that inheritance. There are no permanently superior races, and there are no permanently inferior races; there are developed races and un-developed, but no permanently superior or inferior. The median scores in the intelligence tests given to the American Expeditionary Forces of World War I were as follows: Southern whites in Mississippi, 41.25; in Kentucky, 41.50; in Arkansas, 41.55. Northern Negroes in New York State scored 45.02; in Illinois, 47.35; in Ohio, 49.50. The reason for this inferiority and superiority was, not in inherent inferiority, but in the fact that the Negroes who came out superior had a better cultural and educational opportunity where they were. The whites had an inferior educational opportunity and hence turned out men-tally inferior.

Russia and now India have both made discriminations based on caste or class or color illegal. India, the home of caste, has made it illegal, and discriminations are subject to fine and im-prisonment. America and South Africa are the remaining strongholds of caste, and both profess the Christian faith.

The early Christians under the Spirit's touch had their hearts and eyes open to the fact of the oneness of humanity.

O Spirit of God, I thank Thee that Thou hast uncovered the worthwhileness of a person as a person. The future belongs to this. Help us to belong to it. For Thou art sifting the nations on this. Sift us. In Jesus' name. Amen.

AFFIRMATION FOR THE DAY: *I shall look on every man today, not as a problem but as a possibility.*

"I DON'T KNOW; I'LL LOOK TOMORROW"

We must spend another day on the Spirit's deliverance from race snobberies.

These snobberies are not born within us; they are socially imposed at an early date. They are not in the child. A little boy was talking to his family circle about his friend Joe—his powers, how he could make better paper airplanes than any other. At a ladies' club meeting a woman suggested to his mother: "Did you know your child's best friend is a Negro?" So the mother raised the question with her boy: "Did you know that Joe is colored?" "Colored, what's that?" "Why his skin is darker than yours, isn't it?" The little boy thought a moment and said: "I don't know; I'll look tomorrow."

A neighbor saw a pastor's boy playing with a Jewish boy and said: "As a good Lutheran you must hate the Jews." The boy looked at him and calmly replied: "Jesus was a Jew wasn't He?" Children get race prejudices from society. A white boy said: "I was sixteen years old fore I knowed I was any better'n a Negro." Bill Mauldin caricatures this is one of his cartoons: "My pop says I shouldn't worry if other kids is smarter than me. He says I got race superiority."

A member of the Naga, one of the most backward of the hill tribes of Assam, when expressing contempt for another says: "You smell like a Nepali." The Nepali is culturally superior to the Naga! We make a black sheep the symbol of the bad boy of the family, but in Africa it is the white sheep that is the bad boy!

The Christians under the Spirit's sway saw straight through all this make-believe of superior races and looked on man as a man, a man "for whom Christ died." That was a revolutionary thought; and had it been followed, it would have created a new world. In a certain section of America a Negro tried to ride on a train which had no segregated coach and was refused. His son was ill, and he wanted to get to see him. A cultured lady suggested he sit with her. He did. She got him everything he needed. Someone watching it suggested it was strange that she did that—why did she do it? Her reply: "I serve a Master who is color blind." The early Christians were color blind and class blind.

O Spirit of Truth, give me eyes to see a brother in every person, "a man for whom Christ died." Take out of my inmost being all lingering prejudices and fears. Let me catch Thy attitudes, and then I shall be free. Amen.

AFFIRMATION FOR THE DAY: *Today, I shall see not a man's color, but his character.*

UNITY IN MATERIAL GOODS

We continue our study of the unities that came into being with the coming of the Holy Spirit.

6. *Unity in material goods:* "All who believed were together and had all things in common; . . . and distributed them to all, as any had need." (Acts 2:44-45.) "There was not a needy person among them . . . ; distribution was made to each as any had need." (4:34-35.) Here is a unity of the Spirit that resulted in a unity of economic interests and goods.

Along with this passage must be put another to complete the total picture: "If any one will not work, let him not eat." (II Thess. 3:10.) This passage corrected the possibility of one getting according to his need and then refusing to work. If you do not contribute to the collective good according to your ability, you will not get according to your need. So the early Christian position was: To each according to his need, and from each according to his ability.

These passages have become an embarrassment to us in an individualistic society where distribution is, not according to need, but according to greed. We have tried to take the edge off these passages in two ways: (*a*) It was an interim ethic, for men expected the near coming of Jesus, so they distributed their goods in this reckless way in view of that event. (*b*) It failed. They soon had to take a collection for "the poor saints at Jerusalem"—they had impoverished themselves by distributing what they had. In regard to the first objection, it is obvious that the impulse which gave rise to this practice was not the near coming of Jesus—it was deeper, for it was part of the experience of God in the Holy Spirit. Life to them was all of a piece—it was not compartmentalized as with us. So the impulse came from an experience instead of an expectation.

Second, it did fail; but it failed, not because it was wrong in principle, but because it was only partially applied. They applied the principle of co-operation to distribution but failed to apply it to production. We must rediscover the principle and apply it to both production and distribution.

O Spirit of God, Thou art shining upon our relationships and making us to see life in Thy light. That light is always our highest interests. Thy ways must become our ways. For Thy ways work. Amen.

DISTRIBUTION BY COLLECTIVE CONSENT

We saw yesterday that with the Spirit's impact upon life two principles emerged: To each according to his need, and from each according to his ability. But this is socialism, or even communism, says my reader in inner hesitancy. If the distinction between socialism and Marxian communism is that in socialism changes are to be brought about by consent, by constitutional means, and that Marxian communism is to be brought about by force, by a minority, using any means that will get to the goal, then of course the kind that emerged in Acts has kinship with socialism but little or no kinship with Marxian communism. For whatever brand may be put on this New Testament society, it was voluntary and not compulsory. Peter said to Ananias when he kept back part of the price: "While it remained unsold, did it not remain your own? And after it was sold, was it not at your disposal?" (Acts 5:4.)

Lenin gives the dictum: "Great problems in the lives of nations are solved *only by force.*" Against this monstrous doctrine the New Testament and democracy stand in complete opposition. For once you introduce force to gain an end, you will have to keep force to retain it. That means dictatorship. If you believe, as Marxianism does, that anything is right that gets you to your goal, then what is to keep someone else from considering anything to be right that ousts you from that goal? Your moral universe is gone, and the principle that might makes right has been substituted. That means the end of a free society for free men. Lenin also says: "We must be ready for trickery, deceit, lawbreaking, withholding and concealing truth"—anything is right that gets you your goal. But you can't use a wrong means to get to a right end and then dismiss the means. For the means pre-exist in, and determine, the ends. So a wrong means will corrupt your ends as sure as fate. Stalin says: "Dictatorship means unlimited power resting on violence and not on law." Dictatorship either by an individual or by the proletariat means just that. In the Christian Way God is dictator, but His rule rests on law which He observes; and when we obey His dictatorship, we find perfect freedom.

O Spirit of God, help us as we thread our way through these mazes of thought and attitude, and help us to come out at Thy thought and attitude. Then we shall be safe—and free. For we are made for Thy ways. Help us then to obey them. Amen.

AFFIRMATION FOR THE DAY: *Force holds the hour, God holds the day.*

TOO LITTLE AND TOO MUCH MAKE PROBLEM CHILDREN

Is need the ultimate basis for society? I think it is, and that the Christians discovered this basis by divine inspiration.

For need is basic in life. It is written into our bodies. If you eat less than you need, you are unhealthy; but if you eat more than you need, you are also unhealthy. Someone has said that "we live on half of what we eat, and the doctor lives off the other half." Need is written into our bodies. It is also written into society. A friend has charge of the problem children in a certain city. The economic life of that city is divided into three classes: (*a*) 25 per cent below the privilege line—the under-privileged. (*b*) 25 per cent above the privilege line—the over-privileged. (*c*) 50 percent between these two—the middle classes, not having too little or too much. Invariably, my friend says, the problem children come out of the 25 per cent below the privilege line or out of the 25 per cent above the privilege line. The 50 per cent in the middle represent the normally adjusted American children. Too little and too much both produce problem children. Need is also written in our psychological make-up. Having too little creates worries, and worries and consequent psychological disturbance. Two classes have to think too much about money: those who have too little and those who have too much. The best adjusted people are those who have just enough money so they can forget it and get on with the business of living.

Each person has a right to as much of the material as will make him more mentally, physically, and spiritually fit for the purposes of the best living. All beyond that need belongs to the other people's need. That need includes old-age and sickness provision until the government takes over provision for both. How shall we arrive at that basis of need? Since both the individual and society are involved, the decision must involve both. The decision must rest primarily with the enlightened conscience of the individual, approved or corrected by the enlightened conscience of society. Where the conscience of the individual does not function properly, the conscience of society must function through legislation.

O God, Thou who hast made the material and didst declare it good, help us now to distribute it wisely and according to Thy will and our need. We know that Thy will and our need are one. Amen.

AFFIRMATION FOR THE DAY: *We save or lose our souls at the place of the material.*

REDISTRIBUTION THROUGH FOUR WAYS

When we come to the methods by which material things may be distributed according to need, four ways can be suggested: (*a*) By the individual's own efforts to earn sufficient for his needs; (*b*) by profit sharing; (*c*) by co-operatives; (*d*) by legislation.

An economy of a personal attitude that doesn't give a man an incentive to work hard to supply his needs produces a slave mentality which leans on society. Anything that takes away personal initiative hurts personality and thereby weakens society.

But you cannot expect personal initiative and hard work unless the man shares in the profits of the enterprise. He will inevitably slow down and slacken if he thinks that the more he works, the more capital gets. That is a brake on his motive machine. To give him a motive for more initiative and harder work, there must be a sharing of gains and losses. A management engineer, who takes hold of sick businesses and puts them on their feet again, said to me: "Profit sharing works like magic. I am using it everywhere I can." It is based on a higher principle: "Thou shalt love thy neighbor as thyself." Our present system says: "Thou shalt love thyself." The universe works with one and against the other. But the direct corollary to profit sharing is capital-labor management. If both are to be represented in the profits, they should both be represented in the processes.

The third method of distrubiting wealth widely is through cooperatives. For as profit sharing is valid for the producer, so profit sharing is valid for the consumer. It distributes wealth without revolution. And it trains us in the working of a cooperative order.

The fourth method of distribution according to need is the method of legislation. This method can be reduced to a minimum if the first three methods are in operation and are really being worked. To depend on legislation without the other three is to produce hopes in the people that cannot be fulfilled. Only if the other three need correction and supplementation should legislation be used. It should be the last, and not the first, resort.

O God, our Father, give to us intelligent attitudes toward Thy material gifts, for we cannot impoverish others without getting hurt ourselves. Help us to take Thy ways, for Thy ways work. Ours do not unless they coincide with Thine. Amen.

AFFIRMATION FOR THE DAY: *Contribution —God's part; distribution — our part.*

UNITY WITH THE UNBROTHERLY, EVEN WITH ENEMIES

We come now to the final unity that came into being with the coming of the Holy Spirit:

7. *Unity with the unbrotherly, even with enemies:* "And now, brethren, I know that you acted in ignorance, as did also your rulers." (Acts 3:17.) Here Peter and the rest of the disciples called the people who had crucified their Lord "brethren." And they echoed the forgiveness of Jesus on the cross when they said, "You acted in ignorance." Here was a brotherly attitude toward the unbrotherly and a spirit of forgiveness even to men whose hands were red with the blood of the Son of God. A chasm, an impassable chasm, had been bridged, by their bridging in it the only possible way—overcoming evil with good, hate by love, darkness by light, and the world by a cross. They turned enemies into friends by inexhaustible good will.

They struck the deepest note in the moral universe. And struck it without hesitation and without effort. It welled up from within as a natural expression of this new life of the Spirit. I was talking with a Hindu agnostic. As the conversation came to the Cross, I said that Jesus' praying for His enemies, "Father forgive them, for they know not what they do," is the high-water mark of moral life. He thought a moment and said: "High-water mark? The highest-water mark of moral life upon our planet." The agnostic was compelled to bow before the shrine of this moral and spiritual grandeur.

The verse that India quotes more than any other is just this verse: "Father, forgive them, for they know not what they do."

The idea that we are to be brotherly only to brothers runs counter to the Christian concept. Jesus said: "If you love those who love you, what reward have you? . . . If you salute only your brethren, what more are you doing than others?" (Matt. 5:46-47.) We are to give out love and only love, no matter what the other man does. If he takes it, well and good; but if he doesn't take it, then love like "peace will return to you again." You will be made loving, for you are born of the qualities which you habitually give out. The loving become lovely.

O Spirit of Truth, who art also the Spirit of Love, help me to be loving to the unlovely. Help me with infinite patience to wear down all hate, all resentments with inexhaustible good will. Amen.

AFFIRMATION FOR THE DAY: *Forgiveness of injuries is the cardinal Christian virtue. May I manifest it to all, today.*

PENTECOST—ZENITH OR DAWN?

We have surveyed what happened at the birthday of the Christian Church. But there are many who look on Pentecost, not so much as a birth, a dawn, but as a zenith. They feel that this was noontime, and from henceforth the light fails toward the dark. They look on Pentecost as an event in time instead of an uncovering of a principle and power available for life now—and now more than ever. For life needs it more.

But suppose Pentecost means only what Charles Foster Kent says: "Among the disciples themselves the first dejection had been followed by a joyous reaction, characterized by intense religious emotion. On the day of Pentecost this pent up feeling broke out into an irresistible wave of spiritual enthusiasm that marked the beginning of the worldwide Christian missionary movement." If Pentecost means only that—a pent-up feeling breaking forth into an irresistible wave of spiritual enthusiasm—then of course it belongs to the past, because it belongs to a set of circumstances peculiar to that day. But Kent skirts around the central fact—the coming of the Holy Spirit. This was, not an enthusiasm worked up by circumstances, but an infusing of human nature with the ultimate divine intention—the Holy Spirit. How could God have come so far and draw back at the place where it counted—the divine Presence and Power within? He came a long way in His approach to man: He spoke to man from a mountaintop—Sinai—and gave a Law; He dwelt in a temporary Tabernacle and gave a Glimpse; He dwelt in a permanent Temple and gave a hidden Presence; He dwelt among us in Incarnation and gave a Life; He now takes the ultimate step, and moves within our hearts, and gives us Himself. The coming of the Spirit is Christianity's consummation—it is redemption where it counts—within us. To stop short of this is to stop short of a met need. The Holy Spirit is the cutting edge of redemption—it is redemption penetrating to the depths. The depth psychology probes; the Spirit probes, purifies, perfects, and points all the powers to great ends. Where the depth psychology gets beyond its depth, there the Spirit is at home, for the depths are made for Him. He is the Deep that answers deep.

O Spirit of God, I thank Thee that Thou art the answer to all my questions and the end of all my quests. And yet Thou art, not the end, but just the beginning. For now having Thee, I am ready for all. Amen.

AFFIRMATION FOR THE DAY: *My depths are shaped for God, and shall be shaped by God.*

EVENT OR CONTINUING PRINCIPLE?

We saw yesterday that the coming of the Spirit was an event in time and a continuing principle. It happened once, and it can happen again—can happen wherever the human heart meets the conditions.

The atmosphere presses upon every one of us, but only those who breathe it get the benefit. The Holy Spirit presses upon us in loving, redemptive pressure; but only those who open the depths of their being in surrendered, appropriating receptivity receive the Benefit. Were I to pick out a text for this book, it would be this one: "He yearns jealously over the spirit which he has made to dwell in us" (Jas. 4:5). That is the picture which the practical-minded James gives of the ultimate purpose of redemption: the Divine Spirit yearning jealously over the human spirit, eager to dwell within it, more eager than we are to be indwelt. If that is true, then God's skies are full of Pentecosts, for the coming of the Holy Spirit is founded on the very nature of the Divine. God couldn't be what He is if He didn't want to be where we are, in spite of what we are. He wants to dwell in us that we may dwell in Him. He comes to where we are that we may be where He is.

The benediction most used in Christendom is this one, for it is the most complete: "The grace of the Lord Jesus Christ and the love of God *and participation in* the Holy Spirit be with you all." (II Cor. 13:14, italics marginal.) Note the steps: Grace introduces you to the love of God, and that eventuates in the participation in the Holy Spirit. Grace and love are not enough if they do not lead you to a participation in the Holy Spirit. And this was for "all."

It is the destiny of every Christian to participate in the Holy Spirit—the only thing that can block that participation is our refusing will. And participation in the Holy Spirit doesn't mean participating in His gifts—love, joy, peace, and so on—it means participating in the Giver. The gift without the Giver is bare—ultimately we must partake of Him or stop at a dissatisfaction. He yearns; we yearn—one down and the other up. We meet and Life begins. But the beginning is so wonderful we sometimes think it the end!

O Spirit Divine, Thou art the very ground of my seeking, for Thou art inspiring the quest in order to satisfy it. How could I seek Thee if in a measure I had not already found Thee? I thank Thee. Amen.

AFFIRMATION FOR THESDAY: *Today my anticipations are changed by faith into participations.*

THE BLASPHEMY OF THE SPIRIT?

We said yesterday that "all" can be partakers of the Holy Spirit. But there are tied-up souls who think they are exceptions. They get obsessed with the notion that they have sinned against the Holy Spirit and therefore are under perpetual self-condemnation. It seems absurd that we should stop and look at this after these centuries of Christian teaching, and yet we do not want to go on without the last, lamed straggler.

In all my varied travels I have never seen anyone who I thought had really committed the sin against the Holy Spirit—the one that Jesus mentions: " 'Truly I say to you, all sins will be forgiven the sons of men, and whatever blasphemies they utter; but whoever blasphemes against the Holy Spirit never has forgiveness, but is guilty of an eternal sin'—for they had said, 'He has an unclean spirit.' " (Mark 3:28-30.) Now note the "for"—"for they had said, 'He has an unclean spirit.' " The scribes had said, "He is possessed by Beelzebub" (3:22). Beelzebub literally means "the lord of filth." To blaspheme against the Holy Spirit was to say that the Spirit that was in Jesus, the Holy Spirit, was an unclean spirit, the lord of filth. That sin is seldom committed. Ordinary sins that bring contrition do not come under that category. This sin is so distinct and devastating that if anyone is troubled about committing it, then that shows, by the very fact that he is troubled, that he has not committed it. For if he had committed it, he would not be troubled; his conscience would be dead.

There is another passage: "How much worse punishment do you think will be deserved by the man who has . . . outraged the Spirit of grace?" (Heb. 10:29.) Outraging the Spirit of grace is seldom committed. Anyone who is worrying about it has not done it. For the very upset over it is the Spirit of grace calling you to repentance and forgiveness.

There is a more frequent sin in all of us: "Do not quench the Spirit" (I Thess. 5:19). We often quench the creative Spirit within us by fears, by self-assertion. He would make us creative, and we quench the Spirit—we dampen the fire of the Spirit. But that is far removed from the blasphemy of the Spirit. It is a difference in kind.

O Divine Fire, burn within me. I would throw my all upon this Altar Fire. For I know when I am consumed by Thee, I am alive forevermore. No more dampening of Thee. In Jesus' name. Amen.

AFFIRMATION FOR THE DAY: *Today I shall "maintain the spiritual glow."*

THE LAW BECOMES A LIBERTY

Instead of the coming of the Holy Spirit being an isolated event happening at Pentecost, it introduced us to a "religion of the Spirit." Sabatier says that there are two types of religion — the religion of authority and the religion of the Spirit. The religions of authority impose their codes from without; the religion of the Spirit puts the authority within. In the latter you do things, not because somebody commands, but because Someone from within commends. Religions of authority are kindergarten, immature religion; religion of the Spirit is mature religion. The outer law becomes the inner you, since you identify yourself with it by surrender to the author of that law, God. Hence the law becomes a liberty. Instead of dancing attendance on an autocratic God or on an autocratic religious system, you dance to the rhythm of a law which you gladly accept from within. It is, not a suppression, but an expression. You are free—to obey. And you obey—to be free. The Christian faith in its reality is, not a religion of authority, but a religion of the Spirit.

Everything is done "in the Spirit." When the Galatians turned from the religion of the Spirit to a religion of authority, Paul cried out: "O foolish Galatians! . . . Let me ask you only this: Did you receive the Spirit by the works of the law, or by hearing with faith? Are you so foolish? Having begun with the Spirit, are you now ending with the flesh?" (Gal. 3:1-3.) They turned from an inner surrender to an outer struggle—they tried by struggle to obey an imposed Law, instead of by surrender to Christ becoming identified with that Law within and therefore fulfilling the Law because it was they. One of the most important verses in Scripture is just this verse: "Did you receive the Spirit by the works of the law"—by struggling to obey imposed authority? "Or by hearing with faith"—by surrender and acceptance of Grace? A Hindu visitor to our Ashram wrote: "I came to the Ashram expecting to find you in earnest endeavor and prayer; instead I found you a God-intoxicated child of nature." He expected to see a religion of authority and found a religion of the Spirit.

O Spirit of God, I am weary with struggling and trying to reach goals that ever recede, and now I see it is unnecessary; I can surrender, and trust, and be at the goal—now. I thank Thee. Amen.

AFFIRMATION FOR THE DAY: *Today I shall walk in the disciplined freedom of the religion of the Spirit.*

"THERE IS FREEDOM"

The religion of the Spirit is wonderfully expressed in this passage: "Now the Lord is the Spirit, and where the Spirit of the Lord is, there is freedom. And we all, with unveiled face, beholding the glory of the Lord, are being changed into his likeness from one degree of glory to another; for this comes from the Lord who is the Spirit." (II Cor. 3:17-18). Note: "With unveiled face"—nothing covered, no hidden conflicts, no unsurrendered areas. "Beholding the glory of the Lord"—making Jesus "Lord," controller of every area of our lives. "Are being changed into his likeness"—becoming like that which you look at constantly. "From one degree of glory to another"—under an endless growth, always arriving, but never having arrived. "For this comes from the Lord who is the Spirit"—He is the divine Sculptor, working from within, making us into the image of Jesus. That is redemption. And that is release. The only free people in the world are the people who live in the religion of the Spirit. The religion of authority brings knitted brows, tense muscles, tied-up spirits—bondage. The religion of the Spirit brings a lighted brow, relaxed muscles, a released spirit—freedom!

I stood a few days ago in Dumaguete, Philippines, in a room which was used as a Japanese-prison death chamber. Men went out of there to their death—and they knew it. On the walls of the room are written various statements that reveal the very depths of the men held there: (*a*) "I live to eat, not eat to live—Hungry Prisoner." (*b*) "If I am to die, please send my love to my wife." (*c*) "O Liberty, why have you been denied us?" (*d*) "If I am to die, I forgive my enemies." (*e*) "I hear the footfalls of the coming of the Japanese. My time has come. May God bless us all."

These cries sum up the needs of the human heart: (*a*) Food. (*b*) Love. (*c*) Liberty. (*d, e*) God. All four of these are found in right relations to God. If we obeyed God, our food would be guaranteed; love would be glorified; liberty would be found. God is the ground of our liberties.

O Spirit Divine, I feel Thee within as the Creative Urge heightening everything and bringing everything to its best—Thy best. A growing loyalty is meaning a growing life. Amen.

AFFIRMATION FOR THE DAY: *If God is the ground of my liberties, then I am free unless I stray from that ground.*

"SEALED WITH THE PROMISED HOLY SPIRIT"

Early Christianity was living, not on a remembrance of Pentecost, but on a realization of it. Pentecost was, not a sigh for yesterday, but a song of today. Everything was being done "in the Spirit." Paul could say: "Does he who supplies the Spirit to you . . . do so by works of the law, or by hearing with faith?" (Gal. 3:5.) "Supplies the Spirit to you"—that is present continuous. God was working by a law—the law of redemption. In that law of redemption is the intention to give the Holy Spirit to every open, receptive heart.

Peter said: "And you shall receive the gift of the Holy Spirit. For the promise is to you and to your children and to all that are far off, every one whom the Lord our God calls to him." (Acts 2:38-39.) Here the promise of the gift of the Holy Spirit is to "every one whom the Lord our God calls to him." It is a promise to those who are called to him—to believers. It usually, almost uniformly, is a gift subsequent to conversion. Out of two thousand examined, only eighty or ninety, according to Wesley, received the fullness of the Spirit at conversion; the rest received it as something subsequent. That corroborates my own experience in many parts of the world. It works out that way. And we can see why this is: For in coming to Christ we want forgiveness, restoration; but after we come to Him, we feel the need of a deeper cleansing and a greater power. In conversion we are adopted into the Home; in the fullness of the Spirit we are adapted to the Home—we become at Home. Everything is ours.

The promise is to "all that are far off"—and that reaches into this needy, nerve-shattered, conflict-ridden present. The Holy Spirit is God's offer now, and He is our need now. That offer and that need can meet and can meet now.

In Ephesians 1:13-14 we are told: "In him you also, who have heard the word of truth . . . and have believed in him, were sealed with the promised Holy Spirit." Here those who "heard" and "believed" were "sealed"—the hearing and believing were conversion; the sealing was later. If you are not sealed by the Holy Spirit, your letter, being open, easily drops out or is stolen. The Holy Spirit seals, brings permanence.

O Spirit of God, seal the open places in my life, places where grace leaks out; save me from the fallings away I am prone to until sealed. If the sealing means searing, let it come—but seal me. Amen.

AFFIRMATION FOR THE DAY: *I am saved by Grace, sealed by the Spirit, sent by Love.*

TIRED OF WORKING ON THE CITY OF GOD

Yesterday we quoted only part of a passage: "Were sealed with the promised Holy Spirit, which is the guarantee of our inheritance until we acquire possession of it." (Eph. 1:13-14). The Holy Spirit is not only the seal of our spiritual life but the guarantee of it—the guarantee of its permanence. The inheritance is guaranteed by the Spirit. For in Him you possess that inheritance now. You have heaven in which to go to heaven. If there is no heaven, something like heaven would have to be created to house and environ what you have in the Holy Spirit.

The bane of the spiritual life is its impermanence. So many are sighing over lost ecstacies, lost touch with God, lost victory. It is largely because they are living, not "the life of the Spirit," but the life of following an ideal with their own resources, stirred by emotion through a sermon or plagued by a demand laid upon them. So they grow tired and give up. A Chinese scholar was working on a translation of Augustine's *City of God* and sent the following message to the mission board: "I'd like another assignment. I'm tired of working on the *City of God.*'" A lot of people are tired because they are working on the City of God, instead of the City of God working in them. The Holy Spirit is the City of God working in us. We don't work at the City of God; we let the City of God work in us, take possession of us. The Holy Spirit is the guarantee of the City of God. Not that we cannot fall, but the chances are minimized, for by the sealing the guarantee can be applied. Spiritual permanence sets in. The wobble is taken out of us. I have watched it across the years: Where people come to India through romance, or through duty, or through wanting to serve, they often fall by the wayside, get tired, and give up. Only where there is a surrender to, and a possession of, the Holy Spirit do people have that "stickability" that makes them, not only endure to the end, but enjoy to the end. The Holy Spirit guarantees to keep us in repair, guarantees enough gas for the journey, guarantees the course we take, and guarantees arrival.

O Spirit of God, I thank Thee that Thou hast taken out of me all nervous fear of the future, all fear of losing this precious Gift, for in Thee I have a guarantee that is a divine guarantee. Amen.

AFFIRMATION FOR THE DAY: *Guaranteed by the Spirit I think victory, I act victory, I am victory.*

A HOLY SPIRIT—LESS CHRISTIANITY

Last week we emphasized the gift of the Holy Spirit as a continuing fact. Someone has said "the Holy Spirit makes Jesus contemporary"; and we may add Jesus makes the Holy Spirit contemporary.

The rest of the Acts of the Apostles, after Pentecost, throbs with the Holy Spirit. And so do the Epistles. He is their pulse beat. Take Him out, and you have a body of doctrines, a corpse. Anywhere you press upon this body of literature, you can feel the heartthrob, but especially in Romans 8. This chapter begins with condemnation and ends with a hallelujah chorus of permanent victory. And the secret is the Holy Spirit.

The sixth chapter of Romans mentions grace or its equivalent eighteen times; the seventh chapter mentions sin or its equivalent eighteen times; and the eighth mentions the Holy Spirit eighteen times. It is possible to talk grace and then to fall into a seventh-chapter experience of defeat. Why? For in the seventh chapter the Holy Spirit is not mentioned. It is all a human struggle to fulfill duty without divine reinforcement within. It is all pre-Christian and sub-Christian. If it is possible to emphasize grace and live in the seventh chapter, how much more will we live in the seventh chapter if we talk seventh chapter. The neo-orthodoxy which emphasizes sin is depicted by Paul Scherer as saying: "Where grace abounded, sin doth much abound." If you talk sin, you will probably take sin, for whatever gets your attention gets you. But it is possible to talk both grace and sin and yet to live defeated unless the Holy Spirit is an integral part of that grace.

We note, first of all, that the Holy Spirit is described as "the law of the Spirit of life in Christ Jesus" (Rom. 8:2). The Holy Spirit is so closely connected with this historic Jesus that He is called "the Spirit of life in Christ Jesus." He projects the Spirit of life which was in Christ Jesus—projects it straight into the depths of us, even into our subconscious. The work of the Holy Spirit is to make character Christlike. He has the highest work in the world. No greater redemption and reconstruction than this—to make sinful men Christlike.

O Holy Spirit, I'm grateful that I'm under a reconstruction that is breath-taking—I'm being made into the image of the most beautiful Thing that ever appeared upon our planet. I gladly yield to this process. Amen.

AFFIRMATION FOR THE DAY: *The Holy Spirit will chisel me into Christlikeness today, if I let Him.*

"THE LAW OF THE SPIRIT OF LIFE"

We began yesterday to note the working of the Spirit as found in Romans 8. The first statement is: "The law of the Spirit of life in Christ Jesus has set me free from the law of sin and death." (8:2.)

The Spirit works with the certainty of law: "The law of the Spirit of life in Christ Jesus." This introduces a surprising element for to many the Spirit is without law: "The wind [or Spirit] bloweth where it listeth." (John 3:8, K.J.V.) Are there laws underlying the spiritual life as definite as the laws that underlie our material universe? Yes. Psychologists are beginning to discover those laws; and when they really do, they are not different from the laws the Christian gospel reveals. For instance Carl Jung, the famous psychiatrist, says this: "I venture to arrange the sum total of findings under the four heads: Confession, Explanation, Education, Transformation." But these are the four steps our faith has always insisted upon: (*a*) Confession—"If we confess our sins." The confession brings a catharsis. (*b*) Explanation—explaining the steps of confession, and surrender, and faith. (*c*) Education—putting ourselves under the tutelage of the Spirit. "Take my yoke upon you, and learn from me." (*d*) Transformation—"If any man be in Christ, he is a new creature." (II Cor. 5:17, K.J.V.) As psychology probes deeper, it will find deeper laws, and they will always be Christian laws—revealed in Christ because implanted by Christ.

For instance, Paul speaks of the law of sowing and reaping as operative in the spiritual life: "For he who sows to his own flesh will from the flesh reap corruption; but he who sows to the Spirit will from the Spirit reap eternal life." (Gal. 6:8.) Here he says: Just as you by faith entrust the seed to the earth, surrender it to the process of dying and living, so if you sow to the Spirit—surrender yourself to the processes of life in Him, die to live—then you will reap results, and the results will be life everlasting. But just as surely as you trust yourself to your own flesh—surrender to it—you will reap corruption; life will decay, disintegrate.

O Spirit of God, we see both of these laws operating now before our very eyes with an almost mathematical precision. So help me not to be afraid of a complete entrustment of myself to Thee. I sow my life to Thee. Amen.

AFFIRMATION FOR THE DAY: *I am adventuring into law, not Divine whim; therefore I expect results—precise results.*

SUN AND DEATH—TWO SIDES OF A COIN

We saw yesterday that the life of the Spirit is as much under law as the law of sowing and reaping—put in a certain amount, and you get out certain results multiplied. You sow life, and you reap Life. You sow a self, and you reap a Self. On the contrary, there is the law of sin—"the law of sin and death." The two go together. Sin and death are connected as two sides of a coin. Take sin and you get death—get it now—decay sets in. A lot of people hope to cheat the moral universe—to take the sin and to avoid the death. It can't be done.

How does this law of the Spirit of life in Christ Jesus make me free from the law of sin and death? Just as the bird in flying takes advantage of the law of wing lift and the law of air resistance and is therefore free from the law of gravitation, so we take advantage of the higher law—the law of the Spirit of life in Christ Jesus—obey it, and so we are free from the law of sin and death. The introduction of a higher law frees us from the operation of the lower law. But the moment we cease to take advantage of the higher law, the lower law begins to operate—we come under the sway of the law of death.

The second step in the life of the Spirit in Romans 8 is: "Who walk not according to the flesh but according to the Spirit" (8:4). The first step is freedom from the law of sin and death. The second step is, not a freedom from, but a freedom to—a freedom to walk. The life of the Spirit is not a negative deliverance only—it is a positive doing. You align yourself to outgoing and ongoing life. You become a creative personality. Your ideals and longings begin to walk—incarnated in you. But you walk "according to the Spirit"; not your impulses and cravings, but the Spirit is now in control.

Then a further step sets in: "Those who live according to the Spirit set their minds on the things of the Spirit. To set the mind on the flesh is death, but to set the mind on the Spirit is life and peace." (8:5-6.) You don't merely walk according to the Spirit—your actions. You also live according to the Spirit—He becomes the source, not only of your deeds, but of your very being—you live, and move, and have your being in Him. He is your Life. Amen.

O Spirit Divine, I thank Thee that I have no life apart from Thee. I have only death apart from Thee. So I would live in Thee with everything attuned to Thee. Amen.

AFFIRMATION FOR THE DAY: *Today all my ideas shall walk.*

TO THINK FLESH IS TO THINK DEATH

We continue our study of the work of the Holy Spirit as found in Romans 8. We saw that to set the mind on the flesh is death, but to set the mind on the Spirit is life and peace. To think flesh is to think death, for those who pay too much attention to the flesh will have a diseased, decaying flesh on their hands. Those who think most about their own health are least healthy. Physically, as well as spiritually, you will have life and peace. And note, it is, not "spirit," your own spirit, but "the Spirit" upon whom you are to set your mind. That turns you in, but not in upon yourself—it turns you in upon another Self, the Spirit. That releases you from preoccupation with yourself and yet rescues from the thought-control movements the truth that is there: namely, that thought can determine you. But it saves the thought from self-centeredness, which is poison, and applies it to the Spirit, which is Health. To set your mind on the Spirit is life and peace—first life and then peace. Peace comes as a by-product of adequate life.

Another step: "You are not in the flesh, you are in the Spirit, if the Spirit of God really dwells in you." (8:9.) This is an efficient and operatable way to get out of the flesh: let the Spirit dwell in you, and, lo, you are released from the flesh. No tense struggling, no sitting on a lid, but just letting the Spirit of God dwell in you—and by that very indwelling you are a released person. The flesh is in its place when the Spirit is in His place: namely, within you. It is the expulsive power of another occupant. You have Him, so you don't want the flesh. "For if you live according to the flesh you will die, but if by the Spirit of God you put to death the deeds of the body you will live." (8:13.) Here you are not tense and struggling and tied-up in the struggle with the flesh, for by the Spirit of God you put to death the deeds of the body. You give willingness, and He gives power. This saves the Spiritual life from being a fight and turns it into a faith. You expect, and He executes. This is a relaxed warfare, poise in the midst of life's most intimate battle—the battle within.

O Indwelling Spirit, I turn over to Thee my struggles. Thou hast them, for Thou hast me. I am released and relaxed in Thee. I've learned the secret of victory, Thy victory. Amen.

AFFIRMATION FOR THE DAY: *Relaxed receptivity—my theme song for today.*

ACID IN HER, NOT IN THE PEACHES

A further step in our study of Romans 8: "If the Spirit of him who raised up Jesus from the dead dwells in you, he who raised Christ Jesus from the dead will give life to your mortal bodies also through his Spirit which dwells in you." (8:11.)

There is a putting to death of this body of sin, the flesh, and a quickening with life of this physical body. The one is quenched, and the other is quickened. Everything unnatural, the flesh, the body of sin, is cleansed; and everything natural, the physical body, is brought to its best—and beyond its best, for it becomes God's best. A woman came to one of our Ashrams allergic to peaches; the acid in the peaches upset her. She surrendered herself to God and found that the acid was in her, not in the peaches. When she got rid of her conflicts, she began to eat peaches without harm. A very intelligent Negro said at one of our Ashrams: "I thought I couldn't eat this, that, and the other; and now here I'm eating everything, including onions—and I've never eaten onions in my life." One woman said that she had eighteen allergies; she surrendered her conflicts to God and now has conquered all those supposed allergies but two. And she expects victory over them!

The Spirit of God is health. When He indwells us, then life is poured into every fiber of our being. We become alive—to our finger tips. The diseased portions tend to become well; the normal portions become better—all become quickened. A health tendency takes possession of us. We think health; we breathe health; we are health—and we give health. When I was going through a physical crisis about thirty years ago, I heard a Spirit-filled Indian say: "When the Spirit of God dwells in you, then you can preach five and six times a day without being tired." I wondered at it then, for I was spiritually and physically floundering, but today I do not wonder at it. It is a fact. There is a physical rejuvenation taking place constantly when we are in tune with the Spirit: "So that the life of Jesus may be manifested in our mortal flesh" (II Cor. 4:11). Christian bodies are healthier and more rhythmical than any others.

O Spirit of God, who art the Spirit of Health, I yield my untouched portions to Thee for Thy quickening, healing power. For this body as the temple of the Spirit must be kept at its best. It is—in Thee. Amen.

AFFIRMATION FOR THE DAY: *Today, my body will be at its best—in Thee.*

THE GUIDANCE OF THE SPIRIT

We come to another stage in the Spirit's work within us: "For all who are led by the Spirit of God are sons of God." (8:14.)

This is a stage which many Christians never attain—they are not Spirit-led Christians. They are led by self-interests, physical impulses, the actions and attitudes of the group, or the occasional pressure of ideals upon them from sermon or book. But they have not put themselves at the disposal of God to be led of Him in the outlines and details of their lives. Hence they lack direction, therefore goal.

The Spirit leads us through the revelation of God in the Scriptures, through the counsel of good people, through opening providences, through the heightened moral intelligence, through the discoveries of science, through conscience, and through the Inner Voice. All of these are authentic ways of the leading of the Spirit.

To cultivate the guidance of the Spirit by the Inner Voice one must learn the art of lowly listening. And when the Inner Voice speaks, test it by the other methods of guidance. In general it will be in harmony with the other ways. For God does not speak with contradictory voices. He will not speak one thing through the revelation in Christ and another thing through the Inner Voice. They will morally coincide.

And don't get discouraged if occasionally guidance turns out wrong. Go back and examine to see where the wires were crossed so that the wrong message got through. As a friend put it: "I cannot always trust my guidance, but I can always trust my Guide." Don't lose faith in Him if guidance goes wrong; lose faith in your method of guidance and re-examine it.

But if we are honest, basically honest, the guidance will seldom go wrong. Then tune yourself to hear His voice. He is the God who speaks. A Quaker woman inquired of a young man she knew: "Hast thou heard God speak lately?" And when he answered, "No," she commented: "Thee must have forgotten to be still." "Be still and know"; be unstill and you will not know. God guides everyone who really wants to be guided. Only those who are led by the Spirit are children of God.

O Spirit of the Living God, I attune my heart to listen to Thee, for in Thy guidance I find direction and mission. I am not at loose ends. Take the reins of my life and guide me. Amen.

AFFIRMATION FOR THE DAY: *"When God guides, God provides."*

OUR SUPREME WEAKNESS—PRAYERLESSNESS

We come to the last and the very climax of the Spirit's work as found in Romans 8: "Likewise the Spirit helps us in our weakness; for we do not know how to pray as we ought, but the Spirit himself intercedes for us with sighs too deep for words. And he who searches the hearts of men knows what is the mind of the Spirit, because the Spirit intercedes for the saints according to the will of God." (8:26-27.)

It is interesting that the climax of the Spirit's work is to help us to pray. For the "weakness" is at the point of praying. For if we are weak in praying, we are weak in power and poise. The central weakness of the Christian world is that we have lost the art of prayer. If we accept the Spirit within the depths of us, then we find the urge to pray heightened. It becomes acute. We begin to have the Spirit of prayer. He is the up-pull of the heart, the stretching forth of invisible hands to the infinite resources of God—He inspires prayer. And if He inspires, He also insures, prayer. For the Spirit-aroused prayer is the Spirit-answered prayer. Then we can pray with confidence and faith, for we know we are in line—we are not butting into the universe with a request; we are praying with the sum total of reality behind us.

The work of the Spirit as seen in Romans 8 lead to the highest stability possible. The inner life has caught its tranquillity. It has learned that "in everything God works for good"—the thing itself may not be good, but God works in that evil thing and makes it contribute to the ends for which we live. So we harness evil itself to our purposes and use it. That possibility gives us inner steadiness of heart. Of one prominent and dynamic minister it was said: "He always talks as if he held four aces in his hand." The Christian can face life with a supreme confidence knowing that he has resources to meet anything—literally, anything, for God works in everything, good, bad, and indifferent, and makes it work for good. Life may deal you a very bad hand, but you know that you can turn all evil into a good. You are in complete mastery.

O God, my Father, I thank Thee that I have found the secret of mastery—the Spirit within. Fortified by Him I am ready to say, "Let life come on." For I can stand, and more, can use everything that comes. I am grateful. Amen.

AFFIRMATION FOR THE DAY: *Today I shall pray in the Spirit, and then the Spirit shall pray in me.*

"IN ALL THESE THINGS"

We ended last week with a note which brings us to the very heart of the Christian victory. "No, in all these things we are more than conquerors through him who loved us." (Rom. 8:37.) This is a complete expression of power and poise.

Note the phrase "in all these things." These things were not pleasant, agreeable things. On the contrary, they were the kinds of things that upset human nature deeply: "tribulation, . . . distress, . . . persecution, . . . famine, . . . nakedness, . . . peril, . . . sword" (8:35). A worse combination is scarcely imaginable. And yet the writer says that in all these things—not in some of them victorious and in others defeated, but in *all* these things—we are not only conquerors but more than conquerors: conquerors with a margin, a plus, ready for another encounter, with resources intact.

And further note: it is "*in* all these things." The Buddhist word is: *Indifferent* to all these things. The Hindu word: *Apart* from all these things. The Moslem word: *Beyond* all these things. Modern hedonism: *By* all these things. Modern cults: *Mentally deny* all these things. The Christian word is: *In* all these things. Every one of these answers wants a victory apart from these things. Only the Christian wants a victory "in" all these things. Hence there is no escape mentally, no playing tricks on the universe, no side-stepping of any issues. The victory is *in* all these things. That is in line with the Christian Way—it is *in*, never apart from, above, or beyond. The Incarnation is the center of that in-ness. The answer came by God entering flesh and demonstrating all the answers by identification. He took on Himself everything that man meets and showed the victory from the inside. It makes the Christian Way the Way of realism instead of the Way of idealism. All the answers are wrought-out answers instead of verbal answers. That puts the victory right where everybody can get it. For if we are told to have victory "apart from," then that makes victory impossible for most people; for they cannot get apart from—they must get the victory "in" or not at all.

O Father, I thank Thee that I need not strive for goals that always recede, nor sigh for the impossible. I can have the victory now, where I am. I need not run away. I can realize Thee and Thy victory where I am. Amen.

AFFIRMATION FOR THE DAY: *Today, all my victories "in," not "apart from"—real victories.*

"IN EVERYTHING GOD WORKS FOR GOOD"

We saw yesterday that the victory is "in," not apart from, not above, but in. But some of the things in the "in" are evil. How can we get victory in and through evil? This verse tells us: "We know that in everything God works for good with those who love him." (Rom. 8:28.) Note the thing itself may not be good—its source and its content may be evil, but God works in that evil to turn it for our good. The very genius of the Cross is that. The Cross is evil, and yet God works in that evil and makes it redemptive. The Cross is sin turned saving. With that at the heart of our gospel we will expect to be saved, not from trouble and evil, but through them.

Here is a victorious young mother who has every reason to get a divorce from her husband. He has broken every single code of honor and morality that it is possible to break, and he has made a hell for her. At least what should have been a hell, but strangely enough it wasn't. She was inwardly victorious and even gay. The spiritual experience she had found made it impossible for her husband to torment her any longer. He lost all power to give her pain. For all her pains furthered her. "You are not being hurt by all this?" I asked. "Strangely enough, no," she answered; "I'm even growing under it." "Then you don't want to get away?" "No," she said, "I want to stay just where I am and demonstrate the victory." She and God together are working out the answer through the evil. Note: she and God together, for the passage says: "in everything God works for good *with* those who love him." God doesn't work out the answer by an imposed miracle apart from us—it is "with those who love him." Don't sit down and with folded hands look for God to "pass a miracle" of deliverance, but listen to God, and together work it out.

I do not say that one should not change his circumstances, if possible, when the circumstances are hurting the deepest within him, but that should happen only as one of God's solutions. "Apart from" is a lesser victory—not *the* victory.

O, my Father, I thank Thee that Thou dost not bid me have victory, but Thou dost offer to enter it all with me, and the victory then becomes ours. We are working together for victory. Amen.

AFFIRMATION FOR THE DAY: *I shall not look for miracles today; I shall be one—a miracle of grace.*

"I WANT ROOM TO GROW UP IN"

We saw yesterday that the victory was "in" and "through" everything. The Christian way does not bear things in the way of Stoicism; nor does it make you indifferent to things as in Buddhism; nor deny the reality of things as in Hinduism; nor bend under things as in Islam; nor expect to escape from these things if you are righteous as in Judaism; nor become immersed in these things as in modern materialism; but it does offer the possibility of *using* everything that comes, good, bad and indifferent, and making something else out of it. That is a completely workable faith. And workable for anybody, anywhere, at any time. This is the answer.

But to be sure that every hole has been stopped up and every possibility of exception eliminated, Paul tells us of ten things that cannot separate us from the love of God in Christ Jesus our Lord. When he calls the roll of these ten things, he really just about exhausts the possibility of things that might break us. In reality he says: "Nothing can break you if you don't break with Him! "For I am sure that neither death, nor life, nor angels, nor principalities, nor things present, nor things to come, nor powers, nor height, nor depth, nor anything else in all creation, will be able to separate us from the love of God in Christ Jesus our Lord." (8:38-39.)

These are the Ten Horses of evil, intending to ride us down and trample us under their feet. Instead of letting them ride us down, we grasp their bridles, swing into their saddles, and ride these very evils to our own destination. Take the first: "Death." He puts the worst first, for death is the consummation of all earthly evils. William Randolph Hearst, the publisher, will not allow anyone to speak of death in his presence—it is taboo. He hopes thus to postpone it. Death to him is the supreme evil. On the contrary, one of the radiant members of our Ashram, a gracious lady of sixty-four, said: "I look forward to death and immortality, for I want room to grow up in." In the living Christ she knew she had an immortality, for the pulse beat of immortality was already beating within her. She lived in a deathless One and was therefore herself deathless.

O Deathless Christ, alive forevermore, why should I be afraid of death? I am in Thee, and death becomes unbelievably unimportant, a mere transition, a veranda that opens to the Home of Many Rooms.

AFFIRMATION FOR THE DAY: *I no longer belong to those "who through fear of death are all their lifetime subject to bondage."*

FACING DEATH AND LIFE

We saw yesterday that "death" could not separate us. Deliverance from fear of death is a central deliverance, for the lesser fears are inherent in this. The writer of Hebrews speaks of Him who will "deliver all those who through fear of death were subject to lifelong bondage" (2:15). Subject to lifelong bondage. For the shadow of death falls upon every earthly thing; and until we are delivered from the fear of that shadow, we live in perpetual shadow. But the Psalmist says: "Though I walk through the valley of the shadow of death, I will fear no evil: for thou art with me."

Then the writer takes up another thing that might separate us: "Life." Many are not so much afraid of death, for that is remote; but they are afraid of facing life, for that is near, at hand, must be faced every moment. On-going life holds unnamed terrors for many. A man wrote: "I seem to be afraid of meeting people and going places. If I know I have to go downtown to meet an appointment, the closer to that appointment the worse I feel. The instant I turn around and come back toward home, that instant I feel better and keep feeling better the closer I get to home." Here was a man with everything, except one thing—the power to face life. He needed inner Resources so he could say to himself: "In him who strengthens me, I am able for anything" (Phil. 4:13, Moffatt). Look at that picture of the man afraid of ordinary life, and then look at this picture of General Booth, the founder of the Salvation Army, going blind, and his son Bramwell breaking the news to him: "You mean that I am blind?" said the General. "I fear you must contemplate that," his son answered. "I shall never see your face again?" asked the General. "No," said Bramwell, "not in this world." The old man's hand moved across the counterpane until he grasped his son's: "Bramwell," he said, "I have done what I could for God and the people with my eyes; now I shall do what I can for God and the people without my eyes." Life, even when hard and cruel, could not separate him from the love of God. He had power and poise—in spite of what life could do.

O God, I thank Thee that nothing now can make me afraid—I am possessed by Life; what can life do to me? I can do anything that ought to be done through Thy Spirit within me. Let life come on. I am ready. Amen.

AFFIRMATION FOR THE DAY: *Life holds nothing within it which Christ has not conquered.*

"LIFE IS FEARFUL; REFUSE IT"

We studied yesterday the victory over "life" as one of the things that might possibly separate us. A brilliant young Indian lawyer said concerning his conversion: "I despised the Christian way—I admired Hitler, for he was power. And then when Hitler went down to a miserable death amidst the rubble of Berlin, my faith crashed with him. I was empty. Then Christ came and said: 'Life is joy; take it.' The Tempter replied: 'Life is fearful; refuse it.' 'No,' said Christ, 'Life is joyful; receive it.' And I did. And was new from that moment."

So we need not be afraid of life, for "Life is joy," and we can take it and make it into joy even when the path of sorrow is ours.

Then the Apostle goes on and says that there is another thing that will not separate us: "angels." It is not stretching the meaning of this to say that angels could stand for the good things of life that come to us—love, joy, happiness, prosperity, friends. Some are afraid of the good things of life—afraid that they will separate us from the love of God. Why should they? God made us for joy, put laughter in our hearts. Would such a God be happy when we are unhappy? Someone has said there ought to be another Beatitude: "Blessed are they who cure us of our self-despising." And we may add; "And of our joy-despising, of our love-despising, our prosperity-despising." So when joy, or love of God. I am safe, for I can stand prosperity or penury, the them at the feet of Christ exactly as I lay my burdens of grief there—they are both His. And these joys, and love, and friendships, and popularity must be used for the purposes of the Kingdom exactly as our sorrows and our griefs. The Christian way is life-affirming, world-affirming, joy-affirming. So if anguish or angels come, I will make them both messengers. "He maketh his angels messengers." Everything carries the same message—the love of God. I am safe for I can stand prosperity or penury, the good things or the evil things. I am insulated against disaster, for everything serves.

O Father God, I thank Thee for the angels that come to me day by day and night by night. I welcome them. For they are straight from Thee and lead me to Thee. Give me a confidence in joy, in the good things. Amen.

AFFIRMATION FOR THE DAY: *My joys, as well as my sorrows, shall take me by the hand and lead me to His feet.*

"BIG ENOUGH TO SPREAD OVER TWO WAVES AT ONCE"

We go on to study the list of ten things that might separate us: "Principalities." It is a strange term and might possibly stand for the dominant things, the things that everybody obeys in a civilization. Principalities might stand for the mores, the customs which the herd obeys. The herd instinct is probably the most determinative of the instincts. "Everybody does it" settles it for many people. But surrender to God brings a supreme loyalty into which the lesser loyalties must fit. Instead of the herd custom being our supreme loyalty, the Kingdom of God becomes our principality. We obey it supremely and the herd only when it fits that Kingdom. The herd has lost its power to separate us.

Then the account says: "Nor things present." A great many are separated from God by things present—things as they are. The monotony of work and the monotony of the home life gets on the inside of us and makes us intrinsically monotonous. That tyranny of monotony can be broken, for there is a stimulus in Christ that puts a tingle into life and makes it creative amidst the noncreative. It redeems man not only from sin but from the spindle, not only from evil but from the anvil: "By all the stimulus of Christ." "Things present" have no terror for you, for you do not belong to them—you belong to Christ and receive creative stimulus from Him. So you are creative—in spite of.

The next: "Things to come." Many are afraid of the oncoming future. They fear the unknown and especially if that unknown holds within it as a certainty oncoming old age. People should be taught how to grow old just as we teach young people to grow up. For the shock of retirement is devastating to those who are not inwardly prepared for it. Those who studied a landing place in mid-Atlantic said the problem was to get a barge big enough to spread over two waves at once. It would be steady if it could do that. To have a way of life that can spread over the wave of youth and the wave of old age is to bring security and stability. The stimulus of Christ can rejuvenate and adapt old age and hold it steady.

O God, even down to old age I expect to prove the might of Thy strengthening and steadying. Through the tempests of youth thou hast held me. Through the serenity of old age Thou wilt hold me. Amen.

AFFIRMATION FOR THE DAY: *The barge of my life is large enough to spread over youth and old age—so I am safe.*

"NOR ANYTHING ELSE IN ALL CREATION"

We continue the study of the things that might upset our inner stability. The next is "Powers." They might differ from "principalities," in that the latter might refer to a corporate dominant entity and "powers" might refer to a personal dominant entity—power vested in, or acquired by, some person, a dictator in public or personal situations. Many of us have to live under tyrannies collective or personal. We must be able to adapt ourselves to this tyranny by not being adapted to it. Surrendered to the supreme totalitarianism—the Kingdom of God—we are free amidst any tyranny, for we are inwardly free. Then the "powers" have lost their power—over us.

Then the next: "Height." Many are afraid of the heights, afraid of success, for it brings responsibility. "If any man can draw back, my soul shall have no pleasure in him"—the creative God cannot approve of those who draw back, cease to be creative (Heb. 10:38, K. J. V.). But the Christian Way is the way of affirmation; and if success is affirmed, we can take it and use it. All is laid at His feet. Success doesn't go to our head—it goes to His feet.

Its corollary: "Depth." If "height" will not separate us neither will "depth"—depression. For we have victory over both. "But when some were stubborn and disbelieved, speaking evil of the Way before the congregation, he withdrew from them, taking the disciples with him, and argued daily in the hall of Tyrannus. This continued for two years, so that all the residents of Asia heard the word of the Lord, both Jews and Greeks." (Acts 19:9-10.) Here was something that should have sent Paul into the "depths," but the evil speaking sent him from a synagogue to a lecture room where not only Jews heard him, as in the synagogue, but Greeks as well. The depression was a wider expression. He *used* evil.

And then finally: "Nor anything else in all creation." This throws a blanket over the left-out things. Nothing, absolutely nothing, can separate us except our own consent. We have perfect security as long as we have consent. This brings power and poise—both.

O God our Father, I thank Thee that Thou hast swept the boards with Thy promises and Thy provisions. My willing consent is the only unsure thing. And I make that sure now. Amen.

AFFIRMATION FOR THE DAY: *The decks are swept of possible failure; I stand on them a conqueror.*

THE FRUIT OF THE SPIRIT WITHOUT THE SPIRIT

We saw last week that the result of the impact of the Spirit was to create an inner serenity and steadiness of spirit which nothing can separate or destroy. The last section of the eighth chapter of Romans comes out of the first section. The first section emphasizes the work of the Spirit, and the second section emphasizes the fruit of that work: namely, inner security and poise. A great many try to take the second section without the first—the fruit of the Spirit without the Spirit. It all remains an unfulfilled promise—a quest instead of a realization. The Holy Spirit is introduced after the defeat in the seventh chapter. The tide is turned by the introduction of the Holy Spirit—we are made free from the law of sin and death; but not only are we made free *from*; we are made free *to*—free to the life of inner poise and security. But the eleven verses of victory from 8:28 to 8:39 are dependent for their base on the twenty-seven verses describing the work of the Spirit within. One is root, and the other is fruit. If the first of the fruit verses (8:28-39) begins, "We know," and the last ends, "For I am sure," it is because having the Spirit within meant a life of certainty and security. Take the Spirit out of the eighth chapter, and it will be as flat and dead as the seventh chapter. No Spirit, no serenity.

The same thing can be said of the thirteenth chapter of First Corinthians—the love chapter. That chapter is quoted in isolation from the preceding chapter, which is a chapter entirely devoted to the work of the Holy Spirit. The central verse of that twelfth chapter is: "To each is given the manifestation of the Spirit for the common good." (I Cor. 12:7.) The chapter is devoted to the various manifestations of the Spirit and ends, "But earnestly desire the higher gifts. And I will show you a still more excellent way" (12:31); then follows the love chapter. The Spirit chapter is the root, and the love chapter is the fruit. For the first thing mentioned in the fruits of the Spirit is "love" (Gal. 5:22). To struggle to show the fruit of the Spirit without the root of the Spirit is to make of this chapter a whip of duty instead of a natural manifestation of the Spirit of love.

O God, I've looked on this chapter as a burden instead of a natural overflow. Help me to be so possessed by the Spirit within that the very outgoing of life will be love, and only love. For this is the very heart of my faith. Amen.

AFFIRMATION FOR THE DAY: *All my roots are in Thee; all my fruits are from Thee.*

I AM NOTHING

Years ago at my first meeting with Mahatma Gandhi I read the thirteenth chapter of First Corinthians to him from Moffatt's translation. When I got through there were tears in his eyes, and he exclaimed: "How beautiful, how beautiful." He organized love into a national movement for independence and made it a working force. And as we look at Gandhi's corporate translation of love in terms of a national movement for freedom and see it in its higher manifestations, we exclaim: "How beautiful, how beautiful—and how powerful, how powerful." For this love chapter is the power chapter—a description of the only abiding power on earth. All else fades and fails; love alone abides and holds the field.

That ancient world of the Mediterranean was divided into three nations with three emphases: The Greeks, the emphasizers of the power of speech, the orators; the Hebrews, the emphasizers of prophetic powers, understanding the mysteries of God, and holding a faith in God as thus understood; the Romans, the emphasizers of action, a willingness to sacrifice themselves for the nation's honor, the doers. Paul stepped into the midst of these partial emphases and said: "If I speak in the tongues of men and of angels [the Greeks], but have not love, I am a noisy gong or a clanging cymbal. And if I have prophetic powers, and understand all mysteries and all knowledge, and if I have all faith, so as to remove mountains [the Hebrews] but have not love, I am nothing. If I give away all I have, and if I deliver my body to be burned [the Romans], but have not love, I gain nothing." Here he says: "If I speak, I know, and do, but have not love, then I speak nothing; I know nothing; I do nothing; I am nothing. A more devastating judgment never fell upon whole systems of thought and life than this judgment, done in the name of love. A more excellent way had arisen, and beside this way of love the lesser ways seem detours—this is the arterial highway of life. Life founded on half-truths perishes for want of inner sustaining power; so life in these nations perished or it lives on as remnants, little side-eddies. The future is with love as it is organized into the total life. For only love abides.

O Father, who art love, and who therefore remainest amidst the change and decay of things, give to me this persisting love, that all my values may be intact, preserved by love. For I live in vain if I do not love. Help me. Amen.

AFFIRMATION FOR THE DAY: *Today, unless I love, I speak nothing, know nothing, do nothing, am nothing.*

THE JUDGMENT OF LOVE

We saw yesterday the three great emphases of that ancient world—the Greek, the Hebrew, the Roman. We saw that love took over where they left off. That world was weighed and found wanting.

India in her search emphasizes three ways to realize God: the Gyana Marga, the way of knowledge; the Bhakti Marga, the way of faith or devotion; the Karma Marga, the way of works. The Hindus were thus searching along the three ways which the Mediterranean world searched. Here Paul's judgment of love is just as devastating: If I have all knowledge (Gyana), all faith (Bhakti), all deeds (Karma), but have no love, then I know nothing; I am devoted to nothing; I do nothing; I am nothing.

But the judgment of love falls closer home. Modern psychology divides man into intellect, feeling, and will. Some lay emphasis on the intellect, the thinkers; some lay emphasis on the emotions, the emotionalists; some lay emphasis on the will, the men of action. Each has its devotees, and each is insufficient, even when carried out. For if I think everything, feel everything, do everything, but have no love, then I think nothing, feel nothing, do nothing, am nothing.

The ancient world of East and West were, and the modern world is, running into futility. Only one Man hit the nail on the head, who, when asked which was the greatest commandment, answered: "Thou shalt love the Lord thy God with all thy heart [the affectional nature, the feelings], and with all thy soul [the volitional nature, the will], and with all thy mind, [the intellectual nature], and with all thy strength [the physical nature]." (Mark 12:30, K. J. V.) The total man—feelings, mind, will, body—was to be attached to God in love. Then, animated by love, we will feel right feelings, think right thoughts, will right actions, and become the right person. Love is the bond that holds the whole into coherency—without love life falls apart, incoherent. And incoherent life is not life—it is chaos. So it is love or chaos—and that in the total life, individual and collective. The stone which the builders of civilization have rejected has become the head of the corner.

O God our Father, we have missed the way—the way of love. Our confusions and our clashes are witness that life is off-center. Bring us back to the center—love. Then we shall live and live abundantly. Amen.

AFFIRMATION FOR THE DAY: *All my ways are ways of futility unless I take Thy way—the way of love.*

SINGING OUT OF THE HEART OF PAIN

To get the background of this thirteenth chapter of First Corinthians we must be reminded that this letter was written out of pain: the pain of a divided Church, one going to Apollos, another to Cephas, another to Paul; the pain of Christians turning to pagan practices and attitudes; the pain of Christians getting off on the marginal, tongues, signs; the pain of personal criticism: "His letters are weighty and strong, but his bodily presence is weak, and his speech of no account." With that background of pain Paul takes up his pen, dips it in the blood of his broken heart, and writes of love—love for them even when they were doing these things. You simply cannot write such literature as this except out of the heart of pain—a pain which is no longer a mere pain but an instrument of redemption. This chapter is pain set to music. The heartstrings are drawn so tight by pain that they are thus tuned to the higher notes of love.

But before love can sing, it has to cut. So it cut in the first three verses: cut away all fancy speaking in tongues of men and of angels as a sign of the Spirit of God, cut away all boastful claims to prophetic powers and secret knowledge, cut away emphasis on miracles such as removing mountains, cut away all secret boasting about special zeal in giving and sacrificing—cut these all away unless at their basis was love. Where love is not, the Spirit is not. If the first fruit of the Spirit is not love, then the other fruits are rotten to the core. Love makes all the other fruits sound. So if the joy is not a loving joy, the peace not a loving peace, the patience not a loving patience, the kindness not a loving kindness, the goodness not a loving goodness, the faithfulness not a loving faithfulness, the gentleness not a loving gentleness, and the self-control not a loving self-control, they are sterile virtues, springing from self instead of the Spirit. Love is creative and makes all the other eight fruits creative—the joy a contagious joy, the peace a contagious peace, and so on. Love must be the soul of every virtue, or that very virtue turns to a vice.

O Spirit of Love, take possession of me as I go into Thy meaning, for without Thee I am dead, and all I do is dead. So make me alive—with love. Help me to begin this day with nothing but love. Amen.

AFFIRMATION FOR THE DAY: *Love will be the soul of all I do today—all else will be body, an instrument of love.*

LOVE IS ALWAYS MORE POSITIVE THAN NEGATIVE

The Apostle now turned to an exposition of what love is. Even in telling what it is, he had to tell them what it is not. But even so, he was more positive than negative. He said eighteen things about love—eight things it does not, and ten things it does. Love is always more positive than negative. But it is negative—there are some things it does not do, but only in order to do some other things. To put no negatives in love is to make love maudlin and sentimental. Said the head of an institution which was very redemptive: "We like you, Johnny, but we don't like the thing you did today." That is love—not sentimental, but sensible. The negatives in love are hedges along the way, so love will not stray. It is saying these "Noes" in order to say a great "Yes." No man can say "Yes" who hasn't said a "No." Say "No," but not too much.

The first thing Paul says about love is that it is patient: "Love is patient" (1 Cor. 13:4). The dictionary definition of patience is: "The suffering of afflictions, pain, toil, calamity, provocation, or other evil, with a calm unruffled temper; endurance without murmuring or fretfulness." The root of patience is *pati* (suffer). The first emphasis, then, is that love can suffer, can take it. Since love is outgoing, and since by its very nature it insinuates itself into the sins and sufferings of the loved ones, its very first capacity must be to be patient, to have a capacity to take suffering and sorrow patiently. The very first step takes us to the Cross at once, where, in a supreme way, Love showed its capacity to take on Itself everything that would fall upon the loved one. So if love can go to the Cross straight off, it can go anywhere. It meets the supreme test, and all the other tests have been met in this initial test. A Chinese doctor walked from Peiping to Chungking, which was bombed throughout the war. He went on to Amoy and found sixteen members of his family wiped out by bubonic plague, his house a shell. He said: "We Christians can take it. We know no discouragement. We must show the non-Christians the Way." He had the first requirement of love—the power to take it, and to take it without discouragement.

O Christ, Thou who didst show ability to meet the supreme test, the test of the Cross, help me to have that love which is, not tender-minded, but tough-minded with a capacity to take it, and to take it cheerfully. In Thy name. Amen.

AFFIRMATION FOR THE DAY: *I shall take all that comes today with unruffled temper.*

RESPONDING NEGATIVELY TO SORROW

We looked yesterday at the very first quality of love—the power to take it, and to take it cheerfully. The first thing in love is poised power—the power of not only taking what happens but reaching out and deliberately taking on yourself the pains and sins of the loved ones and making them your very own. A girl of nineteen writes: "It's been a habit of mine to respond negatively to sorrow. For the life of me, and though I try, I can't, in the midst of tragedy, react with faith, with a positive attitude." She was responding negatively to sorrow because the roots of life were in herself: "Though I try, I can't." She was trying—trying to bring forth the fruit without the root.

In a crisis the three greatest personalities of the New Testament—Jesus, Stephen, and Paul—all three prayed for enemies in the end crisis of their lives. Jesus said on a cross, "Father, forgive them; for they know not what they do." Stephen prayed amid a shower of stones: "Lord, do not hold this sin against them." Paul said: "For I am already on the point of being sacrificed; the time of my departure has come. . . . At my first defense no one took my part; all deserted me. May it not be charged against them!" (II Tim. 4:6, 16.) It was the crowning act in the life of all three.

Why can love take it, be patient? Because love with a Christian content of faith in it knows that the universe is behind it; then in spite of what the present says, the future belongs to Christ. So it can afford to be patient. For nothing right can come out wrong, and nothing wrong can come out right. A. N. Whitehead says: "Negative and evil factors are neither the stable nor the victorious elements in the sweep of history." The Christian believes profoundly that "the world has a character which justifies hope and serenity." The Christian can wait—and wait on, and keep on waiting on. In the end the universe will not let him down. It guarantees his faith. The outcome is inherent in the very act, so "having done all, to stand"—to stand and wait with infinite patience that wears down all opposition, all hate, all that is not love. Where patience is not, love is not.

O living Spirit of Christ, give me Thy infinite capacity to take it, and to take it with a cheer, for Thy word is to be the last word. I can wait for it, and can wait for it with joy. Amen.

AFFIRMATION FOR THE DAY: *My love can take it, and nothing can break it.*

THE SPIRIT OF THE PATIENCE

We saw yesterday that the first capacity of love is to be patient, the power to take anything, for it can use everything.

There is another portion to patience: "Love is patient *and kind*." Love not only can be patient but can be kind in the patience. There is the act and attitude of patience, and being "kind" in the midst of that act and attitude is the aroma. If the aroma of kindness is not in the patience, then the very patience may smell bad. You have seen patient people who did not leave a good flavor in the mouth. The patience wasn't a gracious, kindly patience. Even a dog knows the difference: Throw it a bone, and it will take the bone and go off without a wag in the tail. But call it to you, pat it on the head, and then hand it a bone, and the dog will go off with its tail wagging in gratitude. There was the deed—and the aroma. The hard-lipped patience of some women—and men—fails to win out, for it is not winsome. This type is patient, but not kind in the patience; therefore it is something less than love. The kindness is the spirit of the suffering and transforms the victim into a victor. For in the kindness you assume the offensive—the offensive of love. You give back kindness when life isn't kind. Therefore you are on the moral and spiritual offensive. You are not negatively patient—you are positively kind amidst the patience. That is the victory.

The hymn "Are Ye Able" has been paraphrased this way:

> Able to suffer without complaining,
> To be misunderstood without explaining;
> Able to give without receiving,
> To be ignored without any grieving;
> Able to ask without commanding,
> To love despite misunderstanding;
> Able to turn to the Lord for guarding,
> Able to wait for His own rewarding?

Love, then, instead of belonging to the tender-minded type belongs to the tough-minded type. Instead of being a clinging vine, it is a sturdy oak, gnarled but not knuckled under the storms of life. A love that is patient and kind is the most formidable thing on our planet.

O Father, I thank Thee that I find at last the real thing— real poise and power. It is the power and poise of love. Let it come to illustration in me this day in all my thoughts and relationships. Amen.

AFFIRMATION FOR THE DAY: *As the violet leaves perfume on the heel that crushes it, so let me leave the perfume of kindness on all that hurts me today.*

LOVE HAS NO INFERIORITY COMPLEX

We come now to look at four statements of what love is not. The first is: "Love is not jealous or boastful." Both jealousy and boastfulness show one thing—a sense of inferiority. Obviously if you are jealous of another, you have feelings of inferiority toward that person. Boastfulness is the obverse side of inferiority—you boast to cover up feelings of inferiority. J. S. Bonnell says: "If a man is blatant about his atheism, we may expect to find a desire for belief in God. If he is constantly protesting his faith, we may look for an inclination to doubt. If he is suffering from impulses to suicide, we may expect to find in him a marked desire to live and to accomplish something in which he has been thwarted. If he induces conceit, we may expect to find inferiority. If he is distressed by a feeling of humiliation, we may be sure that pride is also present."

The Apostle says: Love has no inferiority complex, jealousy; nor has it a superiority complex, boastfulness. It is natural, and normal, and even. An inferiority complex keeps you in the dumps, and a superiority complex also ultimately lands you in the same dumps. For it is an attempt to lift oneself up out of an inferiority by loud assertion of superiority, by boastfulness. But the boastfulness ultimately gives way, and the dumps set in again.

Love, being power and poise, saves you from the depths and from the false heights which drop you into the depths. For the person who loves another cannot by the nature of things be jealous of the other. And the person who loves himself as he loves his neighbor can neither despise himself nor attempt to put undue value on himself. For the love of the Spirit within makes him know that he is not worthless, but worthful; and that same love of the Spirit gives a sense of deep humility that precludes all boastfulness. Maimonides, a noted Jewish rabbi, said: "Humility is the mean between arrogance and self-abasement." Love is humility, so it is neither up nor down—it is even.

O Spirit within, save me from the depths of false inferiority, and from the heights of false superiority, and give me the balanced, even-tempered heart that is so sure it is serene and unruffled. Amen.

AFFIRMATION FOR THE DAY: *The even-tempered heart shall be mine today—not exalted by success nor depressed by failure.*

NOT ABOVE, NOR BELOW, BUT WITH

We saw yesterday that love gives an even temper of mind by saving you from inferiorities or superiorities. Kahlil Gibran puts it this way:

Only those beneath me can envy or hate me,
I have never been envied or hated; I am above no one.
Only those above me can praise or belittle me.
I have never been praised nor belittled; I am below no one.

In one of the service clubs they sing in a song: "Not *above* you, nor *below* you, but *with* you." The love of the Spirit delivers you from the "above" and the "below" and holds you at the "with."

Another pair of assertions of what love is not: "It is not arrogant or rude." These terms seem a repetition: boastfulness and arrogance. They are, but deeper. Boastfulness is outward and verbal; arrogance is inward and may never be expressed in words. Arrogance usually expresses itself, not in words, but in attitudes—attitudes of rudeness.

Perhaps the most widespread arrogance resulting in rudeness is racial arrogance. The newspapers of India carried an item telling of a religious conference in the United States where a resolution was passed putting God behind racial arrogance as seen in segregation—it was His will. But He is not our puppet to sponsor our arrogance. His hand of judgment is upon everything that arrogates to itself superiorities based on race. For the so-called inferior race is thereby stimulated and over-compensates and surpasses the arrogant.

The arrogant and the rude are unsure of themselves. Only the humble are sure of themselves, and only those who are sure of themselves are humble. The account says: "Jesus, knowing that the Father had given all things into his hands, and that he had come from God and was going to God, . . . girded himself with a towel . . . , and began to wash the disciples' feet." (John 13:3-5.) The consciousness of greatness was the secret of His humility. One less sure of himself would not have done that. The great are humble; they have to be in order to be great. You know no secrets of life unless there is low humility, a willingness to be teachable. So the judgment upon the arrogant is that they become more arrogant to cover up an increasing inferiority. It is a vicious circle and ends in disaster to the arrogant.

O Father, give me the lowly heart and the kindly attitude. Make me inwardly so great that I can afford to be humble in speech and act. Make me gentle within and without. Amen.

AFFIRMATION FOR THE DAY: *"Thy gentleness has made me great."*

"LOVE DOES NOT INSIST ON ITS OWN WAY"

In the paragraph beginning at the fourth verse and ending with the seventh of the thirteenth chapter of First Corinthians—a paragraph which describes what love is, and what it is not—there are seven statements. At the center of those statements is this one: "Love does not insist on its own way" (13:5). At the very core of the love victory is the victory over insisting on your way.

There are two ways of trying to get victory over always wanting your own way. One is to retreat into empty silence, where you become a nonentity, everybody's doormat. Many take that way and become household drudges, or married suppressions. They accept it very often as a kind of self-punishment for wanting their own way, a kind of masochism. Or they sink into silent, sullen resentment. Either case is a disaster to the personality. There is the other way of not wanting your way, and that is of so surrendering yourself to something beyond yourself that your self is caught up into a higher purpose and plan, and you want only the furtherance and triumph of that something. When that something is the Kingdom of God, then you are safe, for your self is fulfilled in the Kingdom. You don't care what happens to you and your way, just so the Kingdom is furthered. That saves the self from insistence on its own way, and it saves the self itself.

Love is the law of our being; and when we love, we fulfill our self. But to turn that love in on itself makes it like an ingrown nail—the nail is healthy and right when it grows outward but becomes festering if it turns in toward itself. A self that is preoccupied with itself and its own ways is a festered self. It is living against the law of its being. It has broken the law of love, and you cannot break the law of love any more than you can break the law of gravitation and not get hurt. It is just as inexorable and just as exacting.

Insist on your own way, and your own way will turn to ashes in your hands. You will do as you like; then you won't like what you do. Be a loving person, and you will be the kind of person you can safely love and a person you can live with—gladly.

O Spirit of Love, live within me and break the tyranny of self-preoccupation and give me the outgoing heart; and in that outgoing it will find itself released, and happy, and fulfilled. Amen.

AFFIRMATION FOR THE DAY: *Since love is the law of my being, I will have to love others to fulfill myself.*

LOVE "IS NOT IRRITABLE OR RESENTFUL"

We saw yesterday that "love does not insist on its own way." But we saw that it found its way by renouncing its own way for the way of love. People who love always get their own way—in the end. They get it because they don't want it.

We come to another step: Love "is not irritable or resentful" (I Cor. 13:5). The center of the irritation and resentfulness—the self—is surrendered to the Kingdom, and so the irritability and the resentments drop away. Don't fight the irritations and the resentments—surrender the root, the self, and then the fruits drops off.

A touchy, resentful self is as bad as a porcupine as a bedfellow. The punishment for being touchy and resentful is that you grow quills that stick others, but stick you worse. For they are ingrowing quills. A radio executive sat at the telephone and blistered the man at the other end of the line. A friend sitting near listened with amazement at this outburst, and when the executive put down he telephone said to him: "If you keep that up you'll get a stomach ulcer." To which the executive snapped: "I don't get ulcers; I give them." And he said it with an air of finality. But was it final? Was he only giving ulcers and not getting any? Perhaps his stomach had a tough lining that resisted ulceration, but his spirit was being ulcerated, and that was the worst punishment. That which did not show in the physical showed in the spiritual—he had an ulcerated spirit. Irritation toward others produced increased irritation toward himself. He was hanged on the gallows he prepared for others.

You are born of the qualities you give out. If you give out resentments, you become a resentful person. That is the pay-off. And if you give out love and only love, then you become a loving person. That is the pay-off. Said a Kansas farmer: "If you know how to surrender to God and let His power get hold of you, then you ain't shortchanging yourself." The irritable and resentful are always shortchanging themselves. The loving in loving become loving. They don't shortchange themselves.

O Spirit of Love, be the spring of my loving. For without Thee within I become an ugly, touchy, resentful person. But with Thee within I become beautiful with love, and beautify all I touch. I would be love filled. Amen.

AFFIRMATION FOR THE DAY: *All my irritations shall become interpretations of the grace of God, and by the grace of God.*

DO I BECOME A MORE LOVING PERSON IN THE PROCESS?

We come to another step in the unfolding of the way of love: Love "does not rejoice at wrong, but rejoices in the right."

There is a subtle falling into a rejoicing in wrong on the part of many religious people who seem to be fighting wrong. It is entirely unconscious, but it is nonetheless devastating. For a good many people, earnestly religious, have fallen into the attitude of always looking for wrong, and often finding it where it isn't, finding it often in other Christian workers. What is the unconscious motive behind all this mote picking? The motive is: If I can find something wrong in others that proves my superiority, their wrongness boosts my rightness. Who hasn't seen, as I have, a man or woman concentrating his or her attention on fighting obscene literature and in doing so rejoicing secretly and unconsciously in the finding of it, for it satisfies their own unconscious sex curiosity and at the same time boosts their own estimate of themselves: "I wouldn't do that."

The test of whether we are acting through love or through a desire to boost oneself? It is simple: In pointing out wrong, do I become a more loving person in the process? If so, then love is at the basis of my work. But if I become unloving, censorious, and critical, then the spring of my action is self-interest. The pay-off is in what I become—the pay-off and the revelation. The self-boosting critical person has, in time, a telltale drawn, hard face. That is the pay-off. But if in the fight with wrong, you are deeply suffering because of that wrong, and you are bearing it in vicarious love all the time you are fighting it, then you become a loving person—and your face shows it; your being breathes it; you become it.

Love rejoices in the right and by its attitudes produces the thing it rejoices in. Francis of Assisi, in his marvelous love, felt sorry for thieves and the generally bad because they couldn't give expression to the holiness within them. And that attitude produces the very thing it believed in. Thousands threw off the old life and followed—followed a creative love.

O Father, save me from secretly rejoicing when others show weakness and sins, and help me to rejoice in nothing but good. Then I shall become what I rejoice in. For I would be good—good to the core. In Jesus' name. Amen.

AFFIRMATION FOR THE DAY: *Severe toward self, tender toward others, loving toward both.*

HEADS I WIN: TAILS I ALSO WIN

Four positive things love does: "Love bears all things, believes all things, hopes all things, endures all things." (I Cor. 13:7.)

The first and the last are similar: "bears . . . , endures." The two central ones are also similar: "believes . . . , hopes." The two at the center save the first and the last—save them from being just bearing and just enduring. They become believing and hopeful bearing, and believing and hopeful enduring. It is not dead, unlighted-up bearing and enduring; it is bearing with a smile—the smile of belief and hope—and it is enduring with a pulse beat at its center, the alternate beats of which are belief and hope. That saves the bearing and enduring from being stoical and makes it Christian. The Stoic endures; the Christian exults.

But the reason why Love bears all things and endures all things with belief and hope is because Love knows it cannot merely bear and endure all things—it can *use* them. Love is so creative that even out of wrongs it can create a good. Evil put Jesus on a Cross, and Jesus being love made that Cross redemptive. Evil saved Him. So there is nothing that comes to us—good, bad, or indifferent—but when it comes, we can take hold of it and make it into something else—can make it redemptive.

Someone has defined democracy as "that madness which believes about people that which isn't true, and yet without that belief they will never become what we believe them to be." It creates the very thing it believes in. If this is true of democracy, how much truer it is of love. For love sees an Augustine in every libertine, a Kagawa in every sorrowfully confused schoolboy, a Carver in every slave boy. And love has a deathless hope at its heart. The only faith that uses "hope" as a working force is the Christian faith. "We are saved by hope." "May the God of hope fill you with all joy and peace in believing, so that by the power of the Holy Spirit you may abound in hope." (Rom. 15:13.) Love believes and hopes because it knows that God will have the last word, and that last word will be victory.

O God of Hope, live within me so that the things around me which seem hopeless may become alive with hope, for I am alive with it. Let me "by the power of the Holy Spirit ... abound in hope," because I abound in love. In His name. Amen.

AFFIRMATION FOR THE DAY: *"Let us hold fast the confession of our hope without wavering, for he who promised is faithful." (Heb. 10:23.)*

"INCORRIGIBLE LOVERS"

The last paragraph of this love chapter begins with, "Love never ends," and concludes with, "So faith, hope, love abide, these three; but the greatest of these is love." The paragraph before this ends by saying love "endures all things," this paragraph begins and ends by saying love is enduring—it "never ends"; it abides. Why? Because in loving you become loving; so that even if no response comes to that love, you have not loved in vain; you are loving for having loved. That remains, and it never ends.

Take Mary Reed. She lived for fifty years among the lepers of the Himalayas. She poured out her life for them—life, and substance, and love. When she died, a faithless, trusted "son" had stripped everything from her, was so afraid he wouldn't get the very bed she lay on that he requested that too, so she gave it and lay on a hard, inferior bed—to die. After fifty years of loving serving that was her reward. Her love was a vast failure. Was it? It produced Mary Reed, and she is deathless. She lives on, immortal amidst the wreck of hopes. And her spirit even then does not fail; for beside the lepers she has helped, an English lady doctor, inspired by her, walks midst that wreckage, takes over, and says to me with a joyous laugh: "I wouldn't be anywhere else for the world." And that place is three days march beyond where a motor can go on the borders of Tibet. What incorrigible lovers these Christians are—and how prodigal with their love. They are gamblers, knowing that they can't lose. For if there is response, they win; and if there isn't response, they still win, for they become loving as they have loved. And that is the reward.

No wonder the chapter ends: "The greatest of these is love." So those who can foretell the future, "prophecy"; those who can speak eloquently, "tongues"; those who know many things, "knowlege"—if they have only these, they pass away, for these things leave little or no deposit within the person. But those who love abide forever, for in loving they become loving, and loving character is the universe's most precious value, and it will survive. It holds the field when everything else dies.

O God, my Father, this is my real poise, and this is my real power—the poise and power of love. This will hold me steady, and this will make me creative. Therefore give me love—Thy love, and yet more love. Amen.

AFFIRMATION FOR THE DAY: *Love holds the field when all else dies.*

COLD POTS MORE DANGEROUS THAN "HOT-POTS"

We have now come to the last week of the half-year in our quest for power and poise. In this week we will sum up the Christian answer to that quest.

We have seen that poise is not to be sought first—it is a by-product of power. But power should not be sought primarily, for power itself is a by-product of something deeper—the Holy Spirit within. When you have Him within in full possession, then power and poise flow naturally.

I say in full possession, for it is possible for you to possess the Spirit and yet the Spirit not possess you. Dr. Handley Mowle says: "The difference between a soul filled and one that is un-filled is the difference between a well in which there is a spring of water choked, and a well in which the obstruction is removed, so that the water springs up and fills the well." If we are choked by resentments and fears and self-centeredness, then we will always lack a sense of fullness.

I know that many are afraid to let go to the Spirit, afraid they will become a "hot-pot." But the danger to the present-day Chruch is not from hot pots, but from cold pots. Our churches are more in danger of freezing out than of burning up. There are three types of life: men of the flesh, men of the mind, and men of the Spirit. Men of the flesh and men of the mind greatly preponderate over men of the Spirit. It was said that the devil preached a sermon, but it did no harm, for it had no unction of the Spirit in it. Too much of our Christianity is stale and flat and lacks power to win, for there is no unction of the Spirit in it.

The Acts of the Apostles can be divided into three portions: *preparation, power, production.* The preparation is seen in chapter one, the power in chapter two, and the production in the rest of the book. The peak from which to see the whole book is Acts 1:8—the key word is "witnessing." Witnessing in Jerusalem covers chapters 2-7; witnessing in Judea and Samaria chapters 8-12; witnessing unto the uttermost parts chapters 13-28. The Holy Spirit produces an amazing poise and an amazing power—to create.

O Spirit of God, I thank Thee that Thou art my Resource for everything I need. I can draw heavily on Thee for adequacy for life and for the creation of life in other souls. Amen.

AFFIRMATION FOR THE DAY: *I have witnessed Thy saving power; now I shall witness to Thy saving power.*
176

"YOU'RE NOT AS GOOD AS YOUR BOOK"

We continue to gather up the loose ends of our thinking in regard to the Christian answer. The Holy Spirit makes Jesus contemporary. When we think of God, we often think of Him above us, in heaven; when we think of Jesus, we often think of the past, of Palestine; but when we think of the Holy Spirit, we think of the within, of the here. And that brings it all where we need it—within.

A Hindu said to me one day: "Sir, I do not want to appear presumptuous, but have you found what the Acts of the Apostles records? I see there a strange power making weak, ineffective men into strong, effective, radiant men. That seems new and central—have you found that?" And that is the central question we can ask ourselves. We are taken up with little marginal things in religion and miss the central power. Some children on the way to the ocean got occupied with a pond they had made in the sand. One little fellow, seeing the real ocean, called out: "Come on, Billy, that ain't the ocean, that's only a pond." And we may well call to people gathered around their little denominational pools and thinking them the ocean: "Come on, brothers, that isn't the real thing; here is the Ocean of Divine Life and Power." It all awaits us.

A Hindu said to a Christian missionary: "Sir, we have found you out. You're not as good as your Book." The Book speaks of, and offers, power and we live in weakness; offers victory and we live in defeat; offers us the miraculous and we live in a dull routine. A little girl came into a drugstore, laid a quarter on the counter, and said anxiously to the man behind the counter: "Mister, I want to buy a miracle." "Buy a miracle? What do you mean?" he asked. The little girl explained: "My little baby brother is very sick, and I heard the doctor tell my mother that only a miracle can save him, so I want to buy a miracle." Only a miraculous type of living faith can save a very sick humanity. And God has the miracle for the asking. A very radiant missionary said: "I don't pray for power now, but only to be obedient. There is plenty of power."

God is saying: "Lay down your life on the Counter and take the Miracle." It is yours now.

O Father God, I am eager to live in the sanely miraculous, to be full of poise and full of power. Take all my powers and put them under Thy schooling and they shall emerge adequate and creative. Amen.

AFFIRMATION FOR THE DAY: *Today I shall be a miracle.*

THINGS NOT ESSENTIAL IN RECEIVING THE SPIRIT

We come to the very crux of our search: How do we receive the Holy Spirit? Let us look at ways we do not receive Him. 1. *We do not receive Him by joining an institution.* The coming of the Holy Spirit may coincide with the joining of the Church, but the act of joining did not do it. A self-surrender does. A Roman Catholic professor wrote, saying: "I invite you to find Christ in the Church." I replied: "I invite you to find the Church in Christ." You don't find Christ by surrender to the Church, you find the Church by surrender to Christ. When you make a surrender to Him, then you find the living Fellowship. Some would say, as the Roman Catholics do: "Where the Chruch is, there is the Holy Spirit," but the Christian position is: "Where the Holy Spirit is, there is the Church."

2. *We do not receive the Holy Spirit by undergoing a rite or ceremony.* The coming of the Holy Spirit may coincide with the rite or ceremony, but does not happen because of it. That would make Christianity mechanical and magical. The Holy Spirit comes by self-surrender and faith—that makes Christianity moral and personal.

We may receive the Holy Spirit at the time of "the laying on of hands," and we may not. If we do, it is not because of the laying on of hands, but because the laying on of hands created in us the accepting faith. To tie the Holy Spirit to a special group of people or to a line of succession is to turn Christianity from the moral to the mechanical and to destroy its nature. It then becomes a religion of a succession instead of a religion of the Spirit, but not because of it.

3. *You will not receive the Spirit because you are worthy, or because you have "tarried" a sufficiently long time.* Neither your worthiness nor your waiting will bring Him. The disciples "tarried" ten days, but not because it took God ten days to become willing—it took them ten days to get to the end of themselves. You can get to the end of yourself in ten minutes or ten seconds. The Holy Spirit is a "gift"—a "gift" of grace, and all you can do to receive is to empty your hands of yourself and receive Him. That puts Him in reach of all.

O Father God, I thank Thee that I too, unworthy though I be, can take this Gift of gifts. My heart is eager to take the steps and the Gift. I stand upon the threshold with my hand upon the doorknob. Amen.

AFFIRMATION FOR THE DAY: *Any child can take a gift; today I am that child.*

STEPS TO RECEIVE THE HOLY SPIRIT

We saw yesterday how we do not receive the Holy Spirit. We come today to look at—and I trust to take—the steps that lead into the fullness of the Spirit.

1. *Remember, the coming of the Holy Spirit is the aim and end of redemption.* God having come so far along—having come through Incarnation, through Crucifixion, through Resurrection—will not stop this side of the final step: the Indwelling. All His barriers are down—the barriers are with us.

2. *Remember that the Holy Spirit is "the promise of the Father."* Three times this phrase is used: "wait for the promise of the Father" (Acts 1:4); "the promise of the Holy Spirit" (2:33); "You shall receive the gift of the Holy Spirit. For the promise is to you" (2:39). This is His promise of promises. To go back on this would be to reverse His very nature, which is impossible. The character of God is behind this promise. You can bank your all upon it.

3. Since God, in the giving of the Holy Spirit, is giving Himself in the final Self-surrender, namely, the Self-surrender of coming in to live alongside of our imperfection and capacity to blunder and to sin—*since God is willing and eager to surrender Himself, then we in turn must be willing and eager to surrender ourselves.*

4. *Mind you: "eager and willing to surrender ourselves"—not merely this thing, that thing and the other thing, this person, that person, the other person, but the central, fundamental self.* From this moment you don't belong to yourself—you belong to Him. And belong to Him forever. What a relief to get a crooked, frustrated, unmanageable self off my own hands and into His hands. He's got me and got me forever! I own nothing—not even myself.

A father was explaining the coming of the Holy Spirit to his little boy and the little fellow said: "I see, the Holy Spirit is the auto driver—he does the steering." Yes, He does—from this time forth He has the wheel. He knows the Way and He knows me. I'm safe in His hands—and assured: I go His way, not mine.

O God, my Father, I'm grateful that the supreme crisis of life has come and I've met it—met it fairly and squarely. I've closed the bargain: I belong to Thee and Thee alone—and forever. I am grateful. Amen.

AFFIRMATION FOR THE DAY: *Today I am moving over and am letting God do the steering.*

THE PHILOSOPHY OF "AS IF"

We came yesterday to the step of self-surrender. This self-surrender is no easy make-believe. A sign in a Manila church read: "Calling all men for a breakfast. Christ your King, your Friend, your Buddie requires your presence at the communion rail. Requirement: a good confession. Easy, ain't it?" But self-surrender is no "Easy, ain't it?" proposition. It means a basic change of the center—from self to Christ.

5. *Since you have made the surrender now accept the Gift by faith.* "We might receive the promise of the Spirit through faith." (Gal. 3:5.) "Through faith"—that puts the Gift in reach of everybody. The simplest child can take a gift. Become childlike and take it. Don't look at yourself and your feelings—look at Christ and His faithfulness.

There is a philosophy of "as if." You become the hypothesis on which you habitually act. Act "as if" you are going to be defeated, and you will be. Act "as if" you are going to be victorious, and you will be. "Reckon yourself dead unto sin"—act as if you are dead unto sin and self, and you will be. "Put ye on the Lord Jesus Christ and make no provision for the flesh to fulfill the lusts thereof." Put on Christ and don't mentally provide for failure. Act "as if" you are even now in the possession of the Holy Spirit, or better that the Holy Spirit is in possession of you, and He will be. "Faithful is he that calleth you, who also will do it." "Whatsoever things ye desire when ye pray believe that you have received them and ye shall have them." Note: not will receive them, but "have received them"—you have now on the authority of God's character which is behind "The Promise." Don't try to believe—just believe. Don't struggle—accept.

A British major, very strong, was a poor swimmer. He said: "I'm much stronger than you and yet you swim better. I'm a dud." I told him the difference was this: he fought the water and struggled with it as something to be overcome. I trusted the water to hold me up—I was relaxed and therefore released. Cease struggling, let the Spirit in by faith. And He is in—forever.

O Father, I'm grateful that my fear has given way to faith. I can't trust myself, but I don't have to—I'm trusting Thee and I can do it with abandon and joy. I thank Thee that Thou hast taken the initiative. I respond by faith. Amen.

AFFIRMATION FOR THE DAY: *Today I shall experiment with the attitude of "as if."*

A LIFE SET TO OBEY

We continue the steps in receiving the Holy Spirit. As you take the step of appropriating faith, a faith that says it is settled—now, then walk by that same faith. Believe that from now on there will be Resources when you need them and whenever you draw upon them. Have the boldness to take what is *there*. But if there is no emotional evidence? The Gift is deeper than emotion, though it often produces emotion and very deep emotion. But if God gave us too much emotion in the acceptance of the Gift, we would always associate emotion with the Gift and always depend on it. That would put the Gift on a shallow basis. Those who are truly married are married whether they feel like it or not. It is something abiding amid emotional changes. So He comes to abide forever—to abide forever amid the emotional changes that come and go.

6. *Set your life to obey the Holy Spirit.* We "receive the promise of the Spirit through faith," but we retain the Spirit through obedience. "The Holy Spirit whom God hath given to those who obey him" (Acts 5:32, K. J. V.). There are these obediences: a belief-obedience, a surrender-obedience, a faith-obedience and a daily-obedience. The center of this new life is in the will, not the emotions. The emotions become a by-product.

This verse gives the attitude: "But he who sows to the Spirit will from the Spirit reap eternal life." (Gal. 6:8). To sow to the Spirit is to do what you do with grain—you surrender it to the earth in faith that something will happen, and the thing that happens is the golden grain. If you sow your life to the Spirit—respond every moment to the Spirit, as the sowed grain responds to the creative caresses of the earth, then you reap an eternal life, here and hereafter. You are under the law of creation.

7. *In your obedience obey the law of sharing.* Now that you have launched out by faith and have become possessed of the Spirit, share Him with others. Humbly and simply share this whenever the Spirit prompts you to share with those in similar need. The Holy Spirit is like electricity in this: He will not come in where He cannot get out. "Freely ye have received, freely give."

O Father, how can I thank Thee enough for Thy bringing me to the consummation and to the beginning, for I feel this is the Beginning. I know life is ahead of me for Life is within me. Amen.

AFFIRMATION FOR THE DAY: *Today I shall not be a reservoir; I shall be a channel.*

WISDOM AND REVELATION

We have come to the end of our inquiry into the Christian answer to power and poise. We have seen that the Holy Spirit in possession of us and all our faculties and powers brings cleansing, co-ordination, and creation. We become outgoing, creative personalities. Someone has said: "Perfect function is perfect health." The Holy Spirit within brings perfect function when the obedience is perfect. In Him we find ourselves. And in finding ourselves we find our power and our poise. This is the Answer.

And it is a growing Answer which makes us growing persons. This expresses it: "May the God of our Lord Jesus Christ grant you the Spirit of wisdom and revelation." (Eph. 1:17, Moffatt.) Note the two: "wisdom and revelation." Wisdom is that which is developed through human search and experience. That puts us in line with the whole scientific unfoldment of truth, the method of experimentation. The Holy Spirit is in this unfoldment of truth, and wherever men find truth it is His truth. He hid it away during the creation of the universe and this unfoldment is His primary unfoldment. It is of Him wherever it leads to real truth. But in addition to this "Spirit of wisdom," there is the "Spirit of revelation"—the direct impact of the Spirit upon our faculties revealing truth to us. Wisdom is the result of the patient search upward and revelation is the result of the Spirit's downward coming. To take one or the other, to the exclusion of either, will lend to mental and spiritual unbalance. There are those who can see nothing of "revelation"—they are earthbound in their wisdom, blind to the highest things. And then there are those who are afraid of this search upward, afraid of the scientific approach and depend only on "revelation." Very soon their revelations don't reveal—reveal nothing except mental and spiritual sterility. Just as the Hindu ascetic ends in physical and mental and spiritual sterility, so if you practice mental asceticism you will end in the same sterility. We are to have "the Spirit of wisdom *and* revelation." These are the two wings on which we fly into the great adventure of living.

O Spirit Divine, in Thee I find my complete power and my complete poise—in Thee I am complete. Outside of Thee is death, inside of Thee is life and life abundant. I am at Thy feet. I stand straight. In Jesus' name. Amen.

AFFIRMATION FOR THE DAY: *Today I shall be open to receive in two directions: wisdom from life, and revelation from God.*

AN EMPTY UNIVERSE—A CAUSE OF UPSET POISE

We now turn to the things that sap power and upset poise. We are now in a position to look at them, for our eyes have already seen something beyond them. We need not be paralyzed by them, for the Great Hope beats within us. There is a way out. These are some of the things that break our power and poise.

1. *An empty universe, devoid of meaning, purpose, and goal.* A man can stand anything if he feels there is purpose and meaning to what he is doing. But when meaning drops out, not merely of the marginal things, but out of the center, the universe itself, then that breaks the inner spirit of man. If there is no God back of and in things, then there is no meaning to life, and if there is no meaning there is no value. A vast sense of futility comes upon life and topples it over. So the modern man, without God, turns to the outward and tries to find meaning there. Someone has said of the modern man: "If he is in a tight spot, he borrows money on the furniture; if he is low, he lights a cigarette; if he is lonely he goes to a movie; if he is maladjusted, he goes to a psychiatrist; if he has a headache, he takes an aspirin. All from the outside in. The Christian remedy is from the inside out."

But the biggest "headache" that man, without God, has is just this empty universe. How can you live in a universe dead—of meaning? The very thought of it sends man into an inward tailspin.

The symbol of immortality with some ancient peoples was a snake with its tail in its mouth. But that queer picture of immortality better depicts what life is now for many—a vicious circle, life swallowing itself. The end is a fiasco.

So the modern man turns to anything that will give him a sense of direction. It is said that one-fifth of the people of America now direct their lives—if you can call it direction—by astrology. When God died in the minds of people, they turned toward anything to put direction into life. So they turned toward the stars to hold them inwardly steady amid the flux of things. Lumps of matter floating in space are supposed to decide human destiny. When the Inner Light fails, then men turn to any light—to stars, anything, for guidance.

O God, my Father, help me to turn not to Thy creatures, but to Thee for light upon life. For Thou hast the answers and those answers answer, and do not let us down. I thank Thee. Amen.

AFFIRMATION FOR THE DAY: *No turning to anything today which will ultimately let me down.*

ASTROLOGY—THE REFUGE OF THE WEAK AND CONFUSED

Yesterday we saw that when God goes, men turn to almost anything to fill the vacuum—anything to put meaning and direction into life. Astrology, a pseudo-science, is one of them. There are 185 newspapers in the United States featuring an astrological column. Five national astrology magazines have a combined circulation of one million. The latest edition of an astrology handbook, which cost one dollar, sold more than a million copies. Many drug and dime stores handle printed horoscopes.

This is a pathetic revelation of vast multitudes spiritually adrift and grasping at any straw to save them from sinking into a meaningless universe. Astrology is always a sign of decay. When men have lost their nerve, are afraid to make their own decisions, they turn to the stars to make their decisions for them. The Hindu mind, a wonderful mind producing the great Sanskrit literature, was sterilized by astrology's laying its dead hand upon it. Men ceased to think and let the stars decide. A minister of education in an Indian State would not set out on a journey, long or short, unless a species of hawk, a kite, was circling in an auspicious direction. He had a servant watching the heavens and when the auspicious kite would appear, he would rush into the office where the minister of education was busy and announce: "Now, sir, you can go." And when he returned from a journey, the minister would circle and circle around his house in his car until the kite was in the right direction, and then he would enter. A highly educated man in the grip of a superstition, and because of it robbed of power and poise, for he went up and down with a kite! An intelligent Hindu said to me: "I was about to start for the railway station, looked up and saw it was not an auspicious moment to travel, waited for the auspicious hour, rushed to the train, but, alas, the train pulled out without me." Any individual, or group or nation, that waits for auspicious moments to do things will find the train of life pulling out without them. Astrology inevitably produces a backward, weakened people. It falls like a palsy on the soul and mind. To try to read your destiny in the stars is to cancel your destiny.

O God, I thank Thee that Thou hast put my destiny not in the stars but in my choices. Help me to have the courage to make those choices under Thy grace and wisdom. For I want inner steadiness of soul. Amen.

AFFIRMATION FOR THE DAY: *My ultimate destiny is my ultimate choice.*

A UNIVERSE THAT CARES NOTHING FOR YOU

We turn again to look at the inner upset that comes to those who have no inner anchorage in God. Listen to Bertrand Russell as he tells from his own experience what life is without God: "We see, surrounding our narrow raft illumined by the flickering light of human relationships, the dark ocean on whose rolling waves we toss for a brief hour. From the great night without a chill blast breaks in upon our refuge. All the loneliness of humanity, caught amid the hostile forces, is concentrated on the individual soul, which must struggle alone, with what courage it can command, against the whole weight of the universe that cares nothing for its hopes or its fears." Note these two phrases: "the individual soul, which must struggle alone . . . against . . . the universe that cares nothing." A "universe that cares nothing"—in that phrase is summed up the meaning of life without God. No wonder Bertrand Russell said that we must have "an unyielding despair." That is a counsel of impossibility, for in trying to have "an unyielding despair," you have already yielded—to despair.

Take Nietzsche. He said: "This is my way—what is yours? There is no The Way." If there is no The Way—God's Way—then life is a trackless jungle, where we ultimately get lost. And everyone who takes any way, other than God's way, does get lost. The modern man is lost, for he has lost God.

The ancient Greeks said: "Whirl is King, having driven out Zeus." When Zeus, their god, died, then Whirl, a fierce activity around a central emptiness, tried to substitute for the loss. Today God is gone from many lives and a fierce activity is the substitute. That fierce activity makes men forget, for the time being, the central emptiness. But life cannot keep up this devastating activity, the flame dies down and life is a central ash.

Kathleen Raine says: "Jazz and swing music are the typical expression of unsolved happiness." All of these things we turn to are, as Evelyn Underhill says: "A little whirl pool of disturbing and distracting influence." They are attempts at distraction—from emptiness.

O God, my Father, from our insane attempts to run away, bring us back—back to sanity, back to meaning, back to Thyself. For in Thee is meaning, value, direction. When I find Thee, I find all. Amen.

AFFIRMATION FOR THE DAY: *Today, Peace is king, having enthroned God.*

THE GENERAL NEUROSIS OF OUR TIME

We continue to study the upset in poise and power when God goes. An architect said: "I'm changing this twelfth century building into a modern house. Here I am changing the chapel into a sitting room." The modern man in modernizing the house of man-soul has changed his chapels into sitting rooms. Result? They can't sit in their sitting rooms—they become too jittery to sit. The sitting room has become a passageway from the dining room to the door—to the latest diversion, to anything that will help men to forget. When the place of quiet—the chapel—goes, then the unquiet steals within the breast and turns it to an inner bedlam. Someone has described "the profane yogis who mortify their souls in behalf of the flesh." The result? The soul passes on its sicknesses to the body. Half, or over half, of the sicknesses of the body are the result of soul-sickness.

Dr. Jung, the famous psychiatrist, says: "About a third of my cases are suffering from no clinical definable neurosis, but from the senselessness and emptiness of their lives. This may be described as the general neurosis of our times. Fully two-thirds of my patients have passed middle age." The "general neurosis of our time" is the loss of God resulting in a central nostalgia, a homesickness for God. Jung again says: "We have come to understand that psychic suffering is not a definitely localized, sharply defined phenomenon, but rather the symptom of a wrong attitude assumed by the total personality." That wrong titude is trying to live life without God. Dr. Luccock said once about traffic accidents: "If I die on the street you can put up on my tombstone: 'Died of looking the wrong way.'" Life is bound to hit you and bowl you over if you look to an earthbound existence and not to God.

Again Dr. Jung says: "A patient often exclaims 'If I only knew that my life had some meaning and purpose there would be no more silly story about my nerves.'" So loss of God means loss of nerve, loss of nerve means loss of nerves, and that means a sick body—a vicious circle.

O Father, I come to offer not only sins, but my follies—follies which become sins. I see the folly of trying to live without a sense of direction. Give me back direction—give me back Thyself. Amen.

ALCOHOL—AN ATTEMPT TO ESCAPE

We look today to some of the things to which men turn to fill a central emptiness and make them forget. A judge once told me that most of the people who come before him are trying to prop themselves up with all sorts of subterfuges—drugs, alcohol, excitement, anything to hold life together for the time being. For life has no inner cohesion—nothing that holds it together.

So men turn to anything that will divert them. Take alcohol. The increase in its use is the increase of the sense of inner insecurity. Alcoholism is now about one-third of the health problem of America. Dr. R. W. Kullberg, M.D., says that the mortality rate is twice as high in alcoholic families as in temperate. The Gallup Poll shows that 59 per cent of women drink. Dr. Eugene Fisk in a study of 6,000,000 policy holders found one-fifth more deaths among those who drink than among the abstainers. There was a 50 per cent greater mortality rate among drinkers than among total abstainers. The British Medical Association says that one glass of beer increases the incidence of error by 21 per cent by lessening eye-hand motor co-ordination. One-third of all fatal automobile accidents in the United States are due to drink. The Yale University estimates from 750,000 to 900,000 alcoholic addicts in the States. In addition there are 3,000,000 excessive drinkers approaching the stage of addiction. About 60 per cent of all chronic alcoholics end their days in psychiatric hospitals or drink themselves to death. Dr. Seldon G. Bacon says: "Two-thirds of the nation's inmates in jail are alcoholics."

Psychiatrist Robert V. Seliger, Johns Hopkins University, says that there are three reasons why women use alcohol to excess: *(a)* As an escape from a real life situation the drinker cannot face. *(b)* As a result of a defective personality or inadequate adjustment to normal life. *(c)* As a development from controlled social drinking to abnormal drinking.

As we review the above, we see that some inherent defect or personality lack resulting in a desire to escape a life situation is largely responsible for drinking among men. It is not smart. It is weak. Only the frustrated turn to it for crutches.

O God, my Father, save me from all subterfuges and escape methods in finding power and poise. Give me the real thing. For I can rest ultimately only in reality. In Jesus' name. Amen.

AFFIRMATION FOR THE DAY: *Today, no crutches, no attempts at escape, no pick-me-ups which will mean a drop-me-down.*

DRINK—THE GREAT ILLUSION

We ended yesterday by looking at alcohol as a means that people adopt to forget—to forget the central emptiness of life.

Dr. Seliger gives the illustration of Miss A., aged 44, in an executive position at $15,000 a year. She was in love with her employer and thought he loved her, but when he went off to war and came back he was cool toward her, interested in younger women. Had Miss A. lived in the Victorian period when delicate health was fashionable she might have tried to escape by taking to bed and becoming an invalid. But in 1946 she turned to whiskey.

Mrs. B. had always been dependent on others and had never developed her inner resources. She had no religion and no philosophy to rely upon, and since she couldn't adjust her immature personality to adult life she reached for the first crutch that offered itself—liquor.

One psychiatrist says: "When I began practice in psychiatry twenty years ago not more than one in ten alcoholics were women, now it is four in ten." Soon they will be equal with the men and surpass them, for their more delicately constructed nervous system cannot stand the ravages of alcohol. Another psychiatrist says: "With modern psychiatric treatment thirty to forty of every hundred alcoholics may be helped back to health, but the others are doomed more certainly than if they had cancer. They will end their lives in psychiatric hospitals or literally drink themselves to death."

A letter in this week's mail says: "My brother cannot stand the nagging of his selfish, worldly-minded wife so he has taken to drink for he has no religious resources." A very attractive missionary slipped sexually and to try to resolve the conflict within, took to drink on board ship to forget. She found God and forgiveness and restoration, and the drink dropped off.

Drink is the great illusion. In a dining car I picked up a wine list. At the bottom of the list were these words: "Aspirin, 25 cents." I thought to myself: "Why should I buy a headache?" When life becomes a headache, people turn to liquor to get temporary relief from the headache and add on another!

O God, help Thy foolish children from going into roads with dead ends. And help us to see Thy signals, for Thou art trying to save us by flashing Thy red lights across our pathways. Thou art redemptive—save us. Amen.

AFFIRMATION FOR THE DAY: *Today, no roads with dead ends; I have my feet on the road of the open vista.*

A "LIFT" AND A "LET-DOWN"

Another sign of inward frustration is the astonishing increase in cigarette smoking. There is now a daily consumption of six and a half cigarettes per capits for every man, woman, and child in the United States. It is a very definite sign of frustration. Said a woman in one of our conferences: "I took to smoking because I was frustrated. I find smoking is an outward expression of inward frustration."

There is a town in the United States called "Echo." Many life in that town. Some frustrated person begins to smoke and to cover the frustration makes it fashionable. Then the others—weak-willed and copyists—do the same. And soon that town could be called "Echo"—an echo of a frustration. It isn't smart to smoke; it's weak. I said to an audience of young people: "When I see gray-haired old ladies turning to smoking, because somebody said it was smart, I feel like turning them over my knee and spanking them," and the eleven thousand young people roared their applause!

A young lawyer said in one of our Ashrams: "For three years I couldn't sleep, now since I have seen the Lord Jesus, I sleep like a top. Now my difficulty is that I sleep too much! I used to smoke fifty cigarettes a day. It dropped off."

Dr. William Sadler, the famous psychiatrist, says: "The various drugs such as tobacco, and cocaine, which raise the blood pressure, as well as the alcohol and morphine group which lower the pressure, are all powerful in their deteriorating effect upon the mind. In fact all states of systematic-poisoning or auto-intoxication, result in more or less derangement of the mental action."

To become addicted to a tyranny of this kind is unworthy of free beings. In a prison camp in the Netherlands East Indies, European women, addicted to smoking, tore up their last book and their last Bible to get paper to wrap their cigarettes. One woman in the internment camp, when she had to choose between taking a suitcase with her belongings in it or a suitcase with cigarettes in it, chose the cigarette suitcase. Bondage! They try to gain a momentary "lift," a kind of false poise. But that poise turns to poison!

O God, give me inner courage and clear thinking, that I may not run after illusions. I want something with a lift in it that will not drop out from under me. I want Thee. Amen.

AFFIRMATION FOR THE DAY: *"So whether you eat or drink, or whatever you do, do all to the glory of God."* (I Cor. 10:31)

ILLUSTRATIONS OF ESCAPISM

We saw last week that men take various subterfuges to escape out of a present that has no God in it for them. Not having God means not having adequate life to meet life, so we take various escape methods to get out of the dilemma.

I have just been with one of the most lovable peoples on earth—the Filipinos—and have watched them unconsciously trying to escape out of corporate decision. Across the waters, next door to them, China is going Communist. The Kuomintang said they would put in land reforms—after the civil war. The Communists redistributed the land as a part of their war. They won. The Philippines should see the lesson. Instead they are trying to shoot down the "Huks" (the Communist peasants), give charity to those hurt by them, and then they are buying here and there an estate and redistributing the land to the peasants. It is a temporizing escape. In the meantime, they are furiously transporting each other from place to place in a mad attempt to forget. It is escapism, unconscious of course.

We will look at various methods of escape in the course of these meditations, as answers to the dilemma of living life without God. We will now look at an example of a man who knew there was a God but wasn't prepared to obey Him, so he tried to run away from Him—Jonah. There are many who are doing the same—they try to run away from God by various means, for they think what Jonah thought—they think God's will is bondage and their own will is freedom. That is the central illusion in life. For God's will and our highest interests are one. Our wills against God's will and our highest interests are not one. You go against God and you go against yourself. Every road that leads away from God has a precipice at the end of it.

Jonah represents a psychological study of an escape mentality—he is the man who ran away. He thought that on his own he would be free, but under God he would be in bondage, so he tried to escape—from salvation. He was free—to get himself into trouble with himself and others. He was free to go from tangle to tangle.

O God, we think our ways are ways of pleasantness and peace and Thy ways are hard. So we learn our bitter lessons. We learn by trial and error that Thy ways are really our ways—Thy way is liberty. Amen.

AFFIRMATION FOR THE DAY: *When I try to play truant with God, I only succeed in playing truant with myself.*

JONAH—THE MAN WHO RAN AWAY

We look at Jonah again as the man who knew there was a God but thought His ways hard and his own easy. "This message from the Eternal came to Jonah, the son of Amittai: 'Go to Nineveh, that great city and thunder in their ears that their wickedness is known to me.' But Jonah went away to fly to Tartessus, from the presence of the Eternal; he came down to Jaffa, ... found a ship there sailing for Tarshish, he paid his fare ... avoiding the presence of the Eternal." (Jonah 1:1-4, Moffatt.)

The account says "he paid his fare." We always do, and we pay heavily to get away from God. For God is our life, and when we run away from Him we run away from life. We learn that the hard way—as Jonah did. We pay the fare in inner conflicts and guilts—things which in themselves become our own punishment. God doesn't have to punish evil, for evil is its own punishment. Peter gives this striking passage: "Suffering wrong from their wrongdoing." (2 Pet. 2:13.) A woman with wrong reactions toward life said to me: "I have been beating my own body by my spirit." The spirit punished itself and the body. Sin and its punishment are one and the same thing. Everybody pays the fare—pays it in his own person. So there is no escape. The man who tries to escape doesn't escape—from himself. The fare is a man he can't live with. He wouldn't live with God, so now he cannot live with himself. That is the pay-off. He has short-changed himself. A little boy of five informed his missionary mother in Manila: "Mother, you'll be glad to know that I have decided not to go to hell." Going away from God is just that—going to hell, the hell of conflict and frustration now, the beginnings of hell.

The account says: "But the Eternal flung a furious wind upon the sea; there was a heavy storm at sea, and the ship thought she would be broken." (Moffatt.) Anyone who is running away from God is headed toward a storm. No matter what happens on the outside, there is the storm within. Fears, worries, conflicts, guilts infest the heart that is trying to get away from God. There is a storm in front of every God-deserter.

O God, my Father, I know that Thou art the Home of my soul, and when I run away from Thee I run into orphanage, into loneliness, run into myself and I become my punishment. Save me. Amen.

AFFIRMATION FOR THE DAY: *All my inner storms are home-brewed.*

THE ESCAPE INTO SLEEP, DRUGS, ILLNESSES

We saw yesterday that Jonah, going away from God, was headed for a storm, within and without. The idea that you can find freedom apart from God is an illusion—sheer bunk.

When Jonah got into the storm of his own creation, he reacted psychologically as others do—he tried to escape. He retreated into unconsciousness—he went to sleep. "Now Jonah had gone below and was lying fast asleep." (Jonah 1:5, Moffatt.) He was unwilling or unable to face the consequences of what he had done, so he retreated into the only open door—unconsciousness. Some retreat out of an impossible situation into illness, some into fainting, some into negativism. They spend their lives in running away from life. A friend of mine said: "I don't like this business of riding on planes—I'm a family man, and I shouldn't risk things this way." We plunged over the Sierra Nevada mountains into a thick fog and flew completely blind—the plane had to be navigated by instruments. I glanced at my friend and saw his head was on his chest. I thought he was frightened and was praying. I looked again and saw he was fast asleep. He stayed asleep until the plane neared the runway. When he got to a really difficult place, he retreated out of his uneasiness into sleep. A junior-high-school girl was found wandering over the streets in a state of amnesia. She had an unhappy home condition where there was drinking, didn't want to go home, so retreated into forgetfulness.

Some try to escape through the dulled consciousness or unconsciousness which drink gives. It is almost invariably some unsolvable life situation that leads a man to try to escape from it through drink. Only the weak turn to it, the strong never do. Then the weak dress up this escape-mentality in the habiliments of "the he-man business." It is the reverse side of an inferiority complex. There are others who try to escape through various illnesses. One stammerer became a stammerer through not being able to meet a life situation in the home, and through not being able to keep up with a more brilliant sister. "If I were normal I could do it, but I'm not normal so I don't have to do it."

O God, my gracious Father, save me from trying to escape the consequences of my evils. Help me to come to Thee as my solution, for Thou canst forgive and release and make well. Amen.

AFFIRMATION FOR THE DAY: *Today no attempt to escape into self-pity, illnesses, or alibis.*

WE TRY PENANCES INSTEAD OF REPENTANCE

We saw yesterday that when we get into a wrong situation through our evils we try to escape. Dr. Jung says: "As soon as man was capable of conceiving the idea of sin he had recourse to psychic concealment—or to put it in analytical language, repressions arose." He adds: "We conceal it even from ourselves. It then splits off from consciousness as an independent complex to lead a separate existence in the unconscious, where it can neither be corrected nor interfered with by the conscious mind." That evil hidden in the unconscious must be discovered and confessed. "It is only with the help of confession that I am able to throw myself into the arms of humanity, freed at last from the burden of moral exile. The goal of treatment by catharsis is full confession—no mere intellectual acknowledgment of the facts, but their confirmation by the heart and the actual release of the suppressed emotions."

Whatever the way of escape, it is all futile, except one way—to throw yourself into the arms of God and man, and ask forgiveness and restoration.

But Jonah took a wrong way out again. It was the way of self-punishment. When the sailors discovered him and what he was doing, running away from God, they said: "What are we to do with you, to make the sea calm?' (for the seas were running higher and higher). 'Take me and throw me into the sea,' he said; 'that will bring a calm.'" (Jonah 1:11-12, Moffatt.) He proposes self-punishment as atonement—he was a masochist. One man went to the extreme of burning the hand that did the deed—burning it until it had to be amputated. Another scalded himself in burning hot water because of remorse over a night's carousal. The more religious lay on themselves penances. In some Latin countries the people will approach the church on their knees—knees lacerated by the ordeal. But note: penance is not repentance. Penance tries to make atonement for sin by its own suffering; repentance is sorrow for, leading to turning from. Jonah was practicing penance not repentance.

O God, our Father, we try everything except the one thing that will help us to release—full confession and repentance. Help us to find release by Thy way, for Thy way works. Amen.

AFFIRMATION FOR THE DAY: *Today I shall resist all attempts at trying to make a halfway house a home.*

A HURT EGO

We saw that Jonah practiced penance but did not repent. He was willing to go overboard, but he was not willing to go to Nineveh—willing to do everything except the one thing that would give him release. So God had to get him in a tight place before he would listen—the belly of a whale.

There he talked with God out of his tight place, and God provided an escape and a second chance. "For the second time the Eternal sent this message to Jonah: "Go to Nineveh, that great city, and proclaim there what I tell you.' So Jonah arose and went to Nineveh, as the Eternal ordered." (Jonah 3:1-3, Moffatt.) He went outwardly, but not inwardly. It was not a real conversion. He went but went grumpily. The repentance was a repentance because of circumstances, not from attitudes. He was Jonah still—the inward runaway, while outwardly conforming. He went, and yet he didn't.

He goes and says something which God apparently did not tell him to say: "Forty days more and Nineveh falls!" he shouted. But God had only said that he was to "thunder in their ears that their wickedness is known to me." But Jonah to heighten his own importance put in a time limit—forty days—and then Nineveh falls. That inflated his unsurrendered ego.

Then he "went outside of the city, . . . where he made a hut for himself and sat down under it in the shade, to see what would happen to the city." (Jonah 4:5, Moffatt.) He was not full of compassion for the people, but wanted to see how his word would come out, whether he would be vindicated or not. He wanted a vindication of himself and not the salvation of the people under the sentence of doom. He was egocentric still, even in his preaching and in the after-attitudes. He was a masochist toward himself and a sadist toward others. He was still running away from God even when apparently obeying him.

"But the folk of Nineveh believed God; they proclaimed a fast and put on sackcloth, from the highest to the lowest. . . . When God saw what they were doing, . . . he decided not to inflict the punishment he had said he would inflict upon them. This vexed Jonah mightily." (Jonah 3:5, 10, Moffatt.) He felt that God had let him down. He cared only for himself, not for the people.

O God, Thou art judging us in this account, for often we are more concerned over what happens to our reputation than what happens to distressed people. Give us another chance. Amen.

BLAMING EVERYBODY—EXCEPT ONESELF

We saw yesterday that when the people of Nineveh repented, God relented and that "vexed Jonah mightily." His own importance suffered—he had said that they would perish in forty days, and now they wouldn't. So he began to rationalize his running away and put all the blame on God. "Oh, Eternal One, did I not say so, when I was still at home? That is why I fled to Tartessus." (Jonah 4:1-2, Moffatt.)

A man who is running away from God always rationalizes that running away—it's somebody else's fault. The unrepentant guilty always blame everybody else—everybody except themselves. Here Jonah blames God. The same mentality of the man who hid his talent: "I knew you were a hard man, so I hid my talent"—the master was to blame, not himself. When you are blaming others, you are excusing yourself. So Jonah wants to die: "Now then, O Eternal, take my life away. Better death than life." (Jonah 4:3, Moffatt.) He is still trying to run away, to escape. Since he had not given up his basic attitudes of running away from God, he still manifests them in the crises. Whenever he gets into a jam, he wants to die. He is not only still running away, he also is still punishing himself, or proposing to do so—he wants God to take his life away. Whenever there is no sincere repentance, which means sincere reversal, then we run into all sorts of substitutes, everything except the one thing. That creates the unstable personality, which hops from subterfuge to subterfuge to get temporary relief from an inner ache—the ache of basic disobedience. The guilty are the unstable—nothing backs their way of life, so they try this and they try that. The forgiven and the obedient are the stable, for they feel that the sum total of reality is behind them. They are steady—they know just what to do—they go to God. He is the center of their stability. The outer restlessness of this modern age is the result of an inner restlessness. Modern man is trying to go every way except God's way. So he is frustrated. It is: God or frustration. And there are no exceptions. God's way works. Our ways work—ruin. Jonah wanted to die because he had never died to Jonah. His ego when hurt and peeved had no remedy except to want to die.

O God, we often try ways unworkable and tread paths with dead ends. Thou art speaking through our frustrations. Thy redemption speaks everywhere and in everything. Amen.

AFFIRMATION FOR THE DAY: *He who is always tripping over his ego is doomed for many a fall.*

JONAH—A MIGHT-HAVE-BEEN

We saw yesterday that Jonah wanted to die when in a sour mood. He said he wanted to die, doing it to spite God, as it were: "You see what you have made me do?"

Another episode showed the same unsurrendered ego. "The Eternal then made a gourd spring up to shade his head. . . . Jonah was mightily glad of the gourd." (Jonah 4:6, Moffatt.) He was "mightily glad" of the gourd that shaded *his* head, but was vexed and angry when a nation repented and was saved. He was pleased at the thing that eased the strokes of the sun, but was displeased at the salvation of a whole nation from the stroke of God's doom. Egocentric still. And when a worm gnawed the gourd and it withered and the sun beat on the head of Jonah he "longed to be dead." "Better death than life!" he cried. When faced with a situation, he still wanted to run away, wanted to die. "Are you right to be angry over the gourd?" asked God. "Yes," said Jonah, "mortally angry." (Jonah 4:9, Moffatt.) Peeved with himself, he was peeved with everybody else, including God.

Then God, according to the writer, said: "You are sorry about the gourd . . .—a gourd that sprang up in a night and perished in a night. And am I not to be sorry for . . . Nineveh, with over a hundred and twenty thousand infants, . . . and with all its cattle?" (Jonah 4:10-11, Moffatt.) It was very gracious of God to say that Jonah was sorry for the gourd that died, but in reality Jonah wasn't sorry for anything, or anybody—except himself. When the curtain goes down Jonah was still running away—in spirit. He was an immature, childish person who never grew up.

He might have gone down in history as the prophet who was the instrument of the redemption of a city. Instead he goes down in history as the man who ran away and the man who kept running away even when he was supposed to be obeying. Inwardly he had never surrendered Jonah. And Jonah becomes a byword, instead of a grateful memory—the man who might have been. His unsurrendered self got in the way at every step and in the end tripped him finally.

O God, save me from trying to run away from Thee, for I know I can only try—I really can't. For if I make my bed in hell Thou art there. Help me not to fly from Thee, but to fly into Thy arms and there be released. Amen.

AFFIRMATION FOR THE DAY: *The universe will not back my acting as though I were the center of the universe.*

FOUR WAYS TO FACE LIFE CHALLENGES

We have spent a week on Jonah, the man who ran away. We must now look at the four types of reaction given by Toynbee, the historian. When a civilization—or an individual—gets up against a problem, a life problem demanding decision, it will react in one of four ways: *(a)* archaism, *(b)* futurism, *(c)* detachment, and *(d)* transformation. The first three represent flights from reality, the fourth a facing of reality and transforming everything that comes into something else.

When we get up against a problem, we will probably take one of these four attitudes toward solution. We will try to retreat into the past, escape into the future, retreat into inner detached attitudes, or we will take hold of everything that comes, good, bad, and indifferent, and turn it into something else.

Take the first, archaism. Nations and individuals try to escape present inferiorities and frustrations by escaping into and living in the past and glorifying it. Nations often do that, especially subject nations. They have no outlet in the present, so they turn to the past and glorify it and live in it as mental compensation for a frustrated present. Until India got independence that was the prevailing mood—everything in the past was glorified, the golden age of the Vedic period was far superior to anything found in modern civilization. A Hindu professor with this left-overmentality was lecturing at our Ashram in the Himalayas. He said: "I can find the counterpart of anything in this present age in the annals of ancient India. For instance, we had injections in ancient India." That became an inner salve to a wounded national pride for being behind in many modern inventions and appliances. Another Indian remarked: "That mentality is the most dangerous thing in India today." It is. He was drawn between escape into the past and his scientific realism. It produced a split-personality—one wanting to escape through a flight into the past and the other wanting to face the present and change it. There is no escape from reality. To try to escape means only a nemesis—the nemesis of inner conflict.

O God, my Father, I am weak and I try to escape into refuges that turn into prisons. Save me from everything except the courage of spirit that faces everything and transforms everything by Thy grace. In Jesus' name. Amen.

AFFIRMATION FOR THE DAY: *I must live in the present or not live.*

ATTEMPTS AT FLIGHT INTO THE PAST AND THE FUTURE

We saw yesterday that individuals and nations try to live in the past as compensation for a frustrated present. Many families live on the borrowed capital of their illustrious ancestors: "My grandfather was so-and-so," and the face lights up momentarily in the afterglow of the reflected glory of the past. Many people are like potato vines: The best part of them is underground.

This archaism is characteristic of a sterile old age. The reason why so many old people live in the past is that they have ceased to be creative in the present. So they turn to reminiscing as mental compensation for lack of creative activity now. The old person who is creative does not turn to the past except for reference, for he belongs to the present and the future. The man who is driving a car looks into the mirror at the side to see what is behind while he forges ahead. So we must look into the past as in a mirror while we forge ahead into the present and the future. To glance at the past to learn its lessons is wisdom; to gaze at the past and to try to live in it is folly, it is worse—it is walking straight into a prison. Whole nations have done it and have died in that self-chosen prison.

The opposite of a flight into the past is a flight into the future—futurism. Perhaps there is no past to boast over and the present is frustrated, then many fly into the future and try to live there as mental compensation for not being able to produce the goods in the present. They are the grandiose dreamers who are always going to—they never do. They are the impractical dreamers who don't touch the present, for they are too busy with the future. The present is messy—the future is glorious, so they try to live in it. They live in the never-never land of projected dreams. They have no roots in the present, so they bring forth no fruits in the present—they are parasites on the present as they live in the future. But the flight from today and its problems brings its nemesis—the dreamers about tomorrow who do nothing about today invariably live in a tangled today, for they have increased its tangles.

O God, my Father I know that I must look to that future, but not look too long, so that I overlook the present. Help me to face today, today and bring out of it thy best and my best. Amen.

AFFIRMATION FOR THE DAY: *Yesterday is history, tomorrow a dream, today reality.*

HEAVEN-GAZING INSTEAD OF EARTH-CHANGING

We saw yesterday that futurism may be the life strategy of a frustrated person. This is often true of very religious persons whose religion is not functioning in the present. Take the growing groups that apparently live in the future in ardenthope of the second coming of Christ. Now I believe in the second coming groups that apparently live in the future in ardent hope of itself, and this may be one of the surprises laid up in future history. But if the hope of the second coming takes the place of endeavor to change present conditions either in the individual or society, or both, then it becomes a flight from reality, an escape mentality. Anything that picks you up mentally and spiritually and transplants you into the tomorrow and makes you live on a hope that may not materialize in your lifetime is making you live without roots in the present, which means you are rootless and, of course, if you are rootless then you are fruitless.

The angel said to the disciples: "Why do you stand looking into heaven? ... This Jesus ... will come in the same way as you saw him go into heaven." (Acts 1:11.) They were turned from heaven-gazing to earth-changing and "turned the world upside down."

There are those who rationalize all this heaven-gazing and say that no social or collective change can be brought about till Jesus comes. Why not? If individuals can be changed now why cannot collective entities be changed now? If God's power and redemption can be brought to bear upon the individual to change him, then why not upon corporate entities? Jesus blamed corporate entities for not receiving the Kingdom of God: "Woe unto you Chorazin ... Woe unto you Capernaum"—these corporate entities were guilty of not embodying the Kingdom in their corporate choices and decisions. If corporate entities could embody the Kingdom then, why not now? This saying that nothing can be done to make a new world until Jesus comes is draining off spiritual and moral energy from present-day problems. If the coming does happen, I would like it to find me working at individual and collective change.

O God, save me from any running away from my present sad world and its tasks. Give me nerve to face everything with courage and a song. Help me to be the kind of person who will be at home in any future change. Amen.

AFFIRMATION FOR THE DAY: Any attempt to escape into the future is an attempt to escape into unreality.

THE ESCAPE INTO INNER STATES

We have looked at two attempts at flight from reality—archaism and futurism, an escape into the past and an escape into the future. There is the third—Detachment.

In detachment we try, not to escape into the past or the future, but to remain in the present, detached. There are those who, afraid of reality and wanting to compensate for not going into life and its problems, build up a detached life, apart from and over against the life around them. They often nurse illusions about grandeur and difference to compensate for not being like other people and taking a part in the activities of the world around them. The child that won't play with other children but lives apart in an inner world of its own is taking the first steps into unbalance and off-centeredness and a frustrated personality. The grownup who does the same must be brought back to normal reality or else he may walk from a dream world into an institution.

When one is condemning everybody else as "stupid," he is mentally compensating for not taking part in life as a normal person. "I'm superior—these stupid people around me,"—the dream world of built-up illusions. A man who was spiritually superior, so he thought, would not take an hour in a prayer vigil, for that would make him like the common herd who kept the vigil. He must be superior by being aloof even in a prayer vigil—he could not be regimented along with the rest. As we march back keeping step from a prayer knoll at our Ashram, the individualists who try to live by detachment almost invariably break step. The detachment must be kept up.

In India this attitude of detachment has been built up into a philosophical system. This philosophical system does not really believe in the world. It is life-denying and world-denying. But they are compelled to live life and to participate in the world and its activities. So the philosophy of detachment is proposed: "Do everything, but with no inner attachment to the thing you do. Look for no reward for anything done." This is still the desire to escape—to escape from changing the world. It is defeatism.

O God, I thank Thee that Thou art leading me out of the morass of self-grandeur and leading me humbly to offer myself to be the instrument of Thy power to change people and things around me now. Amen.

AFFIRMATION FOR THE DAY: *If I attempt to escape within, I won't like my within.*

THE WAY OF TRANSFORMATION

We studied yesterday the third method of flight from reality—detachment. A Hindu said to me one day: "I live in the world, but I am completely detached from the world. I have a daughter and she thinks I love her, but I do not, for I am completely detached from such things as love." He felt that was high spirituality. It was a rationalization of an escape mentality. He was afraid of life and the world and tried to step out of it by—detachment. That brings its nemesis, for it brings conflict by its impossibility. There is no possible way to drive out the natural urges. You must use them for higher purposes.

That brings us to the last of the four ways to deal with life—transformation. Of the four this is the only workable way. By transformation we mean the facing of life as it comes day by day and transforming it into something else. Life will come to us as justice and injustice, pleasure and pain, compliment and criticism. We must be ready to take hold of it *as it comes* and make something else out of it. In that way you face life with no subterfuges, no dodging out of difficulties, no rationalization—you face life honestly and simply and masterfully.

Look at Jesus. He refused an escape into Israel's glorious past, refused to escape into the glorious future of the Kingdom of God on earth, refused to retreat into detachment as the Pharisees who were the Separatists did—He marched straight into life and took everything into His hands and made something else out of it. He took the job of a carpenter and as He made yokes and plows made Himself ready for the great mission when He would be the architect of a new humanity. He met temptation in the wilderness and made temptation strengthen Him—He transformed temptation into a tempering of His soul. He took hold of the ordinary garden variety of humanity, chose twelve uneducated men, and made them into the teachers of humanity and the transformers of the destiny of the race. He sat by a well-side with a fallen woman, led her into a new experience, and then made her an evangelist to her village. He touched everything and transformed everything. That is mastery.

O living Christ, I thank Thee that I need not run away from anything. I go forth to greet everything with a song and a song of victory. For everything has been met and mastered and transformed. Amen.

AFFIRMATION FOR THE DAY: *Transformation is my open door into reality.*

TAKING THE WORST AND TURNING IT INTO THE BEST

We look again at Jesus using the method of transformation. He was criticized for eating with publicans and sinners. Jesus took that criticism and transformed it into the three parables of the lost sheep, the lost coin, and the lost son, the most beautiful parables ever uttered, showing the heart of the seeking, redemptive God. He transformed a reviling into a revelation.

He took the ordinary facts of nature—the man sowing his seed, the fisherman casting his net, the woman kneading her dough, the shepherd attending his sheep, the man building his house, the gardener planting his vines and pruning them, the children playing in the marketplace, the merchantmen seeking pearls, the women grinding the meal, the watchman watching his goods, the man threshing his wheat—He took everything commonplace and made it uncommonplace. He glorified everything He touched, and He touched everything.

Sin put Him on a cross, and He used that Cross to save men from sin. Hate nailed Jesus and through that nailing He showed love—the hate producing love. The Cross was man at his worst, and through it Jesus shows God at His redemptive best.

Jesus transformed the world's darkest hour into the world's brightest spot. He took a tomb and made it glow with light and hope. "Light looked down and beheld Darkness: 'Thither will I go,' said Light; Peace looked down and beheld War: 'Thither will I go,' said Peace; Love looked down and beheld Hatred: 'Thither will I go,' said Love, and the Word was made flesh and dwelt among us." And as the Word was made flesh, so the flesh became Word and showed and spoke the Divine Word. Everything is different now, since He came. He transforms our dead souls, our dead hopes, even our dead—He makes everything live.

This is the very opposite of escape into the past, the future, and into detachment, for it faces all, transforms and transfigures all. The material has become the spiritual, because used for spiritual ends.

O living Christ, how can I give vent to this pent-up gratitude! If I hold it, my heart will burst. I spread it all around to everybody, everywhere that Thou art the great Transformer. Thou hast transformed me. Amen.

AFFIRMATION FOR THE DAY: *I calmly face life, knowing I can transform everything that comes.*

MAKING EVERYTHING SERVE

We were meditating yesterday on the way to meet life—transformation. Once I was speaking through an interpreter and told the story of a husband in a car, with a sliding seat in front, calling to his wife in the back seat: "Dear, please kick me forward." I said, "If life kicks you then make it kick you forward—you determine the direction." My translator put it: "If your wife kicks you, make her kick you forward." Well, if "life" or "wife" kicks you, make them kick you forward. Make everything serve you. Then you are set for victory.

Dr. Ambrose Pere, surgeon to the King of France, was the author of the famous saying: "I treated him; God cured him." This famous surgeon was once operating and ran out of oil, which was considered at that time indispensable in operations, found that the patient got well quicker without the oil and that led to its abandonment. He transformed a lack into a benefit. He used a calamity and made it into an opportunity.

"When they had called in the apostles, they beat them . . . and let them go. Then they left the presence of the council, rejoicing." (Acts 5:40-41.) Rejoicing over injustice! When you can rejoice over injustice done to you, then you are incorrigible. You have transformed the worst into the best. An incorrigibly happy Christian was arrested for preaching on the street. He put his arm through the arm of the policeman as they walked away and said: "If you love me the way I love you, then we are going to have a grand time together." The policeman didn't know what to do with such a man and let him go! My friend transformed the situation by an incorrigible spirit of good will.

It is said: "And the patriarchs, jealous of Joseph, sold him into Egypt; but God" (Acts 7:9). That phrase "but God" is at the end of every injustice—He has the last word. And just as God used the injustice done to Joseph to feed the Egyptian people and the family of Joseph, so He transforms every injustice, every sorrow, every bereavement—everything, provided we let Him. This is a working philosophy of life—and a radiant one. Christianity explains little, but transforms everything.

O Christ with this secret in my heart I face everything, assured that life can do nothing to me and I can do everything to it—I can transform it at its cruelest. I fear nothing, for I can transform all. Amen.

AFFIRMATION FOR THE DAY: *I have peace because I have adequacy.*

THE TWO APPROACHES TO LIFE

We have been looking at the ways men take to try to hold life together in poise and power when they have no faith in God. We have seen the emptiness of life without God and the consequent lack of power and poise. There are a great many who have a faith in God but it isn't an adequate, working faith. It doesn't function at the place of poise and power.

A woman wrote me in great distress: "I saw in the newspapers that a telescope was being assembled by which they would be able to tell whether there was life upon the other planets. What would happen to the Christian faith if they did? Science frightens me. It eats into my subconscious mind like a worm. I'm afraid of it." She had a faith but it could hardly be called a faith. It lacked central assurance. Discoveries on stars would upset it. To have poise and power you must be assured that the universe as a universe backs your way of life. Does it?

As we work from revelation down to life—the Christian approach—and as we work from the facts up to conclusions—the scientific approach—we come out at the same place; these two approaches to life dovetail and say the same thing. Not one single fact has been discovered in the heavens above, or in the earth beneath, or in the waters under the earth, neither in the personal, physical, economic, social, political, or international realms, to invalidate a single essential thing as it is contained in the Christian faith that centers in Jesus. Invalidate Him? The discoveries of science have done nothing but corroborate Him. For His laws are written into the nature of reality, and all the discoveries of science are but the uncovering of those laws. The Christian can stand assured and watch with breathless interest the discoveries of science, knowing that those discoveries if they go far enough will lead us to the feet of Christ. The God of nature and the God of grace are not two Gods—they are one God, and that one God is the Father of our Lord Jesus Christ. The laws of our universe, the laws of our minds, the laws of our bodies are turning out to be the laws of Christ. They fit.

O Christ, Thou art the author of my being and Thou art the finisher of it—in Thee I stand complete. Out of Thee I am in discord and disharmony. So I feel the sum total of reality behind me—in Thee. Amen.

AFFIRMATION FOR THE DAY: *"He who has the Son has life."* (I John 5:12.)

"CHRIST IS NO CANDLE—BLOW ON"

We saw yesterday that a good many have a faith, but it is a troubled faith, not serene and assured and joyous. A Hindu said to me: "I feel like committing suicide at times, for I find science undermining my faith." He might well be concerned, for what man has built up by his philosophies about life may be destroyed by man's further discoveries. But what God has revealed in Christ is the uncovering of the nature of reality. Man's discoveries won't undermine that, for it itself is the uncovering of the laws underlying reality. Is that dogmatic? Yes, but it is verified dogmatism—a dogmatism with scars on it, but radiant scars.

A headmaster of a high school in India was asked to come to my meetings, and he replied; "No, I have a satisfactory faith and I'm afraid if I come to the meetings of Stanley Jones some non-Christians may ask some questions that might upset my faith." He did not have a faith—he had a fear, labeled a faith. Someone has said: "The Church is no candle—blow on." That sounds heroic, but it is more heroic than real. The center of our faith is not the Church, for the Church is made up of very human elements and what man has built up other men may destroy. But if the statement is put: "Christ is no candle—blow on," then I can accept it with all my heart. The only perfect possession we as Christians have is Christ. He is the absolute—all else is relative, infallible and absolute, they are running into a false assurance. For when a relative thing makes itself an absolute, then that is idolatry. When a church makes itself an absolute then it doesn't contain idolatry—it is idolatry—it is idolatry by its very nature. The Church behind Christ is the best serving institution on earth, but the Church in front of Christ, obscuring Him and making itself the issue, is idolatry, pure and simple. In Christ all things hold together—in anything else they go to pieces, go to pieces under the impact of life. "Christ is no candle—blow on."

O Christ, those that blow against Thee blow themselves off the edge of things in the recoil. For when we fight against Thee, we fight against ourselves. We cannot rebel against Thee without rebelling against ourselves. Save us. Amen.

AFFIRMATION FOR THE DAY: *"He who spits against the wind spits in his own face."*

THE THREE INFALLIBLES

We saw briefly that many are lacking a sense of assurance from the center of their moral and spiritual authority. Where is the place of authority in the Christian faith? Years ago, I tried to answer that question in one of my books, but again and again the question comes up. Yesterday a Roman Catholic priest in our Ashram put it this way: "The Church produced the Bible, therefore the Church not the Bible is the place of authority." My reply was: "Christ produced both the Church and the Bible, therefore He is the place of our authority." This question of authority must be clarified.

There have been three historic answers to the question of the place of authority: *(a)* The infallible Bible. *(b)* The infallible Christian Experience. *(c)* The infallible Church. Which is it? Someone has said that reality is of two kinds: objective reality and subjective reality. Objective reality is that which takes place in history, and can be proved to a high degree of certainty. For instance, the battle of Thermopylae can be proved to a high degree of certainty from historical sources. But not the highest degree, for the battle of Thermopylae did not go through the stream of my experience. I was not there. But certain things have gone through the stream of my experience. I am sure that I am sure and I know that I know for they have gone through my consciousness and have verified themselves to me there. "He who says consciousness says science." Each of these—objective and subjective reality—can be proved to a high degree of certainty. But a higher degree of certainty would be where the objective reality and the subjective reality verify each other, say the same things.

The Christian faith has these two kinds of reality: *(a)* The objective reality—the historical revelation in Jesus, the Incarnate. *(b)* The subjective reality—the experiential fact that the Jesus of history becomes the Christ of experience, the historical becomes the experiential. What we see recorded as historical fact becomes in us, when we surrender to it, a verified experience. The Jesus of history moves within us as present fact.

O Christ, I thank Thee that I can believe in something that is past and I can find something that is present within me. They are one and speak the same things. They verify each other. I thank Thee. Amen.

AFFIRMATION FOR THE DAY: *My life is one long verification of its central hypothesis—Christ.*

THE WORLD'S GREATEST COLLECTIVE VERIFICATION

In studying yesterday the place of authority in the Christian faith we saw that in it were the two kinds of reality, the historical and the experiential, and that they dovetail, say the same thing. What Jesus was, said, and promised is verified in experience. Whenever the conditions are met, the facts of experience verify the facts of history. The two kinds of reality become one and verify each other.

If the Christian faith were only an experience not rooted in historical fact it would be subject to the vagaries of changing experience; were it only a historical fact it would be a creed about seomthing that happened long ago. It would be weak. But now the two come togehter and give a very high degree of certainty. But not the highest. For the verification of experience rests upon the individual experience. That is precarious. For the individual experience may be a hallucination. Anything that rests upon one's own individual experience alone is resting upon insufficient foundation.

But there is a third element that verifies the individual experience—the collective experience. The collective experience is what is being set forth in the infallible Church. As an infallible Church, a system, it has been infallibly fallible. But as representing a collective verification, then it is valid. The individual experience is verified by the collective experience and that collective experience stretches over all ages, through all climes, among all people. A common language arises—arises out of a common experience. It is the language of an experience of God in Christ. That language is the language of certainty. The accents differ, the language is the same. It is the most joyous, hope-filled language the planet knows. I have heard this language in every land of the world as I have traveled this planet—it is language with a lift in it, with a note of redemption from evil and a note of triumph over evil, the purest human language spoken. And that is not confined to any group or denomination. Anywhere the heart is open to Christ in simple surrender and obedience, it works. And it works with an almost mathematical precision. If collective verification has been tried and found workable, this is it.

O Christ, I thank Thee that Thou didst live long ago and Thou dost live within me—and live within me now. I'm grateful, grateful, grateful. My tongue shall sing and my heart rejoice in life's greatest gift. Amen.

AFFIRMATION FOR THE DAY: *I am a part of the world's greatest collective verification.*

A THREEFOLD CORD WHICH CANNOT BE BROKEN

We saw yesterday that the three streams come together and converge on one thing: the historical, the experiential, and the collective corroboration.

This takes out of each of the supposed infallibilities a truth and makes that truth contribute to a larger truth—final certainty. The infallible Bible contributes the fact of the historical; the infallible Christian experience contributes the fact of that historical verified in experience; the infallible Church contributes the collective verification in experience.

Where then is the place of authority? *It is at the junction where the historical passes into the experiential and where it is corroborated and corrected by the collective experience.* The three kinds of reality come together and say the same thing.

That certainty is a threefold cord that cannot be broken. It is a far higher certainty than any certainty founded on any one of the three alone. Suppose our certainty rested upon the historical alone—upon the Bible alone—then the battle would be around textual criticism and historical evidence. That often brings confusion instead of certainty. If the place of authority rested upon Christian experience alone, then questions would arise as to its validity. If the place of authority rested upon the Church alone, then that would bring up doubts as to whether any institution made up of fallible people can by any stretch of the imagination or faith be infallible. Each one of these taken by itself cannot give complete and final assurance. But all three taken together can and do give that complete and final assurance.

This then gives cosmic backing to our power and to our poise. I have something in the historical—in Jesus—that is rooted in fact not fancy; I have something in the experiential—in Christian consciousness, that speaks certainty in the depths of me; I have something in the collective—in the Church verification of my personal experience, that makes me know I am not off the track. This is It. All these coming together in corroboration give me what I need: total backing.

O historical, experiential, collective Christ, I thank Thee that in Thee, thus coming to me in this threefold way, I find certainty that seeps into the depths of my being and holds me there—holds me finally. I'm grateful. Amen.

AN INADEQUATE FAITH WILL LET US DOWN

We are studying this week the fact that a great many have faith, but not a faith which brings serenity and power.

A famous preacher on the edge of a nervous breakdown went to a psychiatrist. "You've got a philosophy of life of some kind, haven't you?" asked the psychiatrist. "Yes," said the minister, "I have." "Then, why don't you act on it?" the psychiatrist replied. The difficulty was that the famous preacher had a faith that he was holding, but it wasn't holding him—it didn't get across to him as power and poise. It was an intellectual assent to truth but it wasn't the power of the Spirit working in the depths of him.

Very often our faith is founded on an eccentricity in Christianity, and when that lets us down, then our whole spiritual life collapses with it. An outstanding professor, known for the depth of his spiritual life, collapsed when his daughter died. He had the wrong notion that medical aid is incompatible with the highest spirituality. His daughter was sinking without medical aid. In his desperation he took medical aid, but it was too late and she died. The professor blamed his lack of faith as the cause of his daughter's death. For this reason he collapsed spiritually. But his faith, sound at the center, had gathered a marginal error, namely, that faith is only faith when it works without means. That collapsed, and with it his faith.

Another prominent religious worker, at the time of retirement, lost his wife. He was very lonely because of the loss of his beloved wife and he, who had been prominent and looked up to before retirement now found himself out of everything—on the shelf. His blood pressure shot up. But organically he was sound; emotionally he was upset because of inner loneliness. His faith hadn't prepared him for this shock. There is only one sure center and that center is Christ. If we build upon Him and His approval, then we can take attention or no attention, for both are laid at His feet. That keeps us unshockable and unshakable. Nothing can hurt us.

O Christ, Thou art not only my Saviour, Thou art my center of Power and center of Poise. Things and people may come and go, Thou remainest forever. I face everything with Thy calm and Thy serenity. Amen.

AFFIRMATION FOR THE DAY: *I can take everything that comes, for I can use everything that comes.*

FORM BUT NOT A FORCE

We have been looking at those who have an inadequate faith—a faith that won't sustain life in its crises. We have just had a forest fire which raged through the mountains surrounding us here in the Himalayas. The group gathered here is a religious group, without exception. But the faith of some reacted as panic, while the faith of others reacted as poise. Some went to pieces when the fire broke out—reacted into hysteria. Some went calmly to work fighting the fire—they reacted into helpfulness. One professor afterwards lectured to us on religious faith, but it was lost on us for we had seen him react into panic when the crisis was on. His faith didn't hold his emotional depths. One's intellectual beliefs are swept away in the flood of emotion unless the Holy Spirit holds the depths steady.

There is a passage which lays bare this type of inadequate religion: "Preferring pleasure to God—for though they keep up a form of religion, they will have nothing to do with it as a force." (2 Tim. 3:4-5, Moffatt.) A form, but not a force! And the form crashes in the crisis. Too little, and too late! The Chinese have a saying: "You do not try to put out the blaze of a straw stack with a cup of water." Many do not cultivate a real faith and they are astonished that the faith does not hold them when the crisis is on. They try to put out the fires of life's crises with a cup of water. The Samoans have a proverb: "The size of the sea must determine the size of the canoe." We can't expect a Sunday-religion to function through the week of hard knocks and fateful blows. To function in the crisis our faith must be cultimated in the non-crisis days.

Kagawa testifies: "When bullies grabbed me by the collar, prepared to beat me black and blue, I quietly looked at them right in the eye without any sense of fear, resentment, or anger, prayed to God for their forgiveness. Under that cool, calm gaze they soon broke, and walked away muttering: 'It isn't worth the trouble to kill such a fellow.' Again and again this has been my experience." The hours spent in prayer now paid dividends.

O Christ, I know that if I abide in Thee day by day, nothing can upset me in the crisis. For Thou wilt hold the depths and they will remain serene and untouched. I thank Thee for this glorious holding. Amen.

AFFIRMATION FOR THE DAY: *When I cultivate the customary, then I shall be ready for the crisis.*

"I AM UNABLE TO STAND MYSELF A MINUTE LONGER"

We have been studying why people have a faith, but an inadequate faith. The reason usually is that the self has not been surrendered to God. We give up everything, except the last thing—the self.

In the Indian Aluminum Company there are electrical appliances into which so much intelligence has been put that if anything goes wrong a red light is flashed and a sign tells what is wrong! If the human interior worked that way, many an upset interior would put out the red light and the sign would say: "Unsurrendered self." The fact is that the signs are put out. You can see them in the face—an unsurrendered self always brings a clouded, conflict-filled face. Only when you get yourself off your hands into the hands of God does the face light up with lines gone—only then does radiancy reign.

A young woman said: "I have become tired of living within myself. I am so fearful and uneasy that I am unable to stand myself a minute longer. I want all of myself to be submerged in God. There have been so many resentments, annoyances with life and people that it is a blessed feeling to be able to turn them over to God." "I am unable to stand myself a minute longer!" A self on one's own hands is a conflict. A self turned over to God is a contribution. The self centered on itself is off center, for its center is God. Hence there can be no poise or power while on that center. As long as life and people are patting you on the back, you are on top of the world. But when they cease to do so, you are in the dumps. The self is a demanding self instead of a dedicated self. And a demanding self is an unhappy, unadjusted self.

Someone wrote: "I don't know enough about myself to surrender myself." The answer is that you don't have to know everything about yourself to surrender yourself. All you need to know is that you need to change masters—and do it. And don't surrender your problem and withhold yourself—surrender yourself and the problem will vanish. For almost all our problems are rooted in an unsurrendered self. Get yourself onto the hands of God and your problems will be off your hands.

O God, I know that my problem is myself. Therefore I surrender it to Thee. I consent for Thee to be Master, not I. From this time on I listen to Thee instead of to a demanding self. Amen.

AFFIRMATION FOR THE DAY: *I am a problem or a possibility, according to who has me.*

"I USED HIM—FOR MY PURPOSES"

Yesterday we talked about not merely surrendering our problems, but surrendering ourselves, the real basis of our problems, as well.

A highly intelligent woman became resentful over her husband's spending so much time with the Boy Scouts. They had a new home, but he didn't take time to paint and varnish and fix things. That made her resentments rise. Then one of the boys threw an apple through the window, and it squashed on the pink wall paper. She left it there for her husband to see what his scalawags had done! She woke up one night with pain from head to foot and a temperature of 101 degrees. The doctor said it was rheumatoid arthritis. She asked him if Stanley Jones was right about the possibility of resentments producing a thing like that. "Yes," said the doctor, "it can upset the secretion of glands and thus it can upset everything." She surrendered her resentments to God and was well in two weeks. She was a Christian worker. But she had really never surrendered herself. So she said: "I had God, but God didn't have me. I used Him, for my purposes." Then she saw the need of this deeper surrender of herself. She did so and was freed—freed from her central bondage to herself.

Some people in order to get attention to themselves retreat into illness. A grandmother became ill, went to bed, and liked the attention she received, began to be a permanent invalid. She was an invalid for many years, couldn't get up or walk. Then one day a grandchild's clothes caught fire; no one else was in the house, so she jumped out of bed, put out the fire, and never went back to bed as an invalid.

A similar case was that of a woman who was an invalid for fifteen years. The house caught fire. She ran out. She is now doing her own house work and is well!

When these people turned their attention away from themselves, they were well. A self-centered person is sick or on his way to sickness. The tyranny of self-attention must be broken. Self-surrender to God breaks that self-attention and gives you a God-attention.

O God, I am not at home with myself until the self finds its home in Thee. So help me today to find in Thee my permanent Home by a permanent self-surrender. Then I shall be free—free from myself. Amen.

AFFIRMATION FOR THE DAY: *Today my attention shall be, not on my sicknesses, but on my Savior.*

SHOCKED BACK INTO LIFE

The self-centered person has often to be shocked from a self-center to a God-center. That is one reason why conversion is accompanied often by high emotion. It takes high emotion to sweep us from one life-center to another.

The amusing but true story is told of a wife who was dying. The doctor saw nothing that would save her except a shock back to life. For she didn't have the will to live. She kept saying, "I'm going to die," and rather unconsciously enjoyed being the subject of such solicitous and desperate attention. So, in agreement with the doctor, the husband said: "Well, Mandy, it's too bad that you are going to die. I'll have to accept it. And I think when you are gone I'll marry the hired girl." She sat up. "No, you won't. She's too fast now." She got up and lived—shocked back to life!

Electric shocks for mental patients are used to break up old patterns and form new ones. A moral and spiritual crisis leading to self-surrender is a similar process—it breaks up the old patterns of self-centeredness and shifts one to a new center: God. Life then begins to organize itself around a new pattern. The organization of life around a new pattern is conversion, a new birth. It is healing to find a center of life outside yourself, provided that center be God. But even to love someone outside oneself tends toward healing. Dr. Edward Glover of London has laid down four things as the criteria for normalcy: *(a)* free of symptoms, *(b)* unhampered by mental conflict, *(c)* having a satisfactory working capacity, and *(d)* being able to love someone other than himself.

This last is good, but not good enough, for the capacity to love another may have within it a great deal of self-interest, so it is only partly healing. The capacity to love God means a capacity for the purest kind of love, where self-interest is lost in the God-interest. And incidentally found! So surrender to God, which is the necessary condition for love to God (for there is no love without surrender) is the greatest co-ordinating power known. But both Christianity and psychology insist that for health you have to get beyond yourself, and both say love is the way to get released from yourself.

O God, I thank Thee that Thou art lovable. In Jesus I have seen a God who draws my heart at once and forever. In Jesus I cannot but love Thee. So I open my heart wide—take me. Amen.

AFFIRMATION FOR THE DAY: *I love myself in God.*

"I'M ALWAYS SOMEBODY IMPORTANT"

You can love yourself, provided you love yourself in God. But if you love yourself in yourself, then your love is a self-centered love and hence a poisonous love. A little girl said: "My dreams all come out the same way—I'm always somebody important." Her dreams were the uncovering of her subconscious mind. In her subconscious she always wanted to be somebody important—to be at the center of things. She pushed it down during the day, for she saw it brought conflict with others who also wanted to be important. But during the night the lid was taken off and the subconscious mind let the self out and it reigned—in a dream.

Now to sit on an unsurrendered self all the time is to live in a perpetual conflict. A tension is set up between the faith we hold which demands self-abrogation and the subconscious mind which demands self-adoration. So a rough-and-tumble fight sets in. Life is a struggle with the self. So many get sick and tired of themselves and the constant struggle. A little boy got lost in a department store; the mother frantically had his name announced over the loud-speaking system. For hours there was no trace of him. Finally he was found behind a counter watching a woman demonstrating something. When his mother found him, he was completely lost in absorption in the demonstration. The next day she saw him out in the garden, going behind one bush after another and pausing in a kind of absorption with something. His mother called him and asked him what he was doing, and he replied: "Mother, I had such a good time yesterday when I lost myself, that I was trying to lose myself again." That is what people are trying to do when they turn to liquor, get absorbed in movies, in anything that diverts the self and makes them forget themselves. But this is all temporary. As soon as the diversion is over, the self is back on one's hands again. It is a temporary vacation from one's self. But the vacation is soon over and the old conflict or boredom begins again. Only by a self-surrender to God do you get your self off your hands, and then there is permanent release. You are not sitting on a lid, you are at home with yourself because the self has found its home—God.

O God, my Father, I know my Homeland—it is in Thee. There I find myself and love myself and enjoy myself. But myself anywhere else is in an alien land, uneasy and unhappy. I yield myself to Thee. Amen.

AFFIRMATION FOR THE DAY: *I love myself in God; I hate myself in myself.*

TIMES OF STRESS

We have been studying how an unsurrendered self upsets poise and saps power. This verse describes the situation: "There will come times of stress. For men will be lovers of self, lovers of money, proud, arrogant, abusive, disobedient to their parents, ungrateful, unholy, inhuman, implacable, slanderers, profligates, fierce, haters of good, treacherous, reckless, swollen with conceit, lovers of pleasure rather than lovers of God, holding a form of religion but denying the power of it." (2 Tim. 3:2-5.)

This is a sickening description of moral decay. But where did it all begin? At the first item: "For men will be lovers of self." That is the root-evil—self-love; all else is fruit-evil. If the self is out of place, all else is out of place. Get the wrong thing on the throne, and the kingdom of man-soul will be chaos. The self is made primarily for obedience to something beyond itself and when it obeys that law it reigns. But when it disobeys that law and makes itself central, it doesn't reign, it ruins. Self rule is self ruin.

Now note: "There will be times of stress. For men will be lovers of self." The "times of stress" are a direct result of being "lovers of self"—note the "for." Anyone who is primarily a lover of self is at strain with himself—he is under "stress" and his time of life is a "time of stress." He is perpetually in inner turmoil. He is sitting on a lid. But the one who loves God supremely is not sitting on a lid—he has a self at home with itself.

Now note further: This list of things is concerning a people who are religious: "holding a form of religion but denying the power of it." The religion isn't potent enough to bring self-surrender, hence all these things come as a result of that central failure. If we are not saved from self-centeredness, we are saved from nothing. The "power" of our faith is found in its power to induce you to offer yourself to God. Whether your religion is a form or a force depends on its power to produce self-surrender. Live a life of surrender or a life of stress—there are no alternatives.

O God, I would let down this central "stress," which wears me down and wears me out, by turning myself over to Thee and doing it completely and forever. I know when you have me you have my "stress" too. In Jesus' name. Amen.

AFFIRMATION FOR THE DAY: *Today there be no stresses within, for there is nothing there that is not Thine.*

POSSIBLE ATTITUDES TOWARD SELF

We continue our meditation on the block to power and poise which an unsurrendered self produces. There are these attitudes we can take toward ourselves: *(a)* deny yourself, *(b)* decorate yourself, *(c)* deify yourself, *(d)* deceive yourself, *(e)* divide yourself, *(f)* dedicate yourself.

First, you can *deny yourself.* You can "deny" yourself in the sense of saying your self does not exist—only God exists. This is the method of monism. It begins with an initial exultation, since you have released yourself from yourself by denying that the self really exists—only God exists. But this is a verbal release and the facts close in on you and upset your verbal dreamland. You are not God, nor a part of God—you are you, created by God in His likeness, but you are still you.

Again, you can "deny" yourself in the sense of putting brakes on yourself and holding yourself under control. But this upsets your poise. A suppressed self is an unhappy self. It is straining at a leash, always hoping for its own freedom. For it is made for freedom.

Second, you can *decorate yourself.* You can make yourself presentable to yourself—and others. You can dress it up in apparently altruistic garments; you do so many things for others. But down underneath that altruism is the same old self making itself presentable through that altruism, but still there bidding for attention. That does not bring either power or poise, for it sets up an inner conflict with oneself over motives. That brings strain.

Third, *deify yourself.* You can frankly and without apology make yourself central and absolute. For awhile you can get away with it. You can go far with this uninhibited self. It can drive you to success and power, of a kind, for awhile. But only for awhile. The pay-off comes. You will find your success and your power a Dead Sea fruit. A proud, self-assertive man is not punished outwardly—he is punished inwardly. His pay-off is himself. He has himself, and now he doesn't like himself, but he has to live with himself. To have to live with a self you don't like is hell. When you make yourself god, then the devotee despises the god he has set up.

O God, my Father, I know that I am dissatisfied and unhappy until I find Thy way and walk in it. Give me courage to turn around where I've missed the way and come to Thy way. Amen.

AFFIRMATION FOR THE DAY: *I shall carry a heaven or a hell within me today, according to who has my self.*

"THE TROUBLE WITH ME IS . . ."

We continue our study of the possible attitudes toward oneself.

Fourth, *deceive yourself.* You can press the self down into the subconscious mind and put the lid on it and say to yourself that it isn't there. You can be honestly deceived. Your conscious motives may be clear—and good. And yet the unconscious determines the actions. How can we know this? "By their fruits ye shall know them." If in spite of the apparently clear motives there is inner strain and stress, then the chances are that in the subconscious there is conflict—a suppressed self wanting expression, getting it only in self-deception.

Fifth, you can *divide yourself.* You can frankly try to live in two compartments—a "Dr. Jekyll and Mr. Hyde" type of life. You will try to serve two masters and get the most out of both. You will try to be religious and get its consolations and try to be worldly and get the "kicks" such life can give. But those "kicks" will only produce kickbacks. For you won't be able to enjoy the "kicks" of a worldly life or the consolations of a spiritual life. They will cancel out each other. Jesus pronounced the doom of this type of living: "A house divided against itself cannot stand." Simply "cannot" stand.

Sixth, you can *dedicate yourself.* That is the answer, for it fulfills the first law of our being—lose yourself that you might find yourself. There died not long ago an apparently successful woman publisher, Eleanor Medill Patterson, who said of herself: "I just cannot have friends for more than six months. I have to drink because I have to forget all the mean things I have done." That is the pay-off of a life dedicated to herself and to resentments. The moral universe simply did not approve of her and her vain resentments. So it broke her.

But the universe will back you and bless you and further you if you and your powers are dedicated to God. You then have the sense center of all things: God. With the one point of your compass fixed at the Center then the other point can sweep the universe and take in all. For it all belongs to you, for you belong to God. You know how to live.

O God, my Father, I come to Thee to do the one thing I know I must do before I can be at home in this universe—I come to put myself where it ought to be: at Thy feet, forever Thine. Now I'm free—in Thee—and in myself! Amen.

AFFIRMATION FOR THE DAY: *My center is in God, my circumference everywhere.*

"DON'T LET RATS EAT YOUR HARP STRINGS"

We now turn to twin enemies of power and poise—*fear and worry*.

The Africans have much wisdom distilled into proverbs: "Don't be tired tomorrow." "The full-bellied child says to the empty-bellied child: 'Be of good cheer.'?" "Any fool can tell how many apples are on a tree, but it takes a wise man to tell how many trees are in an apple." "Don't let rats eat your harp strings." It is to this last proverb we now turn: Don't let the rats of fear and worry eat your harp strings—take away your music. They are taking away the music of many—all who allow them lodgment in the heart.

Before we look at this type of fear we must look at beneficent fear. For fear is of two kinds: efficient fear and inefficient fear. Says Smiley Blanton: "To fear unwisely is destructive, but to fear wisely is the best of mental hygiene." The driver who has no fear of breaking the rules of the road is an unsafe driver. The pilot who has no fear of the laws that underlie flying will end in a crash. The surgeon who has no fear of cutting into the wrong places is a dangerour person. A druggist who has no fear of giving the wrong drugs is a liability. In each case a healthy fear makes them efficient. Edmund Burke said: "Early and provident fear is the mother of safety." Hatfield puts it thus: "The normal fear leads to efficiency, whereas the abnormal fear leads to inefficiency."

Perhaps this would clarify the matter: *Natural fears* are fears directed to objects dangerous to life. *Anxieties* are fears without an object and are usually due to a threatening impulse within. They are unrecognized fears of ourselves. *Phobias* are fears attached to objects not in themselves dangerous.

In discussing fears it is important to remember that many people who outwardly put on an apparently brave front are filled with fears. They seem poised, but back of the facade, fear is eating at the harp strings. It is not merely the jumpy, nervous type that may be infected with fear—the calm, sedate type may have deep-rooted fears.

O Father God, as I begin this quest for a life free from fear, take away the fear of not finding it. Give me the calm confidence that I shall arrive—arrive at a life completely free from fear and worry and anxiety. In Jesus' name. Amen.

AFFIRMATION FOR THE DAY: *No fear of failure shall deter me in my conquest of fear.*

"DIED OF FEAR"

We are more and more clear about the possibility of passing on the sickness of the mind and the soul to the body and vice versa. Sometimes the body is sick and passes on its sicknesses to the mind and soul. And sometimes the soul and mind get sick and pass on their sicknesses to the body. You cannot touch one without touching all three. There was a time when we tried to divide them—tried to pass the body over to the doctor, the mind to the psychiatrist, and the soul to the minister to take care of. But that division is outmoded.

Some of our symptoms come out of the structural and some out of the functional. Dr. Slaughter says: "These crises in physical symptoms usually coincide with crises in emotional tension. Minor earthquakes of acute mental states shake out the old fears, guilt and resentment from the unconscious and allow them to play upon the sensitive lining of the stomach. . . . Business reverses, disappointment in love, perhaps even the failure to win a golf game—any one may cause the whole flimsy house of cards to topple."

Imagination nearly killed Rex. He applied to a druggist for a vial of poison, and his actions aroused the suspicion that he intended to take his life. The druggist gave him a harmless fluid. Rex wrote a farewell letter to his wife and took the fluid. A few minutes later he was suffering all the agonies of poisoning. He was rushed to a hospital. It took a week to recover from the shock.

A doctor told me they performed an autopsy over a man and found no physical cause of death, and then added: "If we had been honest, we would have put on the death certificate, 'Died of Fear.'" There is not an organ of the body, not a blood vessel, nerve, or tissue that cannot be profoundly affected for good or ill by emotional states. And the effects produced are not imaginary—they are real. Do not tell a sufferer that his pains are imaginary—he knows they are not, they are real. But the cause is not in the organs themselves but in the mental and spiritual states of the person.

O Father, I know that I am one and must be dealt with as one. Then give me a general overhauling. Put Thy finger on me here and there and tell me where I am ailing, for I would be whole, perfectly whole, at Thy best. Amen.

AFFIRMATION FOR THE DAY: *I have nothing to fear except fear.*

219

EMOTIONAL STATES AND FUNCTIONAL DISEASE

Dr. William C. Menninger says: "If you get scared, your blood pressure goes up and stays up, without any apparent cause. Anxiety can cause all sorts of more serious physical symptoms without any organic reason for disease. . . . One-third—possibly one-half—of those who suffer from heart trouble have nothing wrong with their hearts."

The reactions to life produce functional disturbance in the one reacting. For if you react in anger, in resentment, in jealousy or fear, these states will register themselves as functional disturbance in the organs, the tissues, the nerves, the blood vessels, and the skin. The American Medical Association says that the proportion of diseases rooted in the mental and spiritual and those rooted in the physical is about fifty-fifty. Some would say it is higher for the mental and spiritual—up to 85 per cent. One doctor said that the effects of the mental and spiritual are to be found in 100 per cent of cases even where the disease was originally rooted in the structural. If wrong mental and spiritual attitudes are taken, then the disease is augmented or recovery retarded.

Psychologists have shown that the digestive tract is one of the first affected by emotions of fear and hate.

"Peptic ulcers," says Dr. Slaughter, "are practically always a result of prolonged emotional tension. . . . In patients with ulcer, resentment and anger caused increased secretion of highly acid gastric juice, marked increase in stomach contractions and a general increase of the flow of blood through the mucous membrane lining of the stomach and duodenum. These changes are called respectively 'hypersecretion' and 'hyperacidity.' . . . Much of the mucous layer was seen to be washed away when increased acid secretion occurred from emotional causes."

Doctors have been slow to admit that emotional states such as prolonged fear and anger can produce actual structural disease. But psychosomatic medicine has now proved this as scientific fact. The evidence is overwhelming. For instance, attacks of mucous colitis are determined by obvious emotional disturbances in 85 per cent of cases, so we are told by expert authority.

O God, my Father, Thy laws are written in the pages of the Book. They are also written in me—in my organs, in my tissues, in my blood. Since they are so inescapable, help me to obey them and be whole. Amen.

AFFIRMATION FOR THE DAY: *If I am ill, the question probably is, not, "What am I eating?" but, "What is eating me?"*

WHEN HEART DISEASE IS NOT HEART DISEASE

We continue to look at the effects of emotional states upon the body. We have been considering the fact that emotional states register first of all in the digestive tract. They register either as diarrhea or constipation. If the emotion produces a tied-up inner condition then the result is constipation. If it produces a let-go panic then the result is diarrhea. In both cases the result of emotion.

The next place where wrong emotional states register themselves is the heart. It is estimated that 5,000,000 people in America have all the symptoms of heart disease and yet have perfectly normal hearts. One doctor says: "Most patients who come to the doctor complaining of pain in the heart do not have heart disease."

A woman lay dying of heart disease apparently with all the outward symptoms of heart disease—weakness, stabbing pain over the heart, palpitations, short breath. Five prominent heart specialists had examined her, and each said the heart was in perfect condition. This emotional history was revealed: spoiled childhood, unhappy marriage, husband unfaithful, a terrifying fear of divorce. The doctor read the riot act to the husband, the whole matter patched up. There was no more heart disease.

A Kansas City woman remarried, and her heart attacks began soon after her second marriage. Under hypnosis she confided to her doctor: "This marriage is too good to last. My new husband will be killed too." Still under hypnosis she was told that her second husband would outlive her. She woke up, announced: "I feel as if the biggest load was off my shoulders." She hasn't had a heart attack since.

A professor was afraid he wouldn't finish his lifework. He was in a cold sweat over how long it took him to shave. Everything seemed to press on him. The doctor told him to "go to the graveyard and get acquainted with the men there and remember that they didn't finish their lifework, either. Nobody ever does, you know." In a month the professor's heart symptoms disappeared. A soldier with an "irritable heart" caused by emotional conflict said: "My heart flutters like a chicken taken by the legs."

O God, my Father, Thy secrets are hid deep within me. Thou art letting me discover them. Thou art telling me how to live—telling me from Scripture and from my body. Amen.

AFFIRMATION FOR THE DAY: *"In nothing be anxious."*

"ALMOST AFRAID TO BREATHE"

We saw yesterday that emotional states can affect the heart and cause functional disturbance, even disease. "Fear, which is the fundamental emotion from which anxiety springs, has been shown to cause actual changes in the electrocardiograph. Patients examined before a dreaded operation often appear to have coronary artery damage, but the signs disappear when the operation is over. . . . Even so a well-sedated person dies on the operating table, probably from the effect of fear in the heart."

A man was accidently shut into a refrigerator. He knocked, no response. He wrote on the wall: "I am getting colder and colder." "I am passing out." The next morning they found him dead. The temperature was only 56 degrees and there was plenty of air. Fear killed him.

There is the mother who always has a severe "heart attack" when the affections of a son or a daughter seem liable to be captured by someone else. "The fear of the loss of affection and security upset the heart. The death of a loved one, disappointment in love or social ambition, or the shock of induction into the armed forces often produce heart symptoms in perfectly good hearts. They are not heart attacks but neurotic anxiety reactions. They often produce the full-blown picture of the anxious, helpless invalid, afraid to lift a hand, almost afraid to breathe, surrounded by the adoring and pitying family who have become entirely enslaved by this pseudo illness. She is sacrificing the happiness of the entire family on the altar of neurosis. Heart neurotics do not always give up the security of their symptoms easily, particularly if there is much to be gained from illness."

Closely related to heart symptoms caused by wrong reactions to life is high blood pressure. This is said to be the single greatest medical problem in the world today. Half the people who die past fifty are killed by some form of hypertensive disease. The disturbances of blood pressure are closely related to emotional life. Anxiety, fear, and other emotional turmoil reduce the blood flow through the kidneys. Emotional tension, discharged into the circulatory system, can result in high blood pressure. Emotion produces motion.

O Calm Christ, calm me within. Take from me everything that upsets the rhythm of my body. Give me Thy poise, Thy calm, Thy peace, and give it to me now. For without it I succumb to the unrest around me. Amen.

AFFIRMATION FOR THE DAY: *"What time I am afraid I will trust in Thee."* (Ps. 56:3.)

PILLOWS WE PUT UNDER OURSELVES

We finished yesterday by noting the effect of emotional up-sets on blood pressure. We are told that hypertensive patients seem always to be in conflict with authority. They attempt to handle their resentments against it by appeasement, particularly trying to avoid criticism. They may also be driven by amtition to excel, and when the ambition is thwarted then frustration sets in, followed by high blood pressure.

We note another manifestation of wrong emotional reac-tions—diabetes. Not all diabetes is caused by emotion, but as one doctor puts it: "Diabetes is largely influenced in its course by emotions." The increase in the disease from year to year exceeds the annual increase in the population. Dr. Eliot P. Joslin, world-famous diabetic expert, says that two and a half million Americans will have diabetes before they die. Many di-abetic patients have a long series of deprivations, fatigue weariness, and a sense of depression and hopelessness. One thing that characterizes the diabetic group is "unsettledness." In themselves they are rather self-centered, mixing poorly socially and bemoaning their fate most of the time.

Asthma victims have long realized that their trouble is often made worse by emotional tension. Allergy, the real cause of asthma, often lies within the emotional life of the sufferer. A missionary suffering from asthma was about to be sent by the doctors to a warmer climate when it was discovered that these attacks of asthma always came when he was up against a problem which he could not solve. He always developed asthma—as a way out: "If I were well, I could do it, but you see I am not well, so I do not have to do it. I'm excused." Asthma was an alibi.

One patient was allergic to roses and had an attack of asthma whenever she came near them. She had an attack when presented with paper roses. A man who regularly had an attack at five in the afternoon, failed to notice the time until seven, then forthwith had an attack. Asthma for the asking.

O God, I thank Thee that in Thee I breathe and breathe freely. Out of Thee I am out of my native air so I breathe with difficulty. Help me to be at home in Thee. For I would be free—free of all symptoms. Amen.

AFFIRMATION FOR THE DAY:
   "Peace, perfect peace, in this dark world of sin?
   The blood of Jesus whispers peace within."

THE CONNECTION BETWEEN WRONG EMOTIONS AND DISEASE

We continue our study of the effects of emotions on the body. Many people suffer from headaches which are caused by emotional conflict. Often a mother will develop a headache when her apron-strong daughter wants to go out with a possible suitor.

A lady told me that for years she suffered severely from migraine headaches. She now sees that it was always when she couldn't get her way in a situation. She surrendered herself to God, and she hasn't had a headache in ten years.

We are told that the brain itself is practically insensitive to pain. So if there is a headache it is not the brain aching—it is the upset nerves leading to the brain. These nerves are very often upset by wrong attitudes toward life. Dr. Alvarez states that tense neck muscles are a sign of the neurotic, perhaps as definite as the deep sighing intake of breath. Many migraine attacks come as a result of not wanting to go to work on Monday morning, of having a disturbed conscience from Saturday night excesses, from general reluctance to face life.

This case comes from India: A woman bore her husband three daughters, but no sons. Reluctantly she consented to a second wife that a son might be obtained. The second wife bore two sons. But when the third son came she became jealous and upset. She went to a temple and paid the priest to lay a curse on this second wife in the form of a skin disease. The husband found it out and went to the temple and paid the priest to lift the curse. The first wife thought he had transferred the curse to her, and forthwith developed a skin disease. The husband assured her that he had not transferred it to her, that he had only lifted it from the second wife. It was of no avail. The first wife died of the skin disease. Her wrong ideas produced wrong emotions, which in turn produced disease, and killed her.

We have spent this week in looking at the fact that disrupted emotions can produce disrupted bodies. We must now turn to the more pleasant fact that right emotions can produce health and harmony in the body. That is good news.

O God, my Father, I look to Thee to help me to look away from myself to Thee, for Thou art Health and Life and Joy. Give me release from myself by self-surrender and help me to be at Thy best for me. Amen.

AFFIRMATION FOR THE DAY:
"Peace, perfect peace, with loved ones far away?
In Jesus' keeping we are safe, and they."

THINKING SYMPTOMS INTO BEING

We studied last week the effects of wrong attitudes on the body. Two most startling cases come from America and from India. Human nature is the same the world around.

A woman wanted a baby so badly that she convinced herself that she was pregnant and produced all the signs of pregnancy—distended abdomen and all. The doctors examined her under an X ray and found she was not pregnant. The woman insisted she was, went off to another city, found an unwanted baby in a hospital left there by an unmarried mother and adopted it. She then brought it back to her own city and triumphantly showed the baby to prove that she was right.

The Indian woman wanted a baby so much that she too produced all the signs of pregnancy—distended abdomen and all. The missionary doctor put her under an anesthetic to examine her. Under the the anesthetic the abdomen flattened out to normal. When the thought pressure was removed by the anesthetic, then the symptoms disappeared.

Obviously, we cannot be healthy unless our emotions are healthy. And we cannot be healthy if our thought life is controlled by wrong emotions. So fear and worry can throw disruption into the whole physical organism. They can make the body function badly and that wrong functioning can pass into structural disease. And the disease isn't imaginary—it is a fact, but caused by wrong mental and spiritual attitudes.

Here is a missionary doctor, who gave me her story. She went to a crystal-gazer as a young women. The crystal-gazer in telling her fortune gave some beautiful things that were going to happen and then drew back obviously upset, and refused to tell her what she saw. Then imagination began to play. When the doctor married, came to India, and the first baby was to arrive, she began to fear that this was the time for the calamity to strike. She became more and more fearful. The baby was born dead, killed by fear. Then she surrendered herself and her fears to God. The second baby came normally and beautifully. She is today a radiant, outgoing, creative person. But fear had shadowed her life and killed her baby.

O God, Thou art wanting to lift me from fear to faith, from disease to wholeness. Take me and cleanse me from all lingering fear and make me well—even to my depths. For I am afraid of fear. Deliver me. Amen.

AFFIRMATION FOR THE DAY: *I make my thoughts, and then my thoughts make me.*

FEAR DISPOSES TO INFECTIONS

We continue our study of fear and anxiety. The body works well under faith, works badly under fear and anxiety. Dr. William Sadler says that "mental work never kills. Mental work plus worry is highly destructive to strength of brain and health of body. Faith is a material aid in resisting most infectious diseases. Fear predisposes its victims to infections." Those who fear a disease most are most likely to catch it.

In our Ashram at Sat Tal, India, one of the members opened a bookcase and found the bees had made a hive of it; frightened she slammed the door and fled and was stung by the pursuing bees. Then one of the other members walked up to the hive and calmly took out the books one by one with bees crawling all over his face and hands, but he was not stung once. His quiet confidence was his protection. In the first case fear produced the thing feared. "The thing that I feared came upon me." A woman was doing well in life and then came the fear of getting ill and consequently of not being able to put her son through college. This fear became so real that she fell ill—fell ill through the very fear itself. Now she has shaken off that fear and is well.

It has been proved by careful experimentation that by concentrating the mind on one arm the surface temperature of that member can actually be raised considerably above that of the other arm. So fear can produce the very thing it fears. Many a mother engaged in nursing her infant has had her milk dried up and has been compelled to wean the child as a result of chronic fear and worry. Dr. Sadler says further: "It is a well-known fact that anger and fretting, grief and despondency are able to change the character of the mammary gland, so that the milk may become highly injurious or positively poisonous to the suckling child." Doctors say that life in New York unfits many mothers for nursing their babies—the strain and worry and fear of a great city put toxins into the milk and upset the child. "Fear, grief, worry, and fretting invariably decrease the secretion and flow of the gastric juice. Chronic worriers and despondent patients usually suffer from deficient gastric juice and slow digestion."

O God, my Father, I see that Thou hast wrought my inmost being for faith and not for fear. Forgive me that I have allowed this poison of fear and worry to get within me, and cleanse me. Amen.

AFFIRMATION FOR THE DAY: *I shall think faith, talk faith, and live faith today.*

OVERATTENTION AND FUNCTIONAL DISTURBANCES

We continue to look at unnecessary fears and their effects. A man in Bloomfield, New Jejsey, was afraid of fire, so he installed fireproof walls and floors in his house, hose and water outlets, coiled escape hatches and ladders, self-closing anti-draft doors, fire alarms on the stairs, and then decided to install a sprinkling system—just in case! He lived in a fever—an inner fire—through fear of an outer fire!

I sat in a bus about to start on a journey up the Himalaya Mountains. A doctor told me of how he always got carsick. As he talked about it he became pale, and great beads of perspiration came out on his face. Fear was producing the illness already, before we started. A man sued an automobile dealer for $30,000 because the suspense of waiting and waiting for delivery of his new car had given him stomach ulcers. A man had been seasick on board ship, and after that when he looked at a ship in the harbor he became ill again. The fear emotion produced the illness.

Doctors tell us that trachoma, a disease of the eye, is usually caused by emotional upset. Emotions block the canal and the eye doesn't get sufficient nourishment for its needs and the vision is impaired. A doctor friend of mine asked a woman: "Have you had trachoma in your family?" "Yes, father, brothers and sisters." The next day she had it! Fear produced the thing she was afraid of!

If you pay over-attention to your digestion you will probably have indigestion. Nature works well if too much attention is not paid to her. But if fear attention is given to digestion, then that fear upsets the secretions and produces the very things it fears. A woman in our Ashram was tied by fears, developed allergies, broke out in a rash, became allergic to sunlight. But she surrendered herself and her fears to God and she sat in the sunlight for two hours with no ill effects. Fear produced the allergy and the allergy produced the fear—it was a dog chasing its tail! Fear, and the thing you fear will come upon you.

O God, my Father, these fears that possess me are not Thy will and now they are not my will. For I will that they go. I relinquish them into Thy loving hands. Manage them—I can't. Amen.

AFFIRMATION FOR THE DAY: *Faith is my native air—I shall breathe it today.*

WORRY—A CYCLE OF INEFFICIENT THOUGHT

We think of stomach ulcers as a phenomenon especially prevalent among businessmen. Someone asked a farmer why he should have stomach ulcers and he replied: "Farming is big business now. Why shouldn't I have an ulcer?" The incidence of stomach ulcers goes up and down with the stock market. "Fear, worry, and anger are in themselves directly responsible for the production of 'fear toxins' which are exceedingly harmful to the human organism." Stomach ulcers have been called "the wound stripe of civilization." But the Portuguese East African natives have stomach ulcers, too, and the reason is fear of the medicine man. The stomach begins to digest itself and an ulcer is formed.

A Hindu engineer came to our Ashram in India, all tied·up— couldn't sleep. He had seen an infection on a friend, imagined it might strike him, began to worry about it, couldn't sleep from the worry and then he couldn't sleep because he was worrying over not sleeping.

Worry has been defined: "Worry is a cycle of inefficient thought whirling around a center of fear." Another definition: "Worry is a chronic process of making mountains out of molehills." "But if I don't worry, who will hold things together?" said a man to me. He was then in a sanatorium because of his worry!

A lady writes: "My sister worried about everything. She heard you on Sunday night, surrendered herself and her fears into the hands of God, and now she is quite different."

And it is not merely the women who are frustrated by fear—it is very often the "he-man" type who is infested with fears within, all the time acting the he-man stunt to cover up his fears. "This is almost an axiom in psychosomatic medicine that those suffering from the most deep-seated disturbances are much less obviously unstable in their makeup than others. Often, as in the high blood pressure, coronary heart disease and angina pectoris the conflicts are so deep that they do not appear in consciousness at all." Deep-seated fears often work in the "he-man" type making him more he-man to cover the underlying fears.

O Christ of the fearless heart, give to me Thy courage. For I want no false fronts of seeming courage covering fear—I want Thy simple courage to face anything. Deliver me and do it now. Amen.

AFFIRMATION FOR THE DAY: *If I tremble today, I shall tremble bravely.*

FOUR STEPS OUT OF FEAR

We now come to the steps for getting rid of fears and anxiety.

We take the four suggestions of Dale Carnegie: *(a)* Write down precisely what it is you are worrying about. *(b)* Write down precisely what you can do about it. *(c)* Decide what to do. *(d)* Start immediately to carry out that decision.

When you write down precisely what it is you are worrying about you will find that in the writing down about half of your fear will be seen to be baseless. When Justice Oliver Wendell Holmes was in a despondent mood through worry he found a note on his desk written by his wife: "Dear Oliver: You have lived a long time and have seen many troubles, most of which never happened."

> Some of your griefs you have cured,
> And the sharpest you still have survived,
> But what torments of grief you endured,
> From evils which never arrived.

The writing them down will often write them off. For you will find that they won't stand looking at. For instance, many fears would drop away if we simply said to ourselves: "Well, suppose the worst should come to the worst and that thing should happen to me—so what?" Nothing that can happen to you—absolutely nothing—can ever be as bad as the fear itself. There is nothing to fear except fear. You can meet everything that can happen to you, if you meet it day by day and do not let things gang up on you. Meet today today. "Therefore do not be anxious about tomorrow, for tomorrow will be anxious for itself. Let the day's own trouble be sufficient for the day." (Matt. 6:34.) That is profoundly correct. Edward Everett Hale once said: "Some people have three kinds of trouble—all they ever had, all they now have, and all they ever expect to have." Many people go bankrupt paying interest on troubles that never come. Many do come, and you can meet them as they come day by day.

In writing down precisely what you are worrying about you will find that half will dissolve into thin air—worrying about happenings that never happen, about events that never eventuate. The other half have a basis, but not so secure that they cannot be shaken off.

O Christ, I know, I know there is an answer. Thou art the answer and I know that these real fears are no longer real when I face them in Thee. For Thou canst deliver me from all fears. I know it. Amen.

AFFIRMATION FOR THE DAY: *If I worry, I weary; if I have faith, I have freshness.*

SURRENDERING OUR FEARS

We saw yesterday the firs step in getting rid of fear. The second step is: Write down precisely what you can do about it.

You can, first of all, *decide that you do not want to live with fears.* Many have not made that decision. They have lived so long with fears that they are afraid to let go of fear! A cartoon depicts a lady, the kind that enjoys talking about her troubles, saying to a psychiatrist: "All at once I stopped worrying. It worries me." It worried her to get rid of worry! A woman who had a marvelous deliverance from a fear which was upsetting her heart stood up in a meeting and said: "I have been so wonderfully delivered from my fear that I am almost afraid to be without my fear." She had lived with it so long that she missed it when it was gone. And for that reason it came back temporarily; she had not really surrendered it.

So decide that you want to get rid of fear and want to get rid of it now. Then take the next step—*surrender your fear into the hands of God.* Your fear has been in your own hands—now it is in the hands of God. He is going to deal with it with your co-operation. You and God are going to work it out *together.* Now you are not alone facing your fears—you are facing them *with God.* Say to yourself: "Now I am not alone. With God I can face anything—anything." And you will! For that sense of facing life alone will be gone and you'll be able to do things beyond your strength.

A pastor in Hiroshima, Japan, where the first atomic bomb fell, lost his home, his wife and baby—his all. He asked me to autograph his copy of *Abundant Living.* In the fly leaf he had written: "Am starting a new life back at Hiroshima where I lost my all—my all, except Christ, my last hope." He pointed out to me where his house had been and where his wife and baby had disappeared—blotted out. But he was facing the future with calm confidence.

The words "surrender" and "serenity" sound alike. They are alike—they are root and fruit. Have surrender and you have serenity. Now having surrendered your fears to God, listen to see what He will say as to how to get rid of them. Follow His direction.

O God, Thou hast the way out of my fears. I take that way. I am listening and I'm getting Thy answer and I'm ready to obey. And I'm ready now. For Thou art willing the end of my fears. Amen.

AFFIRMATION FOR THE DAY: *When people look on my face today, they shall see the outer reflection of a serene heart.*

BECOMING DECISIVE

We have seen the first and second steps in getting rid of fear. We come now to the third step: *Decide what to do.* Decision is important, for in decision the stage is reached where you go beyond *wishing* the fears to go, you *will* them to go. The moment that stage is reached—they are on the way out.

"Do the thing you fear, and the death of fear is certain," said Emerson. A woman was afraid to go out on a pier, for she was afraid of the water since she could not swim. She asked a man to go out with her. They came back, and the man told her he too could not swim. But with decision they both got through. When teaching to swim, the new method is to get the learner to put his head under water, doing the thing at once that he is afraid of doing. If you are afraid to stand up and speak, then stand up and speak! In the act of doing it strength and courage will come. If you tremble, then "tremble courageously."

The fourth step is: *Start immediately to carry out the decision.* It has been said that 50 per cent of the worries vanish the moment you have arrived at a decision, another 40 per cent vanish once you have started to carry out the decision, and that leaves only 10 per cent to be faced when you get there.

Here is a letter from a lady whom you would not expect to be a public speaker—she was a good listener: "In January 1947 I had a mental picture of a thousand people in our country hearing the message of the Kingdom made clear and beautiful as you have made it clear to me. So my prayer list was headed with this petition: 'If you see fit, Lord, let Brother Stanley make plain your plan and your love to 1000 people here.' For a year nothing happened. In January 1948 I started with the same prayer. It seemed to me I could hear the answer: 'You tell them.' I said, 'I will.' Immediately I began to get invitations to speak to various groups. I never dreamed that people would ever listen so eagerly to me. Up to today I have listed 964 people to whom I have spoken and yesterday an invitaiton came to speak to 1200 students! My fears are gone."

O Christ, I thank Thee that through Thee I can do all things. I hear Thee saying 'Fear not. I am the first and the last and the living one.' Thou art the living One, so I too am alive in Thee—and without fear. Amen.

AFFIRMATION FOR THE DAY: *"In Him who strengthens me, I am able for anything." (Phil. 4:13, Moffatt.)*

UNCONSCIOUS FEARS

We have looked at fear and anxiety as enemies to power and poise. We have looked at conscious fears, but there remains another fear to look at before we pass on to the next: unconscious fear.

Some of our fears have been dropped down into the subconscious and there the lid put down over them. In the subconscious they work against us creating a vague anxiety, the cause of which we are not aware of. We are afraid and don't know why.

Take three steps: First, get alone with God and let down the barriers of your being; take off the lid from the unconscious by relaxing and by letting come to the surface any fear that may be buried there. Don't be afraid of letting it come up, for it is only dangerous as it is suppressed. It may have come from some childhood experience where a fear has been imposed. If it comes up, offer it to God to be cleansed away. If you cannot find your way to release alone with God, then go over things with a sympathetic but wise friend. Relax in the friend's presence and tell all. Only as a last resort should you go to a psychiatrist, and then only to a Christian, for many are left worse off than ever by going to pagan psychiatrists who pick you to pieces and don't know how to put you together again in great affirmations.

The fact is that only God knows the depths. And He has provided in redemption for the redemption of the depths. When we surrender all we know, the conscious, and all we don't know, the subconscious, then the Holy Spirit will cleanse at the depths. He made them and He can remake them. He can cleanse the ego from egoism, sex from sexualism, and the herd instinct from the domination of the crowd and fasten it on the domination of the Kingdom. When these are adjusted to their God-ordained functions and place, then fears which arise from inward maladjustment drop off. They are cleansed away en masse. You will probably not have to deal with them one by one; they will just be dissolved by the inflooding of the Divine life and power. Then the greatest release that can come to a person will come to you—you will be released from a fear-infested subconscious. That is release indeed.

O Spirit of God, Thou who hast fashioned my depths, now refashion them and make them over again, minus my fears. For I cannot go through life weighted with inner fears. In Thee I am free—and free now. Amen.

AFFIRMATION FOR THE DAY: *If I sink, I sink into the love of God.*

TIED UP BY RESENTMENTS

We now turn to look at another set of enemies of power and poise—resentments, hate, and anger. If one person out of ten needs treatment for emotional upset, then fully half of these need to get rid of resentments if they are to be well.

For the inner structure of the life is made for good will, not for ill will. The moment ill will is formed in the emotions, that moment the color of the stomach will change, the gastric juices will stop, and digestion will be at an end. When you say, "He makes me sick," that is a fact, for by your reaction of resentment against him the process of digestion is upset and you are sick—literally sick. Again when you say, "He gives me a pain in the neck," that is literally true, for a tension is set up in the neck, and a pain results. Then again when you say: "He certainly is a headache," that is true, for by your reactions to the person concerned your head begins to ache with resentments. On the other hand, when you say: "You're a tonic," it means that you react favorably with appreciation and love and hence the person is a tonic, your whole being is toned up by good will. Resentments and ill will set you against the structure of the universe, and they will end in frustration and instability.

Take this girl with curvature of the spine. She grew up feeling she was of no use. She was always sick and miserable. She was resentful at her condition. Her doctor told her that this resentment was at the basis of her trouble. She confessed she was resentful, and honestly faced things. In one year she had grown four inches. She got a job in a war factory and was able to devise a labor-saving technique. Now she is happy and useful.

A girl attending to a pastor's children said: "Now I see why I didn't have any appetite. My parents were always quarreling, and in the place I worked before the family was always quarreling, too. But since coming here my appetite has come back. I'm eating normally. I feel well." The rhythm came back when the resentments went out. Resentments tie you up, good will releases you—inevitably.

O God, our Father, Thou hast made us for love in the depths, so cleanse away all hate, all resentments, all that keeps me inwardly at war with myself and everything else. Free me from my self-imposed bonds. Amen.

AFFIRMATION FOR THE DAY: *I will breathe good will, then I shall breathe better; I will think good will, then I shall think better.*

A TRANQUIL MIND IS HEALTH

We continue our study of how resentments and anger upset the total person. The vice principal of a certain college is a fighter—he is always "anti," always stirring up a row. He has stomach ulcers, and his wife has arthritis from having to live with him. He was kicking against everything—mostly himself. It all kicked back in physical upset.

A woman applied for divorce, said that every time her husband came around she broke out in hives. It was the anger and resentment that made the physical manifestation. In a certain city where I held a series of meetings a pastor chose a woman as organist for the meetings. A friend of the woman not chosen was so resentful that her friend was not chosen that she went to bed and was there for a week. The doctors could find nothing physically wrong. The wrong was in the resentments which threw functional disturbance into the system and made her ill.

The Old Testament seers saw this: "A tranquil mind is health for the body; but passion is a rot in the bones." (Prov. 14:30.) Anger registers itself in the very bones. "A loving mind makes for a healthy body," therefore love is the law of our being. Anger and resentments upset the body, and therefore they are not the law of our being.

A cultured Negro lady writes: "I shudder to think what might have happened to me had I not discovered that my self-centeredness and my supersensitiveness were undermining my physical and spiritual well-being. That first Ashram and *Abundant Living* fairly shocked me into the realization that I was emotionally and spiritually immature. And, thank God, they also convinced me that it was up to me to do something about these wrong attitudes. I was resentful of the time and attention my husband gave to his profession as a doctor and not to me. But since I've surrendered all my petty resentments, I'm proud of him and his devotion to his patients. The result is that he and I are really beginning to have a wonderful fellowship." Her resentments had resulted in a facial stroke which left her mouth twisted all out of shape. The face is now normal, for the inside is no longer twisted by resentments.

O loving God, make me loving. O peaceful God make me peaceful—within. I empty out all these ugly resentments and hates that disfigure me within and without. Sweep them all out of my heart. Amen.

AFFIRMATION FOR THE DAY: *Ugly attitudes will inevitably make me ugly.*

"SHE WAS THE PAY-OFF"

We saw how resentments twist the inside and outside all out of shape, and more—they produce disease in the twisted organs.

A doctor friend was talking to a doctor who had resentments against a local hospital which did not have to pay income tax, being a charity hospital, while he had to pay taxes on his own hospital. The result was stomach ulcers. The doctor friend said, "What you need to do is to become a Christian and give up your resentments." "Yes," said the other. "I know it. But I haven't time to attend to it." So he did have to take time to have an operation. A generation that hasn't time for God and His way to poise and power now has to take time off to go to psychiatrists, to spend endless "vacations" trying to run away from oneself, calling it "a change," when the change needed is one's attitude toward life.

This same doctor who counseled his doctor friend told me of a man who had high blood pressure and a heart affliction and hadn't done a bit of work for ten years. The doctor asked him point blank: "Against whom have you a resentment?" The man replied, "Against a nephew." The doctor got him to fix the matter up with the nephew, and as a result his blood pressure is down, his heart normal, and he is back at work, a happy man.

But there are those who chew on a resentment for years, and that resentment poisons their whole life. A friend tells of being at the home of a wealthy, but crotchety old lady, and as she was about to go to bed the old lady said: "Would you mind going down to see if the front door is locked, for I can't trust my niece, for she left the front door open once, and burglars might have entered and robbed us." That omission was 38 years before, and the old lady chewed on it for 38 years—and poisoned herself and her surroundings. One moment of quiet talk and forgiveness and the whole thing would have been cleansed away. But the catharsis never came, and the punishment was the thing itself. She lived with an ugly self for 38 years, upsetting herself and everybody around her. She was the pay-off.

O forgiving God, help me to forgive, for I know with what measure I mete, it is meted to me again. I do not want to live with a self I hate, so help me to surrender the hate that makes me hateful. Amen.

AFFIRMATION FOR THE DAY: *I shall give out love and only love to all I meet this day.*

RESENTMENTS ARE FUTILE—AND WORSE

There are those who feel that they have to hold resentments as a moral correction to a situation. A man said in one of our Ashrams: "I felt I should hold resentments as a means of correction of a situation. But I now see it is a wrong means to a right end."

A man came up to me at the close of a meeting and said: "You almost called my name when you told of a man who had divorced two wives and was in the hands of psychiatrists. For I've done just that. I thought all the time that the wives were at fault. Now I see that is is in me. I've surrendered it all to God, and now I am different." And he looked different! He had been resentful against people, because he was really resentful against himself.

A very cross old lady wouldn't let children roller-skate past her house, and was mean to them in every way possible. Then she took ill. The doctors said she couldn't recover. The children got together, pooled their pennies, and bought her one rose and sent it to her with a note of good wishes. It so moved her that she perked up, got well, was lovely to the children, gave them candy, and they became fast friends. Only good will is strong ill will is intrinsically weak.

Louis Agassiz, the great botanist, said: "I cannot waste my time in making money." How much more could it be said: "I cannot waste my time in holding resentments." It is a costly way to live, for it costs the holder far more than the object of the resentments.

John Watson MacLaren said: "What does your anxiety do? It does not empty tomorrow of its sorrow; but it does empty today of its strength." And what does your resentment do? Empties today of joy and tomorrow of its strength.

A truck driver was fined $10.00 when he did not go to a union meeting. He was so angry and resentful that on the way to the investigating committee his stomach was tied up in knots, and before night he was dead. He poisoned himself by hate.

A woman said her blood pressure was up. The doctor said it was only 180. This made her angry, and in a few minutes the blood pressure was up to 240! And had she kept the resentment it would have stayed there—a self-inflicted upset.

O Father, Thou art trying to save us from our self-inflicted pains. For Thou art love and art trying to impart Thy love to my hate-stricken heart and body. Help me to love Thee and myself by banishing all hate. Amen.

AFFIRMATION FOR THE DAY: *Hate is poison; love is food.*

BURY YOUR RESENTMENT OR IT WILL BURY YOU!

A Chinese saying: "He who is not at peace with heaven cannot be at peace with himself, and therefore he is never at peace with his neighbor." Again: "Wishing to cultivate their persons they first cultivate their own hearts." Another Chinese saying: "The superior man guards against lust in youth, quarrelsomeness in middle age, and covetousness in old age."

A doctor in China told me that he was being examined by the Japanese as a spy. He was not a spy, but had done other things for which they might have caught him. His blood pressure went up as he reacted to this fear and resentment. A teacher was given an apple-picking job—got asthma to escape the necessity. Thought she was allergic to ragweed; now she can sleep with it. She also had arthritis, and doctors told her she would be an invalid. She found resentments possessing her, surrendered them, and hasn't had arthritis since.

A man took a cow a mile against a bitter winter wind, and when he got to the barn door he fell dead of heart failure. His wife came out and found him dead with the cow standing near him, so she thought the cow had killed him. She seized a pitchfork and went after the cow in a fit of anger. She went back to her house, went to bed, an invalid, couldn't lift her arm. And there she lay, a victim of her own resentment.

A young minister had all sorts of illnesses, had his tonsils and appendix taken out, but with no effect. (Bushels of teeth, tonsils, and appendixes have been taken out of people whose emotions are causing pains and upsets. One woman was so full of abdominal pains that after the third doctor had tried to take out an appendix that wasn't there, he tatooed on her abdomen: "There is no appendix here.") Well, the young minister underwent operation after operation in a vain search for an emotional upset. Finally one doctor said: "Ministers ought to be healthy. You should give up the ministry." He did. He went to teaching and is now happy—and well. He didn't like the ministry, had an inner buried resentment against it, but felt he had a duty to stay in it. A buried resentment will hasten your own burial.

O God, my Father, Thou hast taught us to love and we teach ourselves to hate, and therefore we are at cross purposes with Thee and with ourselves. Help me to align myself with love hence with Thee and the universe. Amen.

AFFIRMATION FOR THE DAY: *"My soul is too glad and too great to be the enemy of any man."*

RESENTMENTS LEAVE A DARK BROWN TASTE

I was talking on the subject of resentments and their effects upon the human personality in India, and while I was speaking a woman went out of the audience and lay down under a tree, apparently ill. I could see her through the open window. When I remarked to a friend that I did not feel very comfortable in the thought that I was making my audience sick, the reply was: "Oh, you didn't make her sick; she is making herself sick by her resentments. She is resentful that she has to associate with women of less scholastic ability and attainments in her class. That resentment is making her ill. She is a perfect illustration of what you were talking about." The rats were eating her harp strings.

A girl who had resentments and criticism against her parents because they did not like the thing she was drawn to, namely, drama, said to me: "I've noticed that whenever I am critical and resentful it leaves a dark brown taste in my mouth." Why? For the simple reason that we are made in the very structure of our beings for love and not for hate—one leaves a dark brown taste and the other leaves a song on our lips. So when we fight against love, we are fighting against ourselves. The proverb says: "A cruel man troubleth his own body." The cruelty practiced toward others creeps within his own body as upset. The resentful person succeeds in doing nothing more than making himself resentful against himself. When we go into an emotional debauch against others, in other words, hate another, it leaves a hangover, a dark-brown taste, exactly as does a drunken bout. Both of them are an attempt to live life against itself, and both of them leave an aftermath of devastation behind.

A professor's wife was resentful over her husband's resigning his post and going to another city to work. She loved the first city and resented the second, was ill all the time she was there. She came back to the first city, got a job, and became well and happy. When she went back to see her husband, she lost her breakfast the two days she was there. Resentment upset her whole being, physically, mentally, spiritually.

O Father God, Thou knowest my needs without any signs being put out. For Thou knowest my hidden depths. Cleanse them and let me be free from all resentments and hate. For I would be free—wholly free. Amen.

AFFIRMATION FOR THE DAY: *My soul shall be no culture ground for any resentment today.*

THE CONVERSION OF THE REACTIONS

We must look at the importance which Jesus attached to reactions to what happens to us. He says: "Take heed to yourselves; if your brother sins . . . forgive him." (Luke 17:3.) The verse emphasizes the importance which the Christian Way places upon yourself—"take heed to yourselves"—for you are your own heaven or your own hell. You carry one or the other around in your own bosom. Paul said to a young minister: "Take heed to yourself and to your teaching." (1 Tim. 4:16). First to yourself, then to your teaching, for the teaching cannot rise above the teacher. For you are the teacher. Again: "Take heed to yourselves and to all the flock." (Acts 20:28.) First to yourselves, and then secondarily to the flock, for you can give nothing to the flock which is not within you.

Here Jesus says, "Take heed to yourselves; if your brother sins against you"—be careful of your reactions when your brother sins against you; don't react in resentment and hate, react in forgiveness, unlimited forgiveness. The most dangerous moment is not at the place of your actions, but of your reactions. For your actions are more deliberately chosen, but your reactions are more spontaneous and off guard. And reactions can be more deadly to the character than actions. If you react in resentment or self-pity to what happens to you, then that is just as devastating to your personality as to get drunk or to commit adultery. The younger brother in the parable committed wrong actions and the elder brother wrong reactions. He reacted into hardness of heart, unforgiveness, and resentment at the coming home of his brother. When the parable was over, the younger brother was on the inside of the father's house, and the elder brother was on the outside. The Church today is filled with people who, priding themselves that they do not act in lying, stealing, drunkenness, adultery, nevertheless react in resentment, anger, self-justification to what happens to them. They need conversion from wrong reactions in exactly the same way as others need conversion from wrong actions.

O God, I come to Thee to be saved from unchristian reactions to what happens to me. For if in my actions I am condemned, in my reactions I am also condemned. I need release from both. Amen.

AFFIRMATION FOR THE DAY: *I shall react in a Christian way to all that happens to me today.*

"LET YOUR PEACE RETURN TO YOU"

We saw yesterday that reactions are as important and as far-reaching in their results as actions. If the courts and jails and reformatories are filled with people as a result of wrong actions, then the hospitals and sanitariums are filled with people as a result of wrong reactions. But think of those who never get into these institutions, but remain in the home and office and school-room, reacting in fear, in anxiety, in resentment, in self-pity, in self-centeredness, to what happens to them—they upset their own personalities and those around them in just as devastating a way as those who commit wrong actions.

This is written in Korea, where both State and Church are being devastated by an attempt to pick out and punish the collaborators with the Japanese. It is an attempt to apply an eye for an eye and a tooth for a tooth. The result is a general entanglement. A general forgiveness would right the situation overnight, and a new era would begin.

Since revenge entangles, Jesus said: "Be careful of yourself when your brother sins against you," for if you react wrongly, then all life goes wrong with that wrong reaction. That is why religious people often need conversion as much as irreligious people. They react badly to what happens to them. When one reacts in wounded sensitivity and resentment, it throws monkey wrenches into the machinery of life as much as what is known as a moral fall. Both are bad, but the badness of the bad reaction is often covered by self-justification: "Look, what he did to me!" In both cases the personality is shattered, robbed of poise and power.

So Jesus said: "If the house is worthy, let your peace come upon it; but if it is not worthy, let your peace return to you." (Matt. 10:13.) Note: "Let your peace return to you"—do not let resentment return to you. For if you let resentment return to you, it is as bad as the action of rejecting your peace. And it is for you to decide your reaction—*"let"* your peace return to you." Open your heart to peace and forgiveness. Actions have slain their thousands, reactions have slain their tens of thousands.

O God, make me truly Christian in my reactions to life. Injustices will come—bound to come—to me, as they did to Jesus. Help me to react to them as He did. Then I shall be like Him. Amen.

STEPS OUT OF RESENTMENTS ·

We have seen how devastating both wrong actions and wrong reactions may be. One may produce the other. A wife may react to the wrong actions of her husband—may react in jealousy, nagging, self-pity, and resentment, and they may drive him into further wrong actions to escape the wrong reactions of his wife. He may drink more to deaden himself to the situation he meets when he gets home.

A young man was getting over the results of a drunken bout, and his mother and a pastor sat with him. The pastor, called in to help, was giving the young man a severe moral scolding—a scolding which he deeply deserved. He wilted under it, but was unchanged. Then his mother, who had sat silent through it all, went over and planted a kiss on his bloated face. That was all. But her reaction wrought a miracle. The minister represented the law, the mother represented grace. And grace won. That kiss broke his heart. He rose never to touch liquor again. Her reaction was of loving forgiveness, therefore power.

In getting rid of resentments take the following steps. 1. *Make up your mind that in a world of this kind you are not going to escape injustice and unmerited pain.* Jesus didn't, Paul didn't, why should you and I? The idea that the good will be exempt from the injustices of the world is responsible for more heartache and wrong reactions than almost anything else. "Why should that happen to me?" Well, why not—it happened to Him. Are you better? You are not promised exemption as a Christian. The Christian gospel doesn't promise exemption, but it does promise something better—it promises power to *use* everything that comes, good, bad and indifferent, and to make something else out of it. That is the Christian reaction to injustice—not whining self-pity, but a positive reaction of forgiveness and a further taking up the injustice into the purpose of the life and making it contribute to the ends for which we truly live.

So banish from the mind the idea that injustice ought not to come. It will come. But Jesus said to Paul: "For I am with you, and no man shall attack you to harm you." (Acts 18:10.) He didn't say: "No man shall attack you," but "no man shall attack you to harm you."

O God, I know that the harm is not in the attack, but in my reactions to the attack. So keep me intact within by right reactions to wrong actions toward me. Then nothing shall harm me. I'm safe. Amen.

AFFIRMATION FOR THE DAY: *I'm safe in love, very unsafe in resentments.*

BLESSING THOSE WHO WRONG US

Make up your mind that in a world of this kind you will not escape injustice and unmerited pain.

2. *Pray for those who do you wrong.* Don't pray *at* them—pray *for* them. Meet all invasions of resentment with a barrage of prayer, not for yourself, but for the one who does you the wrong. Jesus said: "But I say to you, Love your enemies and pray for those who persecute you." (Matt. 5:44.) Note the connection between loving your enemies and praying for those who persecute you. You cannot love your enemies unless you pray for them, unless you love them in God. By praying for those who wrong you, the resentment is sterilized by the antiseptic of prayer. And get in prayer *first.* Don't let the resentment sit down and be at home and then try to dislodge it by prayer. Meet the resentment at the door—meet it with the uplifted heart and resentment will probably decide that this is no place to call. It will not be welcome.

3. *Not only pray for those who do you wrong, but bless them.* This attitude of blessing them goes beyond praying for them, for in praying you ask God to bless them—that is blessing them in a round-about way, at second hand. But blessing them personally is straightforward and firsthand.

A lady and a group of children were out for a walk. Johnny, aged twelve, was mean to the girls, mean to everybody. The lady suggested that they all broadcast love to Johnny. At this suggestion a thundercloud came over Johnny's face. This was new. He didn't know how to meet it. He became worse. The lady suggested that the evil spirits were coming out of Johnny's head, and fighting hard to stay. Johnny felt his head to see if he could feel them coming out. Then he suddenly changed, asked forgiveness of each one of the party, and was the soul of courtesy and thoughtfulness the rest of the day. A few days later Johnny said to his mother: "Mother, let's broadcast love to Daddy, for he's in a bad mood. You know there is something in this broadcasting love business." There is. For even if the other doesn't receive it, you are the better for giving it.

O Father, fountain of love, give me an unfailing fountain of love in my heart. Help me to love the unlovely and to bless those who would hurt me. For I belong to the Society of Incorrigible Lovers. Amen.

AFFIRMATION FOR THE DAY: *Today I shall broadcast love to everybody and everything.*

SURRENDERING OUR RESENTMENTS

4. *Not only pray for and bless those who do you wrong, but pray with them, if possible.* This praying *with* makes it all the more pressingly intimate. A man, prominent and able, came to a doctor friend of mine, and announced: "I have my stuff in my car. I'm leaving home for good. I can't stand my wife's stubbornness. I'm through." The doctor told him what a fool he was to leave his wife and family in this way. The man replied: "I've tried everything. Nothing does any good." The doctor suggested they try one more thing before he left: "Go home, leave your things in the car, take your wife alone and get down on your knees before God, and first confess your own sins, leaving your wife to confess hers." He promised reluctantly to do it. An hour or two later the man called up the doctor: "Doctor, I did it. And it worked. It's heaven. We've settled everything before God." Two things did it: They were both in the presence of God, not just in the presence of each other. He confessed his sins *first.* When we confess the other person's sins first, that puts him on the defensive.

5. *If resentments have taken lodgment in the heart, don't struggle with them, don't even pray against them—surrender them.* It is easy to fight against your resentments and to pray against them and not give them up. A very superior type of woman, striking in appearance, stood up in one of our Ashrams and said: "Today, I went to the woods, stood on a cliff where a hundred feet below me was a pool. I took up a stone, dropped it and said: 'There go my resentments.' Another: 'There goes my pride.' Another: 'There goes me.' And the last for my husband: 'There goes my mother-superior attitude.' I've come back free and new." The husband, an outstanding architect, had been an alcoholic for thirty-five years, treated by psychiatrists and others, and grew only worse. In a half hour of prayer and counsel with a friend, the whole thing was surrendered and settled and he has not even desired it since. His wife was his remaining problem, for she was resentful and superior—and religious. Now both were changed—one from wrong actions and the other from wrong reactions. Heaven set in!

O God, I know that if I live in hate I live in hell. If I live in love, I live in life. I cannot go longer with festering resentments dogging my footsteps. I surrender them all to Thee. Amen.

AFFIRMATION FOR THE DAY: *If I do not forgive, then I break the bridge—forgiveness—over which I too must pass.*

GIVING OUT LOVE AND ONLY LOVE

We note the further steps in getting rid of resentments and hate. 6. *Kill the other with kindness—and more kindness.* If the amount of kindness you give is not effective, then "increase the dose."

Two incidents regarding Hiroshima, Japan, where the first atomic bomb fell: When the first Americans came into Hiroshima after the bombing, they were met by an old man who insisted on shaking hands with them, saying: "I am a Christian." You obliterated my city—shake hands! The other incident was the fact that I found an American war-widow whose husband had been killed in Okinawa, now in Hiroshima to serve the Japanese as a missionary.

There were eleven men in the office of a friend of mine. Their attitude toward each other was cut-throat. One man told my friend that he was going to get him. My friend replied: "No matter what you do, I'm not going to do anything to you." That broke him down. The boss heard of it, and it got him. He gave it to the group and it changed the whole group from cut-throat competition to co-operation and fellowship. This spread to the offices in the towns roundabout. The attitude of this one man changed another and that changed an office, and that changed the offices roundabout.

A young wife found God in the midst of her hell. Her husband had been married three times. The first wife was driven to drink by him, the second to other men, and she was driven to God. One day he said to a friend: "Jane and her group are praying for me, I know, and I have to act like a hellion, or it will get me." In the end it will probably get him, but if it doesn't then she wins. For her very attitudes are the victory. She is getting progressively stronger, and he progressively weaker.

A woman, living on a ranch, said she couldn't stand spuds and beans any longer. Left her husband. On the way back to her home she ordered spuds and beans every place she stopped. It wasn't spuds and beans, but her reactions.

O God, give me that infinite patience that wears down all hate by love, all sin by goodness. Don't let me stop at a half-victory. I would endure to the end and then some. Give me the joy of a final victory, no matter how long the battle. Amen.

AFFIRMATION FOR THE DAY: *With love, anywhere will be heaven.*

LOVE ITSELF IS THE VICTORY

We come to our last step: 7. *Be willing to take defeat in the way of love, for love itself is the victory.* Love is not the preparation for the battle of life—it is the battle. He who retains love, retains the victory, for it is the victory.

Dr. Aggrey, the great African Christian educator, said: "If I am abused, I smile. If abused again, then again I smile. I am seldom abused the third time." But even if he were, his very attitude was the victory. Another great African Christian, Booker T. Washington, put it this way: "No man shall ever narrow or degrade my soul by making me hate him." That spirit itself is the victory apart from what it accomplishes.

A Negro, Ronald, moved too close to a white man to live, and the white man said he was going to drive him out. The Negro on the other hand said he would kill the white man with kindness. Ronald's cow got into the white man's pasture and Ronald had to pay heavily. Then the white man's whole herd got into Ronald's pasture. He would be ruined, he thought, but he sent his son with the large sum to be paid. Ronald sent back the herd—nothing to pay. The white man, convicted of his sin, writhed on the floor in an agony of remorse and repentance, and sent his son for Ronald to pray for him. He came and prayed the white man into the Kingdom. They became fast friends. The white man was killed by kindness, but even if he hadn't been, the spirit of Ronald would have been the victory.

A Christian friend of mine found himself in a position where a quarrel with his neighbor was possible. His peach tree was planted on his side of the fence, but all the peaches were on the neighbor's side. So he said to his neighbor: "The peaches are on your side, you take them." "No," said the neighbor, "they are on my side, but they belong to you, and I'll pick them and send them over to you." He gave up a right to the peaches and found the peaches coming back to him—picked. A high school teacher was insulted by another teacher, so he went to him and said very simply: "I forgive you." The man who had wronged him nearly prostrated himself every time he met him after that. Love is power—the only power.

O God, how can I ever thank Thee enough for showing me the way out of everything—the way of love! When in doubt, help me to do the most loving thing I know. And I can't go astray when I love. Amen.

AFFIRMATION FOR THE DAY: *Armed with love I can walk into any situation unafraid.*

RETREATISM

We come to another enemy of power and poise—*retreatism,* a running away from life and responsibility.

We saw this in Jonah, but we must look at it again to be sure that we are, in our quest for security, running away from nothing. Someone asked a psychiatrist what were the three most important things to a person and he answered: "Security, significance and to be loved." Note the first is security. But we sometimes try to find security by retreating out of life and situations. It is possible to be as much afraid of success as of failure, for success brings responsibilities.

Sometimes we retreat into illness for security. A lady did not want to go to a certain city to interview the head of an institution about a certain position. She felt she ought to go, but did not want to. Each Saturday when the time approached to go she developed a cold. The cold made it possible not to go. It was a retreat into illness—she was secure, for the time being, from having to face that decision. A woman said to Dr. J. S. Bonnell, a prominent pastor in New York: "Lately I have experienced a feeling of fear which distresses me. I have struggled desperately to overcome it. It is not death that I fear, but life itself and all that goes with it." So we try to get out of life by retreating into illness.

A pastor tells me of his wife, who every time she gets into a jam and things get out of her control develops asthma. It offered an open door out of the difficulty. She ducked into it, but of course found herself in a road with a dead end.

I sat in a restaurant in the early morning and a bleary-eyed man began sweeping the place; as he passed me he muttered, half to himself, and half to me: "Gosh, I hate to begin the day's work." During the night he had ducked into the open door of oblivion through drink to forget life and its responsibilities, but now in the morning life was harnessing him to his tasks, and he hated to face it.

Every short cut to security from life and responsibility will let you down, will leave you frustrated and unhappy. Life must be faced and conquered, not escaped.

O God, forgive me that I try to live life in ways which are not Thy ways, but manufactured follies of my own. These ways are ways to disillusionment. Forgive me. Help me to take Thy way. Amen.

AFFIRMATION FOR THE DAY: *Today I shall face success or failure with confidence and poise.*

FROM RESIGNATION TO REGISTRATION

We studied yesterday the subject of retreatism, an attitude of mind that refuses to face reality.

A woman sais to me: "I was frustrated, so I took to smoking." The modern turning to drink and narcotics is a sign of the modern frustration. "Do you see that box full of briar pipes with their handles chewed off?" said a tense, nervous man. "Well, they are a sign of my inner tension." A schoolteacher took refuge in as many as fourteen cups of coffee a day. "If I don't take it, I'm flat." But she surrendered the whole mentality of running away and found herself sleeping like a top.

A business executive came to a doctor on Christmas Eve and said he was going to celebrate. The doctor replied: "I'm glad you are going home to write out checks for needy causes." The man became angry, said he was going out to forget everything, he was going to get drunk. The doctor told him a story of a Negro who did the same thing. That made him more angry to be put in the same class as the Negro. He went away in a huff. But he came back after awhile and said he was a fool for trying to run away from life and duty in this way, he would do as the doctor advised—he would go home and write the checks. He wrote out seventy checks for needy causes. He told the doctor that it was the most wonderful Christmas he had ever spent.

A girl said in reference to the "desk" where registrations are made: "Go up there where the resignations are made." It is one or the other: You register for life, or you resign from it. A woman couldn't walk, not even move her toe. She was examined, but no physical reason was found for her disability. Under a drug she was asked about her life and she revealed a fear that a man was not going to marry her. She wouldn't acknowledge this in her conscious moments. Under the drug she was told to move her toes and to walk, and she obeyed. After she became conscious she was told to walk, that she could—that she had done so. At first she was very angry, but got up and walked and has walked ever since. She withdrew her resignation from life and put in her registration.

O God, Thou hast made me for life. Help me to accept life and to let its healing power course through every portion of my being, cleansing away all feelings of inferiority and escapism. Amen.

AFFIRMATION FOR THE DAY: *Today my attitude shall be registration, not resignation.*

SHORT CUTS OUT OF LIFE

We pursue the subject of facing up to life and responsibility.

A wealthy woman was in bed, an invalid. A doctor friend examined her and couldn't find anything the matter with her physically. He called the nurse aside and told her, to which the nurse replied: "You'd better not tell her that, she will throw a pitcher at you." But the doctor proceeded to get her out of bed into a bepillowed chair, accompanied by many protests, groans, and moans. Then one day a severe earthquake struck California, and the doctor got a distressed call from this woman's husband: "A terrible thing has happened. Come quickly. An earthquake has taken place and my wife is out in the street jabbering away with excited women." The doctor replied: "Well, keep her out of the house till I come." The woman has never gone back to bed as an invalid, but it took an earthquake to get her from resignation to registration!

Dr. Worcester tells of "George" who, in the midst of a building project, suddenly collapsed. His right arm was paralyzed and his right knee was drawn up under his chin so tightly that it could not be straightened out. His right foot began to mortify, so a surgeon had to cut off two of his toes. Dr. Worcester got his confidence, saw that all this was the result of a diseased and burdened soul. "George" confessed to certain sins which he felt were successfully hidden. Under relaxation he went to sleep. Dr. Worcester began suggesting: "George, you are not really paralyzed. You are able to move your arm, and I want you to move it now." He did so. In a few days he was able to walk. He is now radiant and happy.

A pastor said that his mother in order to keep him from leaving home on a trip invariably got a heart attack. An Indian evangelist told me his mother had acute stomach trouble when he answered the call of God to be an evangelist. She wanted him to be with her always. For thirteen years she has been an invalid—an invalid because she didn't want to face life without her "boy." She was unwilling to let her son live the life that God intended him to live. You must face life and live it, or it will tie you into knots of frustration.

O God, my Father, I thank Thee that Thou hast put all things under my control, including life. But how can I control life, unless I am controlled by Life? So give me Life. Amen.

AFFIRMATION FOR THE DAY: *He and I together shall "control everything"—for good.*

WHAT WOULD YOUR BODY SAY?

We continue to look at retreatism.

Jesus said: "Blessed are your eyes, for they see, and your ears, for they hear." (Matt. 13:16.) Blessed is your stomach, your heart, your nerves, your blood—blessed is every organ within you if it is fulfilling its intended function through living the Christian way. But woe be to the stomach, the heart, the nerves, or the blood that is the subject of emotions of retreatism and fear and escapism.

I have sometimes imagined a convention of bodies met to discuss their inhabitants. One body stands up and says: "I wish the man that occupies me knew how to live. He doesn't, so I'm tied in knots half the time. He doesn't know how very sensitive I am, inherently so, to his letting in fears to take possession of him. I go into a spasm every time he lets one in. But he entertains them and I go on a strike." Another body stands up and says: "The woman who inhabits me is afraid to live. She's always inventing ways to escape living. She drinks and smokes hoping that will let her out. But each time I protest by a reaction into dullness and lethargy, she whips me up again. But it's all a losing game—we are under the law of decreasing returns. She has to whip me up more to get out the same result. It's a descending spiral—and some day I'm going to quit protesting, and I'm going to give up and die. It's too bad that these humans don't know how to live." Another body stands up and says: "Look at my condition. I'm all black and blue inside—and I'm showing it on the outside too. The person who lives in me has taken to be resentful toward life and has a chronic grouch. You should see how my gastric juices refuse to flow under these conditions. And now this silly person is dosing himself with medicines and running from doctor to doctor, who can't find a thing wrong with me. I know what is wrong: I don't work well with resentments. I like good will. One is sand in my machinery and the other is oil."

If our bodies could talk, what wouldn't they say! But they are talking—talking in the only language they know, the language of protest through upset and disease and pain.

O God, I thank Thee for my body. I'm grateful that it is such a good body that it protests against wrong treatment and wrong ways of life. Give me sense to listen to it. Amen.

AFFIRMATION FOR THE DAY: *Today, I shall treat my body in a Christian way.*

THE STEPS OUT OF ESCAPISM

We come now to the steps out of Retreatism and Escapism.

1. *Sit down with yourself and ask, What is it I am trying to escape? Anything? Just what is it?* Give yourself a good look in the face, honestly and straightforwardly, and don't allow any excuses, any rationalizations. You will be as sensitive as a boil at the real thing when it comes up, and you will try a mental detour. When I got to the real issue in a young man's life—he was retreating into illness to escape responsibility—he flushed, pulled at his collar, and said, "It's terribly hot in here." So he wanted to open a window instead of opening his sore.

2. *If you find the attitude is a desire to escape, then deliberately do the thing you don't want to do.* Walk right straight up to it and do it.

Perhaps you will have to do as the little boy who looked at the food on the table and was asked to say grace, and he prayed: "O God, I don't like this food, but I thank you for it anyway." And he ate it. That last part of the prayer saved the situation. If he had said: "O Lord I don't like this food"—full stop, he would have been left with a grouch and a dislike and a frustration, but when he filled out the prayer of thanksgiving for it, that turned the whole thing from a rejection to a redemption. Moses didn't like the call to go down to deliver the people, but he thanked God for it, and went and became the deliverer. Jesus didn't like the Cross, but He thanked God for it, took it, and redeemed a race. Paul didn't like the thorn in his flesh, but he thanked God for it, turned it from a pain to a paean. Take the thing you don't like and thank God for it and eat it! A woman had refused to eat strawberries all her life—was allergic to them. This spring she ate three quarts without any wrong result. Perhaps you're like the woman who looked through her binoculars, saw a lion loose, and called the police, who came with screaming sirens and found a scared fox in the corner of the yard. The woman remarked: "Those binoculars are stronger than I thought." Perhaps your fear of life is turning foxes into lions.

O God, if I've been making mountains out of molehills, lions out of foxes and making difficulties where there are none, except within me, help me this day to walk up to them all—unafraid. Amen.

AFFIRMATION FOR THE DAY: *Today, through faith I shall turn all my lions into foxes.*

FROM NAY-SAYING TO YEA-SAYING

We continue to study the way out of an escapist mentality.

Samuel Armstrong says: "The glory of life lies in doing the thing that can't be done." Malinda Rankin says: "The word 'discouragement' is not to be found in the dictionary of the Kingdom of God." The Panama Canal Diggers' song runs:

> Got any rivers that are uncrossable?
> Got any mountains you can't tunnel through?
> We specialize in the wholly impossible,
> Doing the thing no man can do.

And when you decide to do it, then the moral resources are behind you and with you and within you. A girl in a sorority found herself fitting into a group that was sagging morally and intellectually. She felt she ought to oppose this drift and stand up and be counted. But she was afraid of the herd, afraid she would be unpopular. But she decided to do the right thing, cost what it might. It turned the tide, the sorority from being the worst in morals and scholarship became the best, and this girl found herself the president of the sorority.

3. *Not only do the thing you are trying to escape but do it with prayer.* The prayer part of it will give you a sense that you are not alone. You are working with God and God is working with you. That will make the doing of the thing not a tense struggle, but a quiet, poised co-operation. Over a booth in a lawn party was this: "What do you want? We've got it." We smile at the pretension. But prayer is no pretension. Prayer is power. God has what you want. Paul's letters are weighty and powerful. Why? Because God and Paul had joined forces.

A saintly friend puts it: "Let Him love you into loving." And we may add: Let Him will you into willing, and, let Him encourage you into courage. Then I am not able to do it, but I am enabled to do it.

A young man stood up in our meetings, handsome, strong, and positive, and said: "You will hardly believe it, but I've tried to take my life, I was so afraid of life. But now I am free and I want to face everything—I have dedicated my life to be a medical missionary." All his nay-sayings had turned to yea-sayings.

O God, I thank Thee that Thou hast put nerve within my nerves, Thou hast put quiet amid agitation, Thou hast made me the inadequate into me the adequate. I thank Thee. Amen.

AFFIRMATION FOR THE DAY: *Today, no conferences with fear, only with faith.*

"IN GOD I AM SUPERIOR"

We continue the steps to freedom from escapism and inferiorities.

4. *Keep saying to yourself: "In God I am superior. I can do all things through Christ who strengthens me."* This is not mere "kidding yourself," for in God you *are* superior.

A minister arose in one of our Ashrams on the last day and said: "My pet phrase has been 'I can't.' Now it will be 'I will.' I've had an inferiority complex. I've surrendered it to God and it's gone." Another said: "I've never seen so much positiveness. Everybody is saying, 'I know,' 'I can,' 'I will,' 'I see.' " Another, a layman, said: "We've got the battle of Jericho all mapped out, and next Sunday morning we begin." Another, a woman, said: "I've been afraid of love. Whenever I contacted love I got hurt, so I asked for love to go. I wanted a home and I frustrated myself, for fear I would get hurt." Another said: "I've been running my own life. I've been like a person learning to drive a car, flooding the carburetor, choking up things, starting and stopping. Now I've moved over and let God take the wheel. It's different now." Another, a minister: "My ministry was falling down, something down underneath was wrong. I surrendered, it is gone! I've been a minister for eight years. I've never had more than two minutes alone in quiet at a stretch. I've been able to forgive some, in order to pour my resentments on a few. But it's all different now. I can do anything I ought to do." An African student in India at our Ashram: "I said to myself, 'It is all magnetized here. I am, I will be magnetized.' I was. Jesus said to me: 'If you bow to me, then all things will bow to you.' I find it so. A new mastery has come over me." He was strong and adequate *in God.* Another said: "I've been under the shadow of an inferiority. I'm leaving it here." A Polish minister, saddened by the happenings in his native land: "We can make an idol of our sufferings. I've gotten here a large dose of Christian optimism." Another: "I came here to get my face shined up. I live in Washington and had begun to get that bored look."

Gracious Father, I thank Thee that in Thee I am able for anything—for anything, anywhere, at any time. Help me to draw heavily on Thy resources, for in myself I am weak. Amen.

AFFIRMATION FOR THE DAY: *Today, "God will not allow anything to come to me that He and I together can't handle."*

THE THREE LEVELS OF LIFE

We are looking at the enemies of power and poise. We come to another: *Wrong attitudes toward sex.*

We mentioned briefly the three levels of life without elaborating them: 1. The level of instinct. 2. The level of duty. 3. The level of grace.

The first level is the level of instinct, where the three driving urges, self, sex, and the herd, are given full play without inhibition. This is the level of the animals. But on the level of the animals, sex, for instance, is not without inhibition, for it is governed by the mating seasons and the cycle of procreation. Nature imposes inhibitions. But with man there is often the attempt to live on the level of instincts without any inhibitions either from nature or from social morality. This runs him into difficulties.

For on the level of man we enter the realm of moral law. The lower animals survive as they respond to their physical environment. When they are no longer able to do so, they die. But on the level of man the secret of survival is not merely a response to physical environment—he must respond to a moral environment as well as to a physical environment, or he will perish. This moral environment is not built up by man in the form of codes of conduct—it is built into the nature of reality. Break these laws and you will get broken. As someone has said, if you jump out of a ten-story building you do not break the law of gravitation, you only illustrate it! Anyone who tries to cheat a moral God, in a moral universe, is a moral imbecile.

This introduction of moral law at the level of man puts restraints on the use of the instincts. You find them in a certain way or you lose them. When the devil showed Jesus the kingdoms of the world, he said: "It shall all be yours," if you listen to me and take my way. That phrase: "It shall all be yours," is the basis of all temptation—the temptation to find yourself, to find sex, to find the herd in some way other than in God. But nothing is yours unless you find it in God.

O God, I try to find this, that, and the other in myself and not in Thee. But when I do not find it in Thee I do not find it at all. Out of Thee all things decay. Amen.

AFFIRMATION FOR THE DAY: *Everything found in God will be illumined; everything outside of Him will be illusion.*

"IT SHALL BE YOURS"

We saw yesterday that the center of Jesus' temptation and ours is: "It shall be yours"—yours, if you seek it for yourself, instead of seeking it in God. That is the master lie.

Take yourself. If you seek yourself in yourself, apart from God, you will lose yourself—it will decay. You won't like yourself. A metaphysician, giving herself to self-cultivation, turned to me bitterly and said: "I don't like myself." Why? She was finding herself in herself, instead of finding herself in God.

Take sex. When sex is found in God, then sex finds itself fulfilled. One man and one woman live together in moral faithfulness, a home is set up, children come, love is the bond. That is sex fulfilled and sex beautiful and beautifying. Then sex is "yours." But suppose you listen to this lie: "It shall be yours, take it, for it belongs to you apart from morality and apart from God." What happend? Is sex "yours"? No, you do not have sex, sex has you. It dominates your thinking, your acting, you. You become its slave.

Pagan psychiatrists, seeing people struggling with sex on the level of law and duty and ending in a frustration and a conflict, and knowing nothing of the possibilities of grace, advise people to go out and find "your man" or "your woman," regardless. What happens? I have talked with many to whom this advice has been given. Has it cured the conflict? It has precipitated a worse conflict. For the moral closes in and upsets you. No more dangerous idea has been dropped into the soul of the sexually chaotic to make them more chaotic. A girl came up to me at the close of a meeting and said: "You told of a girl who was a civil war. That's nothing—I'm a world war." And she told how she became a world war—she listened to the deadly talk about having a right to taste all sex experience apart from morality, acted on it, and became a world war. It is all like producing more war to get rid of war, or introducing cancer cells to get rid of cancer. One of the reasons why this age is very sex-conscious and increasingly neurotic is this teaching.

O God, our Father, when we take Thy way we find peace, when we take our own ways against Thy way we find unpeace. Forgive us that we make ourselves God—and ridiculous and disrupted. Give us sense. Amen.

AFFIRMATION FOR THE DAY: *Today, all my urges harnessed to God's creative purposes.*

WE CANNOT LIVE ON THE LEVEL OF INSTINCT

We continue our meditation on wrong sex attitudes as the way to weakness and upset instead of the way to power and poise. Honest psychiatrists are seeing this and are trying to set people on the road to the right use of sex.

"Dr. Alfred Adler, in common with many other physicians and psychiatrists, brands as utterly false the notion that it is necessary for young people to have sex relations in the interests of their health. There is no sound medical basis for the contention, says Dr. Adler. The cult of the postwar moral sophisticates, which taught that full expression must be given to the sex instincts, regardless of the consequences, is losing its appeal and chastity is once again coming to its own."

Why are these psychologists and psychiatrists discovering that you can't return to the level of the instincts in order to be unified? We all have to recognize sooner or later that when we come to the level of man we are introduced to a world of law and morality. The animal survives as he responds to environment—to physical environment. But man survives by fitting not merely into physical environment but into moral environment, to this universe of law. The moral universe and the Ten Commandments both say: "Thou shalt not commit adultery." And our inner being, made for this moral universe, chimes in and says, "Thou shalt not commit adultery." So the one who breaks this moral law is in conflict with himself—inevitably. Hence the advice to break one's sex frustration by breaking the moral law only ends in a breaking of oneself inwardly. The moral breakdown has resulted in an inward breakdown. Our hospitals and sanatoriums are filled with people who thought they were free to break law and found themselves only free to break themselves. They were trying to do the impossible, namely, trying to live on the level of law and morality as though they were living on the level of instincts. Man can't be an animal, for the moral law won't let him. He must come to terms with the moral law or perish.

O God, my gracious Father, I come to Thee to have my eyes washed in Thy light. Save me from stumbling in the half-lights that turn out to be whole darkness. In Jesus' name. Amen.

AFFIRMATION FOR THE DAY: *Today, not: "Everybody does it," but: "God wills it," shall be my standard.*

THE LEVEL OF GRACE

We are considering the three levels of life: instinct, duty and grace.

We have seen that we cannot live on the level of instinct, nor can we live well on the level of duty. For duty is a strained attempt to live according to law. Those who live on the level of duty live lives that are strained, hence drained. They get no joy out of their faith—it is a whipping up of the will, and a constantly whipped will is a tired will. Hence a lot of people get discouraged and let go and sink to the level of instinct. Alas, they have not seen the possibility of rising to the level of grace, or better still, of being lifted by grace to the level of grace.

The level of grace is the level where we take these driving instincts which we cannot control, and with which we cannot live without control, and surrender them to divine control. That act of self-surrender, involving sex-surrender, does the trick. First of all, there is an inner relaxation of spirit through the surrender. That relaxation allows divine grace to get through, for without relaxation we are tied up, and hence the power cannot get through to our need. The person who is fighting sex with the power of will nearly always fails, for in fighting sex your attention is concentrated on sex and the imagination is aroused, and in any battle between imagination and the will the imagination always wins. You have to set your imagination on something else. Surrender of sex sets the imagination not on sex, but on the One to whom sex is surrendered—on Christ. That means a higher imagination is aroused, and that higher imagination wins; for the center of loyalty is now Christ, not sex. But sex now in its proper place as servant, not master, becomes contributive, not combative—it tones up the whole life, so that the whole life becomes creative. Sex becomes the tonic that tones up the whole of one's being. The strongest and most creative people in the world are the people who are highly sexed, but with their sex powers under divine control and direction. They have a drive, no longer against themselves, but for themselves.

O Father, I thank Thee that Thou hast made it possible that my most dangerous powers can become my most contributive. So I surrender them to Thy purposes. Now I am free—free in Thee. I thank Thee. Amen.

AFFIRMATION FOR THE DAY: *The most strongly sexed, dedicated to God, are the most creative in the higher realms of life.*

GRACE FULFILLS THE INSTINCTS

When we come to the level of grace a profound change takes place—we do not give rein to our impulses as on the level of instinct, nor do we suppress them through strained effort as on the level of duty; we surrender all these urges into the hands of grace. Grace takes hold of them, purifies them, redirects them and unifies them—with our consent.

This takes the strain out of our moral striving. We are no longer fighting with ourselves and our instincts. In the hands of God they are fulfilling their God-appointed destiny and use, and hence they are rhythmical and harmonious. This expulsive power of a new affection gives freedom from the dominance of the instincts. Sex is no longer in the saddle, but grace is in the saddle and sex is harnessed to the purposes of grace. Hence sex becomes constructive. It is constructive in the purposes of procreation within the family. It is constructive in that it serves the higher purposes of a deeper fellowship within the family when not used for the purposes of procreation. It is further constructive in that it is sublimated for other uses, becomes creative on another level. The person who has surrendered sex to God finds himself creative still—creating newborn souls, movements, hope. In other words, the power of sex is now at work in the purposes of the Kingdom. The poise that results is the poise of conscious fulfillment. Life is no longer a fight—it is a freedom.

And this sublimation of the sex urge can make us creative clear up to the end of life. If sex is used only on the physical level for procreation, or if it is used only for physical pleasure, then its limits are obvious. In the case of the woman phsyical procreation ends in the mid-forties, but if the sex instinct is sublimated, then one can be creative clear up to the end of life in old age. Creation never stops. And there is no reason to believe that it will not continue through eternity. But those who use it only on the physical level are doomed to a road with a dead end. When the physical is dimmed or dies then creation is dimmed or dies. There is frustration.

God, my Father, I would be creative for eternity. Therefore take my sex urges and fasten them upon that which will make me eternally fruitful. For I want the open vista, not a dead end. In Jesus' name. Amen.

AFFIRMATION FOR THE DAY: *"He that doeth the will of God abideth forever"* —in fruitfulness.

STEPS TO VICTORY IN SEX

We come now to the steps in sex victory.

1. *Make up your mind whether you want defeat or victory at th place of sex.* This is important, for if you don't make up you mind then your un-made mind will un-make you. Here is th place where there must be no dallying. For any dallying will b the Trojan horse that will get on the inside and open the gate to the enemy. God can do anything for the man who has mad up his mind; He can do little or nothing for the double-minded.

2. *If you really want victory, pay the price of victory.* Victor doesn't just happen. It comes as a result of a planned lif strategy. A Spanish proverb says: "Take what you want and pa the price for it." There is nothing worth while gained unles there is a price paid for it. There are no short cuts taking you t your goal without price. God works in the spiritual realm b certain laws, and those laws are inexorable. Vague wishing wil leave you vague—and vacant. A spurt of passing desire will le you down unless it gets control of your will and becomes a life desire. The Africans have a proverb: "Don't hunt two birds a once, for you'll probably get neither." Don't have mutually ex clusive desires competing within you for the mastery. It wil leave you cancelled out—a cipher. Make up your mind to pa the price of victory, for if you don't you'll have to make up you mind to be a house divided against itself that cannot stand.

3. *The price of victory is the surrender of these sex powers to God control. Do it—and do it now.* The "now" precipitates a crisis an makes for decisiveness. The "yes and no" period is over. It is "yes." You no longer bend the knee to sex, you bend the knee to God, and then sex bends its knee to you. You are master—i God. When you belong to God, then everything belongs to you including sex. And when it does come back to you it will ad luster to the eye, a bloom to the cheeks, a firm tread to th steps and a general tone of well-being. The first place where will become creative will be in you—it will create you into new person.

O Christ of the surrendered powers, give me Thy sur render, for I want Thy powers. I want creative power t work in me that I may be no longer the flat minus type, bu the positive, plus type. Amen.

AFFIRMATION FOR THE DAY: *The Cross is my "plus" sign—I die on on level to live on another.*

BEING GOD-GUIDED REGARDING SEX

We come now to continue our steps in sex victory.

4. *Train your ears and your heart to listen to His voice in regard to the use of sex.* Since your sex life has been surrendered into the hands of God for His guidance in sex matters, you will now have to sensitize your ears and your heart to listen to His voice. For under His guidance sex becomes a sacrament—a sacrament of love. Without His guidance it becomes a desecration of love; everything within you will feel outraged and ravished and prostituted.

But to get guidance in sex matters is not an easy thing. For the subconscious desires will frame themselves into the voice of God. And then they can deceive the very elect. You will be tempted to listen to the voice of self-pity: "Others are doing it, why cannot I?" That will mean that the crowd instead of the Christ is the arbiter. You are now Christ-controlled, not crowd-controlled. You are different, and your actions must be different.

5. *Remember that God has created sex and He wants to make it a constructive force in your life. He is not just a No—He is a Yes.* Since God is author of sex, He knows how to guide to its fulfillment. Outside of God, sex ties us in knots. "It keeps the word of promise to our ears, and breaks it to our hope." Inside of God sex is one of the greatest single joys of life, if not the greatest. To sex God is the Yes, and everything else is a No. Your creative life cannot come to its own except in the Creator. A very highly intelligent woman who thought otherwise kept saying: "I was a fool. I was a fool." She was.

6. *Hold steadily in mind that your Master was tempted in all points like as we are and yet without sin. Under His control and guidance He can keep you without sin.* He was the most natural man that ever lived in his relationships with the opposite sex—the most natural and the most restrained. His poise and power at this place were unique. The victory He gives, then, is the victory of the natural. It isn't strained. It is released and free and happy. It makes you so you can move freely and masterfully down through life. If you win at the place of sex, all life is toned up by that victory.

O God, our Father, I know that the battle of my life as a whole will not rise above my sex battle. Give me victory there, and then victory will spread all down the line of life. Reinforced by Thee I am adequate for anything. Amen.

AFFIRMATION FOR THE DAY: *I am natural in God.*

LACK OF SECURITY

We turn to another cause of a weakened power and poise—
lack of security.

You recall the answer of the psychiatrist who when asked
what was the most important thing people wanted replied:
"Security, significance, to be loved." People who live in an age
of crumbling values feel the need of security. And in addition to
crumbling values, there are the crumbling defenses. We thought
we were secure behind national defenses. But the discovery of
atomic energy makes all our physical securities insecure. There
is a feeling of nakedness, of openness to attack, of being at the
mercy of anyone who may seize power and use the atomic
bomb. If war comes, both sides will be ruined in four hours.
And if inflation comes, our savings will vanish into thin air.

A man was wearing a button with the letters B.A.I.K. on it.
When asked what they meant he replied: "Boy, am I konfused."
When it was pointed out that "confused" is not spelled with a
"k" he replied: "That too is a sign of my confusion." We laugh,
but there is a heartbreak in the laugh, for we are confused,
because we are insecure.

When the center of an earthquake is at the margin of the
earth's crust, then the area of disturbance is marginal. But if the
center of the earthquake is at the center of the earth, then the
whole earth is an earthquake area. In a moral and spiritual sense
if the center of your earthquake is the center of the universe—
God—then the area of disturbance is universal. The universal
unrest and uneasiness comes out of the fact that there is an
earthquake at the center of the universe—God. We've lost our
sense of God, hence all life feels the shattering effect of that
loss.

We need an unshakable order. Can we find it? Yes. The
writer of the "Hebrews" says: "Therefore let us be grateful for
receiving a kingdom that is unshaken amid a world shaken to its
depths—the Kingdom of God. When we enter and are related
to the Kingdom of God, the absolute and final order, then we
feel that we are in the midst of a vast Security amid insecurity.

O God, I thank Thee that the Kingdom environs me both
within and without and that my security is there. For amid
the shakings of things Thy Order is unshaken and unshak-
ble. I thank Thee. Amen.

AFFIRMATION FOR THE DAY: *I may shake, but the Kingdom in which I*
stand does not shake.

OUR SECURITY IS ULTIMATE REALITY

We saw yesterday that the only security that is real security is "the Kingdom that cannot be shaken."

This Kingdom must not be identified with the Church. For the Church is a relative order; the Kingdom is the absolute order. The Church is shakable because made up of shakable persons. But the Kingdom is unshakable because while shakable persons are in it, nevertheless the Kingdom itself is unshakable. It is God's Kingdom—not ours. Those who have fled into the Church for security are leaning on a stick that may break and pierce the hand and the heart. For suppose the Church turns out to be less than infallible, as it is sure to turn out, then your faith is due for a shock.

A Roman Catholic priest told me that while studying in Rome he memorized the whole of the Epistles of Paul in Latin. Another priest warned him: "I wouldn't do that. If you do it, you are liable to become a Protestant." That was significant. For the priest saw that to shift the emphasis from Peter to Paul was a shift from using Peter as the basis of security in supposedly founding a church—a church security—to emphasizing Paul, who proclaimed that our security lies in a divine Kingdom: the Kingdom of God, a Kingdom whose center is in the human heart, but whose circumference is everywhere. There is no other security—none whatever, except in this Kingdom which cannot be shaken.

This gives an over-all security and in-all security. For all systems—church, state, world government—can contribute to security, but they in themselves are not security—they give security only as they share the ultimate security: the Kingdom of God.

Here is the center of our modern confusion and sense of insecurity—we are leaning on less than the ultimate for security, and nothing relative is secure. We lean on philosophies, on momentary accumulations, on human associations—churches, clubs, families. All of them represent relativeness. In our heart of hearts we know they are all shakable, and hence we shake inwardly with a sense of insecurity. We can have inward power and poise only if we are sure that Ultimate Reality, the Kingdom of God, is working in us and for us.

O God, I thank Thee that at last, at long last, Thou hast brought me to security: Ultimate Security—the Kingdom of God. Here I rest—rest only to be fired with a sense of direction and mission. Amen.

AFFIRMATION FOR THE DAY: *In the Kingdom all my securities are secure—and I am secure.*

THE KINGDOM IS ULTIMATE SECURITY

We continue to emphasize the fact that our personal security cannot be held except in a framework of ultimate, cosmic security. That security is the Kingdom of God. Where God rules there is ultimate security: "He that doeth the will of God abideth forever."

If I am to go forth with the inner air of a conqueror, I must have the sense that though I fail, the thing with which I am connected by inner allegiance cannot fail. I am shakable, the society in which I live is shakable, the church to which I belong is shakable, the family in which I am rooted is shakable, except one thing: the Kingdom of God. And only as I relate myself to that Kingdom by inner self-surrender and obedience do I find myself unshakable too. Everything may go down in a crash, but amid the wreckage of things I can lift my two fingers with a *V* sign of victory, for the Kingdom is not wrecked—it is not even shaken, for it *"cannot* be shaken."

When Jesus stood before Pilate as the crash of outer events was going on around Him, He quietly said: "My kingdom is not of this world"—it was not rooted in this world, hence the shaking of outer events did not shake Him. He belonged to an unshakable Kingdom, and the ages have justified His calm security. The "powers" that held Him have gone down in a crash, but He goes on from power to power, the only unshaken power in a shaken world. His security was secure.

Those who are identified with this Kingdom can stand the shocks of life better than those who are on their own resources. Said a doctor: "Patients who go to the operating table with a confident faith in God have far less dread of the operation, take less anesthetic, recover from it and with far less of the distressing aftereffects. They have little or no restlessness or postoperative fever. They go through the crisis of acute disease more easily and have quicker and less eventful convalescence." Their kingdom is not shaken. The center holds.

O Christ, I thank Thee for introducing me to this unshakable Kingdom. Without it I would be at the mercy of the next happening; with it I am at the mercy of nothing! I thank Thee. Amen.

THE INDIVIDUAL AND COLLECTIVE ANSWERS

We are looking at the lack of security as a potent means of upsetting power and poise. We have looked at the over-all security of an all-embracing and unshakable order, the Kingdom of God.

But when we come from that unshakable Kingdom to the shakable kingdoms around one, has the Christian way any word on how to make less shakable these orders closely environing man? Has it any word about the economic order, which causes a great deal of insecurity?

Let it be borne in mind that the Christian answer does not identify itself with any of the passing phases of economic life— capitalism, communism, socialism. If it identifies itself with any of these, then when these decay, it decays with them. The Christian faith takes hold of any good in any of these which has an affinity to itself and uses it, but it does not identify itself with any of them. It has its own Answer. And that Answer judges these lesser answers, even at their best.

But the Christian Answer would strike at the insecurity, both in the environmental factors and in the individual will. It proposes to change both. I rode along in a car in Cuba on un-paved roads, and when our car would approach, the pedestrians would put their handkerchiefs to their nostrils, knowing they would soon be enveloped in a cloud of dust. That was one answer to the dust nuisance—each person to put his individual handkerchief to his individual nose. That is the answer of individualism. The other way to meet the dust nuisance was to pave the roads. That is the answer of collective action. In this the Christian Answer would lean toward the collective answer as embodying more sense. In an audience of three thousand people everyone was provided with a fan, and the audience looked like a sea of animated butterflies flapping their wings. Each was working hard to keep cool individually. But all the windows were shut! It had not occurred to them to open the windows by collective action and reduce the temperature for everybody. When they did, the fans stopped, and they had collective comfort by collective action. The Christian faith would commend *that*.

O God, help us to have a consciousness of collective as well as individual need, and help us to meet collectively what we cannot meet individually. Give us the sensitivity we need. Amen.

AFFIRMATION FOR THE DAY: *My securities can only be secure when others are secure too.*

WORLD GOVERNMENT A MEANS OF COLLECTIVE SECURITY

We see that insecurity in the economic and social orders works its way into the individual and makes him inwardly insecure. Environmental depressions create individual depression. We must make a social order free from boom and bust, if we are to help create poise in the individual. And by collective security we must do away with the anxieties and fears which come from insecurities because of unemployment, old age, and sickness. If our present social order cannot deal with these, then it will be replaced by one that can.

Then again, we must help individual poise by taking away the nightmare of impending war from a defenseless humanity. As long as war is an imminent possibility, the poise of the individual is under a strain too great to bear. And when war comes, that poise cracks except in very exceptional cases. War is our chief collective enemy, our chief collective sin. Our chief enemy is not communism, or Russia, or fascism—it is war. Get rid of war, and these other problems can be solved. But how do we get rid of war? By world government.

The French, Germans, and Italians have fought each other for centuries under separate governments, but under one government in Switzerland these same French, Germans, and Italians live in peace, and have done so through two world wars waging around them. Why? They have a government over them to which they are all loyal. We have everything in America that produces war between nations—sectional, race, religious differences, and a citizenry made up of people from the nations of Europe that have fought each other for centuries. Then why don't we go to war? Because we have a government over us to which we are all loyal. That is lacking in world affairs. We have no government over us to which we can all be loyal. Hence every nation has to go around armed and fearful, and ready to fight it out at the drop of the hat. We must have a world government over us under which we will all be secure. It will not be any more impossible than it was to make the contending, suspicious thirteen colonies come together in a union. The entire plan of federal union was considered "utopian," "a visionary project," "an indigestible panacea." But they did it, and it worked.

O God, we are on the greatest watershed of history, and we need Thy help if we ever did. Save us from nearsightedness that sees only the problems and refuses to see the possibilities. Amen.

AFFIRMATION FOR THE DAY: *I am all for that which is for all.*

HOW WE STRUGGLED TO FEDERAL UNION

We were meditating yesterday on the necessity of collective security through world government. We continue to look at the hesitations through which the thirteen colonies went before they came to a federal union. One writer of that period said: "With such vain and delusive hopes are the minds of many honest and well-meaning people fed, as by these means are they led to contend for a Government which is made to promise what it cannot perform; while their minds are diverted from contemplating its true nature, or considering whether it will not endanger their liberties and work oppression." Pinckney, during the last week of the Constitutional Convention, expressed this atitude and it was not uncommon: "He was not without objections as well as others to the plan. . . . But apprehending the danger of general confusion and an ultimate decision by the Sword, he would give the Plan his support."

They did not expect the Union to last even after being adopted. When Madison objected to the ratio of 1 to 40,000 on the grounds that future increase of population would lead to a legislature of unwieldy proportions, Nathaniel Ghorum replied that the worry was premature: "It is not to be supposed that the Government will last so long as to produce this effect. Can it be supposed that this vast Country, including the Western territory will 150 years hence remain one nation?"

Many voted for it through despair of the old. Madison weighed, in April 1787, the possibilities of reaching agreement on the amending of the Articles of Confederation: "The probable diversity of opinions and prejudices and supposed real interests among the States, renders the issue totally uncertain. The existing embarrassments and mortal diseases of the Confederacy form the only ground of hope that a spirit of concession on all sides may be produced by the general chaos." Again he wrote in 1787: "I find men of reflection much less sanguine of the new than despondent of the present system." Just as necessity laid its hand on them and compelled them to form a union because the old was breaking down, so necessity is laying its hand on us to form a world union.

O God, Thy hand of necessity is laid upon us. We learn the hard way. But hard or easy, help us to learn before it is too late. Amen.

AFFIRMATION FOR THE DAY: *We are now finding out how not to live. Soon disillusionment shall drive us to God's ways.*

IN SPITE OF FEARS FEDERAL UNION CAME INTO BEING

We continue to look at the difficulties through which our Union came as it struggled to come into being.

Gouverneur Morris thought federal taxation was not possible since it was "idle to suppose that the General Government can stretch its hands directly into the pockets of the people scattered over so vast a territory." The federal government has succeeded in doing it—and how! George Mason was dubious about the election of a president, since "the extent of the country would make it impossible that the people can have the requisite capacity to judge of the respective pretensions of the candidates." The candidates have succeeded in putting up their "pretensions" before the people—and how!

And then again the people of the different colonies were just as prejudiced against each other as we are against the people of other nations. Carter Braxton, a Virginian, remarked of New Englanders: "I abhor their manners, I abhor their laws, I abhor their government, I abhor their religion." When Washington took charge of the army surrounding Boston he wrote that the New Englanders "are exceedingly dirty and nasty people." On the other hand, Eldridge Gerry of Massachusetts found Virginians overconscious of their own importance and Ephraim Paine of Vermont considered Southern members "nabobs" "who behave as though they viewed themselves a superior order of animals when compared with those at the other end of the Confederacy."

A contributor to a New York newspaper in 1784 said, "The fact is by the interests of America we mean only the interests of that State to which property or accident has attached us. Thus a citizen of Philadelphia when he harangues on the rights and liberties of America is not aware that he is merely advocating the rights and liberties of Pennsylvania."

In spite of narrow provincialism and fears and distrust we came together and formed a union. We can do the same in the world situation. We must. Now the insecurities of our world situation invade our personal poise, and if we have poise it is in spite of the collective insecurity. Some day we will make a collective order which will work with us and not against us as now.

O God, we ask for help in building an order which will work with and not against us, for we believe Thou dost will this. Help us to will it. Amen.

AFFIRMATION FOR THE DAY: *I can work for my own good only as I work for the good of all.*

INSECURITY THROUGH APPROACHING AGE

We come now to look at another enemy of power and poise—insecurity from the thought of approaching old age. This disturbing thought projects itself into middle life and upsets the inner poise as an undertone of anxiety.

A lady, very able and accomplished, had a fear that someone was trying to steal her manuscripts, which she kept in a safe-deposit vault. She was afraid that someone was always trying to snatch her purse, in fact someone was trying to steal everything she had. Down underneath those fears was one central fear—the fear that life was snatching away her youth and with it her powers. She transferred that central fear to these other things, but they were only symptoms of the central fear of approaching old age. It was an undertone which produced these overtones. She was fighting old age. And to fight old age is to give old age a fighting attention, and what gets your attention gets you. So old age got her—sent her into the jitters.

In the daily paper was a picture of a ninety-two-year-old man, his jaws set, his face defiant, and his fists doubled—squared off fighting old age. The paper commended the spirit. To get rid of old age is to fight it.

But if you fear it or fight it, in the end it will get you and master you. The old man was pathetic in his defiance. Everyone who saw it must have inwardly smiled, for he was fighting a losing battle. Old age would whip him—had whipped him. This was all a dying kick, at best a pose.

The thing to do is neither to fear old age nor to fight it, but to accept it without tension and use it. When I say "use it," I do not mean bear it, accommodate yourself to it, but take hold of it and make something beautiful out of it. That's what nature does—she does not die drably; she puts on her most gorgeous robes in autumn, her yellows and her flaming reds, and dies gloriously. She goes down with her gay banners waving. So we can face approaching age with serenity and gaiety, and make the last years the most beautiful. And that isn't using words to cover up reality—it can be a sincere, honest fact. Old age can be the crown.

O God, our Father, I thank Thee that the years have not dimmed Thee, nor decayed Thy powers. In Thee I, too, can be undimmed, and my real powers undecayed. In Thee I am life. I thank Thee. Amen.

AFFIRMATION FOR THE DAY: *Every day I live, my inner serenity shall deepen till old age shall be serenity itself.*

A NIGHTMARE OR A GOLDEN SUNSET?

We saw yesterday that the best thing is neither to fear approaching old age nor to fight it. The only thing to do is to use

In Matsuyama, Japan, which had been bombed out with only five buildings surviving, a man said to me: "I lost my only child of five and one-half years by a streetcar accident. I was surprised at my inner peace. I didn't know till then this saving power of Christ. I was a surprise to myself." That is what will happen when old age comes—you will be surprised at Christ's saving power, keeping you from decay and from regret.

In this same city a girls' high school chorus sang beautifully the "Hallelujah Chorus" in a concrete basement—the only thing left when the frame school building was burned by the bombing. The "Hallelujah Chorus" from a basement! When only the basement of life is left—old age—then you can still sing the "Hallelujah Chorus"!

When the prophet said, "They shall mount up with wings as eagles": youth; "they shall run and not be weary": middle age; "they shall walk and not faint": old age; he was describing a fact. Old age need not be a period of fainting—you can go down with your real powers unabated as you "walk" from one life into another.

I know that life often belies that, for old age is very often not a beautiful thing. As W. B. Yeats says:

> An aged man is but a paltry thing,
> A ragged coat upon a stick, unless
> Soul clap its hands, and louder sing
> For every tatter in its mortal dress.

It is the spirit of old age that determines whether it be a nightmare or a golden sunset. A psychiatrist said: "I have never seen a case of senile psychosis in the aged where they have a faith in God, and are free from the fear of death, and are active." But if the spirit droops, then the shoulders will droop with it. If the soul loses its music, then the body will lose its vibrancy. "For of the soul the body form doth take." Keep the soul alive and growing, and it will quicken everything it touches. And it will keep the body alive until its work is done. "He that liveth and believeth in me shall never die."

O God, I thank Thee that in Thee I am deathless. For in Thee death has died. And I am no longer subject to it. I shall use even it—use it for the purposes of larger life. I thank Thee. Amen.

AFFIRMATION FOR THE DAY: *Even my decays, like falling leaves, shall be fertilizer for the tree of life that I am.*

NEVER BELOW "TOPS"

Has what we have been saying been a mere talking loud to allay the inner fears of the ghost of approaching age?

Scientists have shown that the capacity of the brain is highest between the ages of forty-five and sixty; then there is a slight downward trend until eighty, but it does not go below what it was at forty-five. So you need never go below what you were at forty-five. And forty-five is supposed to be "tops." This was taken from the ordinary run of humanity, but the Christian, who can have a planned old age, can go on with a renewal constantly taking place. Those who know say that the earth would run down and decay, but there are cosmic rays which are renewing and creative, constantly bombarding us from a creative center somewhere in the universe. So we can be constantly bombarded by the healing rays of God's creative grace—and so never run down.

Old age can be looked forward to with anticipation and with a sense os adventure. For it is from old age that we step off into the supreme adventure—the Great Beyond. A wren made a nest in the pocket of a scarecrow. That which was supposed to scare it away became the place where it was secure, and where it produced its young and reared its family. So in the pocket of the scarecrow of old age we can be secure and become creative. I saw another wren make its nest in the cross standing by the side of Green Lake, Wisconsin, and at eventide, as the sun would set gloriously across the lake, it would sit upon that cross and sing. If we nest in the cross, make it our refuge and our home, then when eventide comes to life we can sit upon that cross and sing and sing until it melts into the heavenly "song of Moses and the Lamb." As Henry van Dyke put it:

> So let the road wind up the hill or down,
> O'er rough or smooth, the journey will be joy:
> Still seeking what I sought when but a boy,
> New friendship, high adventure, and a crown.
> My heart will keep the courage of the quest,
> And hope the road's last turn will be the best.

So we prepare for life's climax—serene old age.

O God, my Father, I thank Thee that I can look forward with Thee to the days to come and can greet them with a song and a shout. For in Thee is nothing but life—endless life. Amen.

AFFIRMATION FOR THE DAY: *I shall make my nest in my scarecrows and there hatch my hopes.*

A LADDER TO SERENITY

A woman said in one of our Ashrams: "I am about to jell into the kind of a person I don't want to be." Many of us are about to "jell," become fixed in the kind of person we would not like to be. How can we remain flexible and growing even through old age? Here is a ladder to reach an old age of power and poise:

1. *Surrender into the hands of God your fear of old age and death.* This is basic. For if you hold to an inner fear of old age and death, then all attempts at victory are a whistling in the dark to keep up courage. It will be putting make-up on faded cheeks.

Go aside and on bended knee say to God: "You have promised to 'deliver all those who through fear of death were subject to lifelong bondage; now I will be in fear of old age and in bondage unless you take out this fear. That you may take it out I surrender it—surrender it once and for all. It is gone—gone forever. I thank Thee." And believe that He takes it away.

Serenity has its roots in surrender. But it is not a mushy serenity, it is a creative serenity. For now approaching old age is not something to be dreaded, but something in the hands of God to be beautified. You and God co-operating can make old age beautiful—the most beautiful portion of life. Can that happen? Yes. Mrs. L. C. Nisbett of Colorado, now 78, at 62 went totally blind. That is a devastating combination for you—approaching old age and blindness! She met that combination and met it victoriously. When blindness came, she left her daughter's home and went back to her ancestral home to live alone. "I wanted my family to keep on liking me, so I didn't want to burden them. I get along beautifully with myself . . . I haven't given up a thing. In fact I've loaded on twice as much." She keeps house, attends meetings, plays the piano, acts as organist to a church, makes hooked rugs and colorful afghans. She is 78 and blind—and radiant and loved. She surrendered the whole thing to God, began to co-operate with Him and *uses* old age and blindness.

O Father, I thank Thee that Thou canst make my approaching age beautiful and blessed because I am surrendering it into Thy hands to make it creative and serene and joyously contagious. Amen.

AFFIRMATION FOR THE DAY: *I shall walk into my sunset with my shoulders back and head up.*

KEEP GROWING CLEAR UP TO THE END

We are now taking steps to keep old age fresh and green and creative.

2. *Having surrendered your fear of old age into the hands of God, co-operate with God who is the creative God and will make you creative.* Someone has suggested that you "take your minds out and dance on them, they are so caked up." You do that. If your attitudes are becoming inflexible and hardening into rigidity then dance on them and break them up. How? The Greeks kept young, they say, by learning something new every day. Why does one's memory tend to fail in old age? It is not that the mind is wearing out, but that the attention is dimming. You remember a thing to the degree that you pay attention to a thing. So don't say, I have a bad memory, rather say, I have bad attention. If you apply your attention, even in old age, then you will remember things. Apply attention through an aroused curiosity, and your memory will be in proportion to the attention.

A missionary from Burma, 107 years of age, bright and sparkling, used to read her Burmese Bible aloud each day so she would not lose the accent. Mary Elizabeth Ferndale, also 107 years of age, was asked what was her secret of a long, useful life and replied: "Plenty of exercise, wholesome food, and freedom from worry." The first was plenty of exercise, and that meant not merely exercise of the body, but of the mind and imagination. Because of a growing inflexibility vast races become extinct. Break up your growing inflexibility by undertaking new tasks and adventures.

"Mother, don't go to college at your age. You're fifty-seven, and you'll be in classes where these young people will make you look ridiculous. They're bright," said Mary. But Mary changed her tune when her mother got all *A's,* far better than Mary got, and the professors said she was the best student in the class. Grandma Moses started painting and selling landscapes at Hoosick Valley farm at the age of 79. Dr. Lilliam Martin learned to type at sixty-five and learned to drive at 77. "He who thinks he has arrived, has." But you must not arrive, but always be on the way—forever!

O God, Thou who art within me, break up old molds, old words that have lost their meaning, old habits, and jolt me out of my ruts and make me a creative being, creating forever. Amen.

AFFIRMATION FOR THE DAY: *I shall never arrive—I shall be forever on the Way.*

LIFE'S QUICK WAY OF DISPOSING OF NONWORKERS

We continue our steps for a victorious old age:

3. *You must not only learn something new every day, but take on yourself tasks that will make you grow every day.* "Your work is your life preserver." Don't retire to idleness and expect to enjoy yourself. You won't. Don't retire, just change your occupation. Dr. Clarence A. Neymann, professor of psychiatry at Northwestern University, said: "No matter what social position a person has, it is a fact that life has a quick way of disposing of non-workers and non-toilers." . . . "Retirement should be the most active part of one's existence. It should be the culminating effort of one's career, and the attainment of goals previously sought but hindered by the five-day week routine." He describes symptoms of senile dementia as "a growing narrowing of the mental horizon, with interests in the outside world giving way to the preoccupation with the immediate surroundings, a disregard of today's happenings in favor of those of yesteryear, and eventually the confining of interest to the primordial stimuli of food, sleep, warmth, and other bodily needs—a childlike state." Get and keep interests outside of yourself or else you'll become a prisoner of yourself, and in the end you'll be strangled by yourself.

A wealthy man, retired, nothing to do, had three friends die of high blood pressure and a stroke. Afraid he was going to get one, he became terror-stricken, and sat awaiting the blow. When a doctor examined him and told him his blood pressure was normal, he said: "You're a liar." "Then look at it for yourself. Man, ideas are things." It didn't sink in. So the doctor went to the door and came back and said: "A messenger at the door says your wife has been crushed under a car and is dead." The man collapsed. The doctor then called: "It's a lie. Your wife is well." He recovered. "Don't you see that thoughts can send you to the jaws of death and bring you back again?" Softened, the man put his hand on the doctor's shoulder and wept. He began to take an interest in life and people and work, got well, and is now happy and adjusted. Go to work, be creative.

Thou creative God, I take into every pore of my being Thy creative power. Keep me alive to my finger tips. Help me to take on myself tasks that will keep me vital and growing. In Jesus' name. Amen.

AFFIRMATION FOR THE DAY: *I shall doubt my doubts, believe my beliefs, and affirm my affirmations.*

"ETERNALLY CREATIVE"

We continue our steps to poise and power in old age.

4. *Be the "grand old man," if not of your city, then of your community, or of your family.* Old age will find you the "grouchy old man," or the "grand old man." You decide. Destiny is not chance but a choice. Now plan to be the best that God can make you. Ruskin says: "Their power is not *in* them, but *through* them." God's power and poise can work in you and through you.

Then you will be under the law of an endless growth. But you must co-operate. Luis Rich of South Orange, New Jersey, started as a freshman in college at the age of eighty-five. "Can't keep occupied with movies and radios," he said. H. S. Curtis, age seventy-six, ran a hundred yards in eleven seconds. Remember at eighty your brain power need not dip below what it was at forty-five. Banish the word "can't" from your vocabulary and substitute: "I can do all things through Christ, who strengthens me." I once saw a "stop" sign, not on the road but standing in a garden. I laughed. I said to myself: "You can't stop that garden from growing by putting a 'stop' sign in it. For the garden is growing through the power of *life*." If old age puts a "stop" sign in the garden of your life, laugh at it and keep on growing.

Even if you are bedfast, you can reach out through the power of prayer and touch the ends of the earth and change things. When you are linked with God by prayer, then you can loose God's power on situations and persons everywhere. You are not confined to that body, you are walking the earth and are infusing new life everywhere.

You can live life on two levels at once. When talking to a person, you can be in an undertone of communion with God. When walking the streets you can be walking with God—within. When lying on a bed, you can drop down beneath the level of your physical weakness to the eternal Strength, relate yourself to It, and loose it through prayer upon your immediate circle and upon distant persons and places. To your last gasp you can be creative through prayer. And you will wake up eternally creative.

O God, I thank Thee that I am never stymied, I always have a way out—of everything. For in Thee my inner man is renewed day by day, and that inner renewal creates outer renewal. Amen.

AFFIRMATION FOR THE DAY: *Today, I shall live on two levels, and my deeper level shall be my real level.*

"A DISRUPTED INTERIOR AND A LUSTERLESS FACE"

We come this week to explore further the results of wrong reactions we take to life. Also the result of right reactions. Your actions may upset your power and poise. But your reactions can even more definitely affect your poise and power.

Religion has been occupied in large measure with right actions—do this, don't do that. This is important. But even more important are your reactions to what happens to you. For if wrong actions can throw disruption into the personality, wrong reactions can just as definitely disrupt the person, often more so. And wrong reactions often are found in people whose actions are correct. They don't lie, steal, commit adultery, get drunk—they are outwardly correct in actions, but they may be upset and inwardly disrupted by wrong reactions to what life and other people do to them. Drunkenness and dishonesty and adultery can and do cloud the countenance, make the lines of the face sag. But just as definitely will the same thing happen to you if you react in self-pity, in resentment, in fear, in jealousy, in retaliation, in an effort to escape—all of these reactions will make a disrupted interior and a lusterless face.

Take the actions of Jesus. They were wonderful, but His reactions were even more wonderful. About half of the New Testament is taken up with a description of His actions and the other half with His reactions. And His reactions reveal Him even more than His actions. His reactions were just as redemptive as His actions.

Take His reaction to temptation. The temptation in the wilderness for forty days should have left Him spent and exhausted. On the contrary, the account says that Jesus went into the wilderness "full of the Spirit" and came out "in the power of the Spirit"—mere fullness turned to power. His reaction to temptation was so sound, so decisive, so uncompromising that the temptations furthered Him. It must be discouraging to the devil to tempt a Man like that, for He uses the very temptations to further Him. If His actions furthered Him, His reactions furthered Him further.

O God, I thank Thee that not only my actions can be redeemed through Thy grace but my reactions also. Help me to victory in my reactions, too; then I shall be victorious. Amen.

AFFIRMATION FOR THE DAY: *Today, even my temptations shall strengthen me, for I shall come out on the right side of them.*

274

EVERYTHING FURTHERED HIM

We continue to look at the reactions of Jesus. When a lawyer "stood up to put him to the test," He answered his question and then gave the unforgettable parable of the Good Samaritan. Through it humanity hears the words ringing down through the ages: "Thou shalt not pass by on the other side, away from human need." The lawyer asked a question about the Law, and Jesus, through that attempt to discredit Him, showed something beyond the Law—the law of love. Everything furthered Him, for He reacted in love.

Take His reaction to the attitude of the Pharisees when they watched Him to see whether He would heal a man with a withered hand on the Sabbath, that they might accuse Him. He "looked around at them with anger, grieved at their hardness of heart"—here He defined anger: an anger that had grief in it at what was happening to another, not a personal resentment at what was happening to Him. That reaction was a revelation— He uncovered the nature of righteous and unrighteous anger, and did it not by a definition but by a deed. Everything furthered Him. Every interruption was an interpretation.

They murmured against Him because He ate with publicans and sinners—"He's like them, therefore He associates with them"—an attempt to take away His good name. How did Jesus react to that? The account says, "So"—note the "so"—"he told them this parable," and then He gave the parables of the lost sheep, the lost coin, the lost son, all revelations of the seeking, redemptive God. He uncovered the very nature of God and the ground of the universe—it is redemptive. What a reaction to an accusation—He reacted into revelation.

Then take the events of the closing days. Life acted with terrifying severity against Him—denied, betrayed, forsaken, crucified, mocked at, and spat upon. What was His reaction? To Peter He looked in pity and broke his heart; to Judas He said, "Friend"; for His crucifiers He prayed, "Father, forgive them, for they know not what they do"—the highest reaction ever seen upon our planet. That reaction revealed the nature of God as redemptive love in final terms. All of His reactions were revelations.

O God, how can I thank Thee enough for these reactions? For they reveal to me Thee and Thy universe. Now I have the Key. I am grateful that I see how to live: to react redemptively to everything. Amen.

AFFIRMATION FOR THE DAY: *No reactions into self-pity, all into deeper self-dedication.*

USING OPPOSING WINDS

Since we have seen the reactions of Jesus to what happened to Him we will now note what happened to some of His followers.

A Korean pastor had two earnest Christian sons, both intending to go into the ministry. The Communists brought them before the People's Court and asked them to recant. Instead they began to preach to the Court. The younger son, seeing that his brother was about to be shot, begged that he be allowed to die in his brother's stead so he could support the family, but the older one refused, saying "No, it is me they want to kill." As they covered the face of the boy, he was heard to pray, "Father, receive my spirit and forgive these people." The younger son said his faith was the same as his brother's, so he too was shot, praying the same prayer: "Father, forgive them and receive my spirit." The pastor asked that the youth who shot his sons be released, and also offered to adopt him as his own son. This so impressed the parents of the boy who shot them that they asked that the sister of the boys come and stay in their home with their daughter. She has gone. Many have been won to Christ through the pastor's reaction.

One little boy in giving himself to Christ said: "I think I know what I can do to please my parents—I can eat cabbage." He did. Another little boy, hearing of this said: "Now that I have given my heart to God, I want to eat lady's finger." "But you hate lady's finger," his mother said. "Not now. Since I've given my heart to Jesus, I'm going to like them." The mother, so struck with this changed reaction of her little boy, was herself converted.

All of these things mentioned above were unpleasant to the taste until another reaction made them pleasant. The negative reaction of dislike did actually make them disliked, but the positive reaction of liking them made them likable.

In the train I saw the windmills turning swiftly and lifting the precious water for the dry prairie. If the windmill had acted stiffly against the wind and had fought it, then it would have been an enemy, but it reacted by seemingly yielding, and in the yielding it used the wind to lift the water. It used the opposing wind.

O God, my Father, help me to react to everything that comes in such a way that out of every opposition I shall take power to lift water from my wells. Then everything serves. Amen.

AFFIRMATION FOR THE DAY: *Since I love Thee, today I shall like a lot of things I haven't liked.*

COINING HEAVEN OUT OF HELL

We continue to meditate on reacting in a Christian way to everything that comes.

Five years ago a woman asked me if she should get a divorce from her husband. After I heard her story I reluctantly said: "Well, if ever a woman had a right to a divorce, you have one." There wasn't a single thing left to do that he could do to make her miserable. And there wasn't a single moral law which he had not broken. So she instituted proceedings, but when it came down to signing the last papers, something within her wouldn't let her do it. Then she went through five more years of hell— literally. He would lock her out of the house in his drunken fits and even nail the doors. For as much as a week she would be at the home of a friend. He took her clothes, tore them up, threw some of them out of the window and the rest he smeared with cosmetics and shoe polish. He lost his business and was a wreck. All this time this woman went prayerfully and patiently on reacting in loving pity. She worked and supported her family and put four children through college. Her patient love broke him. For a year now he has not touched a drop, has begun his business over again, is pathetically grateful to her, and clings to her sustaining faith. She has pulled herself, her family and her husband out of hell into heaven. One daughter said: "Mother, I don't think you could do a wrong thing if you tried." She reacted in a Christian way against hell, and transformed it into heaven. The serenity on her face and in her heart is the result. The words of Tennyson come to mind: "Well roars the storm to him that hears a deeper Voice above the storm." She made the storm roar "well," for she heard the Voice above the storm and, steadied by it, she came through the storm unscathed. Unscathed? It beautified her. And strengthened her. Every fiber of her being was toughened and her roots have gone deeper. And how proud her husband is of her.

After a service club meeting I was introduced to a lawyer, who, after he went blind, studied law and is now a leading member of the bar. He might have reacted in self-pity and become a pitiful self.

Gracious God, give me grace to react to everything that comes in Thy way of creative love. For then I can make my infirmities into inspirations, my lacks into fullness. I thank Thee. Amen.

AFFIRMATION FOR THE DAY: *I've set my sails—all winds that blow shall drive me forward.*

UNCHRISTIAN REACTIONS PRODUCE
ABNORMALITY

We continue our meditations on Christian reactions to unchristian actions. In a world of this kind the Christian is bound to be treated unchristianly, for it is an unchristian world. Therefore his reactions to unchristian treatment become even more important than his actions.

For instance, here is a woman, correct and Christian, but because her family is treating her in an unchristian way she is developing an undertone of self-pity, a near-martyr attitude. It crops out here and there in tones of semi-complaint. She suddenly sees as in a flash the inner drift away from the Christian position and attitude, and surrenders this attitude of self-pity just in time to keep herself from jelling into a querulous, complaining, self-pitying old lady.

Here is another young woman who finds herself as she teaches school growing drowsy, so drowsy that she goes to sleep on her feet. The doctors thought probably it was sleeping sickness, but could find no physical symptoms of it. Down underneath were working two things: She had been rejected as a missionary candidate and was also rejected in several other situations, which created an inferiority complex. In addition there was a deep-seated resentment. These two combined to make her want to run away, to get out of life. The sleepiness was an outer symptom of her desire to dull the pains and problems of life—she took unconscious refuge in uncontrolled sleep in exactly the same way as others would try to take refuge from the pains of life in narcotics. The sleep was the narcotic. When these inferiorities and resentments were surrendered to God, she came back to normal. The drowsiness and oversleepiness have dropped away, and she is alert, normal and effective. The unchristian reactions of inferiorities and resentments threw functional disturbance into her system. The opposite of this is the case of a young lawyer, smoking fifty cigarettes a day, unable to sleep. Now since his surrender to Christ he finds himself sleeping normally and the cigarette tyranny dropped off, the desire gone. In both cases unchristian reactions produced abnormality.

O Father God, I know I can be normal only as I'm in Thee and adjusted to Thy will. I give up today every unchristian reaction which has kept me from being at my best, Thy best. Amen.

AFFIRMATION FOR THE DAY: *I shall play nurse to no resentment or wrong reaction today.*

THE SPIRIT OF INFIRMITY

"Do you see that little woman?" said a pastor of a certain city. "She is the greatest moral and spiritual power in this city. She is quiet and effective and dynamic." A few years ago this little woman was an invalid, for two years on her bed with a bad heart. The basis was not structural disease, but emotional upset through fear and resentment at what her husband was doing. When she surrendered her fears and resentments to God, the lines on her face relaxed, she began to go around doing what other people were doing. She drove home five hundred miles without being tired, showed herself to the doctor, and when he exclaimed, "Something has happened, what is it?" she told him and got this comment: "If half of my patients had what you have, they'd be well." The actions of that woman are much the same—her moral life was correct, but her reactions were incorrect, and that made her an ineffective invalid. She surrendered those reactions and became an effective, vital, contagious person.

Dr. William Sadler, the psychologist, says: "Beware of aggravating your troubles and of making your position worse by your complaints. Pain is slight when not aggravated by the idea; if we encourage ourselves by saying: 'It is nothing,' or at least, 'It is of little account, let me endure it, it will soon be over,' we render the pain slight by thinking it so." He tells of those who get a morbid pleasure in exaggerating their pains: "As she told of her 'unbearable suffering,' or her 'excruciating agony' her face wore a beautiful smile, and her whole countenance beamed with delighted joy." She enjoyed ill health. Because through it she was bidding for attention and sympathy. In the New Testament there is the woman who had a "spirit of infirmity." Some have infirmity, others have the "spirit of infirmity," it becomes an attitude and an atmosphere and an actuality. Dr. Sadler tells of a woman who had a local disturbance which kept up through attention to it. She had "attention pains." A man was examined under elaborate laboratory tests, but no physical basis could be found for pains in his knees. But he gave up his business and devoted his attention to his knees. He was suffering from "attention pains."

Gracious Father, I thank Thee that when I take Thy way, I take my way. For when I react in Thy ways, then my whole being reacts soundly to life. I am well and whole in Thee. I thank Thee. Amen.

AFFIRMATION FOR THE DAY: *Today, my pains and sorrows shall die of inattention; my joys and gratitudes shall grow through attention.*

STEPS OUT OF WRONG REACTIONS

We have been studying this week the effects of wrong and right reactions to life. We now take steps out of wrong reactions into right.

1. *Get quiet before God, let down the barriers of your being, and there go over your life to see if you are reacting wrongly in any area of your life.* Ask the Holy Spirit to help you see yourself as He sees you from within. You have been looking at life from a certain angle, and it will not be easy to see yourself from a different angle. You'll need Divine aid to shift your viewpoint.

2. *You will tend to defend yourself since defenses have been built up to justify your reactions.* You will have argued yourself into self-justification of these reactions, so it will not be easy to say that you are wrong. It is easier to confess wrong actions than wrong reactions, for wrong reactions are the vice of the virtuous; they can point to wrongs being done to them as justification. But there can be no justification for wrong reactions, for whether justified by the actions of others or not, they are devastating to you. To justify them will not take away their evil effects.

3. *Be relentless and leave no roots behind to sprout again.* Don't chop off the branches, get at the roots. For a partial surrender of them will mean a whole defeat. A man said that he felt he should be resentful against another as a means of redemption of the other. But resentment is a false means that will get you to a false end. Can Satan cast out Satan? Can you by acting like the devil, get the devil out of people? Like produces like. And resentments produce resentments.

4. *Remember that the redemption of Christ extends to wrong reactions as well as wrong actions.* He is a Saviour from both. The father in the parable of the prodigal son was willing to restore his younger son who had sinned in his wrong actions, but he was also just as eager to save his elder son from wrong reactions of unforgiveness, hardness of heart, self-righteous complaining. If in the end the younger son who sinned in his actions was inside, and the elder son who sinned in his reactions was outside, it was not because the redemption was not extended to both.

O my Father, I thank Thee that Thou art wanting to save me totally, from wrong reactions and wrong actions and make me perfectly whole. I consent and I surrender both. And I do it now. In Jesus' name. Amen.

AFFIRMATION FOR THE DAY: *All my steps today shall be away from wrong reactions toward right reactions.*

UPSET BY TRIANGLE SITUATIONS

At this point in my writing I received a letter from a distressed woman: "I can't root out the fears that possess me. I am reacting to my fears as the woman who touched the hem of Christ's garment had been reacting to her's—with bleeding each time the fear gets too bad. Sometimes I wish I would bleed to death and get it over with. I do have faith in God, but the trouble is I have lost my faith in men, particularly my husband. The agony and torture of knowing my loved husband is faithless to me is more than I can bear. . . . There is a baby by the other woman. . . . What shall I do?"

So I have had to turn aside in my plan of writing to try to answer this question: What is to be done in a triangle situation? How do you keep poise and power then? An increasing number find themselves in that situation.

In order to try to answer it, let us step off from the situation and try to see what it is that sets up the triangle. Often it begins in a desire for fellowship with another, a fellowship often not found at home. The first steps seem innocent and justified. I say "justified," for I would not rule out friendships between men and women who are not husband or wife. They may be kept on a very high noble plane. Jesus "loved Mary and Martha"—a statement that would have damned any other religion teacher. But we feel its beauty, for we see its inner discipline. That is possible among Christians—and very wholesome and contributive.

But the line between that and setting up a triangle is very thin and many step over it without noticing that they are on slippery ground. Soon they get deeper and deeper into the mire of a triangle. Once the triangle is set up, hell sets in. The Y. M. C. A. has as its symbol a triangle—body, mind, and spirit, with God at the center. But when the triangle is man, wife, and another woman, or woman, husband, and another man, then hell is at the center and all three are liable to slip into it. At least two will, the third may or may not according to the reactions of the sinned-against party. The woman writing the above letter reacted in fear and partook of the central hell.

God, our Father, we tie ourselves in knots and tie situations in knots by our actions and our reactions. And we become caught. Help us out of our self-made hells. In Jesus' name. Amen.

AFFIRMATION FOR THE DAY: *"If thy right eye offend thee, pluck it out and cast it from thee."* (Matt. 5:29, K. J. V.)

WRONG WAYS OUT OF TRIANGLES

We continue our looking at triangles and the way out. One way is to justify them frankly and openly. A famous philosopher of our day has done this. He has advocated trial marriage and has justified living with a woman without marriage. But even he, with all his learning and eloquent pleading, could not stifle the subconscious. He became ill, and in his delirium he kept saying: "O Mary, this isn't right. We've got to make it right before the world." The nurse, who told me this firsthand, said to him later: "You were talking in your delirium." He looked at her and said: "Then you know all my heart." When the conscious controls were taken off and the subconscious depths began to speak, they spoke the truth: "This isn't right." He had to live with a suppressed conflict and to live with a suppressed conflict is hell. No wonder he pronounced this judgment: "Life is like a bottle of very nasty wine." It was—for him. For he tried to justify the unjustifiable, and it can't be done. The moral universe always has the last word, no matter who has the first or the intermediate word. Try to disprove that, and you're going to get hurt—inevitably. Perhaps one reason this philosopher was so ardent in his defense of the indefensible was that he was trying to convince himself that wrong was right. But Jesus said, "There is nothing covered that shall not be revealed," and this philosopher's distaste of life was the revealing of a suppressed conflict.

The way of dismissing, or trying to dismiss, the moral demands of life as a way out of a triangle is no way out. The moral laws do not bend to your whims. They stand foursquare. You don't break them, you break yourself on them. Put them out of the door, and they will come back by the window.

Another way out is to excuse yourself by saying other people do it. A man, untrue to his wife, excused himself to me by saying: "I did exactly what other men in my position would have done." That may be true, and yet that doesn't solve anything. Two tangles never made a solution. To know that you have company in the tangle doesn't make you free. Life works one way—God's way.

Father, I know that life is made to work in Thy way and in Thy way alone. Help me to find that way and to work it out, for in doing so is life. All else is death and I know it. Amen.

AFFIRMATION FOR THE DAY: *No rationalization of questionable things shall put my feet on a slippery road today.*

WAYS THAT DO NOT LEAD TO THE WAY OUT

We are studying the ways out of triangles. There are those who try to get out of the triangle by nagging the offending partner. Correction by nagging is a failure—always will be. The offending partner reacts by justifying his or her action: "Look how unlovely my partner is. I'm justified in going where I can get love and understanding." The Pharisees tried to correct the world by disapproving of it. But it was a failure—wasn't redemptive.

The opposite attempt is the attempt to solve the problem by forgetting it. A doctor advised a woman who faced the problem of "another woman in the case" to "go off on a cruise and forget it." That is the doctor's prescription when he doesn't know what else to prescribe. You never solve a problem by running away from it. I asked a jeweler if he could mend my watch and he replied: "We mend everything here except broken hearts." Broken hearts cannot be mended by watchmakers or by cruises. For cruises that go out have to come back—to the same old problems.

Another method is trying to correct the offender by the threat of exposure. That may restrain, but it does not remake. For the attitudes must be changed and not merely the actions, and a threat of exposure does not change the attitudes. They are not redeemed.

There is another method that is sometimes tried—the method of defending the offender. That, too, is a failure. For it is based on unreality. To defend the indefensible is to stand on sand. The offender knows in his heart of hearts that he or she is wrong, and to find someone defending him or her in that wrong confuses the moral issues and leaves the whole thing a blur and hence unredemptive.

There is another way that is often tried—a sullen silence. There is a silence that is understanding and loving, and there is a silence that is sullen and bitter. This sullen, bitter silence may be rooted in pride. In any case it is not redemptive. The offender knows its meaning and is driven further away by it. It creates an atmosphere that blocks redemptive processes. None of these ways work, for they are not God's way.

O God, show me Thy way, for my ways leave me with dead ends. I must find a way that is Thy Way, then and then only shall my tangled mess begin to find its sure way to release and clarity. Amen.

AFFIRMATION FOR THE DAY: *Today, I shall have more intelligence than a fly that puts its feet into tanglefoot, thinking it to be sweet.*

TRYING TO JUSTIFY THE UNJUSTIFIABLE

In the midst of writing the above I was called on to try to straighten out this: A Christian worker has an unsatisfactory home life, and yet his wife wanted him to stay. He fell in love with a woman, also a Christian worker, whose home life was also unsatisfactory, and yet her husband was willing for her to stay and children would be involved. They promised to marry after two divorces were secured, and on the basis of that promise began adulterous relations. Then they tried to justify it morally. Scripture was appealed to and twisted: "If anyone thinks that he is not behaving properly toward his betrothed, if his passions are strong, and if it has to be, let him do what he will, he does not sin; let them marry." (1 Cor. 7:36). But this Scripture has nothing to do with two people married to others. Sexual intercourse between two such people or between unmarried people is adultery, and no rationalization can change it. And God still says, "Thou shalt not commit adultery."

Another rationalization was brought in: "We decided to part and break this relationship. But the woman began to get sick at the stomach and vomit, and I began to feel a terrible depression. If it were the right thing to part, why should she have had that physical upset, and why should I have had that terrible depression? The right thing should bring the right reaction, physically and mentally." Obviously, the reason for the upset was that they had only outwardly given up each other, inwardly there was no renunciation. So the conflict brought nausea and depression.

No, the way out of a triangle is not to try to justify it on religious or rational grounds. The moral universe doesn't back it, and it will fall to pieces like a house of cards. For instance, a couple, one married and the other not, had sexual intercourse but tried to sanctify it by holding a quiet time of prayer together at a certain hour each day. But the thing was seen for what it was, and it was broken up. To try to set up a new home by breaking up two other homes as in the first instance mentioned today would have ended in failure. For you cannot found a right on two wrongs.

Our Father, I thank Thee that the right way is the right way for us. Thy ways turn out to be our ways, the ways for which we are made to live. Help us to take Thy ways—always. Amen.

AFFIRMATION FOR THE DAY: *If I think I can cheat moral laws in a moral universe, then I am a moral imbecile.*

SOME WAYS THAT WORKED

We have looked at wrong ways out of a triangle. We shall look at several who have taken the right way—and succeeded.

A couple were parted by the war. The man, a doctor, fell in love with a nurse and in a weak moment they gave way and a child was born. In the birth of the child the nurse-mother died. The man wrote the whole thing to his wife, confessed everything honestly and straightforwardly. The wife immediately went out to where he was and adopted the baby as her own. They were reconciled and began again. Today they are living together happily. Both of them, working together, pulled the situation out of a very bad hole.

Another. A prominent man in a community began to be infatuated with a married woman, wife of another prominent man. If the illicit relations had been known, both families would have been ruined. The wife of the first man found it out, and then began a battle of alternatives. Would she leave him, expose them? Her first battle was with herself. The resentments, anger, uncertainty were breaking her physically. She broke out in a disease that baffled the doctors. That disease was rooted in her mental conflicts. She said to me after hearing me speak: "If I believed the things you believe in, I wouldn't be in the mess I'm in." And then she added: "In our home we have everything—and nothing." She turned to God and found Him. She decided she wouldn't leave her husband, wouldn't nag him, wouldn't hold anything but good will toward them both. She began the experiment of living "in spite of," so that if she received no response from her husband she would be on top anyway. So heads she would win, tails she would also win. She *is* on top, unsoured, unembittered, and is slowly but surely pulling that situation within the home and the community out of a hell into a heaven of reconciliation and redemption. Neither the children nor the community know how close to skirting the brink of ruin they were. Only two know—the guilty ones—and in their hearts admire her for the spirit that kept everybody from slipping over. She listened to God's answer, found it, followed it, and it worked—worked marvelously.

O God, I thank Thee for the healing that comes to those who listen to Thee and who obey. Thou art redemption—redeeming us from the results of our sins and follies. I thank Thee. Amen.

AFFIRMATION FOR THE DAY: *"The way of transgressors is hard"*; *"His commandments are not burdensome."*

A BUNCH OF "DON'TS"

If you are caught in the meshes of a triangle what are you to do? Let's look at some of the things not to do.

1. Don't retreat into glum self-pity. That defeats its own purpose, makes you less lovable, and less capable of loving. For the end is to love the erring loved one back to a new position and attitude. That is never done by glum self-pity. It only gives justification to the loved one in seeking solace and companionship elsewhere.

2. Don't take the offensive of nagging. Just as many a man takes refuge in drink from a nagging partner, so many take refuge in a clandestine relationship as escape from a bitter tongue. No one is ever corrected by nagging—no one. It is a bitter failure. A woman, who had tried giving back to her mother-in-law what she got, found it a bitter failure, gave it up and began to give out love, and relationships healed.

3. Don't alternate between tongue-lashing and boot-licking. Some who find nagging won't work turn around and try excessive affectation of devotion and love. Both defeat themselves. For the second makes the erring partner inwardly disgusted. He or she knows he is not worthy of this and doubts the reality of it all. An alternating blistering and blessing is a failure—always.

4. Don't go around seeking sympathy by telling your sad story to a lot of people. That drives the erring ones away all the farther. For they feel they are abused and maligned and that covers up the real issue. Tell your story to a well-chosen friend or advisor, but don't syndicate your sorrow. Often you'll have to exaggerate it to get the required sympathy.

5. Don't forget that if your erring loved one sins in this, that you are sinning in other ways. He may be sinning in the flesh and you in the disposition. Each is wrong and deadly—equally deadly. Approach the whole thing in humility of heart, asking why you have failed to hold the love of the loved one. That humility of approach will help you to gain the right attitudes to win the other to a new life. Even if it doesn't succeed, it sets you right.

O God, help me to approach this whole thing in a spirit of penitent humility so that I can be at my best—Thy best—in winning through on this. I cannot do it alone. Show me, I follow. Amen.

AFFIRMATION FOR THE DAY: *I shall cast no stones today, for I am not without sin.*

CONFESS YOUR OWN SINS, NOT THE OTHER'S

We continue the steps to power and poise in the midst of a triangle situation. A letter in this morning's mail from a woman says: "You enabled me to crawl out from under the debris of my life and sing." I didn't enable her—I only introduced her to the power of Christ that did enable her. And then she adds: "It humbles me to think I go about talking on the home and parents when I know what our own came very close to being. God does work in mysterious ways." Yes, when we co-operate with Him—as she did. Now she is running a city-wide class on the family. She has a right to speak, for she pulled her own self and her family back from the brink of a break-up. How? We have seen the "don'ts"—now we shall look at the "do's."

6. Keep believing in your partner in spite of his or her actions. The very belief will create the thing you believe in. Suspicions are unredemptive, faith is redemptive. Suppose you are let down? It is better to believe redemptively than to disbelieve unredemptively. The believing redemptively does something for you, even if the other doesn't respond, while disbelieving unredemptively corrodes you and blocks the process of healing.

7. Fasten your thoughts and affection on the good qualities in the other instead of magnifying the bad. This bad may be a speck in the apple and not the whole apple. You don't throw away the whole apple because of a local rotten place.

8. Remember that these triangle situations are often temporary, and that infatuations often grow fast and wither just as fast. The infatuation will probably taste sweet in the mouth but will be bitter to digest, for it cannot be assimilated to life. The guilty ones often realize that, and the infatuation passes.

9. Confess your own sins and let the other confess his or hers. Don't confess the other's sins. That is fatal. Have a quiet time each day together, if possible, before starting out in the day, and there talk humbly to God about yourself and leave it to the other to talk to God about himself or herself. Don't pray *at* the other. If this prayer together is impossible, then hold the other believingly to God alone.

O God, my Father, I thank Thee that Thou hast an answer to all my problems—even this triangle problem. I give myself to seeking Thy answer. Give me infinite patience and infinite love. Amen.

AFFIRMATION FOR THE DAY: *Today, God's answer shall be my answer.*

"THE SHADOWS DUE TO CHANGE"

We study this week the way to power and poise through and on account of the "shadow due to change." We looked at the shadows due to our own wrong actions and attitudes and due to the wrong actions and attitudes of others. We must now look at the "shadow due to change."

Life changes and the very changes cast their shadows over us and make many lose their poise and power. We don't like change and cling to the old even when it is worn out. I sat in a private dining room in the House of Commons in London and an official put his head in the door and called out, "Anybody going home?" They explained to me that this was a left-over from the days when the members of the House of Commons in going home would be beaten up and robbed either by thugs, or by paid agents of the House of Lords, so they were taken home in convoys under police escort when the House of Commons adjourned. This question, "Anybody going home?" announced the closing of the session of the House in language left over from an outgrown situation. They preferred not to change.

We tend to go back to the same seats, to do the same things over; it all sinks into habit. We are disturbed by change. And yet life is change. There is nothing changeless about life except change. Our ability to adjust to change determines our poise and power. We can only do that if we have a changeless center of life. That changeless center is God. When that center remains intact, then we can stand change for we have a changeless Center. Without that changeless Center we get jumpy and jittery and afraid when change comes.

Take, for instance, the changes that come with adolescence and youth. There the securities of the home give way to a demand that life be met personally. Responsibility has to be assumed. There many get panicky and retreat into excuses, into braggadocio instead of accomplishment, into inner states of illusions of grandeur or of martyrdom, into illnesses—anything except meeting the change with quiet courage and poise. They are under "the shadow due to change."

O God, Thou changeless One, help me to be centered in Thee so entirely that no change on the outside can disturb this changeless Center. So shall I be changeful and changeless. Amen.

AFFIRMATION FOR THE DAY: *I shall accept change, for I cannot change the fact of change.*

288

AFRAID OF CHANGE

We continue to look at the loss of poise and power through "the shadow due to change."

After adolescence we come to the great change due to the necessity to decide on marriage and the bringing into the world of a family. Many sheltered souls are afraid of the responsibilities of marriage and draw back, some into illness, to escape those responsibilities. A young lady, not certain she wanted to marry a man, though he was excellent in every way, had a nervous breakdown seven days before the marriage. She was afraid of the "change" that marriage would bring and retreated into a nervous breakdown as a way out. The man was very patient and waited for her to come out from under this cloud. I pointed out to her that her fears were baseless, and that she should surrender the whole thing to God and then go on and marry. The lines of her face relaxed, and she rose up with joy and anticipation and is happily making her plans to marry, inwardly released.

Sometimes it is the parents that find "the shadow due to change" coming over their lives when the son or daughter is engaged and is making plans to marry. A bishop told me that he burst into tears when the only daughter announced her engagement. The cloud quickly passed and he regained his inward poise, but it might have settled down upon him as a permanent gloom. A very attractive woman who had everything to make a beautiful home and an excellent mother was asked why she did not marry, and gave the sad reply: "My mother kept us sheltered and wouldn't let us have any normal contacts with the other sex, through fear that a calamity might come upon her girls such as came upon a grandfather and grandmother who were compelled to marry because of a moral slip." She justified herself morally but nevertheless perpetuated a great wrong upon her daughters. Even after marriage parents often will not accept the "change" and nervously try to manage the lives of married children. This produces conflict and unhappiness. The changes will produce no "shadow" if we accept them gladly and dedicate them.

Gracious Father, I thank Thee that life is change and that I can accept change and make every change an open door to Thee and to fuller life. Help me to throw away my fears of change. Amen.

AFFIRMATION FOR THE DAY: *Today, I shall accept with good grace the changes I cannot change.*

ON MAKING CHANGES CONTRIBUTIVE

We pursue the matter of "shadow due to change." When marriage comes with the prospect of children coming, many are afraid of this "change," begin to get panicky and try to avoid the responsibilities. One strong, able married woman told with deep sorrow how she became afraid with the coming of the baby, gave way to panic and allowed an illegal operation. "And now my arms are eternally empty and I want a child in them." That was the pay-off—an eternal regret.

Many couples fear what the coming of children will do to their settled habits of personal pleasures and entertainment and pull back from the responsibility of parenthood—and lose eternally the joys of creation. They take the pleasures of recreation and miss the joys of creation. They grow small with the smallness of their purposes and lose their power and poise.

Then another "shadow due to change" comes over many lives when they approach the period of change of life, the cessation of the physically creative period in women. When single women see this period approaching and find themselves facing the fact that they will be forever deprived of fulfilling the function of motherhood, many get bitter, querulous and frustrated. There is only one way to face this change, and that is by surrendering it to God and through that surrender realizing an inner poise from the fact that you can be forever creative—on another level. Let me emphasize what I have already mentioned, namely, that when creation is blocked physically, it can continue spiritually. Some women have been most creative when physical creation is at an end. They create newborn souls, new hopes, new movements, and a new and radiant personality in themselves. This type of creation can continue clear up to the end of life. This obviously is a far more important type of creation than physical creation, for physical creation is over a span of about twenty-five years, but this creation continues throughout life. To be physically creative over a period of twenty-five years and then be barren the rest of the life is tragedy. But to be creative throughout life is a thrilling possibility.

O God Thou hast worked hitherto and will forever work in me Thy creative power that I may be able to be creative throughout my life, through Thy creative energy within me. Amen.

AFFIRMATION FOR THE DAY: *If I live in the creative God, I shall live creatively.*

CHANGING CHANGE INTO THE CHANGELESS

We come to another "shadow due to change"—the change from middle age to maturity and old age. People are poised or not poised, according to the way they meet this change.

The Koreans wore white clothes almost universally until recently. It is said that they wore white, which is the color of mourning color perpetually. But to wear white clothes took a after the death of a near relative they found it easier to wear a mourning color petpetually. But to wear white clothes took a large part of the time of the housewife to keep her family in white. It was an economic waste. The Japanese, when they took over Korea, forbade the wearing of white. When the people did not obey, the Japanese would go around and daub with a tar brush every white-robed Korean they found. A doubtful method of reform. But now that the Japanese have gone, the people are voluntarily taking to colors in dress. Will you accept gladly the changes that coming age brings, or must you be compelled? Why not do as nature does—as autumn comes she dresses in her gayest colors and meets decay and falling leaves gloriously.

One who is being perpetually renewed in God in the inner man can look with poise on the decay of the material substance that surrounds him, knowing that the real person is alive forevermore. Someone asked John Quincy Adams how he was and got this reply: "John Quincy Adams is well, thank you. But the house that John Quincy Adams lives in is falling to pieces; the doors are falling in and the windows are sagging and soon John Quincy Adams will have to move out of this house. But John Quincy Adams is well, very well, thank you." "Though our outer nature is wasting away, our inner nature is being renewed day by day." (2 Cor. 4:16.) There is no real change in the real man except a change for the eternally better.

Then there comes "the shadow due to change" when death comes. We can await it with calmness and even joy and enter it "like one who wraps the drapery of his couch about him to lie down to pleasant dreams." For in Jesus we have died the only death that can come to us—the death of ourselves by a voluntary act of self-surrender. Since we have died there, there is henceforth no death anywhere.

O God, my Father, I thank Thee that no "change" can touch me to hurt me for I am in Thee, the Changeless. So I watch the passing panorama of life, secure in the Eternal Securities. Amen.

AFFIRMATION FOR THE DAY: *If life passes me day by day, nevertheless Life passes into me day by day.*

ON MAKING FAILURE A STARTING POINT

We continue to look at the shadows "due to change." Some of us have to face "the shadow due to change" when we pass from success to failure.

Dr. Russell L. Cecil said that the four things that most commonly bring on arthritis are: *(a)* marital shipwreck, *(b)* financial disaster and grief, *(c)* loneliness and worry, *(d)* long-cherished resentments. Note that the first three are connected with failure and the fourth is possibly the result of failure. These four things upset the balance of nature, and arthritis results. How can we have poise and power amid failure?

First, by realizing that success is not the aim in life. The most influential person who ever lived on our planet was Jesus of Nazareth, and He died an apparent failure. So failure in itself is not so bad, after all.

Second, we must do what Jesus did with His failure—accept it and make something out of it. When Judas had decided on the betrayal the account says: "He immediately went out; and it was night. When he had gone out, Jesus said, 'Now is the Son of man glorified.'" (John 13:30-31.) Note that Jesus accepted the failure: "What you are going to do, do quickly." And then He proceeded to turn the failure into victory: "Now" (note the "now")—at the very moment of failure—He announced that He is glorified. Not "will be," but "now is the Son of Man glorified." He assumed charge of the wreckage and proceeded to make out of it a victory for Himself and others. On the turnstile of His spirit the whole thing turned from failure to fruitfulness.

Willis H. Carrier, the creator of the air-conditioning industry, tells of his failure: "I was stunned by my failure. My stomach, my insides, began to twist and turn. For awhile I was so worried I couldn't sleep." And then he took three steps: "I analyzed the situation fearlessly and honestly and figured out the worst that could possibly happen as a result of this failure. I reconciled myself to accepting the worst, if necessary. From that time on I calmly devoted my time to trying to improve upon the worst which I had already accepted mentally." Then he won through.

O God, I accept the worst that can happen to me. And by Thy strength and grace I will now work with Thee to make the best we can out of the failure. Thou and I will work it out together. Amen.

AFFIRMATION FOR THE DAY: *No failure is failure if it succeeds in driving me to His side.*
292

THE ARMS OF FORGIVING LOVE

We come to another "shadow due to change"—the shadow due to the change from goodness to sin.

The modern attempt to get rid of this shadow is by denying that guilt has any basis except in social disapproval, that morality is built up by custom and not built into the nature of reality, that it therefore can be dismissed from the mind. The moral universe cannot be waved out in this cavalier fashion. You must come to terms with it and get its approval. How? By forgiveness!

Here was a woman who twenty years ago spent a month in adultery—and the twenty years following in self-reproach and penances. She felt herself unclean in any company she was in. I assured her that God forgives and forgives now, and that He wipes it out of the book of His remembrance, that if God forgives her she must forgive herself. The lines of her face relaxed, the tensions of twenty years gave way, and she arose released. She called me long distance to tell me she was living in heaven, after years in hell. As she put it: "Sixty-two years in the flesh and a month and two days in the spirit."

A medical student raised this question: "Doesn't contact with religion deepen the guilt complex, and isn't it therefore a danger?" Yes, unless it introduces you to forgiveness that is real and self-verifying. If it stops short of, "there is therefore now no condemnation to those who are in Christ Jesus," then it stops short of our need—it increases a sense of guilt without giving release from it through forgiveness and change of heart. But the real gospel specializes in that very thing. It is its native air. Jesus, seeing a man with an illness that was rooted in a sense of guilt, said to the man: "Son, thy sins are forgiven thee," and then he said, "Rise up and walk." The sense of guilt had thrown functional disturbance into his body and that guilt had to be lifted before health returned. This connection between guilt and disease is seen in this passage: "He that sinneth before his Maker, let him fall into the hand of the physician." (Ecclesiasticus 38:15.) There is not always a connection but there often is, and that connection can be broken by forgiveness and reconciliation.

O God, my Father, I thank Thee that my deepest malady, guilt, can be cured by Thy forgiving grace, that I can stand before Thee, myself, and the world as though I had never sinned. Amen.

AFFIRMATION FOR THE DAY: *There is only one open door out of guilt— my confession, God's forgiveness.*

A CENTER OF MORAL AND SPIRITUAL CONTAGION

We come now to the last "shadow due to change"—the shadow of discouragement. A minister prayed: "O God, save me from the blight of discouragement." It is a blight.

It is said that the devil had decided on retiring, laying down his arms, feeling that he had done enough damage. When he was on the point of retiring he decided to keep one weapon, discouragement, knowing that is he could discourage a man then he was ready for any other evil.

Those who are in contact with Christ find a constant quickening of faith in life, in one's self, and in others. I know that Christ believes in me when I can't believe in myself. So I have to respond to His faith in me. "I live by the faith of the Son of God"—not by my faith in Him alone, but by His faith in me.

I have just come from a conversation with a woman who is a convert of only four months; she is still in the Roman Catholic Church, but her spiritual conversion is so real that she is radiant and alive with God to her finger tips. Her priest quotes a passage of scripture to prove his point, and she goes to work and through investigation and moral and spiritual insight shows that the priest is wrong in his interpretation. Here she was with a quiet self-assurance, coming from a God-assurance, that made her a real person in four months. She was a dead personality until touched by the life of Christ, and now she is winning others around her. Defeatism and discouragement have no place in her.

Here is another: A business woman, changed six months ago, has organized in her home a class in "abundant living" and no one can come unless he brings a "pagan." They have sixty or seventy there each week, with games before and after the study group. In six months a disrupted person at war with herself is the center of moral and spiritual contagion in her community. Moreover, she is being called on to help organize these groups in other communities. In the community where I am, a man converted by visitation evangelism is now the head of the whole movement among all the churches of the city.

O Thou living Christ, I thank Thee that Thy touch upon us is awakening, quickening and creative. Thou dost make us alive in every cell, in every nerve and tissue. Our blood runs faster under Thee. I thank Thee, thank Thee. Amen.

AFFIRMATION FOR THE DAY: *Discouragement and defeat are not my lot, for my lot has been cast with Christ.*

IT CAME TO PASS

We come to a steadying influence in our search for power and poise—the realization that almost all the upsetting things that strike us are temporary, and if we just hold steady they will pass.

A Negro, very steady and poised, was asked what verse of Scripture he loved the most and replied without hesitation: "And it came to pass." When pressed for his reason for choosing that verse, he replied: "Well, things that are hard come, but they come to pass, they don't stay." His interpretation was unsoundly sound! It is a fact that troubles come, but they are temporary—they come to pass. The ancient writer saw this and said: "Weeping endureth for the night, but joy cometh in the morning."

I fly a great deal, and the thing that strikes one is how temporary storms are—you run through a storm cloud, there are some bumps, a blinding rain, and then you are through it and back into the sunshine again. The area of sunshine is infinite compared to the small patches of storm clouds. Even when in an area such as Chungking, China, where the arctic and tropic currents meet and form almost perpetual clouds, still we found we could get down from Chungking to Hankow by going through the gorges of the Yangtse by plane—an exciting adventure, as hour after hour the plane flew through the gorges, around the cliffs, the wings seemingly just tipping them. Even when clouds hang perpetually over the spirit, sorrow will cut gorges through which you can get to your destination. So whether you go over the clouds, through the clouds, or under them they always come to pass. Life has a way of meeting dark clouds by cutting gorges by sorrow and pain through which you can fly to destinations. Had there been no gorges cut through the centuries we, cloud-bound, could not have come down. So "sorrow expands the heart for joy." The sorrow comes and then passes, the joy remains forever.

So when a sorrow or a problem confronts you, simply look it in the face and say, "You come, but you come to pass. I'll hold inwardly steady. It will pass." Remember the verse: "Their strength is to sit still."

O God, my Father, I thank Thee that my passing light afflictions which are but for a moment are working out for me a far more exceeding and eternal weight of glory. I can sit still. Help me to do so. Amen.

AFFIRMATION FOR THE DAY: *There is a way through, around, or over everything.*

RELAXING IN MID-AIR

We saw yesterday that we can remind ourselves constantly that troubles come but they "come to pass."

This paragraph is written in Nanking, China. The Communist forces are on the opposite bank of the river. Their forces, victorious in the North, are now poised ready to strike at this capital city. The one big question is: When will they strike? The inner attitude of the missionaries who are staying after many, both Chinese and foreign, have fled, is this: "Well, we will bow our heads to the storm, and after the first fury is over we will put up our heads. It will probably come, but it will come to pass." As a bishop put it: "The Chinese are past masters of not doing what they don't want to do." They know how to sit still and wait. For five thousand years they have ridden out every storm. The missionaries, learning this from the Chinese and from their gospel, are sitting still—with poise and confidence. They can still laugh—in spite of!

So we await the coming and going of events and can await them relaxed. Sometimes we will have to learn how to relax in the very midst of the crisis. A very radiant Christian, who has to wear braces because of a weak back, tripped on the top step of a stairway and fell from the second to the first story of her house. As she began falling through the air the Inner Voice said: "Relax." She did, in mid-air—she simply let go. She hit half way down and then landed in a heap at the bottom. By all the rules of the book, she should have broken a number of bones, for she is no longer young, but she got up without a bone broken, nor were her glasses broken. She was bruised and sore for a few days, but nothing was permanently injured. To be able to relax in mid-air was her salvation, for had she hit taut and afraid she would probably have been a wreck.

Dr. John Biegeleisen, a professor in a theological college, a converted Jew, now a very radiant Christian, tells of having a tomato hit him in the face while preaching; he felt no resentment and no upset, only pity. He lived on two levels at once, and the inner level held the outer steady.

O God, my Father, cleanse my depths from all fears, all resentments, all tensions, so that in the crises of life I may be able to be calm within no matter what happens on the surface. I let Thee have them now. Amen.

AFFIRMATION FOR THE DAY: *To the degree that I am relaxed, to that degree am I released.*

"IT DIDN'T EVEN HURT ME"

We continue to look at the possibility of living on two levels at one time. When one has learned to live at a deeper level, then in a crowd he may be talking to people and communing with God at the same time. So the depths are occupied with God, while the surface is occupied with man. That is the secret of not being depleted by outer happenings and strains, for at the depths you are calm and being renewed by contact with the resources of God. The surface is being drained and the depths are being renewed, so you are not exhausted by outer happenings. Like the railway train scooping up water from the trough between the rails as it flies along, so you go through the outer happenings of life. Then these outer happenings leave few marks upon us, for the real living is below. There you keep tryst with God and the depths are at peace.

Paul knew this secret when he said: "Have no anxiety about anything, but in everything by prayer and supplication with thanksgiving let your requests be known to God. And the peace of God, which passes all understanding, will keep your hearts and your minds in Christ Jesus." (Phil. 4:6.) Here the peace of God which passes all understanding, and all misunderstanding, will keep—or "garrison," as one translation puts it—the depths in tranquility. You have "settled down in God," as the Quakers say—"settled down" at the depths so the surface is not unsettled, no matter what happens.

Take the case of M—. She is living in heaven while living in hell—literally. Her husband hit her a blow with his open hand on the cheek with such force that it knocked her out of the chair. She says: "I was possessed by such an inner peace that I wasn't even ruffled on the inside, and though the blow was brutal it didn't even hurt me or leave a mark on my face. It was uncanny." The depths were held by the peace of God, and that peace guarded the outer ramparts and kept them intact too. Now she has a power of laughter—the ability to laugh, a reverent, triumphant laugh, at anything that happens to her. It is a laugh that laughs at the rhythm and joy and peace of God which holds one "in spite of." *That* is victory.

O God my Father, I thank Thee that Thou hast provided for the depths, that there they can be held steady by Thee. Then my depths are Thine. I need not worry about the surface, for the depths are in Thy keeping. I thank Thee. Amen.

AFFIRMATION FOR THE DAY: *The blows of life won't even hurt me —I am in God.*

A PEACE THAT PASSETH UNDERSTANDING

We have been considering the possibility of living on two levels at once. If the depths are held by prayer and communion with God, then the surface takes on that inner calm. Jesus said: "Praying that you may have strength" (Luke 21:36); if you pray, you have strength; if you don't pray, you don't have strength. That's the whole secret in a nutshell. For if the heart is held by prayer, the surface is held by peace. As George Adam Smith says: "Prayer is not preparation for the battle—it is the battle." For where quiet prayer is there worry and fear are not.

A lady who had read my statement that "the area of the work of the Holy Spirit is largely, if not entirely, in the subconscious mind," made up this prayer: "O Holy Spirit of God, with my conscious mind I invite Thee to come into my unconscious mind and by Thy pure light and power cleanse all those areas which my conscious mind cannot touch and bring to my conscious mind those things which Thou knowest I must deal with, through Jesus Christ our Lord. Amen."

When you are held at the depths, then it is permanent. So many who have been living on the surface suddenly find themselves with unutterable peace at the depths, and they are afraid it is temporary like the surface happenings they have been used to living in. One woman said: "I have such peace and rest within that I am afraid." She was afraid of the unusual and the permanent! A Roman Catholic woman, wife of a doctor, found God, and was so utterly transformed and happy that she said: "I was afraid to go to sleep, afraid this would leave me." Starr Daily had been twenty years in the underworld and had spent many years in prison, a hopeless criminal. While he was in solitary confinement, skin and bones from the punishment inflicted on him, suddenly he was converted, an unutterable peace took possession of him. He was so enveloped with peace and joy that he was afraid they would take him out of solitary confinement and this peace would leave him. It seemed too good to be true that this was a lasting depth-peace and not a fleeting surface-peace. It was a peace that passed all understanding.

O Father, I bow my heart and my head in deep gratitude for this exquisite peace that makes me quiet at the depths. This is no passing peace—this is it! I'm grateful to my finger tips. Peace, peace, peace. Amen.

AFFIRMATION FOR THE DAY: *"The peace that passeth understanding shall guard your hearts and minds in Christ Jesus our Lord."* (*Phil. 4:7, K. J. V.*)

THE DEPTHS HELD BY THE SPIRIT OF GOD

We are looking this week at the fact that we can live on two levels at once—the surface tides may come and go, but the depths are held by the Spirit of God.

Here is a pastor's wife who was subject to the currents of life that flowed around her, for in the depths there was no peace—conflict reigned there. She says: "I was reading where Peter said: 'Repent, be baptized, and receive the gift of the Holy Spirit.' I had repented of my sins and now here was a gift—the gift of the Holy Spirit, to be taken by faith. I accepted by faith. All day Wednesday I stood on the promise. Thursday morning was a beautiful sunny day, and I was standing at the ironing board looking out at the sun and I prayed and said: 'I wish I had that sun in my heart—so bright and warm and glorious.' The answer came. Christ said: 'I am there,' and I stood there wrapped in the most glorious feeling from head to foot. The ache in my heart let go and I felt a great physical release of all tensions. My husband came in from the church, and I was standing there smiling and tears rolling down my cheeks. He came to me and asked, 'What's happened?' and I replied: 'Darling, the armistice is signed.' Before, my devotional periods, which were limited, were forced and the Bible never meant much to me. Now I am trying to keep two devotional periods, in the morning using the Bible and in the evening *Abundant Living.* I can hardly wait for these times. I used to run the radio all day to keep my mind away from my inner conflicts and on something else. Now I want the house quiet so I can talk with God, and I find my thoughts and prayers being led as I work." She was living on two levels at once and the lower level sweetened the upper level.

Your lower level can sweeten or sour the upper level. If the lower level is held by unsurrendered, hence conflicting, self then it is off center, and the upper level will be off center, full of conflicts and dissatisfactions in general. When the two levels are at one you live in a two-story house equally at home in each and equally happy in each.

O God, my Father, I thank Thee that with Thee at home in the depths, I, too, am at home there. And with Thee guiding the surface I, too, am at home there. I am at home—anywhere. Amen.

AFFIRMATION FOR THE DAY: *The Holy Spirit has taken over my lower level; I am not afraid of anything that can happen on the surface level.*

HURTS CAN BECOME INOCULATIONS

We began this week by saying that sorrows, problems, disappointments come, but they come to pass. They do not remain—long. That is, if we let the healing process operate. For the healing processes are always there ready to rush in with first-aid and with permanent care. Dr. Cannon says that when we understand how nature has provided for recovery from injury and illness and is ready to prevent possible injury and illness then one wonders that anyone should ever be sick. It is all there ready to operate preventively or healingly if we clear the way. That is all medicine or surgery can do—clear the way. They do not heal—they only clear the way for God's healing.

So the redemptive processes of God operate within the mind and soul when we allow them. We don't have to beg them to come, nor force them—they are there and are ready to make us whole if we cooperate. And just as every physical infection leaves a deposit of inoculation against another possible physical infection, so everything that hurts us spiritually leaves a deposit of inoculation against a possible future hurt—provided we let it. Our reaction determines whether it leaves germs of infection or inoculation. If we react with resentments and self-pity toward passing events, then they leave germs of bitterness and self-pity within. And they will fester. Or if we react in the right way, God's way, then we leave a deposit of inoculation against that thing hurting us again. The calamity comes, but it comes to pass—it departs. But it does not depart—it leaves within us a deposit, a deposit of moral and spiritual inoculation against the things happening again. So each hurt when handled with God leaves us an insurance policy that covers the risk of having it happen again. While every calamity comes to pass, nevertheless it comes to stay—it comes to stay as inoculation or insurance against future hurts. Then we should welcome these hurts as we welcome inoculations—they both hurt at the time, but they save from larger future hurts. Every calamity well taken is not just an occurrence—it is an inoculation against future occurrence. So after awhile you are immune.

Dear Father, I thank Thee that Thou hast provided for my continued redemption from all that happens to me. It is so wonderful I am awed. For I see now purpose—redemptive purpose—in all that happens. Amen.

AFFIRMATION FOR THE DAY: *I am safe. My little sorrows inoculate me against bigger ones.*

THE GAME OF TIMING YOURSELF

We continue to look at those things that come but come to pass and yet come to stay—to stay as inoculation.

The wisdom of life is in reducing the length of the period of shock when hard things hit us. We described it in the beginning of our study as a period of inner adjustment to outer changes. Some people take long periods for recovery—a grief lays them prostrate for weeks and months and even years—a sign of immaturity. Others straighten up and are on the victory side of their sorrows in an hour. I have often said before public audiences that I hadn't "had a blue or discouraged hour in thirty years." Since this statement is liable to be misunderstood, I take this opportunity to explain: I have had shocks, hurts, sorrows in those thirty years, but I cannot remember any of them to have lasted for an hour. Within the hour it was possible to gain equilibrium, to surrender it to God and to find a way through to peace and poise. So the hour covers the period of inner adjustment from any upset. Usually the time is very much shorter, in fact only momentary. There is the blow, then the inner recoil, then the surrender, then the victory. And they more and more follow upon the heels of one another. And you feel you are not doing it, you feel you are only letting the redemptive grace of God, which is always there, operate in healing. So you are not boasting of your own attainments, but of your obtainments. You are letting grace work—your credit is that you have learned sense enough to do so!

Perhaps you can play the game of "timing yourself"—see how long it takes for you to go through a period of adjustment to a given type of pain, sorrow, and calamity. An hour should be par—all under that is sheer progress. Perhaps you will learn in the beginning to laugh a jittery laugh, it is there but precarious. Then you will laugh a jujitsu laugh, knowing that the very fury of your opponent is going to be used to lay him low. Then you will learn to laugh at everything that comes to you, knowing in your heart of hearts that you will rescue out of this calamity an inoculation against any future contingency. Then you will get to the place where calamity only jolts the glory out.

Father God, I know that Thou art teaching me hour by hour the way to complete victory. Help me to seize on everything that happens as a textbook in this school of living. Then everything will train me. Amen.

THANKFUL FOR THE WORST THAT CAN HAPPEN

We must take one more step in this matter of inner poise mid unhappy circumstances. Speaking on Thanksgiving Day in the morning on, "What things I am thankful for," I knew that all my thankfulnesses were vulnerable unless I could accept this, and accept it with real acceptance: "I am thankful that I can be thankful for the worst that can happen to me." I preached on that at night, and because I really meant it, felt that my thankfulnesses were safe—safe if I could be thankful for the worst.

For unless I can be thankful for the worst that can happen, then all my thankfulnesses are unsafe. For at the heart of every good in our lives is this worm eating: suppose that thing is taken away, lost or destroyed—then? In other words, you cannot really be thankful for a thing unless you can also be thankful for the worst that can happen to that thing. When I say "worst" I mean to except one "worst," that is, you yourself or the loved one sinning. Apart from that moral worst it is possible to be thankful for everything, including the worst, that can happen to us. If so, then we are really safe.

For instance, take a happy home. You cannot be truly happy in that happy home unless you can stand the loss of that home, and be thankful for the worst that could happen to it. If you can't be, then your happiness is not safe. You must have a happiness that can stand the loss of the thing you are happy about. Does that sound impossible? No, for if you are a Christian your ultimate happiness is in a center which can't be hit nor hurt by any earthly loss. That center is God. Strip away everything but leave God and you can come back from anything and come back thankful, for the loss of that thing borne gladly deepens your center, God. That means that all calamities are contributive.

When the worst came to Jesus—the Cross—He came back from it by two words: "My God." Those two words were intact. Nothing could snatch them out of His heart. On the pivot of those words He came back from the worst. With God intact within you can look with equanimity on anything that can happen. For anything that happens, taken in the right way, deepens the Center.

O God, I thank Thee for the ultimate thankfulness—the thankfulness that can thank Thee for anything that might happen. Now I am safe, for nothing can touch me. I am hid in Thee. Let life come on. Amen.

AFFIRMATION FOR THE DAY: *Since I am safe if the worst comes to the worst—death—so all my safeties this side of that are safe.*

BUILDING YOUR NEST TOO LOW?

We pursue the thought of being thankful that we can be thankful for the worst that can happen. An outstanding philosopher giving his philosophy of life ended his volume by saying: "Goodbye, dear reader, I'm going out in the garden and play with my children." That was the center of his life—the simple joys of human relations. My inner comment was: But suppose your children should be taken away by death? Then? You have built your nest too low—the floods may reach it and sweep it away. Your philosophy of life is vulnerable. In order not to be vulnerable you must be able to be thankful for the loss of that relationship because you have a relationship which cannot be touched by any human happening.

This week in coming out of a luncheon meeting at a Y.M.C.A. I noted the bright smile on the face of a man of sixty. When I shook hands with him, his hands were hard and rough from doing hard work. Someone pulled me aside and said: "That man was a wealthy silk manufacturer. When rayon and nylon were invented, his silk business was ruined. He was reduced to this. But he has met it with simple joy. One of his greatest pleasures is to go and play on the organ of a church for which he contributed $25,000 in the days of his wealth. He is victorious." As a businessman the worst that could happen to him was the complete loss of his business, but since he was able to be thankful for the worst that could happen, all his other happinesses were safe.

While I was on my first journey to India forty-one years ago, a chaplain said to me on board ship: "You don't drink? You can't live in India without drinking." My reply was: "Well, I don't have to live. I can die if it comes to the pinch. If I die, I'm really better off. Some of you have to live, or you're in for trouble." I said it half-humorously, but I really meant it. A Christian doesn't have to live. If he couldn't die and die gladly, then a worm would be eating at the heart of every earthly relationship and every earthly thing—the worm of possible death. But when that very worm can become a butterfly—death can become immortality—then worms are no longer worries. Everything has possibility in it. You wring the best out of the worst.

O God, my Father, I thank Thee for the worst that can happen. For by Thy redeeming power everything can be redeemed. Through hell and high water I can go with head up and heart singing. Amen.

AFFIRMATION FOR THE DAY: *All the worms I am afraid of have butterflies in them.*

"EVERYTHING IS GRIST TO HIS MILL"

A very regal type of man who had been a superintendent of
olice in India and was used to having everyone dancing at-
ndance on him was converted and came to our Ashram in
dia. As he left he said: "Having done the worst job, the
reeper's, now I am ready for anything." No greater self-
miliation could have been imagined, but having met that he
as literally ready for anything.

That is the meaning of the Christian's consenting to die to
mself. Having died there—the central death—then none of
e little deaths can touch him. He has inoculated himself
ainst death by dying voluntarily.

This week I heard a letter read from a missionary wife whose
sband had been taken by the guerrillas in Sumatra, bound,
indfolded, and then thrown over a bridge into the river. While
e struggled in the water, they shot him. His body was never
covered. His box of belongings was sent to his wife and she
id the son opened it. The clothes were ruined and worthless,
it there were five Bibles in five languages and sermon notes in
re languages—priceless mementos. The mother quietly said:
Well, your father didn't leave much, did he?" To which the boy
plied: "But mother, he left a great deal—he witnessed for
hrist in five languages." And then the boy quietly said:
Mother, I'm going back to Sumatra and take up Dad's work.
m going to be a missionary." He has been accepted by the Mis-
on Board. That is thanking God that you can be thankful for
ie worst thing that can happen. For nothing worse could
appen to a family than that and nothing more beautiful could
appen to a family than that—the son taking up his father's
ork under those circumstances.

In Jesus everything is opportunity. For everything can be
irned from the worst to the best. When Professor Royce says:
No man is safe unless he can stand anything that can happen to
im," then the Christian is more than safe, for he can use
verything that can happen to him. Everything is grist to his
iill. He makes filthy rags into beautiful paper, makes his tears
ito telescopes, coins heaven out of hell. He is incorrigibly
appy.

Father God, I thank Thee that I stand immune and un-
ioved. I am in Thee. All else is marginal. As long as Thou
rt my Center the circumference is secure. Thou art my
ecurity. Amen.

SERENITY AND POISE

Yesterday I said that in Jesus everything is opportunity. I mean that. Even your sins can be used to help others get past those sins. Your infirmities become inspirations. William Axling quotes Kagawa: "Having so largely lost my eyesight the power to see has extended into every part and parcel of my person." Eye-blindness meant a wider seeing.

Kagawa continues: "Criticism, abuse, ridicule, slander, all these serve as polishing powder in the process of further burnishing the mirror-like calm in my heart. Even I stand amazed at this calm! This tranquility within is so composed and sustained that it borders on the absurd." Again he says: "Even in the midst of the most chaotic scenes there will be a stillness of soul which is undisturbable." Again: "It is by no means sinful to make our way through the world with as much peace of mind as possible, laughing as we go, maintaining an unhurried heart and with a pace that betokens time to spare. He who considers this as a sin is a self-inflicted maniac." "This lively consciousness that every moment and in every move he is adventuring with God has produced a serenity and a poise that baffle the uninitiated."

The secret of this serenity? In Rochester, New York, when a Protestant clergyman denounced Kagawa as a menace and his gospel of social and economic reconstruction as moonshine, Kagawa retaliated by spending a whole night in prayer for his denouncer. When you can do that, then serenity is a by-product. Nothing corrodes your soul, nothing steals away your calm. When you love everybody and everything, then all things are yours. Kagawa says: "Both Fuji and the Japanese Alps are but wrinkles on my brow. The Atlantic and the Pacific are my robes. The earth forms a part of my footstool. I hold the solar system in the palm of my hand. I scatter millions of stars across the heavens. The whole creation is mine. God threw it in when He gave me Christ." That is it! All things are yours if you are Christ's. "As long as I love the whole creation I can travel about it with the utmost freedom."

O God, my Father, I thank Thee that my soul has found its calm in Thee. It exults in all because it exults in Thee. I take in the whole universe because I have taken in Thee. I thank Thee, thank Thee. Amen.

AFFIRMATION FOR THE DAY: *"All belongs to you ... the world, life, death, the present and the future, and you belong to Christ."* (I Cor. 3:21, Moffatt.)

FED FROM THE OIL THAT NEVER FAILS

We continue to sit at the feet of Kagawa.

He shared his bed with a beggar and through that sharing contracted trachoma, the dread eye disease which almost robbed him of his sight. " 'It's inconvenient, isn't it?' 'What?' 'Your blindness.' 'Yes, but it is inconvenient for people not to have wings, isn't it? If, however, they invent airplanes, these take the place of wings.' The same is true regarding external eyes. If they go blind it is simply a matter of inventing internal sight. My God is light itself. Even though every outward thing is shrouded in darkness in the inner chamber of my soul, God's eternal light shines on.

> "Burn! oh, thou inner light, burn!
> Burn on, oh light, fed from the oil
> That never fails.

"Prayer continues! Prayer continues! Daily my prayer continues! Back of the blinded eyes prayer continues.

"With the thought of comforting me, a friend remarked: 'Because of so many things waiting to be done you must find this long illness tedious.' I, however, was compelled to confess that I was not conscious of any ennui. I realize that a lot of work is waiting. But work is not the purpose of my life. I am given life that I may live. I am not thinking of tomorrow or the next day, nor even of this day's sunset hour. I am concerned only with being, this present moment, without any sense of tedium, with God. And for men constantly praising God for the joy of the moments lived with Him there is no such thing as tediousness."

But back of all that calm is something more — a complete surrender to God: "There is nothing more exhilarating than to walk through the world unencumbered. If possessions abound there is the haunting fear that they may be stolen. If you are beautifully gowned you worry lest your garments be soiled. If you are high of rank you are anxious lest you be thrown down. If you pride yourself on being erudite, you are cut to the quick if someone makes light of you. Stripped to the skin! Stripped to the skin! That is the way to walk!"

O God, this full surrender to Thee brings a sense of joyous calm, an undisturbed calm amid the coming and going of things and persons and events. It is the center of calm. Amen.

AFFIRMATION FOR THE DAY: *Today I shall milk from each passing event the milk of peace and opportunity.*

"I MUST LAUGH TWICE AS MUCH"

We have been looking at Kagawa, the great Japanese Christian, and have tried to find the secret of his poise. His poise is in God. He says: "I find no necessity for pessimism. Have I not strength in abundance to lay temptations low? Who says that the flesh has a mighty influence over the spirit? My experience is just the reverse. If I may be allowed a confession in which there is no conceit, I see no need for concealing the fact that I am surprisingly strong. If there is literary merit in sincere confession, I will glory in my strength. . . . Since I became God-possessed it has become impossible for me to commit my soul to wanton thoughts. I glory in the might of the Almighty who dwells within me."

If you think this is very high and impossible, then look at this out of very ordinary happenings, amid contemporaneous life. A woman publicly throws a barb into the soul of another woman. She sat there in silence "inwardly bleeding," but calm and without resentment. Another woman, friend of both, came to the one who was hurt and said: "Do you know why she is after you this way? You have the fun of being what you are and N—— is miserable trying to keep up with you. People catch your spirit and ask you to do things, while they flee from hers." The woman who threw the barb was talented and very wealthy, but she didn't know "the fun of being what you are." She got her fun—the meager bit that came her way—through attention, through compliment, through favorable circumstances, but not from inner being, hence her poise was nil.

When Dr. George Carver lost his life savings through a bank crash someone asked if he knew he was bankrupt and he replied: "Yes, I heard," and went on with his teaching as though nothing had happened. A pastor had the fun of being what he was when his only child, a little girl, was taken from him. "Now," he said, "I must laugh twice as much, for now I have to laugh for both of us."

A salesman was showing a new car and said: "Under that hood is 120 h.p. Why that car laughs at mountains." That is the Christian: he laughs at everything, for he has the fun of being what he is.

O Father, I thank Thee that I can lie back and laugh at everything that comes, knowing that I have the secret of fun within me. This heart of mine in tune with Thee has caught the music of the spheres. Amen.

AFFIRMATION FOR THE DAY: *Today, I shall enjoy to the full the fun of being what I am in God.*

THE TWO PILLARS OF OUR PEACE

We look today at the two pillars upon which our peace rests.

Jesus said to His torn and troubled disciples after His death and resurrection: " 'Peace be with you.' When he had said this, he showed them his hands and his side." (John 20:19-20.) Note the connection of "peace" and the showing of "his hands and his side." The peace was based on the worst being met and overcome. The hands and the side bore the marks of the worst that life could do to Him. But they were marks of victory—the worst had been met, and the worst had been turned into the best. Our peace then rests not on a smiling, Pollyanna optimism that has its head in the clouds and refuses to see evil. It has looked life straight in the face and has taken the worst that life can give. At that place it can say, "Peace be with you." It is peace *in spite of!* Your optimism has been won out of the heart of pessimism. It is therefore no cheap optimism. This peace, then, is not the back-slapping type that says, "Buck up"; it is the kind of peace that, having seen the worst, sings!

There is another side to this peace: "Peace be with you. As the Father has sent me, even so I send you" (20:21). The first peace, in verse 20, was based on what Jesus had done for them—"He showed them his hands and his side"—but this second peace is based on what they are going to do for Him: "As the Father has sent me, even so send I you." The Christian peace is based not only on what He does for us but also on what we do for Him. There can be no real peace unless it is based on what He does for us, plus what we are to do for others. It is based on the rhythm of receptivity and response. We receive what He accomplishes, and we respond in our own accomplishments for others. Just to receive without responding will bring an emptiness; just to respond in effort without receiving will also bring an emptiness. The rhythm of life is Take and Give, and the two should be equal.

This peace is soundly based in Scripture and soundly based on the laws of our being which demand intake and outgo in order for us to be healthy. Reality is behind this peace.

Gracious Father, I thank Thee that my peace in Thee is firmly based in Thy Word and in Thy works—in the Scripture and in me. My being demands what it commands. So I am at rest—a rest full of dynamism. Amen.

AFFIRMATION FOR THE DAY: *Peace is, not the absence of conflict, but the presence of God.*

"THE EARTH CAME TO THE HELP"

Last week we ended by saying that reality is behind this peace. Any peace not based on the nature of reality is a precarious peace and will let you down ultimately.

Emerson said many profound things, but this is among his profoundest: "Virtue is adherence in action to the nature of things." A lady told me she had copied that statement and had put it over her kitchen sink so she could look at it many times a day. And no wonder! For if virtue is adherence in action to the nature of things, then sin is departure in action from the nature of things. The nature of reality is behind virtue, and nothing is behind sin except its own inherent drive. This soon expends itself and leaves you flat.

The root meaning of virtue is strength. Virtue has the strength of the universe behind it. It needs nothing around it to bolster it up to make it strong—it is strong in the strength of reality. It has cosmic backing. The idea that evil is strong is pure illusion. It talks big and blusters—it has to, for it knows that at the center it is weak. The superiority complex of evil is the inverse side of its inferiority complex—it asserts outwardly, for it sinks inwardly. But virtue doesn't have to assert anything loudly—it can wait for the revelation of the nature of reality. It therefore has a basic poise.

A little boy read the verse: "Blessed are the meek, for they shall be persecuted"—read it that way out of his limited experience. But Jesus said: "Blessed are the meek, for they shall inherit the earth"—the earth is theirs for the earth is a part of reality and all reality is with the meek. "The earth came to the help of the woman, and the earth opened its mouth and swallowed the river which the dragon had poured from his mouth." (Rev. 12:16.) The earth, the nature of things, comes to the help of those who act according to the nature of things—the virtuous. Every evil is swallowed up sooner or later. The universe is not built for lies, dishonesties, selfishness. It is built for truth, honesty, and unselfishness. The earth swallows up evil; look at history—and believe! The earth sustains good; look at history—and believe!

My God and Father, how can I ever thank Thee enough for the feeling of being sustained by everything real. I walk the earth a conqueror; for I fear nothing, since everything real is on my side. Glory be, glory be. Amen.

AFFIRMATION FOR THE DAY: *The sum total of reality is conspiring to help me to power and poise.*

"THAT I MAY NOT BE SHAKEN"

In the most triumphant moment of human history, in the flush of the first days of the Resurrection, Peter quoted this triumphal passage to express the mood of the hour:

> I saw the Lord always before me,
> for he is at my right hand that I may not be shaken;
> therefore my heart was glad, and my tongue rejoiced;
> moreover my flesh will dwell in hope.
> For thou wilt not abandon my soul to Hades,
> nor let thy Holy One see corruption.
> Thou hast made known to me the ways of life;
> thou wilt make me full of gladness with thy presence.

In the preceding verse he said: "But God raised him up, having loosed the pangs of death, because it was not possible for him to be held by it." (Acts 2:24.) The resurrection of Jesus was not based on the sovereign act of God raising Jesus, an act imposed on reality—it was based on the nature of reality: "Because it was not possible for him to be held by it." It was impossible for a man like Jesus, who held death in His grasp, to be held by death. The nature of things would be reversed if Jesus should be held captive by death. So the resurrection was not based on an extraneous act of God; it came from the intrinsic fact—He had to rise, being what He was.

So the words "That I may not be shaken" are based on the same inherent facts—you are not shaken because the nature of things is with you; you will rise over every circumstance, including death, because death is a circumstance and not an inner-stance.

We can now look at the verses quoted above: "I saw the Lord always before me"—He is "before me"; He holds the future. But He also has the present: "He is at my right hand." If I knew He held the future and not the present, I would be shakable. The psalmist puts it: "Thou hast beset me behind," the past; "and before," the future; "and laid thine hand upon me," the present. The basis of my poise is that God buries the bad past, preserves the good intact; He guarantees the future and is "at my right hand" in the present. I'm safe!

O God, this is too wonderful for me. I am awed and bow with grateful heart before the wonder of Thy perfect preservation. What can life—or death—or anything do to me? Amen.

AFFIRMATION FOR THE DAY: *"Thou wilt keep him in perfect peace, whose mind is stayed on thee."* (Isa. 26:3.)

STRENGTH THAT BECAME WEAKNESS

We continue our meditation upon this passage: "The Lord . . . is at my right hand." The right hand represents the place of power. For the Lord to be at my right hand is for Him to be at the place of my strongest point. We have thought of the Lord being at the place of our weakness to strengthen that weakness, but is He to be at the place of our strength to strengthen that strength and to save that strength from becoming weakness? Yes.

Our weaknesses get us into trouble, but our very strength gets us into trouble even more. Take the sins of the good people in the New Testament—they came out of their very strengths. Paul was anxious about the purity of the Church and hence he insisted on not forgiving and restoring Mark, for he had turned back on a previous journey at Pamphylia. This strong desire for a sifted purity—this strength turned to weakness—made Paul hard, censorious, bordering on the pharisaical. Paul needed the Lord to be at his right hand to make his goodness tender, forgiving, and redemptive. Peter fell at the place of his faith. "Though they all fall away because of you, I will never fall away"—his right hand, his faith, became the place of his weakness; he lacked humility. His faith was such a driving force that it drove him past humility into spiritual pride, and his pride went before his fall—his denial. He needed the Lord at his right hand to make his faith humble.

Those who are in Christian work are so anxious to see that work succeed and prosper that they often exaggerate that success out of the very desire to see it—they produce it, often out of their imaginations; they border on the untruthful. They need the Lord to be at their right hand to make their yearnings honest, and realistic, and truthful.

Take prayer—the right hand of many good people. But prayer may so aborb them in itself that it becomes an end in itself. They end up—in praying! The means stops them this side of the end—the end is an outgoing, creative person.

So love may become sentimentality, purity become prudity, truthfulness become thorny, unless the Lord is at our right hand.

O God, set a watch not only at the place of my weakness but also at the place of my strength. For I want my strengths to be strong through Thy eternal correction. Redeem my virtues. Amen.

AFFIRMATION FOR THE DAY: *No light in me shall become darkness today.*

LAUGHING EVIL OUT OF COUNTENANCE

We continue our meditation: "Therefore my heart was glad" (Acts 2:26). A "glad" heart is the secret of poise and power.

A Chinese student, who was so slovenly in his life that one teacher said, "The very sight of that boy makes me angry," was suffering from a bad habit about which I told an illustrative story in a meeting. He walked out of the meeting, lay back, and laughed, and said, "Then this is the end of my habit." It dropped off then and there. That slovenly, no-account young man is now a doctor of philosphy and is one of the most outstanding Chinese leaders. Someone said of him: "To have won that man to Christ was worth a lifetime of endeavor." But note that laugh that broke the spell of the old. He laughed evil out of countenance and was released. A central joy is the greatest toning-up tonic.

This quaint prayer hangs in a cathedral at Chester, England.

> Give me a good digestion, Lord,
> And also something to digest;
> Give me a healthy body, Lord,
> With sense to keep it at its best.
> Give me a healthy mind, Good Lord,
> To keep the good and pure in sight,
> Which seeing sin, is not appalled
> But finds a way to set it right.
> Give me a mind that is not bored,
> That does not whimper, whine, nor sigh;
> Don't let me worry overmuch
> About the fussy thing called "I."
> Give me a sense of humor, Lord,
> Give me the grace to see a joke,
> To get some pleasure out of life
> And pass it on to other folk.

A woman of ninety-one zrites this as her secret: "I live alone, have no near relatives, but life is full and rich and satisfying, growing better every year, as it always does when we let God have His way in our lives, especially when He gives us a task that is so big that we can do it only in His strength."

O God, my Father, give me the glad heart, and then I shall be able to smile my way through everything that comes. Then I shall be free. Amen.

AFFIRMATION FOR THE DAY: *Today I shall give the glad hand, show the glad face, because I have the glad heart.*

THE TONGUE AND THE HEART CO-ORDINATED

We continue to meditate upon:

> My heart was glad, and my tongue rejoiced;
> moreover my flesh shall dwell in hope.

In addition to the "glad" heart we must have the "tongue" that rejoices, we must express what is within the heart, or soon the heart will not be glad. If there is no outgo, there will soon be no inflow. For the outside and the inside will sooner or later be the same. Hence if there is no expression, there will soon be nothing to express.

"Out of the abundance of the heart the mouth speaks," and if the mouth doesn't speak then there will be no abundance to speak of. No one can be poised who isn't going forward—strange but true. When we walk, we get off balance by stepping forward, and then catch our balance by the other foot. All movement forward upsets balance and recovers it at the next step, so off-balance plus catching of balance equals progress. In our spiritual life it is by adventure and conquest that we keep poise. We get off balance by adventuring in witnessing, and we catch up by an act of faith, and thus we go forward poised. If one stops and says: "Now I am poised and calm; I'll do nothing to destroy this calm and poise," then he will soon find that he has no poise or calm. This is where the ascetics of India missed the way. They thought poise and calm was the cessation of activity. This meant withdrawal. The Christian way teaches, not withdrawal, but witnessing as the way to poise and power. If we do not create, we cut across our own nature and are frustrated.

A businessman of Des Moines, Iowa was only a nominal Christian, but this verse spoke to him: "The Spirit and the Bride say 'Come.' And let him who hears say, 'Come.' " He had been hearing all his life, but he had never said, "Come." So he went to his pastor and said, "My business can run on half my time. I'll give four hours a day to business and four hours to Christ. Give me a job." He gave him a list of nominal Christians. He called on them; won many to Christ. Then he was given a list of students in the local college, not Christian; called on every one; won many. Then he took a list of those in the city not Christian. He is winning them. Hundreds have been won. He has poise and power.

O God, I've been hearing and hearing and hearing; now let me say "Come," and let me never cease to say "Come." For the Spirit within me—the creative spirit—is saying "Come." Amen.

AFFIRMATION FOR THE DAY: *Today, calm because creative.*

"THAT'S STILL IN THE PENCIL"

We saw yesterday that when the heart was glad, the tongue should rejoice—should share with others. The very end of the atonement is to get us out of ourselves and released in loving service to others: "And he died for all, that those who live might live no longer for themselves—a saving of one from himself. This is the central release. The end of evangelism is to produce an evangelist. We all propagate something. When men see us, they get a dominant impression—an impression of self-preoccupation, or an impression of serenity and poise, or an impression of conflict, or an impression of impurity. The dominant impression which we leave is our evangelism. So we are all evangelists—of something. If this be true, then I choose—I choose Christ. He shall be my evangelism. And this shall be not merely by act but by tongue as well. For if I act and do not speak, then I am a half-witness; just as I am a half-witness if I speak and do not act. To be a whole witness I must witness with my total life—deeds and tongue.

A boy of twenty-three, dying in a hospital, said to a pastor friend of mine: "Everybody has been so good to me. I haven't a thing in the world to leave to anybody. Couldn't I leave my eyes to somebody?" He offered his all. And was happy in the offering. John says: "We are writing this that our joy may be complete." (I John 1:4.) John's joy was complete in the creative, sharing urge. So our witnessing helps others, and it helps the helper.

A little girl was asked where the dot was that goes over the *i*. She replied: "That's still in the pencil." Perhaps we have bottled up our witness—it is still in us. Then get it out quick; for if you don't, you'll probably have little to witness to. But your witness is, not to you, but to your Redeemer. Witness to Him, and then you'll have more and more to witness to within yourself. Give, and you will soon be running over with something to give.

O Christ, open my lips in testimony—not to myself but to Thee. Give me the open lips about Thee, and then I shall have the open heart to Thee. Give me courage, knowing that in that hour it will be given me what I ought to speak. Amen.

"MY FLESH WILL DWELL IN HOPE"

We continue our study of the passage:

> moreover my flesh will dwell in hope.
> For thou wilt not abandon my soul to Hades,
> nor let thy Holy One see corruption.

When "the Lord . . . is at my right hand," and our "heart" is "glad," and our "tongue" rejoices, then we are not "shaken." Moreover, our "flesh will dwell in hope." The effect is seen on the body—the flesh dwells in hope and in health. And the hope produces the health. Doubt and despair produce ill health. Therefore you must talk health to your body, not illness. People ask me if I'm tired, and my reply usually is: "If I should say so, then I'd be more tired. No, I am fresh in God." The affirmation of freshness in God produces, or tends to produce, that freshness. Is that autosuggestion? Yes, and very good autosuggestion. You are autosuggesting either illness or health, then why not the better?

A woman said in one of our Ashrams: "I'm tired of being dictated to by my body." The alternative is: Dictate to your body, or your body will dictate to you! That dictation to your body can be along the line of your faith in God.

An outstanding Christian worker said with a sigh: "Last night I was tired to extinction." In saying that, she became more tired that day. For the expression left an impression.

Now take the case of a girl who dictated to her body: She had a spine infection which made her an invalid. She graduated from high school and was chosen the valedictorian of her class—gave the address over a phone while lying on her bed. She set up an employment agency and did war work, fitting parts together. She dictated to her body and made it serve her purposes.

If we get our souls out of the "Hades" of conflict and fear and selfishness, our bodies will be saved from "corruption." But if we let our souls slide into the Hades of conflict, fear and selfishness, we will pull our bodies down too—they will "see corruption."

Dear Lord, be at my right hand, that I may not be shaken. Take over the center, and the margins of life will be safe and sound. Take my inner attitudes, and my outer life will take care of itself. I know that. Help me. Amen.

AFFIRMATION FOR THE DAY: *Today, not tired but fresh in God.*

ON PUTTING UP WITH IMPERFECTIONS

If we are to live a life of power and poise, then we must put up with imperfections in ourselves and others. Those who are always demanding perfection in themselves and others are always upset souls, for they never find it either in themselves or in others.

The other night after an important broadcast in the Town Meeting on the Air, reaching probably ten million people, I came home saying to myself: "Why didn't you say this? And that?" I felt myself slipping into a bad night, when I pulled myself up and talked to myself: "Stanley Jones, you're not perfect and you never do a perfect job. When you record a talk and it is played back, there are your hesitations, your wrong words, your false steps, sprinkled through the whole. And yet you get your message across. You've got to put up with imperfection in yourself and others and to get on with the work." I dismissed it, went to bed and slept, and was fresh for the coming tasks.

"Remember Lot's wife." She looked back and became a pillar of salt. If you look back at your mistakes and shortcomings, then you'll not be a pillar of salt, but you will be a pillar draped in sackcloth and smeared with ashes—a sorry sight. I know a brilliant pastor with very high ideals for himself and others; and when he doesn't reach them, he goes to bed for three days, ill over his own imperfections. Correct your imperfections, but don't make yourself more imperfect by getting sick over your imperfections. It's a losing game.

A man said to Dwight Moody: "Mr. Moody, your grammar is poor." "Yes," he replied, "I know it. But I'm making the best of what I have. Are you?" He got his message across, poor grammar or no poor grammar. And multitudes responded. When someone said to Henry Ward Beecher: "You made three mistakes in grammar this morning in your sermon," he replied, "Madam, I feel sorry for the grammar that gets in my way when I'm preaching." He was preaching a perfect Christ, not trying to demonstrate his own perfection.

If, as Emerson says, "Weeds are plants whose virtues have not yet been discovered," then our very imperfections can be virtues in that they drive us to God in humility of heart.

O Loving Father, who hast made us "imperfect masters of an imperfect world," help me this day to forgive imperfection in myself and others, and in the forgiving help me to be furthered. Amen.

AFFIRMATION FOR THE DAY: *My imperfections are my perfections in travail, coming to birth.*

"WHAT IS THAT TO THEE?"

We look at another step on the way to poise and power—be willing to be yourself. Yesterday we saw that we must forgive imperfection in ourselves and others; today we must see that it is futile to try to be someone else.

Peter said to Jesus: "Lord, and what shall this man do?" And Jesus replied: "What is that to thee? follow thou me." (John 21:21-22, K.J.V.) Don't be too much concerned about the other person and what he does—you follow Christ. Marshall Fêng Yü-hsiang and I were talking in his mountain retreat. He raked out the sins and shortcomings of the Christians in the Chinese government, especially Generalissimo Chiang Kai-shek. I stopped him and quoted the passage above: "What is that to thee? follow thou me." He looked at me for a moment and then poured out more bitter criticism. I stopped him again and said, "Marshall Fêng, I'm afraid I must quote my passage again: 'What is that to thee? follow thou me.' " He struck his knee with his hand and said, "Good, you've got me." His eyes were on others instead of on Jesus. That led him down the slippery road to catastrophe. He said, "You've got me," but I never got him, for he continued to the end bitterly denouncing others. When you are denouncing others, you are not announcing Him. "If you are on the judgment seat, you are not in the witness stand."

Whenever I pick up a letter from a certain lady I say to myself: "Whom is she denouncing now?" It is the inverse side of an inferiority complex.

You'll be upset if you look at people too much. "If you look around, you'll be distracted; if you look within, you'll be discouraged; if you look at Jesus, you'll have peace." The account says that when Peter "saw the waves," he began to sink. As long as he had his eyes on something else, he sank. If you get your eyes on people and what they do, you'll sink when they sink. You have one steady spot in your universe—"the same yesterday, today, and forever"—Jesus. You keep your eyes there, and your feet will walk on troubled waves and stormy seas. You'll be held steady, anywhere.

Dear Christ, I know that if my gaze is steady, my gait will be steady. Keep my gaze on Thee. When I tend to get it off on things and persons, bring me lovingly back, for I want poise and I want power. Amen.

AFFIRMATION FOR THE DAY: *Glance at yourself and others; gaze at Jesus.*

ON BEING YOURSELF

We saw yesterday that we must not look at others if we are going to have poise and power. Today we must go a step further and insist that not only must you not look at others; you must not try to be others—be yourself.

A dean of girls was always upset as long as she was measuring herself by the yardstick of another dean. She decided she was fundamentally wrong in doing this—that she was herself and should measure herself by her own yardstick. That let down a tension in her life and freed her from a false bondage.

When God made you, He broke the pattern. He has never made anybody like you and never will again. You are unique and can give a unique contribution to life. Be yourself—in God.

Angelo Patri, expert on child training, says: "Nobody is so miserable as he who longs to be somebody and something other than the person he is in mind and body." Sam Wood, who has directed such great motion pictures as *Good-bye, Mr. Chips* and *For Whom the Bell Tolls,* says: "Experience has taught me that it is safe to drop, as quickly as possible, people who pretend to be what they aren't."

I started out in life as a preacher trying to be at various times various preachers whom I admired. I found myself imitating them. It was ridiculous. I did it badly, and it got me into trouble. My favorite preacher said dramatically from the pulpit: "It's a lie." I tried saying that in a household circle, and it came near disrupting the household. He could get away with it—I couldn't.

A man for a long time was under great bondage because he couldn't be a second Dwight L. Moody—couldn't do the things Moody did. Then one day he came to himself and said: "When God got hold of Moody, he got hold of a bigger man than He did when He got hold of you. You don't have to do Moody's work. Be yourself and do your own work—under God." A tension was let down. He was natural again, therefore effective.

Let God pull out all the stops and play you all over, but let Him play you as you, not as somebody else.

O Father, I would be myself, but myself in Thee. For in Thee I find myself, all my powers heightened by Thee. I would be natural in the Supernatural. For there I am at Home. And there I blossom, and bloom, and am fruitful. Amen.

AFFIRMATION FOR THE DAY: *I shall be myself today, plus all that God can make me.*

"UNBIND HIM AND LET HIM GO"

One of the most beautiful passages in the New Testament is the one where Jesus says regarding the raised Lazarus, "Unbind him, and let him go." Lazarus was alive but bound with grave clothes. Jesus in these words loosed him from inhibiting bondage, made him free—free to go places! That is the key to what Jesus does.

When I think of the freedoms Jesus has brought to men, I am embarrassed in knowing where to begin. Take one at hand. I am writing this in a plane over the Persian Gulf. The man to my left couldn't eat the breakfast offered him because there was pork, and his faith forbade the use of pork. The man to my right couldn't eat the lunch because there was beef in it, and his faith forbade the use of beef. The bondage of what can be eaten and what cannot is enormous when it involves hundreds of millions. And the degradation of religion in the process: you are good if you refrain and bad if you don't. Both smoke cigarettes, for the books say nothing about them, though cigarettes may be physically harmful.

Jesus cleansed the whole realm by saying: "Not what goes into the mouth defiles a man, but what comes out of the mouth, this defiles a man." That simple sentence was one of the most freeing sentences ever uttered. It threw the emphasis of religion from the ceremonial to the moral.

And when we come to the inner, He says the same thing there: "Unbind him, and let him go." For the inner bondage from fear and anxiety, escapism, resentments, conflicting desires sand emotions, is enormous—and enervating. They lay a paralyzing hand on our outer accomplishments.

Take fear and anxiety again. How does He unbind us from these twin evils? By the simple expedient of getting us to meet today today: "Do not be anxious about tomorrow, for tomorrow will be anxious for itself. Let the day's own trouble be sufficient for the day." (Matt. 6:34.) That simple sentence was one of the most freeing ever uttered. It unbinds us from tomorrow and looses us for today. Many are so bound by tomorrow and its foreboding troubles that they are unfit for today. Tomorrow spoils today.

O Father God, Thou hast set my eyes on today and hast freed them from tomorrow. Help me this day to do the right thing at hand, and the right result will follow tomorrow. Amen.

AFFIRMATION FOR THE DAY: *Tomorrow is not yet here; yesterday is gone, today is my day—and Thine.*

"DAY-TIGHT COMPARTMENTS"

We were meditating yesterday on, "Unbind him, and let him go," in relation to being loosed from tomorrow and its troubles by facing today, today.

Sir William Osler, the great physician of my home city, Baltimore, was world famous—the most famous physician of his generation. He said that twenty-one words from Carlyle helped to free him from a life of worry: "Our main business is, not to see what lies dimly at a distance, but to do what lies clearly at hand." Osler adds: "The load of tomorrow, added to that of yesterday, carried today, makes the strongest falter. Shut off the future as tightly as the past. The future is today. . . . There is no tomorrow. The day of man's salvation is now. . . . Shut close, then, the great fore and aft bulkheads, and prepare to cultivate the habit of day-tight compartments." That gives us inner poise and power to meet things one at a time.

Dale Carnegie, commenting on the objection that one must think about tomorrow—must take out insurance, must prepare for old age—says: "By all means take thought for the morrow, yes, careful thought and planning and preparation. But have no anxiety."

Take a personal illustration. Two days ago I felt inwardly called to take a stand before an important conference—a stand that cut across the position of my beloved colleagues, foreign and Indian. I saw it would probably make me decidedly unpopular to take such a stand and would jeopardize my future within the organization and within Christian missions in India. There was a struggle—a begging off, a prayer to be relieved of this responsibility. But when the Voice within was inexorable: "You must," then after an afternoon of prayer before the address I went calmly to the unpleasant task. I deliberately shut off any thought or foreboding about the consequences of what I was doing: "Tomorrow will be anxious for itself." My inner thought was: "Do the right thing, and leave the results with God." I knew if I did the right thing, the right results would follow—eventually. I was astonished by my own divine indifference to consequences.

O my Father, I thank Thee for this unutterable peace that possesses us when we do the right thing. The consequences are safe—in Thy hands. My business is with today. Amen.

AFFIRMATION FOR THE DAY: *Today I shall take the right means; the right ends will take care of themselves.*

"THIS IS ALL THAT LIFE MEANS"

We are looking at the passage, "Unbind him, and let him go," in its relationship to being unbound from the future to be let go into today.

Dale Carnegie in *How to Stop Worrying and Start Lviing* quotes a young man in uniform: "I had worried until I had developed what doctors called 'spasmodic transverse colon'—a condition which produced intense pain. . . . I was worried about whether I would come through all this . . . , whether I would live to hold my only child in my arms—a son of sixteen months, whom I never had seen. I was so worried and exhausted that I lost thirty-four pounds. I was so frantic that I was almost out of my mind. I ended up in an Army dispensary. An Army doctor gave me some advice which completely changed my life. After giving me a thorough physical examination, he informed me that my troubles were mental. 'Ted,' he said, 'I want you to think of your life as an hourglass. You know there are thousands of grains of sand in the top of the hourglass; and they all pass slowly and evenly through the narrow neck in the middle. Nothing you or I could do would make more than one grain of sand pass through the narrowneck without impairing the hourglass. When we start in the morning, there are hundreds of tasks which we feel that we must accomplish that day, but if we do not take them one at a time and let them pass through the day slowly and evenly, as do the grains of sand passing through the narrow neck of the hourglass, then we are bound to break our own physical or mental structure.' I have practiced that philosophy ever since. . . . 'One grain of sand at a time. . . . One task at a time.' That advice saved me physically and mentally."

Robert Louis Stevenson once wrote: "Anyone can carry his burden, however hard, for one day. Anyone can live sweetly, patiently, lovingly, purely, till the sun goes down. And this is all that life means."

If you are fettered by the fears of tomorrow, then surrender tomorrow into the hands of God and do it now, and then go out to live gaily and effectively today. And tomorrow will blossom with joy because you have lived—really lived—today.

Father God, into Thy hands I commend my tomorrows. Now let me live in Thee today like a relaxed and eager child—alive to everything and not numbed by tomorrow. Amen.

AFFIRMATION FOR THE DAY: *Today, alive to God, and therefore alive to every good thing.*

"LOOK TO THIS DAY"

We continue our meditation on meeting today today. If you are biting your fingernails about tomorrow, remember that a diet of fingernails is not nourishing; it gets you into the raw.

Kalidasa, a famous Indian poet, says:

> Today well lived makes every day a dream of happiness
> And every tomorrow a vision of hope.
> Look well, therefore, to this day!

I recall vividly how two years ago there was hanging over Christian missionaries in India a dread uncertainty—would we be allowed to stay in this new independent India? If allowed to stay, could we carry on anything except medical and educational work—would evangelistic work be forbidden? Would they liquidate the whole system we had built up through blood, and tears, and prayers? We could have bitten our fingernails and worried ourselves sick. We had a case for the jitters. Today? There has been put into the constitution of the new India: "The right to profess, practice, and propagate one's faith is guaranteed." Two hundred amendments to modify or nullify that were rejected by the new government. A non-Christian legislator said in the debate: "The Christian community has never transgressed the limits of legitimate propagation of their religious views." Another: "The Christians want this retention of their right, not because of aggressive design of conversion, but because it is a part of their religious injunction to propagate." Here was the right not only to stay but to propagate our faith guaranteed by the constitution, and that right defended by non-Christians, and all amentments swept aside—and this at the center! A bishop yesterday remarked: "Never were our fears more belied than by what has taken place."

Live today on a diet, not of fingernails, but of faith.

Gracious Father, I thank Thee for today and for its adventure. I thank Thee that I can go into it—with Thee. So all day long I shall meet everything calmly—in Thee. Then night shall come in quiet calm. Amen.

AFFIRMATION FOR THE DAY: *No tensions about tomorrow, no turning back to yesterday, but a turning into today—with God.*

UNBINDING THE SUBCONSCIOUS

We continue to study the possibilities of the statement of Jesus: "Unbind him, and let him go." We saw He unbinds us from fear and anxiety about tomorrow by helping us to face to-day today. But many of us are not so bound by tomorrow as we are by yesterday. It is the yesterdays that shadow today—the sense of failure, and guilt, and inadequacy. And deeper than yesterday is the deposit of the whole individual and racial past in our subconscious minds. There is the central bondage—the bondage of the subconscious. It reaches its fingers out of the past and determines the present. We are in the grip of destiny—the destiny of the subconscious. Do the words of Jesus "unbind him, and let him go," do these words penetrate there—there at the depths of us, in the subconscious?

Here I cannot argue—I can only testify. I found myself about a year after my conversion a very divided person. The conscious mind had been converted—radically and gloriously. But the subconscious mind had not been. There the driving instincts of self, sex, and the herd still reigned, driving for their own completion and satisfaction. These urges clashed with the new morality built up in the conscious mind. I was a house divided against myself. My mother remarked: "Stanley, religion isn't designed to make us unhappy." For she saw the drawn look on my face as a result of inner tension. I was like the ship on which Paul was shipwrecked—it was caught at the place "where two seas met" and was battered by the conflicting currents (Acts 27:41, K.J.V.). I was puzzled: Was this the best that Christianity could do—leave you divided against yourself? At that time I came across a book—a book of destiny to me: *The Christian's Secret of a Happy Life.* I read it avidly, for this was telling of the possibility of total victory—victory at the depths. I came to the forty-second page, when the Voice seemed to say: "Now is the time to get it." But I pleaded that I did not know what I wanted, that I would seek when I was through with the book. But the Voice was the more inexorable: "Now is the time to get it." I saw I was in a controversy, closed the book, fell on my knees.

O God, I thank Thee that Thou art the inexorable Lover haunting us to victory. Thou dost refuse to allow us to settle down this side of victory—of complete victory. I thank Thee. Amen.

AFFIRMATION FOR THE DAY: *All my crises are finger posts, pointing me to the Cross.*

THE BEST GIFT FOR THE ASKING!

I continue my story of the inner release from the conflict of the subconscious: As I closed the book and dropped upon my knees I said: "Now Lord, what shall I do?" Very quietly the Voice said: "Will you give me your all? All you know, and all you don't know?" I replied, as simply as a child: "Yes, Lord, I do." Then the Voice: "Then take my *ALL*." I arose from my knees saying, "I do." The pact was verbally sealed on both sides: my all, His All. It was sealed by faith. I walked around the room asserting that faith; and after about ten minutes in which I was literally pushing away doubt, the faith turned to fact and the fact to feeling. I was filled—filled to my depths, and to my finger tips, and to the roots of my hair; I was filled with the Spirit. It was all very quiet—just the silent tears of joy rolling down my cheeks. But waves of refining Fire seemed to sweep my being, cleansing, uniting. The Holy Spirit had moved into the center of my being, and these outer manifestations were the sign of that inward possession. The manifestations may vary from a quiet calm and pervasive peace to strong physical emotion. "To each is given the manifestation of the Spirit for the common good." (I Cor. 12:7.) And it may be added—for our own good.

The Holy Spirit supplies that lack so often found in psychiatry—the lack of an intimate divine Aid. The Holy Spirit within is aid where aid is needed most—down amidst the subconscious drives and urges. With Him within and in control we can relax—relax at the center, for we know we are now being held by a Power not our own, and held from within. The Holy Spirit is the center and secret of our relaxation. We are not sitting on a lid; there is no need to; for the subconscious and the conscious are both under a common control—the control of the Spirit. Released at the center, then we are released at the margins. Life is all of a piece, and it is gay and contagious. Power and poise have come for the asking—and receiving.

The best gift in heaven or on earth can be had on the lowliest terms—asking and receiving. That makes poise and power within reach of you—now.

O Lord God, my Father, I thank Thee that Thou hast provided for my need where my need is greatest—within. I am relaxed at the center, for I am relaxed in Thee—not in myself. I thank Thee. Amen.

AFFIRMATION FOR THE DAY: *The Holy Spirit within is the secret, the center, and the source of my power and poise.*

QUIET PRAYER UNBINDS US

This possibility of having that verse fulfilled in us, "Unbind him, and let him go," may take place in a dramatic moment such as the one described yesterday, but it can also come through the habit of quiet prayer. The fact is that no dramatic experience can take the place of quiet prayer. If it is not followed by quiet prayer, then the experience will fade out and be inoperative. No experience is proof against prayerlessness. A pastor had on his desk: "Nothing can kill a minister except to kill his experience of God"; and we may add: Nothing can kill our experience of God so decisively as prayerlessness. And again we may add: Nothing can unbind you and let you go so wonderfully as a daily time spent in prayer.

I established the habit in college of setting aside an hour and a half—a half-hour in the morning, another at noon, and another at eventide. I've telescoped the last two and spend an hour at eventide. If I see I will not be able to do it at eventide, I push it up into the day. But it must be preserved. For I find without it I'm a bulb pulled out of its socket; with it I'm that bulb attached to the source of power—full of light and power. I find I'm better or worse as I pray more or less. "Little prayer, little victory; much prayer, much victory; no prayer, no victory."

For in prayer you align yourself to the purposes and power of God, and He is able to do things through you that He couldn't otherwise do. For this is an open universe, where some things are left open contingent upon our doing them. If we do not do them, they will never be done. So God has left certain things open to prayer—things which will never be done except as we pray. It is, not a closed universe, but one open to the praying heart.

I sat one day in meditation and the question came: "If God would offer to give you one thing—and only one thing—what would you ask?" After a moment's thought I replied: "Give me a prayerful heart." I have thought about it a good deal since then, and I've come to the conclusion that I could ask nothing better. For if I have the prayerful heart, all else follows.

O Father, give me the prayerful heart. Let prayer pervade my soul as blood pervades my body. And just as blood carries sustenance and brings away impurities, so let prayer sustain and cleanse me. Amen.

AFFIRMATION FOR THE DAY: *The prayerful heart is insurance against petty upsets and assurance of power for the demands of today.*

"THE SOVEREIGN CURE FOR WORRY"

Let us continue to think upon the power of quiet prayer to unbind us and let us go.

The testimony which I have made concerning the power of prayer in my life is sustained by men and women in all walks of life. Listen to William James, the great psychologist: "Of course, the sovereign cure for worry is religious faith." Again: "It gives a new zest for life—more life, a larger, richer, more satisfying life." And again: "Faith is one of the forces by which men live, and the total absence of it means collapse." Then the words of A. A. Brill, the psychiatrist: "Anyone who is truly religious does not develop a neurosis."

Henry Ford, I was told, read my book *The Way* every day to his wife before he died. He said to Dale Carnegie, when asked if he ever worried: "No. I believe God is managing affairs, and that He doesn't need any advice from me. With God in charge, I believe that everything will work out for the best in the end. So what is there to worry about?" But religious faith cannot be sustained without prayer. So prayer is at the heart of religious faith. As Mahatma Gandhi said: "Without prayer I would have been a lunatic long ago." If the years have left no scars on me, except radiant scars, it is that prayer has been my refuge and my strength.

Once thirty-two years ago when I was going through a physical crisis as a result of a nervous break and was faced with the dilemma of finding new power or giving up the ministry and the mission field to try to regain my shattered health, God spoke to a missionary on furlough, Miss Grandstrand, a woman of a deep prayer life: "Pray for Stanley Jones." She was in America, and I was in India, and she knew nothing of what it was all about. But the burden of prayer was laid so heavily upon her that she canceled all engagements and shut herself up in a hotel room for a whole day and prayed. Later on she told me about it, and we traced it back and found that it was the exact time when I was touched in India and made perfectly whole—the turning point in my whole life. Her prayers and mine met at the Throne of Grace. Result? Perfect health.

O Living God, Thou art anxious to breathe calm, and life, and contagion through every portion of my being; give me a receptive heart—the heart that takes that calm, and life, and contagion now. Amen.

AFFIRMATION FOR THE DAY: *Prayer is, not overcoming God's reluctance, but laying hold of His highest willingness.*

NO VITAL LOSSES

I wrote yesterday telling how I was bound by collapse and inadequacy and loosed by prayer into strength and adequacy. But prayer does the same in the lesser crises of life.

One day in Utica, New York, I gave my bag to the porter to take to the train. In all my years of travel in East and West I've never had a porter let me down, but this one did. When I got to the crowded train, the porter and the bag were not there. I deposited my handbag and the manuscript of *The Way* in the day coach—foolishly—and ran back to get my bag. The porter had deposited it by the gate and disappeared. I grabbed my bag and ran back to the train to find it just pulling out with my handbag and manuscript. That manuscript! Years of work on it! The station master wired ahead to the conductor to search the train for the handbag and the manuscript. Then he managed to secure a place for me on the *Empire Express,* on which it had been said there was no place. When I sat in a reserved seat on this streamliner, I said: "Now Lord, this is lovely to have a seat on this streamliner when I would have had to stand in that other train I missed, but what about my bag and manuscript?" The Voice replied: "You and I have traveled a long way through life together, and I've never let a vital loss come to you. The loss of the bag and the manuscript would be vital, so you'll find them at Rochester." I relaxed and buried my fears and anxieties in the love and faithfulness of God. I was at perfect peace. When I walked into the station, there were my bag and manuscript on a table at the center of the room. I was there only a half-hour later than the other train, had a good seat in a streamliner instead of standing up, and found my bag and manuscript as promised—and more, I had found an assurance, corroborated by this incident: "I have never let a vital loss come to you," which meant that none would come in the future *if we traveled together.*

Prayer makes you and God travel together. The Quiet Time starts the day with Him, it ends the day with Him and saturates the day with Him.

Gracious God and Father, burn upon my heart the fact that in Thee no vital loss can come to me if we travel together. This day I put my hand in Thine, and we'll travel together. Amen.

AFFIRMATION FOR THE DAY: *The only vital loss that can come to me to-day will be the loss of the prayerful heart—keep that, and there can be no vital losses.*

TWO DOGS TEACH US

Life in New York City acts like a violent stimulant to one who comes into it from without. Like the little girl who said she "felt in a hurry all over," so I felt in a hurry all over when I went into the rush of that throbbing city. But I noticed how the bus drivers had learned to survive amidst that roar and rush: They would run up to a stop light, throw their clutch out of gear, and, instead of straining and pushing against the light to change, would sit back relaxed and unstrained. They did exactly what the heart does—it rests fifteen hours out of the twenty-four by resting between beats. This traffic-light stopping and relaxing was the resting between beats. That is what the Quiet Time does to the day—it relaxes and rests you between the beats of the day. To pump hard all day and to have no rests between means that we become inwardly tired.

Even a dog knows that. I went to see a dog in the Bronx in New York who had learned a secret and helped a pastor's wife to hold to that secret. Every day this lovely dog, a cross between a Saint Bernard and a collie, would come to the kitchen door at a certain hour, and stand there, and wag his tail, and would keep wagging his tail until she would leave her pots and pans and come with him into the other room for a Quiet Time. He would eagerly accompany her, and would lie down on the floor with paws stretched out, and completely relaxed would enjoy the Quiet Time with her. After the Quiet Time they were both ready for New York again!

A group was talking about whether there would be dogs in heaven, and one remarked: "Well, if there aren't, I wouldn't want to go there," whereupon this dog, Sandy, lying on the floor, flopped his tail upon the floor in agreement! It was his way of saying, "Amen." When I told that story of the dog and the Quiet Time, another woman told me that her husband could not get her dog to go with him to the farm, though he loved to roam the farm, when the Quiet Time came. He preferred to go with her into the Quiet Time and relax. Then he was ready to roam—anywhere! But the Quiet Time must be kept! I would like to loan those wise dogs around to harassed households and burdened souls.

O Christ of the Relaxed, Calm Heart, give me the will to be quiet before Thee, to relax in Thy presence, and to absorb Thy quiet strength and poise. Then I shall be ready for anything, anywhere. Amen.

AFFIRMATION FOR THE DAY: *With my Quiet Hour guaranteed, the day is guaranteed—for victory.*

COBRAS ACROSS OUR BREASTS

We pause again to look upon the power of quiet prayer to un-bind us and to let us go. I have cited a bus driver, a pastor's wife, and a dog all agreeing upon the necessity of a Quiet Time if they are to survive in New York. One more: this time my granddaughter of one year, who has to live in New York too. When the world is too much with her, and she is tired of too much company, she begins to get fretful, and cries, and is qui-eted only when she is taken to her room and laid in her crib, where she lies without sleeping, perfectly happy and relaxed. The doctor commented: "That's smart. She knows when she needs to get away and relax." In citing this I shall be charged with belonging to the Order of the S.O.G. (Silly Old Grand-fathers), and I shall plead guilty—with joy! But a dog and a little child should lead us to the Trysting Place.

After an hour of prayer I went to the meeting place by the lakeside at Sat Tal in the Himalayas to give an address. I was seated on a raised platform of stones, over which pine needles had been placed to make a cushion. As is the custom in India, I left my sandals below, and sat barefoot, and talked on this theme—the way to power and poise. I felt something cold going over my foot, and there amidst the pine needles a snake was crawling across my foot. And Indian snakes usually are deadly! I was surprised at my own calm and poise as I let it crawl across my foot and continued my talk to the end without acquainting the audience with what had happened. After the meeting I told them, and they pulled the platform to pieces to find it, but to no avail. I am not naturally poised—I'm high-strung, but an unut-terable Quiet took possession of me as a result, I believe, of the Prayer Hour.

But a more exciting story is told of my friend, Jay Kingham, a missionary, who was sleeping outside a native house in South India on a mat when he awoke during the night and saw in the moonlight a cobra crawling across his breast. He lay perfectly quiet and prayed, and the cobra crawled on. Had he not been a man of prayer, panic would have seized him. But prayer had given him the quiet mind and heart in the crisis.

O God, when I live in Thee through prayer, then ser-pents of trouble and sorrow may crawl across my foot and even my breast, and yet I shall be at peace in Thee. I thank Thee. Amen.

AFFIRMATION FOR THE DAY: *"If I make my bed in hell, behold, thou art there"*—there, to turn my hell into heaven.

"THEY CAN TAKE IT"

We turn this week to see the power of the corporate life to loose us and to let us go. The fellowship of a group is one of the most freeing things known, provided it is the right kind of fellowship.

The church is designed to provide that fellowship. It is the corporate expression of the Christian life. No corporate life; no Christian life. The idea that you can be a solitary Christian without corporate relation with the church has been proved false by the facts. I have watched it across the years: those who try this soon have Christianity fade out of them, and then they fade out of the picture. Strong, outgoing, contagious character is nourished within the church even with all its faults. I have spoken to thousands of service clubs across the years, particularly in America. These service clubs contain the cream of the business and professional life of a city—the people who have risen to the top. From 80 per cent to 99 per cent of them are members of some church. The average would be about 90 per cent. Success is no criterion of the truth of a faith; but there munity is 53 per cent. But the average of the successful is 90 per cent. Success is no criterion of the truth of a faith; but there is something in corporate religion that makes for stronger, more dependable character.

Moreover, it not only makes people more successful, gives them power; but it makes them inwardly steadier, gives them poise. They take calamity better. A mortician told me that Christians take death of a loved one much better than non-Christians. They don't go to pieces. A doctor told me that Christians face an operation more quietly, go under the anesthetic sooner, and recover more quickly. The head of a Japanese camp in America during the war said: "If I had no other proof of the truth of Christianity, I have it here: those who are members of churches take this uprooting in a superior way to the non-Christians. They can take it—easily and happily. The others go to pieces." Two Caucasian heads of camps told me they were converted to a Christian life by the victorious lives of Christian internees. The Church helps to poise and power.

Dear Father, I thank Thee for the fellowship of those who are faced toward the Light and are striving to walk in it. Walking in that Light, we have fellowship one with another, and that fellowship is saving and loosing. I thank Thee. Amen.

AFFIRMATION FOR THE DAY: *The fellowship of the Church is the highest-level fellowship in the world.*

ON BEING THE ANSWER

Yesterday we saw that the fellowship of the Christian church was freeing and steadying. It is no mere chance that while the divorce rate in general in America is one out of every four marriages, nevertheless among members of churches it is only one out of fifty. Living together in the church apparently makes it easier for people to live with each other in the home.

The church is the training ground for disciplined character. A Hindu police superintendent was astonished that crowds up to fifty thousand could attend the Maramon Convention in Travancore, India, and need no police supervision of any kind. The church discipline carried over into this larger convention.

But while the church is the greatest human-divine power on earth saying, "Unbind him, and let him go," nevertheless the church often lacks the elements of what the early Christians called the *koinonia,* the fellowship. It is often a group of individuals touching elbows on Sunday and then relapsing into their isolated individualism. It lacks being a close-knit fellowship. So group fellowships or movements have grown up within the church to supply that need. The Ashram is one of these fellowships—not the only one, nor do we say the best one, but just one. The word, taken from India, consists of *a* (from) and *shram* (hard work), a cessation of hard work: a place where one would retire for meditation and spiritual discipline. Others would now say the *a* is intensive and would therefore mean an intensification of hard work. Perhaps it is both: a retreat in order for a release; a going aside from life in order to go more deeply into life. We have taken this Indian term and put within it a Christian content.

The Ashram differs from a conference where people confer with each other to get verbal answers to verbal questions. It differs from a retreat, for in a retreat you go aside to listen to an address and then cultivate your spiritual life in the light of what you have heard. In an Ashram we try not to merely *find* an answer but to *be* the answer—imperfect of course, because made up of imperfect people. But to be in some real way the Kingdom of God in miniature, to be the kind of society we would like to see universalized.

O God, the Father, we know Thou art trying to make out of our chaos a family. Teach me this day to live brotherly, not in an occasional act, but in an attitude and atmosphere. Amen.

AFFIRMATION FOR THE DAY: *If possible, I shall find or make today a fellowship of Christian souls—a fellowship of the being-saved.*

GETTING DOWN THE BARRIERS

We were describing an attempt at corporate living, the Ashram.

In order to be the Kingdom, we tell the group, they will have to get down barriers that divide us. The motto over our door is this: "Leave behind all race and class distinction, ye that enter here." So all races and classes live together without distinction. Another barrier down: between those who have titles and those who have none. There are no longer any bishops, doctors, professors, but just plain, "Brother Stanley," "Sister Mary." We use the first name, for it has a psychologically leveling effect. The words "brother" and "sister" are to distinguish the greeting from a back-slapping, surface fellowship—we try to be a family of God. A Hindu remarked that the terms "brother" and "sister" have "an antiseptic effect on our relationships."

The next barrier we get down is between those who work with their hands and those who do not. So we have a work period in which everybody works with his hands. We begin the period with the hymn:

> O Thou, who long didst labor
> With hammer, saw, and plane,
> Teach us this day to serve Thee
> With hands and heart and brain.
> In toil we fain would find Thee,
> O Workman, strong and fair,
> And thus become the comrades
> Of workers everywhere.

Then there is the barrier between the leaders and the followers, so we try to make all leaders and all followers. We have long periods of silence, after which we share what has been coming to us in the silence. In this way we try to help everyone to be creative.

Then comes the deepest place of getting down barriers—within. People come filled with fears, anxieties, resentments, inhibitions, unrest, guilts, self-centeredness. The real barriers are within. The very first day we ask the group: "Why have you come? What do you want? What do you really need?" I would not have believed that a group of from one to three hundred would expose their own needs at once to a group of people brought together for the first time. They do it eagerly.

O God, in this Family we would be frank, and open, and real. Help us to bring up and out all that festers there. And then we shall be healed. Amen.

AFFIRMATION FOR THE DAY: *Today I shall be a co-operative and working member of the Family of God.*

ON GETTING OUR PROBLEMS UP AND OUT

We left off yesterday at the place where we were getting up and out our deepest needs. We suggest to the group that we are "a fellowship of need": There is not one group of the attained working on those who have not attained. God is working on us all. If we act as though we have no needs, then that shows that we have most need. We take hours at this. People seem glad to unburden themselves. In these years I have never known an indelicate thing brought up, nor any exhibitionism shown. Of course, some in the beginning will bring up marginal sins in lieu of the central sin, but usually the center is reached before long. This public sharing is a great catharsis. Some of the more intimate tings are shared with an individual. God does some business in His private office!

But within a few hours we know each other—know each other more intimately than we would have had we lived together for years without this opening of the depths. At once our tensions have been relaxed, and we are natural and unstrained, at least in attitude toward each other. The process of healing beings.

We will look at some of the problems exposed and then at some of the cures that have taken place: (1) I want to get my vision back into focus. (2) My brother came back from the Ashram an inspired personality. My personality has become thin. (3) My recapped tires are out of balance. (4) My ministry is on the surface. I'm an activist. I've been getting by. I'm critical, for I'm not inwardly secure. (5) I'm one of those hurried and harried minister's wives. I need to be a better woman. (6) I have the feeling of having gotten on the wrong bus and of getting off at the wrong place. I've been playing tiddly-winks in the pulpit. I've been off center. I want to be able to say "Hallelujah!" at three o'clock in the morning when the baby needs the bottle. (7) I always seem to be about three persons. I want to be one person. (8) In the period of silence one word, "selfishness," came to the surface. (9) I need charity—need to forgive others.

O Divine Spirit, Thou who art bringing all these things to the surface, not to shame us but to save us, give me grace to follow through—to follow through confession to conversion, exposure to experience. Amen.

AFFIRMATION FOR THE DAY: *Today shall be the day of the honest heart—honest to God, myself, and others.*

"I HAVE A LOT OF UNNECESSARY ILLNESSES"

We continue to look at the sharing of needs at the Ashram: (10) I came because I'm very tired. Virtue has gone out of me. (11) I have talked all my life, now I would like my life to talk. (12) I want to go back and tremble bravely. (13) I feel I've been a rainless cloud. (14) I want to get God back—want freedom from impotence and criticism. (15) I want to react in a Christian way naturally; now I have to remind myself. (16) I want to be redemptive toward those whose names when recalled bring no pleasure. (17) I'm desperately unhappy. I need to be changed. I have nothing to live by. (18) I am here because I'm not all here. (19) I'm having carburetor trouble—dust in my carburetor. Need to get rid of self-centeredness. (20) I'm all mixed up (ex-service man). (21) Have a big job, become frustrated, make false judgments, have never taken off twelve days before to cultivate serenity. (22) I have found everything I have ever wanted and now I don't know what to do with myself (Negro teacher in army). (23) I came to escape from my problems at home.

They continued: (24) I've tried to swim with one foot on the bottom. (25) I have terrific tensions within me—fears and problems. (26) The conflicts in my own life keep me from being the kind of peacemaker I want to be. (27) I want to be loved and admired, and if I were given power I'd be inflated by it. I feel if I knew God I'd get rid of self, and if I could get rid of self I'd know God. I don't know which is cart and which is horse. (28) I'm battered in a battered world. And I'm all afraid too. (29) I'm still more full of fears than I am of faith. (30) I've come to get peace of mind, to get rid of confusion that is upsetting me physically. (31) I'm just living chronologically, not vitally. (32) I'm tired of being dictated to by my body. (33) I'm about to jell into the kind of person I don't like. (34) Not the wolfishness of the wolf, but the sheepishness of the sheep is my trouble. (35) I've come here to get rid of jealousy. (36) I have a feeling of superiority with little basis for it. I'm playing for attention. (37) I have a lot of unnecessary illnesses.

O Christ, as of old, the sick around Thee lie. Help us to touch the hem of Thy garment and be made whole. For we cannot heal unless we are healed. We want to heal, for the world is very sick. Amen.

AFFIRMATION FOR THE DAY: *I look at myself, not to be paralyzed, but to be prodded—to Thy feet for release.*

ON OPENING THE DOOR TO VICTORY

We have looked at the needs of people as expressed in our Ashrams; now we turn to see how those needs have been met.

(1) I decided to do the will of God and not please people— best year of my life. (2) I came here starved and I've been fed. In all my life before I've never been less with myself. (3) In building the cross, I found the cross. I burned two boxes of sermons. (4) Wondered how I could withstand the atheist with whom I'm going to room next year. Now I'm wondering how he is going to withstand what I have. (5) I came here self-sufficient; now I'm God-sufficient. (6) So good to be with people without ambitions, without suspicions, without *skins.* And it's wonderful to hear wonderful things spoken by ordinary people (dean of men). (7) I feel as light as air; something has really happened to me this time. (8) I've thrown off my excess baggage. I've been filled with the Spirit. (9) I had cold feet, so I stood up at once— a remedy for cold feet. (10) I've been inspired and enlightened at other times, but this time I've been cleansed. (11) This is what it would be if we had a Christian society.

They continued their notes of victory: (12) Last year I had a stone of resentment in my heart, but it is gone. Now my spring has been cleaned out and deepened. (13) After twenty years a Communist, five years an agnostic, now I've seen in Jesus the answer, so now I have a closed mind on Him. (14) I've been putting up spiritual umbrellas to keep off showers of spiritual blessing or the sunshine of God's sun. Now I've gotten rid of my umbrella. (15) I would have dropped dead if I had spoken in public—so I thought. To tell me that I would have eaten pancakes and chipped beef I would have said, "You're crazy." I've eaten both. (16) I have a Christian stomach. I'm eating everything. (17) I've given up my resentments to God forty times. But there'll be no forty-first time! (18) I thought I had it—now it has me (returned Negro soldier). (19) Had mountains of resentments, thought it soupy to talk about oneself. Found the key in surrender. I'm a novice, but I'm in.

O Christ, I thank Thee that Thou art alive forever more and Thy ancient power is still here—here to heal and release and fill. I open my heart to its depths and I take all. Amen.

AFFIRMATION FOR THE DAY: *Nothing stands between me and victory— nothing, except my lack of acceptance.*

NOT SOLVED, BUT DISSOLVED

We continue today to listen to the notes of spiritual triumph from those who really touch Him: (20) I thought it unwholesome to expose your spiritual needs, but now see it is unwholesome not to expose them. (21) Never before have I been at the growing edge of the Christian faith. (22) I've lost the fear of getting old. (23) When I came to the Ashram two years ago I was thirty pounds underweight, and a very tied-up personality. I've not been to the doctor since, except to take out the finest kind of life insurance. (24) Now I'm well. All my ailments have dropped away (Chinese). (25) I've gotten rid of fear. I was afraid of everything—afraid of the news that Russia had struck. Now it's all gone (Canadian cattle dealer). (26) I've been like a puppy dog tied to a stake, winding himself round the stake and tying himself more and more in knots. I'm free. (27) I've been under the shadow of an inferiority. I'm leaving it here. (28) Some said to me, "You're coasting." Now I'm shifting gears. I have held the Holy Spirit at arm's length, afraid of being queer.

The story goes on: (29) I was an alcoholic for thirty-five years, was worked over by a psychiatrist for several years, settled it on my knees in half an hour, have never desired a drink since. (30) I tried to take my own life, but I've come through it, and now I've dedicated my life as a medical missionary. (31) My ministry was falling down—something down underneath was wrong. I've surrendered it—it's gone. I've been a minister for eight years and in that time I've never had more than two minutes alone in quiet. I've been able to forgive some in order to pour out my resentments on a few. (32) I was tied up by fear, developed an allergy, broke out in a rash. Was allergic to sunlight. But stayed out in sunlight for two hours and suffered no ill effects. (33) I've been full of home-made poison. It's gone. (34) I've found here the truth—and it's alive. It breathes. I've lost my fears, inhibitions, inferiorities. (35) In this fellowship my problems have not been solved, but dissolved.

The fellowship itself became redemptive. Loneliness and fear dropped away. Here was a group that cared. That caring cured.

Father, I thank Thee for the fellowship of those who care—care without regard to race or class. Help me to find such a fellowship, or make one by caring beyond race and class. Amen.

AFFIRMATION FOR THE DAY: *If God is touching others into wholeness, why not me?*

ON PRUNING FOR POWER AND POISE

We have seen how power and poise can be had initially by surrender and receptivity to God. But they must be cultivated by deliberate intention. Power and poise do not just happen—they come and continue as a result of careful planning. And in that planning there must be pruning. "Every branch of mine that bears no fruit, he takes away, and every branch that does bear fruit he prunes, that it may bear more fruit." (John 15:2.)

There is no way to power and poise except through relentless pruning—a cutting away of non-fruit-bearing suckers that sap our energies, but bear no fruit. The vine-dresser knows that it is possible to have luxuriant growth with no fruit. This useless non-fruit-bearing growth—the suckers that take life but give no fruit—must be cut away. Life depends as much upon elimination as upon assimilation. If you don't know how to give up you don't know how to give out.

Conversion is the grafting of the Divine life within us. We are made partakers of the Divine nature. But this pruning process provides for a continuous conversion—a conversion from the irrelevant to the relevant, from the marginal to the central, from being just busy to being fruitful. There is a cartoon of a girl getting out of her car, walking up to a policeman, and saying: "Can you please tell me where I want to go?" She was going, but didn't know where! A man stood up in a meeting and asked: "Is there anybody going anywhere in a car?" This living without plan and purpose and streamlined intentions results in a lot of running around in circles and getting nowhere.

The account says that the religious leaders tempted Jesus "to speak of many things." He refused. He kept to the one thing—the Gospel. He was not the purveyor of many nice ideas, but the bearer of the Good News. He left a mark. Many of us leave a blur. He cut out the good to get to the better, and He cut out the better to get to the best. Decide what is best and prune everything to that purpose.

O God, Thou seest how things slip in for the moment and then demand to stay forever—things that draw my energies away from the great to the little. Give me the single eye. Amen.

AFFIRMATION FOR THE DAY: *Today I shall not be among the "peddlers of God's word"* (II Cor. 2:17)—I shall incarnate it.

EMPTY OF EVERYTHING EXCEPT EXCUSES

We continue our meditation on the necessity of pruning in order to gain poise and power. Martha lost her poise because she was "careful and anxious about many things," Mary kept hers because she kept to the "one thing needful."

But to be a disciplined person means we must pass from wish-full thinking to will-full thinking. We must will to be disciplined. "For the moment all discipline seems painful rather than pleasant; later it yields the peaceful fruit of righteousness to those who have been trained by it." (Heb. 12:11.)

Go over your whole life and prune from it all encumbering things. Begin at the outworks—the body. *Prune from your body all unnecessary illnesses.* Yesterday I met a woman who has spent her life inventing excuses for not assuming responsibility and doing things—the excuses were illnesses which she called in to relieve her. Twenty years ago she was a nonentity; today she is a nonentity minus—empty of everything except excuses, a tragedy. To do a thing like that is to do in another form what one man did when he said: "I shot myself in the stomach to take my mind off a toothache." To run away from the responsibilities of life through illnesses is to end in running away from life. Life is lost in the process.

A man came up to me in Oklahoma City and said with a radiant face: "I had stomach ulcers. The X ray showed them. No insurance company would insure me. A Roman Catholic hotel owner talked to me and then gave me your book, *The Way.* I saw I was producing my own illness. Today I am a well man and have $35,000 worth of insurance." No one has a right to carry around unnecessary illnesses—to be sicker than he ought to be.

A mother was told that her husband had an accident. While she waited for the car to take her to the hospital she nursed her seven-months-old baby. The baby after nursing turned blue and became rigid as a board in convulsions. Doctors worked over the baby for an hour and saved it. But she nearly killed her baby by the fears which poisoned the milk—and needlessly, for her husband had not had an accident.

O God, help me this day to slough off by joyous, hopeful thinking all unnecessary illnesses. Help me to be open to health, not disease. Help me to breathe health and affirm health. Amen.

AFFIRMATION FOR THE DAY: *No one has a right to be sicker than he ought to be.*

PRUNING ALL NEGATIVE WORDS

We continue to meditate on pruning our lives from all un-necessary illnesses. Prune your life from all fear of being ill. Fears gather illnesses around them as a magnet pulls iron filings to itself. A woman told me she heard shrieks of terror from a bird. There on a limb was a yellow bird in terror, its wings lifted to fly but unable, standing on one foot, then lifting it, then standing on the other, but unable to fly away. A huge black snake was gliding slowly up the branch with its eyes fastened on the bird. It got within a foot of the terror-stricken bird, when the husband shot the snake. With the crack of the gun the atten-tion of the bird was drawn away and it flew away, free.

If you have been fascinated by the fear of some illness that looks you in the face like the beady eyes of a serpent, then look away to Jesus—gaze on His face, and then you can smile in the face of fear. If the fear has caught you and you need an explo-sion to break the mastery over you, then get to your knees until that explosion—a radical change in your emotions—takes place.

Prune from your vocabulary all unnecessarily negative words. There have to be some negatives in order to have positives. But apart from these necessary negatives, are you allowing negative words to weaken your words—words which are the outgoing of you? My friend, a management engineer who takes hold of sick businesses and puts them on their feet again, says that 95 per cent of the difficulties in business are not in business but in the persons concerned. He says he cannot straighten out that business until he straightens out the people; and he cannot straighten out the people until they begin to turn to the positive—away from the negative. So he makes them say "Yes" twenty-five times as a beginning. They have been saying "No" to themselves and others, and that negativism has spread its dis-ease through the situation.

Speak strong positive words and the very using of those words will help to make you positive within. Speak positive; that will make you think positive—and to think positive is to be positive.

Father, I thank Thee that in Jesus the divine Yes has sounded. In Him Thy affirmations have come to expression. Help me to be so close to Him that I too shall be positive and affirmative. Amen.

AFFIRMATION FOR THE DAY: *Today I think positive, speak positive, act positive, be positive.*

PRUNING AWAY ALL NEGATIVE THINKING

Prune from your very thoughts all defeatist, negative thinking. When a defeatist, negative thought comes, do what Paul suggested; "Shut your mind." For, if let in, negative thinking will soon make of you a negative person. "You are not what you think you are; but what you think, you are." Thoughts dye the mind.

Dr. J. A. Hadfield says that he tested three men by having them undergo a test of their strength by gripping a dynamometer. He told them to grip it with all their might and he had them do this under three different sets of conditions. Under normal waking conditions their average grip was 101 pounds. After testing them he hypnotized them and told them they were very weak, and under that suggestion they could grip only 29 pounds. When he tested them a third time, telling them under hypnosis that they were strong, they were able to grip an average of 142 pounds. When their minds were filled with positive thoughts of strength, they increased their actual physical powers almost 500 per cent. If you are suggesting to yourself that you are weak, then you will be weak; but if you suggest to yourself: "I can do all things through Christ who strengthens me," you will be strong.

Dale Carnegie has a chapter on "Eight Words that Can Transform your Life," and the eight words are the words of Aurelius: "Our life is what our thoughts make it." Emerson puts it this way: "A man is what he thinks about all day long."

Suppose you go around thinking negative thoughts. You will soon be a negative person. The Vedantist philosophy affirms about Brahma, God, *Neti, Neti*—Not That, Not That. They feel He is above all affirmations about Him. But you cannot live on a *Neti, Neti*—that ends in a philosophy. You can only live on a great affirmation—that ends in religion. Jesus was the great Yes about God. He affirmed and showed what God was like—in Himself, an Affirmation. We can live on that Affirmation. He is the divine Yes. So keep repeating the divine Yes within your heart and you will become like that Yes. Prune from your thoughts all unnecessary negatives.

Loving Father, Thou art loving me into affirmation, into power and poise. Thy strength is flowing round my weakness, Thy affirmations are absorbing my negatives. I'm becoming positive, outgoing, creative, like Thee. Amen.

AFFIRMATION FOR THE DAY: *No "Noes" today, only a bigger "Yes."*

PRUNING AWAY NONCONTRIBUTIVE HABITS

We continue our meditating on the necessity of pruning in order to gain poise and power.

Prune your habits. Take an inventory of your habits to see if they are working with you, contributing to the purposes of your life; or against you, blocking or slowing down those purposes. Bring everything to the bar of the question: Do you contribute to the highest purposes for which I really live?

Take alcohol. Darwin, the great scientist said: "Through the long experience of my grandfather and my father I have reached the conviction that no other cause has brought so much misery and disease as the use of intoxicating beverages." If sin is that which keeps you from God's highest best for you, then alcohol is sin, for it does just that. For "alcohol inhibits the inhibition. The alcoholic's escape from his difficulties is like a car with poor brakes careening down a hill." Poor brakes? No brakes! For alcohol is not a stimulant—it is a deadening of the inhibitions.

Cigarette smoking can be even more deadly as a habit than alcohol. A friend who spent a long time in a prison camp in the Philippines during the war told that it was more easily possible for western men and women to give up alcohol than cigarettes when it was impossible to get them. He saw bankers going around in the early morning looking for cigarette stubs in the drain, which they would pathetically rescue, dry, and use, and do it with a fierce eagerness. The habit had them—had them to their depths. In America 6½ cigarettes are consumed daily for every man, woman, and child in the country.

No tea taster can smoke or drink, or else his sense of taste would be impaired. No football player—on the Yale team, for instance—could smoke and keep up. He would be automatically out. Then why put the brakes on your efficiency, why slow yourself down with senseless, noncontributing habits? Be relentless and be released. Prune your habits to efficiency.

O God, my Father, I want to be at my best—Thy best for me. For thoughtless moments weight me down with useless habits, and soon I'm a prisoner. Make me free—free to be at my highest best. I give the utmost for the highest. Amen.

AFFIRMATION FOR THE DAY: *My habits are cancerous or contributive. I decide that they shall all be contributive.*

HOW GOD PRUNES

We must go on with our pruning: *Prune from your wills all indecision.* Indecision of the will can produce conflict in the person and disease in the body. Dr. Flanders Dunbar gives the illustration of the man torn between his desire to write a book and his fear of failure, and who found arthritis localized in his fingers so that he could neither typewrite nor hold a pen. As long as he keeps away from his unfinished masterpiece and tends to his own business, in which he is quite as successful as his literary family and acquaintances are in theirs, his fingers remain free from pain, although they are permanently misshapen. But on several occasions when he returned to his dream book, the pain returned, too. Don't allow your indecisions to throw functional disturbance into your body. Be decisive or be diseased.

Prune your motives. Go over your motives and ask: Why am I doing the thing I do? It is not *what* you do, but *why* you do it that is the important thing. Not *that* you preach, but *why* you preach. Not *that* you give, but *why* you give. Not *that* you do things for people, but *why* you do them.

Having touched the center of the pruning, the motive, we must now look at the means. God has many pruning knives, so let Him use them all. *He prunes by a group.* For many years I lived without a disciplined group correction. My life was overgrown with a lot of useless things. But when I came into a disciplined group—the Ashram—the pruning process began. A convert of a few months said in the group: "Brother Stanley, I've noticed that when we give you a question you cannot really answer you take us off to something very interesting and thus make us forget the point. Is that honest?" Now I'm learning to say: "I don't know the answer." It was a necessary pruning. If we fear this group correction, we are living by fear rather than by faith. "I am afraid to get into this group life, for I'm sensitive to criticism," said an upset girl. She was smothering conflict. She would rather be diseased than be disturbed.

Redeeming and relentless God, save me from drawing back—drawing back from the bleeding that blesses. Give me courage to walk up and say, "Cut." And that blood that flows will be cleansing blood. Prune, divine Vinedresser, prune. Amen.

AFFIRMATION FOR THE DAY: *Any knife God uses today shall be acceptable, if it makes me a more acceptable person.*

HE PRUNES BY PAIN

We continue to study God's methods of pruning. *He prunes through the Word.* Jesus said, "Now ye are clean through the words I have spoken unto you." His words cleansed their ideas of God, of man, of woman, of prayer, of sacrifice, of religion, of life itself. He touched everything and He cleansed everything He touched. So expose yourself to His words. Wash your thinking every day in the thinking of Christ. You will arise a cleaner, a more disciplined, a more pruned person.

Then *He prunes through the Spirit.* The Spirit within will become vocal if we are willing to listen and obey. Paul speaks about his "conscience bearing" him "witness in the Holy spirit." His conscience was under the training and tutelage of the Holy Spirit. Then it was a safe conscience—only then. To become a Spirit-led person is to become the highest type of personality. He prunes us up to date. "I've had my insides sandpapered here today," said a lawyer when the Holy Spirit was obviously present.

Then *He prunes us by sorrow and pain.* He allows nothing to be taken away from us except to give us something better. I write this in the midst of a very war-torn Burma. Insecurity hangs heavy over the situation. But through it all there is a turning wistfully toward the Christian faith on the part of non-Christians. The Burmese Commissioner of a city who could scarcely make a speech without turning a barb toward the Christians, came after the city had fallen into other hands and said: "I want to ask you Christians to pray to your God. We need your prayers." That day, just after the city had changed hands, the Christians were dedicating a restored church; and the very people who were fighting each other over the possession of the city—Karens and Burmans—were seated side by side in the packed church. The Commissioner was amazed that this could happen, and when he arose to appeal to them to pray he said, "Jesus died for us all." The Christians lost their security and found moral and spiritual authority. God makes insecurity the instrument of a higher security. He prunes by pain.

Father, I thank Thee that pain becomes my servant when I am in Thee. It drives me to Thy breast. All things push me Thee-ward when I am set to do Thy will. All things serve me who serves Thee. I thank Thee. Amen.

AFFIRMATION FOR THE DAY: *"O Infinite Designer, must Thou char the wood ere Thou canst limn with it?"*

HOW THE HERD CONTROLS US

Another pruning necessary if we are to be inwardly stable—*a pruning from too great a dependence on the herd.*

If we are herd-centered people then we are insecure, for the herd is fickle and may quickly change. The self-centered person and the sex-centered person are off center—on the wrong center. The herd-centered person is also off center, for if we are dominated by the herd we are doomed by the herd—doomed to a life of up and downness. For the herd changes, and if we are centered there we are compelled to change with those changes.

The power of the herd over the individual is more than we think. The things we do because others do them are legion. Look at the things done in the New Testament because of the herd instinct. Jesus was crucified by the herd instinct: "But they were urgent, demanding with loud cries that he should be crucified. And their voices prevailed. So Pilate gave sentence." (Luke 23:23-24.) "Their voices prevailed"—prevailed over justice and goodness. "So Pilate, wishing to satisfy the crowd, . . . delivered him to be crucified." (Mark 15:15.) Peter was thrown into prison as a result of the herd instinct: "And when he saw that it pleased the Jews, he proceeded to arrest Peter also." (Acts 12:3.) Paul was kept in prison because of the herd dominance: "and desiring to do the Jews a favor, Felix left Paul in prison." (Acts 24:27.) And then: "Festus, wishing to do the Jews a favor said to Paul, 'Do you wish to go up to Jerusalem and there be tried on these charges before me?' " (Acts 25:9.) The herd-urge is a powerful drive in determining conduct. A nun in Germany began to mew like a cat. A wave of mewing went through the monasteries of Germany, Italy, and Holland. A nun bit another, and there was an epidemic of biting in monasteries. A girl in La Porte, Indiana, had convulsive jerks in her leg and it went through the school—an epidemic of jerks.

The Russians use this herd-instinct almost entirely as their central drive. Their central motto could be: "By the crowd thou hast been made, and by the crowd thou shalt be redeemed."

O God, our Father, Thou hast made us to dwell in relationships and yet we cannot entirely depend on those relationships for inner security. Give us an unshakable Kingdom. Amen.

AFFIRMATION FOR THE DAY: *I am destined to be surrounded by the herd, but I am not destined to be dominated by it—I decide that.*

THE FOUR ATTITUDES TOWARD THE HERD

We saw yesterday how powerful the herd urge is in determining conduct. Ask yourself the question: How many things do I do because others do them? Someone has said that a preacher often leads like the coach dog leads a procession—the dog looks back to see which way it is going and then leads. Another puts it this way: "There goes the crowd; I must follow, for I'm their leader." The ancient saying, "Like people, like priest" is often true, for the people make the priest in their own image instead of the priest making the people in his image. A woman was losing the love of her husband because he did not like red fingernails. When advised by a friend to give up red nails and retain her husband's love, she replied: "I couldn't give that up—everybody does it." So she kept her paint and lost her partner.

Since the herd is such a powerful drive, what are we to do about it? There are four possible attitudes we can take in regard to it: *(a)* withdraw from the herd; *(b)* defy it; *(c)* succumb to it; *(d)* surrender the herd to God, and then live within it.

(a) Withdraw from the herd. What happens when you attempt to break the herd dominance by withdrawal? You are tied up—you become the queer. A child who will not play with other children will soon be filled with complexes. You cannot withdraw without becoming the queer—the off center.

The second possibility: *(b)* defy it. There are those who do not withdraw from the group, but who live in constant antagonism to the group. They live on the defensive, afraid of the group, and have their bristles up against it. This attitude too is disruptive. You cannot live constantly objecting without becoming objectionable. The defensive person is a defeative person.

(c) Succumb to the herd. If you do and become herd-centered, then you are no longer a voice, you are an echo; you don't act, you only react; you are not a person, but a thing. All three of these roads are roads with dead ends.

O God, these roads run me away from myself and Thee and others. I want Thy Way, for Thy Way is my way. Give me the right relations to Thee, myself, and others. Then I shall live. Amen.

AFFIRMATION FOR THE DAY: *The herd can commend, but not command—I'm the decider.*

GOD-CENTERED, NOT HERD-CENTERED

We have been looking at the four ways to relate ourselves to the herd. We come to the last: *(d) surrender the herd to God, and then live within it—emancipated.*

That is the only way to deal with herd dominance. Just as the self has to be surrendered in order to be found again, so the herd has to be surrendered in order to be found again. When you have surrendered the herd to God, then its dominance is broken—God is God and not the herd. When its dominance is broken then you can make your domicile within it. For you are in it, but not of it. Your roots are in God; therefore you can have your fruits in the herd. The secret of Paul's power over the herd was in his emancipation from the herd. This was inherent in his commission: "delivering you from the people and from the Gentiles—to whom I send you, to open their eyes." (Acts 26:17, 18.) He was delivered from the people, inwardly emancipated from them, no longer afraid of them; therefore he could serve them—open their eyes, turn them from darkness to light.

Until you are delivered from the herd you can do very little for the herd. For until that deliverance comes, you are afraid of offending the herd by insistence on change. But there is no change without disturbance of the status quo. Jesus said: "I came not to send peace but a sword"—He had to bring disturbance before He could bring peace. But that disturbance was a disturbance toward redemption.

Paul "turned the world upside down" because it was wrong side up. He could change society because he was emancipated inwardly from society. He could now love people because he loved something more than people. The man who said he could lift the world if he had a place outside the world upon which his lever could rest was expressing this truth. That resting place is God. When you belong to God then all things, including the herd, belong to you. Your poise and power are insecure if they are dependent on the approval of a fickle herd. If you are herd-centered you are insecure; if God-centered, then secure.

O Father, into Thy hands I commend the herd—Thou hast it. I'm under Thy dominance, not under the herd. Now use my emancipated soul for the redemption of the herd. I serve it, for I serve Thee—supremely. Amen.

AFFIRMATION FOR THE DAY: *Emancipated from the herd, I can now help emancipate it—from itself.*

A SENSE OF TOGETHERNESS

We must come to another thing from which we are to gain emancipation if we are to have power and poise—the emancipation from the sense of working alone—therefore of being inadequate. If we are emancipated from the herd, we must be saved from the sense of being a lone wolf. We must work with a sense of togetherness—with God and others. Solitude heals, but loneliness hurts.

The story of the painter and sculptor, Sir Hubert von Herkomer, who founded the Herkomer School of Painting, is to the point. His aged father, also a sculptor, spent the last years of his life with his distinguisehd son. The father asked for clay that he might while away the evening hours. But with failing eyesight and enfeeblement, the old man would put away his work at night almost in despair—it was so far below his vision. But after the father had gone to bed the son would go and work secretly at the clay. In the morning the father would look at the work of the previous evening, and not knowing another hand had touched it, would exclaim with delight, "Why it isn't so bad as I thought." That is what Christ the Master does with our poor efforts—He touches our imperfections, our blunders, and makes them something else. "The Lord will perfect that which concerneth me." You are not working alone.

I had a singer with me in evangelistic work and at times he rose to very great heights, but sometimes he missed his notes. His wife is a really able musician, an expert at the piano. He tells of a woman who came up to him after a solo and remarked, "You must have missed your wife at the piano tonight. She certainly does cover up your mistakes." That is what Christ does—He covers up our mistakes.

Samuel Butler wanted someone to invent an assinometer—a gadget by which a man could tell just how big an ass he is. But Jesus, knowing what we are, would never use it on us, nor suggest that we use it. He would cover our mistakes—love covers a multitude of sins. So, "Be silent to God and let Him mould you." Let Him mold you in the Silence from mistakes to mastery, from blunders to beauty. He covers by conversion.

O Christ, I thank Thee that I do not toil alone—Thou art working with me, correcting my mistakes, even while I sleep. Thou art redeeming me daily and nightly from my imperfections. Amen.

AFFIRMATION FOR THE DAY: *God is the coverer of my mistakes and the uncoverer of my possibilities.*

"CLINGING TO HIS CREEKS"

We must now turn to another possible blocking of poise and power—the clinging to small, accustomed but outworn ways in the face of the big and adventurous. In Judges 5:17 the account says: "Asher sat still by the seaboard, clinging to his creeks." (Moffatt.) This is a part of the song of Deborah when she told of the response of the various tribes to her call for them to take Canaan. This was the response of Reuben: "In the shires of Reuben were divisions and debates." They were inwardly divided, and debated and cancelled themselves out. That is the type of response that many of us give to the call of life—we answer by division and debate! Then Deborah asks this question: "Why did you lounge by shepherds' cotes, with only an ear for pastoral notes?" When the call of adventure came they were caught by the shepherd tunes and the ease of a shepherd cote. They turned back to the good old soft, accustomed ways and missed their Canaan.

She goes on: "East of the Jordan the Gileadites stayed." There no reason is given. They just didn't do anything—they just "stayed." This is the type that in the call to possess our Canaan just doesn't do anything, one way or the other—they just stay. These are the non-deciders—they do nothing bad and nothing good—they are just negative.

Another response: "Dan held to his ships" (v. 17). He wasn't going to sacrifice his business interests for an adventure in Canaan. He was the solid businessman who is not to be lured from his moneymaking to take part in any Canaan adventures.

Then there was Ahser: he "sat by the seaboard clinging to his creeks"—in face of the vast seaboard with its adventure and possibilities Asher sat clinging to his dear little accustomed creeks. In face of the big he took the little. They were "his" creeks and he wasn't going to let the accustomed go to venture into the unaccustomed, no matter how large the possibilities. Asher is the type today that always plays safe—and always succeeds in doing nothing and getting nowhere. They are creek-minded and not ocean-minded. They take the little and lose the big.

O God, Thou who hast set eternity in our hearts and Thou who hast made us for enlargement, give me the courage to accept that eternity and accept that enlargement and thus fulfill Thy plans for me. Amen.

AFFIRMATION FOR THE DAY: *I shall be afraid of safety when safety makes me innocuous.*

A SEABOARD POWER AND POISE

We meditate further upon the attitude of Asher who "sat still by the seaboard clinging to his creeks"—the attitude of those who try to find poise by clinging to the accustomed little, in face of the adventurous, but disturbing, big. Do we find poise and power by nondisturbance of our little so-called securities, or do we find poise and power by listening to and responding to the call of God's ocean?

In Valparaiso, Chile, there is a beautiful harbor, but it is strewn with the wreckage of battered vessels. The reason is this: When a storm blows in from the Pacific, the vessels in the harbor put up steam and go straight out of the harbor into the ocean and there they can outride the storm. But those that stay in the so-called safety of the harbor are battered and broken and wrecked. Safety lies in the open sea—in adventure upon the deep.

The people who try to find poise and inner security by clinging to the creeks of little securities are invariably wrecked at the point of poise and calm, for unrest and insecurity invade them—invade them, for we are inwardly made for growth and creation and we feel a sense of frustration if we do not grow and create. Since we are made for creative adventure, we are only poised when we are engaged in creative adventure. To try to find poise in retreat and holding only to the little and innocuous is to find our poise turned to poison, and our power turned to pow-wow. The man who will not put out his neck for fear his head will get hurt will soon have no ideas in the head worth thinking about. "The turtle only starts going places when he sticks out his neck." The trying to find poise in nonattachment, as the Hindu does; in nondesire as the Buddhist does; in nondisturbance as the modern play-safe type does—all of these end in defeating their very purposes. The poise of Jesus was the poise of creation and accomplishment amid adventure and consequent conflict. He said: "My peace I give unto you" at a moment when the shadow of the Cross was falling most darkly upon His spirit. His poise and peace came from allying Himself with the creation of God, yes, with the new creation of God through the Cross. We cannot have a creek-poise; we must have a seaboard-poise and power.

O Creator God, give me the Spirit of Thy creative love. Love adventures and love creates, and help me to do both. For not in stagnation and safety do I find my securities, but in boldly launching out with Thee. Amen.

AFFIRMATION FOR THE DAY: *Today shall be an adventure with God.*

ON THROWING AWAY PASSPORTS

We continue to look at people who are creek-minded instead of ocean-minded. There is more wreckage in creeks than in the ocean. Sir Francis Drake was in a storm in the Thames and was about to be sunk, so he cried out: "I, who have sailed the oceans, am I to be drowned in a duck pond?" Many of us are drowned in duck ponds.

A missionary in China in a train had a pop bottle in one hand and his passport in the other. Instead of throwing out of the window the pop bottle as he intended, he threw away the passport and kept the pop bottle. He had to get out at the next station and walk back to recover it. Some of us are throwing away passports and keeping pop bottles.

This is written in Burma, and I am reminded of seeing people fishing in rice fields in about a foot of water when in sight of them the vast ocean was calling. When I listen to debates in some religious assemblies, I cannot help but say inwardly: "Fishing in rice fields." Catching minnows when the ocean is big with big possibilities.

The Pharisees came all the way from Jerusalem to see the awakening under Jesus. But all that the religious leaders of that day could see was that the disciples of Jesus "ate with unwashen hands." They didn't see healed people, raised people, changed people—they saw "unwashen hands." The movement of Jesus swept past them and left them grand relics. The same thing can be seen today as the movement of unity sweeps across the world—many sit clinging to a mode of baptism, a line of succession, other things, and let unity sweep by, leaving them clinging to their creeks. Real union should take in those who believe that ordination is horizontal, from the apostles on through the ages, and those who believe it is vertical, God down; should take them both in and let them function on the basis of equality, a union of diversity.

To cling to our creeks for safety and security is to be upset at every call of the Big. We are made for that Big and are restless in our littleness. We cannot be poised this side of God's purpose.

Father God, Thou art calling me and I must come. I drop my littleness and watch it sink in the bigness of Thy purposes for me. The great calls me and I must come—at any price. Amen.

AFFIRMATION FOR THE DAY: *Thou hast "set eternity in my heart" —how can I tarry with the trifling little?*

THE BASIC LAWS OF THE UNIVERSE

We now try to gather up what we have been trying to say throughout the book.

We saw in the beginning of our quest that the end of the physical organism was to attain an inner stability amid a changing environment. If it did, it survived; if it did not, it perished. Also, the end of the spiritual organism is to find and maintain inner stability amid an environment that is perpetually changing. However, the end is not merely to be stable but to have power to change the environment.

We must be unchanged by environment, and yet with power to change it. Bertrand Russell has said: "Man's greatest triumph is to achieve stability and inner poise in a world of shifting threats and terrifying change." It is. But the triumph must be greater—it must include the power to change a threatening and terrifying environment. This is victory-plus.

This from a recent letter: "How can I ever thank you enough for *The Way?* It has opened my eyes, answered all my questions, and has tied the loose ends of life into one whole which now has meaning. The Christian way is founded on the basic laws of the universe." We are made in the inner structure of our being for stability, and the universe around us is so constructed that it guarantees the instability of evil and the stability of the good. The character of the world justifies our hope of stability. We are working with the grain of reality, not against it. God wills it, the nature of the universe wills it, and our own inner nature wills it—everything good is conspiring to make us poised and full of power.

Then why are we inwardly unstable and weak? The fault lies in us and our attitudes. That is the first thing to nail down. Only as we cease to blame God, others, and circumstances, and put the blame where it belongs—on ourselves and our reactions to what happens to us—only then will victory begin to set in. Lack of poise and power lies in a person—that person: Me.

O God, Thou hast brought the matter to where it belongs—at the door of my will. There I acknowledge my responsibility. And I acknowledge it with hope. I am ready to co-operate. Amen.

AFFIRMATION FOR THE DAY: *My inner structure and the structure of the universe both contrive to make me poised and full of power.*

"WORRY IS A THIN STREAM OF FEAR TRICKLING"

Confusion is one of our greatest stumbling blocks. Dr. Herbert E. Hawkes, dean of Columbia University, who has helped 200,000 students to a straightened-out attitude toward life, says: "Confusion is the chief cause of worry." And worry is the chief enemy of power and poise. "Worry," says Arthur S. Roche, "is a thin stream of fear trickling through the mind. If encouraged, it cuts a channel into which all other thoughts are drained."

Very often confusion comes from confused loyalties. A Chinese came to one of our mission hospitals and said, "I'm worn out. I plant bombs at night for the Communists and in the daytime I pick them up for the Nationalists. So I'm tired and worn out." We smile at this Chinese who was broken by conflicting loyalties. But we are often tired and worn because we try to hold conflicting loyalties within the heart.

In Chengtu, China, there is a building put up partly by the Cadburys, the Quaker chocolate people, and partly by a man who was known as "the opium king"—one wing was built by chocolate and the other by opium. One missionary said she could not teach in the opium wing, as the conflict within her was too great.

A missionary in China told me that during the Japanese occupation she received the covers of two copies of *Victorious Living*. The insides were torn out and only the covers sent—no one but the Japanese were supposed to know anything about victorious living! Many are worried and fearful because the covers of religion are left to them, the substance has been torn out by modern skepticism, materialistic living, and conflicting loyalties. So they are empty of everything but conflict.

Gene Autry, famous singing cowboy, gives this as his prescription for freedom from worry: "First, I have always followed the rule of absolute one hundred per cent integrity in everything. When I borrowed money I paid back every penny. Few things cause more worry than dishonesty." He is right. The first thing is honesty—honesty with ourselves, ceasing to lay blame on others, and then honesty in money matters—honesty in everything.

My Father, I open my depths to Thy honesty. Let it search me and try me to see if there is any wicked way in me—anything that dodges responsibility. Give me openhearted honesty. Amen.

AFFIRMATION FOR THE DAY: *Complete honesty, my part; complete equipment, God's part.*

"THE BELOVED SYMPTOM"

We continue to sum up the message of the book. We saw yesterday that the first step out of confusion, which is the basis of anxiety, is a complete honesty with oneself and others. That hits at the center. When you are honest there, then healing spreads to the periphery.

We may, in that discovery, be as hard on ourselves as George Bernard Shaw is in his description of one who is creating his own illnesses: "A self-centered little clod of ailments and grievances complaining that the world would not dedicate itself to making him happy." And then Shaw adds this: "The secret of being miserable is to have leisure to bother about whether you are happy or not." It is true that circumstances may have a tremendous part to play in our maladjustments to life. But no part of your environment can affect you if you do not choose to let it affect you. A very discerning woman writes: "I thought all these years people had been making me angry, and I've just realized that anger has been my own choice. I thought people deliberately hurt me and now I see that I choose to serve tea to their thrusts. How can people live 40 years and be so dense? So long in catching on?" That "catching on" to the fact that one is at the center of one's difficulties is half the way to the solution.

Most of our ills—physical, spiritual—are what someone said about herself and her ailments; they are "home-grown." Many are filled with homemade toxins caused by wrong attitudes toward life. We have what Dr. Flanders Dunbar calls "the beloved symptom"—a symptom brought on to provide a way out of a problem we are not solving but dodging by illness.

For instance Elizabeth Barrett, the poetess, was an invalid, with a separate room, much attention and sympathy and "half in love with death." Then came along Robert Browning, the poet, and though six years her junior he fell madly in love with her. They were married when she was forty. At forty-one she was climbing mountains and at forty-three gave birth to a healthy child. She no longer had need of her symptom. It dropped away.

Fall madly in love with Christ. Many of your "beloved symptoms" will fall away.

O living Christ, give to me the inner honesty that sees clearly and then the courage to act decisively, and then the faith to accept Thy way and bank my all upon it. Give me the sense to begin now. Amen.

AFFIRMATION FOR THE DAY: *I shall serve no tea to the thrusts of life or of people this day—my attention is Elsewhere.*

ARE WE, OR ENVIRONMENT, THE CENTER?

We are the center of our difficulties. There are those who would say that environment is. Dr. William S. Sadler says, "I am forced to recognize that many of these newly appearing neurasthenias are not based upon any discoverable hereditary taint. They are due largely to a vicious environment. They represent mechanism which has persistently been forced far beyond the measure of human endurance." But while laying it on the environment, Dr. Sadler doesn't stop there. He adds, "In general our character is destined to become what we make it by virtue of the manner in which we allow or compel ourselves to react to our environment." So if our nervous disorders are not inherited but are the result of our reactions to our environment, then the remedy rests with us.

We have seen that our wrong reactions to what happens to us are disruptive to us, mentally, spiritually, physically. Dr. Karl K. Bowman says, "There is nothing more fatiguing than unpleasant emotion; anger, jealousy, rage, envy, fear are thoroughly undesirable and unhealthy types of reaction. One could wish his enemy no more punishment than to have him be in a constant state of anger and envy, because there is nothing that disrupts the individual man more quickly and uses up his energy more uselessly than emotions of this type. We should therefore regard such emotions as anger, envy, jealousy, and fear as emotions we can't afford to indulge in. They are too expensive, they are not worth the price we pay for them." For instance, a bell boy would break out in a rash when he didn't get the tip he expected. He sustained a double loss—he lost the cash and he got the rash! Hypertension, says Dr. Flanders Dunbar, is more deadly than cancer—kills one out of four men who die over fifty. And hypertension is almost entirely rooted in emotional tension. Again, more than 98 per cent of heart patients have been exposed to a serious illness of this kind in someone dear to them. The sight of it suggested it to themselves, and fear did the rest. The greater part of fatigue we suffer, says Hatfield, is mental in origin; in fact, exhaustion from a purely physical origin is rare.

O Christ, Thou art Savior, save me from my self-inflicted hurts and make me free from every bondage within and without. For I am made for freedom and can find myself only in freedom. Amen.

AFFIRMATION FOR THE DAY: *I shall not nurse but starve my mental and spiritual ills. I shall nurse only my faith and my love.*

ON CHEATING OURSELVES

We continue to gather up the meaning of this book. We saw how wrong emotions are deadly. Someone has said concerning gastric ulcers, "It doesn't depend on what the man is eating, but on what is eating him." If fears, resentments, self-centeredness are eating him, then the ulcer. Dr. Alexis Carrel says: "Business men who do not know how to fight worry die young." And then he adds, "Those who keep the peace of their own inner selves in the midst of the tumult of the modern city are immune from nervous diseases." A United States Bulletin speaks of "the hygiene of a quiet mind." "Anger and sadness and a healthy digestion do not go together." "Fear exercises an influence of general depression over the process of digestion, including stomach and bowels."

How do we get rid of the unhealthy reactions of anger and sadness and fear? Surrender them to God. Surrender gets yourself and its wrong reactions off your own hands into the hands of God. God's resources are at your disposal. Your resources are not adequate. A man who had never traveled before was going across the Atlantic in a steamer. Not knowing the food arrangements, and desiring to travel cheaply, he provided himself with peanuts sufficient for the voyage. After existing on peanuts for some days he got tired of the diet, and asked the steward if he could get a square meal. And then for the first time he discovered that he had already paid for all his meals, which were included in the cost of his ticket. He had been cheating himself. Don't cheat yourself by trying to look after yourself by your own resources. Christ has paid your fare and in it is included everything—everything which life needs, including, and including especially, power and poise.

And, moreover, we must remember that health and holiness are the laws of our being. So, "this universal and legitimate desire for health is one evidence of the indwelling Spirit of God," says Franklyn Cole Sherman. And he adds, "We live in a universe that is friendly and helpful to a loving man." It backs him. He is natural. A sign on a garage filling station said: "We don't even trust ourselves." The surrendered Christian does trust himself, for he feels Reality behind him.

Father God, as I yield my all to Thee I have the feeling that there is a homecoming about it. I feel that I am my own as I am Thine. This is the Home of my soul and body. Amen.

AFFIRMATION FOR THE DAY: *Since I go into a universe today that is friendly and helpful to a loving man, I shall be that man.*

REVERENT LISTENING AT THE FEET OF WISDOM

After surrender, cultivate the Quiet Time. Someone has said, "Better a fountain in the heart than a fountain by the way." But there will be no fountain in the heart unless you stop by the way, at stated periods, and drink. Patmore calls this Quiet Time, "that tender and reverent listening at the feet of Wisdom which is the true and acceptable idleness." But it is an idleness that results in a renewed activity. You become alive all over. Worry is running your engine without the clutch in. It wastes your energy and gets you nowhere; but this Life that takes possession of us in the Quiet Time is a heightening of all our powers to efficiency. Self-centered hurrying results in harrowing, but God-centered energy results in harmony. This is "a busy rest." Then, "Thou shalt wring repose from weariness and death." Then you will know a quiet that turns to Joy.

> The deep enthusiastic joy,
> The rapture of the hallelujah sent
> From all that breathes and is.

Ruysbroeck puts it, "Needs must I rejoice beyond the age, although the world has horror of my joy."

This is written in Burma. Yesterday I went to speak to a congregation that packed the building at Insein, twelve miles from Rangoon. They were calm, composed, and happy, ready to laugh at anything. One would not have imagined that these cultured, sensitive, educated men and women had been through a night of horror, when from four sides of the mission compound firing had gone on over them all night—both sides put them between themselves and the enemy. Toward morning, just before daylight, as the firing began to cease, clear voices could be heard singing in parts at morning prayers:

> When peace like a river attendeth my way,
> When sorrows like sea billows roll,
> Whatever my lot Thou hast taught me to say,
> It is well, it is well with my soul.

O Father, loving Father, teach me the inner calm as sorrows like sea billows roll, and teach me to sing, "It is well, it is well with my soul." For if I am in Thee then all is well. Amen.

AFFIRMATION FOR THE DAY: *I shall draw on such deep and secret springs today that the world will be astonished at my peace and joy.*

"TO HOME OURSELVES IN GOD"

We must learn to be quiet and to receive, to accept:

> With an eye made quiet by the power
> Of harmony and the deep power of joy
> We see into the life of things.

Then we may have serenity of soul in the midst of the difficulties of life, "like the peace of a city church with the tides of traffic and noise about it."

> Oh the little birds sang east
> And the little birds sang west,
> And I smiled to think God's greatness
> Flowed round our incompleteness,
> Round our restlessness His rest.

Then, as Franklyn Cole Sherman puts it, we become "quiet enough to think about eternal verities and to home ourselves in God." And then he adds, "How shall we rest in God? By giving ourselves wholly to Him. If we give ourselves by halves we cannot find full rest; there will ever be the lurking disquiet in that half which is withheld." We do not strive to do things—we put ourselves at God's disposal and He does things through us. We know our greatness is not in us but through us. We know our intelligence is not in us, but our intelligence is in being intelligent enough to put ourselves at God's disposal in every situation that arises. Say: "O God, can you do anything with me in this situation? I'm at your disposal. You've got me." Then let spiritual expectancy possess you. Be alert—passively alert. Learn the lowly art of listening.

Think faith, talk faith, act faith. Someone has suggested this for a good model of suggestion to yourself: "Every day, in every way, God is giving me health." That emphasizes the fact that God is giving and you are receiving—the source of health is in God. That relaxes you before God, opens every pore of your being to the health of God. For where God is there is health, if we can receive it. Be on the receiving end, and you will be on the giving end.

O God, I have all barriers of body, mind, and spirit—have them down. Nothing between. Take possession, and where Thy possession is, there health and holiness are. Thou hast me, so has health. Amen.

AFFIRMATION FOR THE DAY: *Every day, in every way, God is giving me health.*

IT WORKS

This last week of our pilgrimage together must begin with a testimony. The writing of this book has been a searching experience to me. I have tried to write nothing in my books which was not operative within me, or at least in the process of being made operative. I have not always succeeded in that intention. But the intention has been there. Again and again when a crisis has arisen, and many arise in my type of life, I have said to myself, "Remember, you are writing a book on poise. Hold steady. And on power. Take it." It has been a cleansing experience.

For the writing of this book was a test of whether one had poise. The book has been written under every conceivable circumstance, and while in three continents—America, Europe, Asia. On trains, in the air, in waiting rooms, in snatches of time between speaking from three to five times a day, between interviews. This book then is not from the cloister to the crowd. It is from the crowd to the crowd. It partakes of the defects of piecemeal writing. But if it has any worth, it is in this: It works! One can have an Isle of Quiet within, anywhere, under any circumstances. Peace of mind can be a fact. This is written between Rangoon and Singapore in a flying boat. The two weeks in Burma were grilling. Crowded with speeches, the night punctuated with explosions—while I tried to bring together the Karens and the Burmans on the verge of a civil war, and wrote on this book in the interstices. But I took off this morning with no trace of tiredness. The Isle of Calm has held steady and the Resources have not failed. This portion of a letter was sent on to me by a doctor, written by someone else: "I thought back to the first time I heard him. He was a very nervous man—not nervous because he was facing an audience—but that type. And now from a nervous young man he has become a calm, serene, trustful servant of the Lord." I can quote that because I was not naturally peaceful and poised; the opposite. It has been a gift of Grace. The only credit I can take is that I had sense enough to take it—and continue to do so.

Dear Father, I lay at Thy feet the tribute of my gratitude. If I boast, I boast in Thee. Across this holy calm within is written, "A gift of Grace." I touch Thy feet, Thy captive. Amen.

AFFIRMATION FOR THE DAY: *"By the grace of God I am what I am."*

"BEHOLD I HAVE SET BEFORE YOU AN OPEN DOOR"

We come now to a verse which I hope will linger long after the contents of this book may have faded. It is a verse that has come to me in a number of crises: "Behold, I have set before you an open door, which no one is able to shut; I know that you have but little power, and yet you have kept my word and have not denied my name." (Rev. 3:8.)

This verse was given to me by a man who had his life organized around it—and what a life! He came to India a British Tommy with no education and no desire for one—an unawakened clod. Then came conversion in a chapel in Hyderabad. This conversion awakened him mentally, spiritually, physically. He walked seven miles each day to get a language lesson, became a Fellow of the Madras University, head of a college in the very city where he had been an uneducated Tommy, became tutor to the Nizam's sons. Had a road named after him. This verse was given him, and he organized life around it: "Behold, I have set before you an open door which no one is able to shut." It gave him drive, serenity, surety.

This verse came to me in the midst of a crusade—a crusade for a united Church. It came again when beginning a six months' evangelistic tour of the West. I gave it to the churches in strife-torn Burma as my last message, and now I would give it to you.

The word "opportunity" in its root meaning is "the open door." *In Jesus everything is opportunity*—an open door. When we are in Him, then anything that ever happens to us can be turned into an open door. If the worst happens—sin, and sin is the very worst thing that can happen to you—then even that is an open door. For your very sin can drive you to the Redeemer. I can now even bless the sins that drove me to His bosom. Without them I might have been content with a dull, dead contentment—without Him.

But, you say, I do not feel so sinful as I feel empty. Even your emptiness is opportunity in Jesus. For "there is the emptiness of the reed through which the musician makes music; the emptiness of the womb in which a child will be nourished; the emptiness of the cup to be filled with the wine of His Presence." In Jesus everything is opportunity. Let that grip you.

O Christ, why do I have eyes except to look at Thee? Why do I have ears except to listen to Thy Voice? Why do I have a heart except to love Thee? Thou art my Open Door. Amen.

AFFIRMATION FOR THE DAY: *Today, in Jesus everything will be opportunity.*

MY BODY NO LONGER A TAVERN, BUT A TEMPLE

We continue to meditate on Jesus as the Open Door.

He is the open door to release from your defeats. In a certain city a pastor was the spiritual nerve center of that city. He said to me one cay, "You will have forgotten, but I came to your room discouraged and beaten. We knelt in prayer. I turned everything over to Christ. I became new. Discouragement and defeat dropped away." Jesus was the open door out of that defeat and discouragement. A woman, an alcoholic, said, "I heard you quote over the radio the words of Ananias: 'Here am I, Lord.' I repeated them too, made a surrender then and there. From that moment I was different." An editor, an alcoholic, was in a sanitarium, he told me. He said to a doctor about another patient, "That man is in a bad way, isn't he?" The doctor replied, "In a year that man will be well. In a year you will not be well. You will never be well." It shocked him. He went out under the open heavens at night and repeated a verse he had heard somewhere: "If Thou wilt, Thou canst make me clean." And the reply came back instantly: "I will. Be thou clean." He said that then and there his chains fell off—he was free. "I haven't even desired drink again. My body was a tavern, now it is a temple."

But Jesus is not only opportunity out of defeat and discouragement; He is the open door into significance. I mentioned a psychologist who said that the three things people want most are: *(a)* significance, *(b)* security, *(c)* to be loved. Jesus is the door to all three. He is the Saviour not only from sin but also from insignificance. He turns senseless situations into significance. "He turns our tedium into Te Deum." A new sense of dignity and direction comes into life when He comes in. A girl in a sorority was tempted to fall in with the low moral standards of her group, decided against it. Did the right thing—against the herd. The sorority was changed through her courage. From being the poorest in scholarship it became the best in the University. And this girl became its president. The insignificant plus Jesus became the significant.

O Jesus, Thou art my Open Door. Everything outside of Thee leads me to dead ends and dead hopes. In Thee everything becomes alive. Thou art the resurrection and the life. Amen.

AFFIRMATION FOR THE DAY: *If any door closes to me today, it will only mean that God is opening a larger one.*

THE NORTH WIND MADE THE VIKING

We saw yesterday that Jesus is the door into significance, security, and love.

No one is secure unless he can stand anything that can happen to him. In Jesus you can not only stand anything that can happen to you—you can *use* everything. Milton said, "It is not miserable to be blind, it is only miserable not to be able to endure blindness." His blindness awakened him and made him see—see with his whole being. Darwin said, "If I had not been so great an invalid I should not have done as much work as I have accomplished."

"The North Wind made the Vikings." Why? Because the Vikings made the north wind blow them where they wanted to go, and it toughened them in the process.

A few days ago I spoke in the Immanuel Baptist Church in Rangoon, whose main sanctuary has not yet been restored after successive bombings by the Japanese and the British. One wall only was left standing, the front wall. On that front wall is painted these words: "Let the people praise Thee, O Lord, Let all the people praise Thee." This was hidden inside the church until a bomb stripped away the covering walls and left this wall open to the gaze of every passerby. The bomb only brought the glory out. And the baptistry hitherto hidden within the church was now open to the gaze of all. And when I saw it, some Chinese non-Christian families were gathered around it being taught how to undergo the rite which would take place the next Sunday, before the open street. That is the victory—bombs only brought out the significance of that wall and that baptistry. Pain only strips us for action, brings our significance, makes life bare but blessed.

Some Muslims told the Christians of a village in Hyderabad to wipe off the cross from their doors. When they refused, the Muslims forcibly wiped them out. The quiet reply of the Christians was: "You can wipe the cross off our doors, but you cannot wipe it from our hearts." And the Cross was deeper in their hearts when wiped from their doors. Everything serves.

O living Christ, I thank Thee that I have Thy secret—the secret of making everything serve. For Thou hast taught me what men could not learn—to make base metal into gold. Amen.

AFFIRMATION FOR THE DAY: *"The prince of this world cometh. He hath nothing in me, his coming will only serve"* —even the devil shall serve me!

GETTING MUSIC OUT OF THE STORM

We continue our meditation on: In Jesus everything is opportunity. Someone has said, "It is practically a law of life that when one door closes another opens. The trouble is we often look with so much regret and longing at the closed door that we do not see the one which has opened." The Christian is never stymied—he knows what to do in any situation. "Our pastor is not a great preacher, but he always knows what to do," said a loyal parishioner to me.

A hurricane was sweeping across Florida and causing terrible havoc. A moving train swayed dangerously under the blast of the wind. Many were near panic-stricken when a girl jumped into the aisle and began to wave her arms as if she were the conductor of a symphony. The crowd smiled a sickly smile, and then laughed outright as they saw her make music out of the storm. That is the secret of the Christian way—the Christian makes catacombs into cathedrals, makes bombs into blessings, and makes everything sing, even a storm. The Aeolian harp, strung between castle towers, was silent until the storm began to rage; then it brought the music out. A saintly old man, Dr. Godby, was getting out of a train, and as the train lurched it threw him first against one side and then against the other. When he hit one side he said, "Glory," and when he hit the other he said, "Hallelujah." The jolting only jolted out the "Glory's" and the "Hallelujah's."

This is the Christian security—the security of making everything jolt you into jubilance. "Now is the time to be a Christian," said a woman when she lost her only daughter.

Dr. Alfred Adler, the famous psychiatrist said, "One of the most wonderful things about human beings is their capacity to turn a minus into a plus." This is a characteristic of human nature, but how much more if human nature has at the center of its faith a God Who does this very thing. When such a God and such a man come together, then anything is possible.

"Please autograph my *Abundant Living*. It's rather water-soaked and dilapidated, but it went through Saipan with me. It works," said a radiant G.I.

Dear God and Father, I thank Thee that my ways and Thy ways are not at cross purposes. We can work together, and in working together can make everything work together for good. We are unbeatable. Amen.

AFFIRMATION FOR THE DAY: *All my bumps today shall only bump the glory out!*

AT HOME IN REALITY

Just what is the source of our maintaining poise and a consciousness of power? It is found in the fact that one who is fully committed to the way of Christ feels that he has cosmic backing for his way of life. He is in line with the deepest purposes of the universe and is working with them and they are working with him. He feels that he and his way are not intrusions into an alien universe, but are the natural expression of that universe. Therefore he is at home in Reality. That makes him tread the earth with a sureness of tread—afraid of nothing, nothing but sin, his own sin.

I never cease to wonder at the seeing-eye doors that open at your approach, nor can I get away from the feeling that this is what happens when you are on the Way: everything opens to you. The universe has a very discerning eye and will not open to hate, resentment, selfishness, dishonesty. It closes up in disapproval at their approach. But it does open to you when you approach life in the spirit of Christ. Therefore Christ is the Way.

Some Hindus were taunting a Christian in a train for becoming a Christian. "Why didn't you stay within your own religion and improve it?" To which the Christian replied, "I do not want a religion which I must improve. I want one that improves me, and that I have found in Christ." This reply was good, but he could have added, "My faith in Christ not only improves me, but, when I obey it, then the universe approves me. I walk under the benediction of Reality." It is then that your goodness turns to gaiety—you laugh a triumphant laugh—laugh it at the rhythm of things.

Take this impossible situation: a woman, who had formerly been very intimate with the husband of a woman, who knew about it, kept sending expensive presents to the husband and wife jointly but intended for the husband. The wife commented, "I have to write polite notes of acknowledgment. She thinks I'm dumb. John sweats it through. Life is funny if you know how to laugh at it." She could laugh a triumphant laugh for she was on the Way. The others were trying ways.

O God, I thank Thee that in Thee I have Thy approval and the approval of everything except unreality. And that doesn't count. Therefore I lift my head and laugh—laugh because life approves me. Amen.

AFFIRMATION FOR THE DAY: *Today I shall laugh a triumphant laugh in the face of evil—it is doomed to disintegration.*

LITTLE POWER—ADEQUATE RESOURCES

We come now to our final meditation. This open door is promised not to the strong: "I know that you have but little power, and yet you have kept my word and have not denied my name." This open door into power and poise is promised to those of "little power." They have taken that little power and have surrendered it into the hands of Almighty Love. Your business then is not to strain for power and poise, but to be true—to keep His word and not deny His name. Then poise and power are by-products.

Before I came to India as a very young evangelist I was impatient and out-of-sorts with the people in a camp meeting because they were so unresponsive. I went out after a meeting and lay down under an apple tree exhausted. The Lord seemed to come to me and say, "You're tired, aren't you?" "Yes," I replied, "I am, for I have worked hard." "And you are out of patience, aren't you?" "Yes," I replied, "I am, and I have a right to be, for these people are hard and unresponsive." Then He quietly said, "Do you see this apple tree? How does it bring forth fruit? Does it work itself up into a stew trying to be fruitful? Or does it simply keep the channels open, taking in life from soil and sky and allowing life to flow through itself into the fruit? And is it not all unstrained? Then if you'll not fret nor worry about results, but simply keep the channels open, letting My life flow through you, then you will bear fruit naturally without strain or drain." I arose relaxed and released. I didn't have to succeed—I only had to keep the channels open. God did the rest.

In the Quiet Time at Sat Tal in the early morning came with power this statement of Ananias, when Jesus called him to go to help blinded Saul: "Here am I, Lord." The Voice said, "If you will say that in every situation, 'Here am I, Lord,' then I'll take care of the rest. If you will put yourself at My disposal in every situation, then you won't have to be anxious about anything— success, power, poise—it will all be yours." A Calm possessed me. Life was centrally simplified. A door was open to me which no man could shut. My "little power" didn't matter—His resources did.

O Christ, I do not know what the future holds, but I know Who holds the future. I walk into that future unafraid—strong in Thy strength, sure in Thy assurance, poised in Thy steadiness. Amen.

AFFIRMATION FOR THE DAY: *Today and every day I shall say: "Here am I, Lord." All else is Thy responsibility.*

SUGGESTIONS FOR THE QUIET TIME

I. Decide on the time you should and can give to the Quiet Time. Hold to it. Don't make it a matter of debate each day. Pray by the clock whether you feel like it or not. Organize the day around the Quiet Time.

II. Come to it with expectancy—this is faith directed toward your Resources.

III. Before you pray, get your thought and affections directed by the Word of God.

IV. Through the reading of the Word take the attitude of lowly listening.

V. Have a pen or pencil ready to write down what comes.

VI. Let your mind circle around some verse that strikes you.

VII. After you have read, relax and say, "Father, what have you to say to me?"

VIII. Then you say to God what you have to say. (Your prayers have now been cleansed and directed by the steps taken so far.)

IX. After you have said what you have to say, surrender it into the hands of God.

X. Thank Him for the answer, whatever the answer may be.

XI. If the mind wanders, make the thing to which the mind wanders an object of prayer or a means of prayer.

XII. Make the Quiet Time occupy the center of the day— the Isle of Quiet within.

XIII. That center of Quiet becomes the center of activity for the day.

THE FESTIVAL SERIES

The Life and Teaching of Jesus Christ by James S. Stewart   **$1.95**
Confessions of a Workaholic by Wayne E. Oates   **$1.50**
Growing Spiritually by E. Stanley Jones $2.25
How to Be a Transformed Person by E. Stanley Jones   **$2.25**
Here I Stand: A Life of Martin Luther
   by Roland H. Bainton $1.75
Too Busy Not to Pray by Jo Carr & Imogene Sorley   **$1.25**
Letters to Karen by Charlie W. Shedd $1.25
The Transforming Friendship by Leslie D. Weatherhead   **$1.25**
Major Religions of the World by Marcus Bach $1.25
The Topical Bible Concordance edited by D. M. Miller   **$1.75**
God Is No Fool by Lois A. Cheney $1.50
Prayer by George A. Buttrick $1.95
Twelve Baskets of Crumbs by Elisabeth Elliot $1.75
The Compact Treasury of Inspiration edited by Kenneth Seeman
   Giniger $1.95
The Partakers by Robert G. Tuttle, Jr. $1.25
Tell Me Again, I'm Listening by Richard B. Wilke $1.25
Who's Who in the Old Testament by Joan Comay $2.45
Who's Who in the New Testament by Ronald Brownrigg $2.45
Abundant Living by E. Stanley Jones $1.95
The Divine Yes by E. Stanley Jones $1.50
The Master's Men by William Barclay $1.50
Bless This Mess & Other Prayers by Jo Carr and
   Imogene Sorley $1.50
The Will of God by Leslie D. Weatherhead $1.25
How Came the Bible? by Edgar J. Goodspeed $1.75
Strange Facts About the Bible by Webb Garrison $1.95
The Greatest of These by Jane Merchant $1.25
Steps to Prayer Power by Jo Kimmel $1.25
A Life Full of Surprises by Lloyd John Ogilvie $1.50
A Diary of Readings by John Baillie $2.95
The Way to Power and Poise by E. Stanley Jones $2.25
Where Is Noah's Ark? by Lloyd R. Bailey $1.95